Other Renaissances

Other Renaissances

A New Approach to World Literature

Brenda Deen Schildgen
Gang Zhou
Sander L. Gilman

With a Foreword by Giuseppe Mazzotta

palgrave
macmillan

OTHER RENAISSANCES
© Brenda Deen Schildgen, Gang Zhou, Sander L. Gilman, 2006.

First published in 2006 by
PALGRAVE MACMILLAN™
175 Fifth Avenue, New York, N.Y. 10010 and
Houndmills, Basingstoke, Hampshire, England RG21 6XS
Companies and representatives throughout the world.

PALGRAVE MACMILLAN is the global academic imprint of the Palgrave Macmillan division of St. Martin's Press, LLC and of Palgrave Macmillan Ltd. Macmillan® is a registered trademark in the United States, United Kingdom and other countries. Palgrave is a registered trademark in the European Union and other countries.

ISBN-13: 978–1–4039–7446–4
ISBN-10: 1–4039–7446–2

Library of Congress Cataloging-in-Publication Data

Other renaissances : a new approach to world literature / [edited by] Brenda Deen Schildgen, Gang Zhou, Sander L. Gilman ; with a foreword by Giuseppe Mazzotta.
    p. cm.
Includes bibliographical references and index.
ISBN 1–4039–7446–2
    1. Literature—History and criticism. I. Schildgen, Brenda Deen II. Zhou, Gang. III. Gilman, Sander L.

PN501.O84 2006
809—dc22   2006044780

A catalogue record for this book is available from the British Library.

Design by Newgen Imaging Systems (P) Ltd., Chennai, India.

First edition: November 2006

10 9 8 7 6 5 4 3 2 1

Printed in the United States of America.

In the wide ocean upon which we venture, the possible ways and directions are many; and the same studies which have served for this work might easily, in other hands, not only receive a wholly different treatment and application, but lead also to essentially different conclusions.

Jacob Burckhardt
The Civilization of the Renaissance in Italy

Contents

Foreword

For many years, at least since the epoch-making interpretation by Burckardt, we have been entertaining a number of ideas about the Renaissance, chiefly among them its view of human mastery, to the point of dizziness for the worrisome consequences, over the world, its will to reach the extreme limits of thought, to think anew the senses of tradition and to open up to new encounters and new cultures. Above all, we have come to acknowledge the uniqueness or singularity of Renaissance thought, which is at one with its irreducible specifics and originality. How can one think of Renaissance singularity in the context of "other Renaissances"? Is there a contradiction between them?

A question, then, is immediately in order. In what does the singularity of the European, or more specifically, the Italian Renaissance consist? Singularity can be understood as a version of individuality, as a project that unfolds in the wake of Petrarch's fundamental claims about the historicity of his own individual existence. The self, so he argues in the *Canzoniere* lyrical poetry, must be understood from within itself, because time and desire's other displacements are internal to it. By setting the self against all objective systems, Petrarch dramatizes it as the ground where all knowledge can appear significant. The sense of singularity, however, cannot be merely reduced to the acknowledgment of a name because Petrarch was perfectly aware of the difficulties of positing a stable, self-identical self. His reflections unsettle any possibility of stable identity and reveal an endless series of shifts, ruptures, and masks concealed within the folds of the self.

If we wish to still persist in speaking of a Renaissance singularity, we should turn to Petrarch's programmatic cultural fervor in willing to retrieve what seemed to be forever lost and which he turns into the *source* of his project: the culture of ancient Rome. But the singularity of Rome is a complex matter and Petrarch reaches to the roots of that complexity. As a matter of fact, he can be thought as the "founder" of the

Renaissance because he grasped the epochality of Rome's unique history, which to him was the blueprint for rebuilding the present on the legacy of that culture. One particular event triggered this far-reaching meditation. The event occurred in 1341 when he was crowned a "poet laureate" on the steps of the Capitol in Rome, and on this occasion he delivered a speech, which is known as the *Collatio Laureationis* (*The Speech on the Occasion of the Honorary Degree*).

The coronation ceremony was a symbolic ritual, but in Rome symbols and images are charged with hidden resonances. In 1341, whatever else the ceremony meant, it was bound to be taken by Petrarch himself as something of a call to future projects rather than a celebration of past achievements. At this time, in fact, Rome is a graveyard of broken pieces. But as he stands on the steps of the Roman Capitol (and he speaks from within the encompassing horizon of Roman history) the language of the Roman past, thanks to the Roman poets and rhetoricians, is still audible and worth retrieving from the depths of oblivion threatening its posthumous existence. The tradition of the ancient poets and intellectuals—Cicero, Virgil, Horace, Ovid, Lucan—speaks to Petrarch and through him, as if they were not dead relics but oracles or prophetic sources of wisdom for the present. He wills to bring them back to life by internalizing their voices and echoing them.

There were in Petrarch's times several efforts or ways of reviving the Roman past. One was the way of the aesthetes, such as Cardinal Colonna, an amateur archaeologist drawn to the lure of the city's ruins. He loved the sense of mortality emanating from the illegible stones/fragments but chose to reduce them to an object of contemplation. Another way coincided with the dream of an antiquarian turned revolutionary, such as Cola di Rienzo who wanted the literal restoration of the Roman Republic. The past, so he thought, can be brought back to life the way it was. The notion can remind one of Aeneas, who travels from fallen Troy and who, on the way to the new land promised to him by the gods, builds several copies of the lost city. Aeneas' nostalgia will ultimately be overcome. He grasps that the future cannot simply be understood as the mirror of the past. Petrarch, who for a while cultivated close ties with both these contemporaries, ends up distancing himself from either a merely political or an esthetic ideology. He understands that the Roman Empire can only be reborn as the empire of culture.

The speech he gave on the Capitol in Rome can be called his "discourse of Rome" in the double sense of the phrase. One sense refers to the actual occasion of the ceremony in Rome. Another, however, alludes to the "discourse" Rome has made to the world—the myths, ideology, and values it has forged over the centuries. In what way are those values of any validity in the present? Two authors serve Petrarch well in this endeavor of bringing to light the discourse Rome imparted to the world: Virgil and Cicero.

Petrarch begins his speech by citing a line from Virgil's *Georgics* (III, 291–2):

> "but a sweet desire hurries me over the lonely steeps of Parnassus". In these lines Virgil states that he will try a poetic path that will enable him to bring the Muses from the Greek Parnassus to the banks of his native Mincius in Mantua. In effect, Virgil acknowledges that poetry can be grafted and naturalized on his native ground: in his ideology poetry is work, the productive transformation of reality and not simply an aesthetic, unrepeatable simulacrum.

The second text Petrarch retrieves is Cicero's *Pro Archia*, which he had discovered some years earlier in his travels through Flanders and Germany. What is *Pro Archia* about? And why would Petrarch deploy it in order to convey the sense of Rome's "discourse" to the world? In 62 BC Cicero made a speech in defense of the poet Archia in what at the time was in Rome nothing less than a *cause celebre*. Archia, a Syrian by birth, had lived in Southern Italy and was widely acclaimed in the Southern cities of Rhegium and Naples. In Heraclea, a city in Lucania, he was granted honorary citizenship. But because he had traveled all over the East with his patron, he could not claim a Roman residence and his name was missing from the census lists. His rights as a Roman citizen were forfeited.

Cicero took the case in defense of Archia and Archia was acquitted. But Cicero's defense makes clear that the legal case went far beyond the personal situation of this particular man. The genuine question lying at the heart of the debate concerns, through the defense of Archia, the defense of poetry in the tribunal of the city. Folded within the explicit legal argument of the speech lies a philosophical reflection on the relation between politics and poetry, and even more poignantly, between poetry and justice. Where does poetry belong within the economy of the city? In effect, Cicero knows that the value of Rome, indeed the meaning itself of Rome's political history depend on how the city's laws answer this question. If Rome is to be a just city and if its rule is to be just, it will acclaim Archia as one of its own. Poets, after all, are always alien and they never belong to a definite birthplace.

It is easy to discern in Cicero's argument a direct echo of Virgil's theory of poetry as a transplanting from a foreign soil. It is even easier to read in Cicero a deliberate reversal of Plato's expulsion of the poets from the ideal Republic. By distancing himself from the beloved models of classical Greece, Cicero acknowledges Rome's singularity, and yet he is supremely aware that this singularity has nothing to do with, say, Varro's myth of Roman cultural purity. Quite the contrary. Cicero acknowledges that Rome is made of alien components.

By so doing, Cicero enacts the peculiarly Roman concept of universality, which is identifiable with the universal principle of natural law, whereby, as Marius and Sulla had shown when they granted Roman citizenship to Spaniards, Gauls, Italians, and the people in the Middle East, all are members of the same city. This principle of universality, in turn, depends on the consciousness that sharp distinctions between "inside" and "outside", "us" and "them", poetry and rhetoric, and so on are blurred. Here lies, then, in this most Ciceronian of philosophical/political concepts, the principle of *aequitas*, the first and foremost peculiarity of the "discourse" of Rome: whereas most cultures establish boundaries between one group and another, Rome never sets up barriers.

It would be inaccurate, however, to read Petrarch's *Collatio Laureationis* as merely an updated restatement of Cicero's *Pro Archia*. He combines the two voices of Cicero and Virgil, and in the process, he etches a theory of culture that accounts for the emergence of the Renaissance and explains its essence. If Cicero explains the universality of Roman law, Virgil's *Georgics*, which is a poem about the cultivation of the earth, articulates a view of culture as a tending to the earth, as an endless process of making and remaking history. No doubt, in this sense the *Georgics* adumbrates the central message of the *Aeneid*. The mythical origins of Rome, as the *Aeneid* relates them, are to be found in the journey, trials, and errors of Aeneas, who has to learn that the fallen city of Troy cannot be simply remade as it was: the new city has to be made anew. More importantly, the founder of Rome, Aeneas, like Archia, is a foreigner, a *peregrinus* who comes from the outside and, thus, he casts Rome's singularity as a hybrid.

Finally, what is common to the two texts of Virgil and Cicero is the notion of *making*. Like poetry, history comes forth as a process whereby the old stones of Rome, though they have become dusty and illegible fragments, ciphers of time's unavoidable devastation, turn into building blocks for the future. Such, after all, was also Petrarch's understanding of the voices of the poets from the Roman past: their sounds, though dimmed by time's passage, can be heard again and be turned into tissues for new texts. In what has become the founding text of the Renaissance, the *Collatio laureationis*, Petrarch has laid the basis for the vast, unending phenomenon known as the Renaissance, whose specificity or singularity paradoxically consists in the universality of the process of making, and whose essence coincides with the establishment of a worldwide culture. It is a small wonder that the Humanists who followed him acknowledged him as their precursor. They, much like Petrarch, envision the modern world as nothing less than the empire of culture which all men and women are called to build and rebuild. The multiplicity of Renaissances, flourishing in different times and spaces, is a tribute to their dream of a universal Rome.

Giuseppe Mazzotta
Yale University

Acknowledgments

This has been a collaborative project among international scholars with specialized academic training and shared interests and passions. In many conversations among contributors either by electronic communication or telephone, the collection emerged as a transglobal discussion of common issues about language and modernization, nationalism, modernism, postcolonialism, and the archaeology of knowledge in the academy, in widely disparate cultural communities. So the editors wish to give the first acknowledgment to the contributors whose excitement and enthusiasm about this project turned it into a reality. Several conferences facilitated the dialogue about renaissance as an idea received and flowing in different directions. Among these, we must thank the American Association of Italian Studies, that met in Philadelphia in 2001 and that was organized by Professor Victoria Kirkham, who applauded the idea of a panel on "Renaissance outside of Italy." The same year Asian Studies on the Pacific Coast sponsored a session on the reception of the idea of the Italian Renaissance in Asia. At the American Comparative Literature Association meeting in California in 2003, Professor David Damrosch encouraged the project as signaling a new direction for Comparative Literature Studies. Several of these chapters were first presented at that meeting. As with all cooperative projects, besides the work of the editors and contributors themselves, others offered help to identify potential contributors. Among these were Peter Gran and Azade Sehan, and Victoria Holbrook. Gang Zhou expresses particular gratitude to Michelle Yeh, Juliana Schiesari, and Margaret Fergusson, her professors at the University of California, Davis, who encouraged her work from the very beginning and to Georges Sheldon, Julia Klimek, Constance Anderson, Victoria Holbrook, and Deyang Wu, all of whom have given essential support and advice. Final work on the project has been completed at the National Humanities Center in North Carolina, where Brenda Deen xvi • Acknowledgments

Schildgen has been a fellow for 2005–2006. Without the generous help from the NHC with computers, programming, formatting, printing, editing, and all the countless details that emerge in the last stages of a book project, the book would have been considerably delayed. Special thanks go to Karen Carroll for editorial support, Phillip Baron and Joel Elliott for computer assistance, and Lois Whittington and Kent Mullikin, all from the National Humanities Center.

Brenda Deen Schildgen
Gang Zhou
Sander L. Gilman

Introduction

Gang Zhou, Brenda Deen Schildgen, and Sander L. Gilman

In *History and Value* (1989), Frank Kermode argued that "[t]here seem to be two main ways in which we try to make history manageable for literary purposes: by making canons that are in some sense trans-historical; and by inventing historical periods (108–109)." The term "Renaissance," often associated with the fifteenth and sixteenth centuries in Europe, has been "invented" and taught in both of these ways. Beyond functioning as both a period designation and as a principle of scholarly and curricular organization in the study of European cultures, however, the term has also taken on thematic dimensions outside of Europe and has been used to describe changes that may have little connection to the historical period and canon usually associated with that particular temporal and geographical space.

While it is impossible not to acknowledge the role of European imperialism and colonialism in the exporting and importing of European cultural terms and epistemologies, the term "Renaissance" nonetheless has been reimagined to declare and designate historical developments in many areas of the world. The term, always capitalized to signal a monumental historical shift, invariably describes developments that radically question social and cultural attitudes and language practices.

Applied to the May Fourth Movement in China by Chinese intellectuals, to the Bengali literary and political movement of the nineteenth century, to the Irish recovery of Celtic culture, to the Harlem cultural flowering in the early twentieth century as well as to the emergence of modern Hebrew as a literary language, the term "Renaissance" has thus proven itself a mobile critical and politico-cultural term, even as its very ability to travel across borders of languages, cultures, and periods has made its significance in those contexts as protean and contested as it also remains in its European setting, as debates about the retrospective application of the concept to the twelfth-century "Renascence" have shown. This "protean" aspect of the term to describe various cultural movements around the world becomes a case study of how the transcultural imagination participates in a complicated network of literary and cultural exchange.

This complexity is only hinted at in this volume. This present volume on *Other Renaissances* represents different geocultural areas: the Arab "Renaissance" [s], the Bengali "Renaissance," Tamil "Renaissance," the Chinese "Renaissance," the Harlem "Renaissance," Mexican "Renaissance," the Maori "Renaissance," the European "Renaissance" as received in the United States during the Cold War, the Chicago "Renaissance," the Ottoman non-"Renaissance," the Hebrew "Renaissance," and the Irish "Renaissance" as well as different disciplines (Comparative Literature, Area Studies, History, and English). In doing so, it examines the complex nature of the adaptation of the concept over the past centuries through the power of the transcultural imagination. Its intention is to indicate the complex rethinking of the "Renaissance" as well as to offer a new and powerful model for the study of literature and culture. As Giuseppe Mazzotta indicates in his preface, all have roots in the early modern evocation of a fantasy of classical culture. Each version of the global idea of the Renaissance includes bits of this and other preceding "renaissances" in making their own claims.

The Birth of the "Renaissance"

The word "Renaissance" (*rinascita*) was first coined in the sixteenth-century writings of the Italian artist and critic Giorgio Vasari (1511–1574). In his long introduction to the *Lives of the Great Painters, Sculptors, and Architects* (1550), Vasari labeled the art of his time *la rinascita*, the rebirth, proposing that "these arts resemble nature as shown in our human bodies; and have their birth, growth, age, and death." He claimed that his book would enable his readers "more easily to recognize the progress of the Renaissance (rinascita) of the arts, and the perfection to which they have attained in our own time." While "Renaissance" becomes the specific word used to designate the historical period in which Vasari lived, its overarching power as a concept causes it to be appropriated in multiple ways that lose something essential from this moment of origin.

The "natural" claim that followed from Vasari's concept comes to be replaced by the notion of an aesthetic stylization. Following Vasari's conception of the *Renaissance des beaux arts* came that of the *Renaissance des lettres*, as crystallized in Pierre Bayle's great *Historical and Critical Dictionary* (1695). For Bayle it was not only the written word that trumped the visual (Vasari would not have been pleased) but also the image of a written word already crystallized in the past that could be reappropriated in the present. By the eighteenth century, the significance of the European "Renaissance" was further elaborated by French Enlightenment thinkers such as Voltaire (1694–1778), who suggested that the "Renaissance," "the time of Italy's glory," was one of only four periods in human history worthy of intellectual consideration. For Voltaire, of course, his own age, so modestly labeled the "Enlightenment," was or at least could be the cultural equivalent of this past "Renaissance." In the nineteenth century, of course, Jacob Burckhardt (1818–1897) picked up on Voltaire (and Vico's) notion of a monumental history, the keystone of which was the "Renaissance." Giuseppe Mazzotta shows how this nineteenth-century reading has its roots in earlier claims but also tills new and unexpected soil. Burckhardt, along with his sometime colleague at Basel, Friedrich Nietzsche, directly shaped our modern conception of the Italian "Renaissance" in his work *The Civilization of the Renaissance in Italy* (1860; translated into English in 1878). He redefined the conventional view of the "Renaissance," which emphasizes the revival of antiquity and added to it what he considered the essence of the Renaissance: individualism and the discovery of the world and of mankind. For Burckhardt it was the visual arts (Vasari smiles) that provided the key. Indeed, it was Burckhardt who first recognized the transcultural implications of the "Renaissance." He begins his book with the following claim:

> To each eye, perhaps, the outlines of a given civilization present a different picture; and in treating of a civilization which is the mother of our own, and whose influence is still at work among us, it is unavoidable that individual judgment and feeling should tell every moment both on the writer and on the reader.

With this view already built into the concept, all future reprisals and interpretations are framed by and frame our evolving understanding of the "Renaissance" period, but they elaborate and distance Vasari's original concept of the "Renaissance."

The "Renaissance" was born as an act of naming and claiming as Vasari declared the existence of a "Renaissance" based on his understanding of the art in his own age. In turn, this declaration also shaped the way his time would be understood by later generations. Both in describing a reality and working toward creating the reality, Vasari's speech act called into being a "Renaissance" both as a period and as an idea. The "Renaissance" was also born as an analogy to the development of the human body. This assumes a transforming process that moves in natural progression from birth, youth, to maturity and perfection. (There is no old age and death in this view even though Shakespeare's monologue on the "seven ages of man" from *As You Like It* will soon point to this moment of cultural as well as physical decay.) The "Renaissance" is an analogy that is optimistic and utopian, sheltering the present age from negative elements such as death and decline.

Vasari was certainly not the first one who invented the idea that his own time constituted a positive, cultural "rebirth" of the best in the past. Earlier Dante (1265–1321) had contrasted Cimabue to Giotto; Petrarch (1304–1374), as Giuseppe Mazzotta indicates in his elegant reading of that text, scorned the "dark ages," just left behind. Lorenzo Valla (1406–1457) remarked that his time was "a harvest of good artists and good writers," while the previous eras were crude, dark, decadent, or moribund. Erasmus, believing his own age a time of revival of arts and letters of which he was one of the prime movers, had observed to a friend in 1489,

> When you look back over an interval of two or three hundred years, be it at metal work, paintings, works of sculpture, buildings, structures, in fine arts, at monuments of every kind of workmanship, you will, I think, both marvel and laugh at the extreme crudity of the artists; whereas in our own age there is again nothing in art which the industry of its practitioners is not able to accomplish.

The dichotomy of death/birth and dark/bright found its best representation in Vasari's "Renaissance" analogy coupled with the image of a utopian moment in the past now rediscovered and restored. Not only is the present better than the immediate past but it also has a point of origin in a moment of perfection in the past.

In the *Other Renaissances* that this present collection explores, it is precisely this act of naming and claiming (the point of origin) that excited the non-European intellectuals (as well as Europeans outside the mainstream of hegemonic European culture), who set out to change things through words. It is precisely the "Renaissance" analogy that is both exciting and tension-ridden that provides them with another means to critique the present, to hark back to a lost past, and shape the present toward an ideal future. What the objects are (art, music, literature, history) in a sense are already set by the value system of the West that sees High Culture as linked to the "Renaissance." Yet the content, the language, the rhetoric, the literary forms, the claims on national and cultural identity, all change through the transcultural imagination.

Reconfiguring World Literature through the Transcultural Imagination

David Damrosch in *What is World Literature?* (2003) proposed an innovative way to articulate the problem of world literature. By investigating the ways literary works change as they move from national to global contexts, Damrosch argues that world literature should not be perceived as a canon of texts but rather as a mode of circulation and reading. He observes:

> A work enters into world literature by a double process; first, by being read as literature; second by circulating out into a broader world beyond its linguistic and cultural point of origin. . . . As it moves into the sphere of world literature, far from inevitably suffering a loss of authenticity or essence, a work can gain in many ways. . . . To understand the workings of world literature, we need more a phenomenology than an ontology of the work of art. (6)

Damrosch discovers an elliptical space that transforms the claims of a single work of art into multidimensional world literature. Instead of perceiving world literature as isolated books on the shelf, Damrosch considers world literature as texts that travel, texts that assume new lives, and texts that manifest differently in different geocultural contexts. What Damrosch has achieved can be seen as another way to open the canon, for he creates a unique perspective that reframes the canon and sees the possibilities and opportunities of a work of art. In other words, to understand world literature is no longer to understand the sum total of all national masterpieces, but to understand how a work of art is opened up by that elliptical space as well as reshaped by a world literary cultural exchange network.

Damrosch's proposal might also help us understand how an idea moves beyond its place of origin and moves into an elliptical space created between the perceived work of origin and receiving cultures. Each chapter in this volume represents a case study of an elliptical space that the "Renaissance" has inhabited. Together all the chapters suggest a new way to open up a conceptual structure quite different from that posited by recent German historians such as Reinhart Koselleck and his

"Begriffsgeschichte" (conceptual history). Here we can see the potential and possibilities of an idea that travels and manifests itself quite differently at different times and in different spaces and that is constantly building on the process of innovative and critical rethinking and restatement.

One needs to address the elusiveness of the term "Renaissance" as it evolves and changes across time and space at each moment referring and reacting to multiple pasts and multiple presents. Lisa Woolley in her chapter on the Chicago "Renaissance" and the Harlem "Renaissance" observes that in the American context, "Renaissance has little authority left; it is used skeptically, with the understanding that a Renaissance is hardly a shadow of the Renaissance." "Movements such as the New York Little 'Renaissance,' Southern 'Renaissance,' Chicago 'Renaissance,' and Harlem 'Renaissance' were short-lived, limited to a small region or demographic group, sometimes involved only a few of the arts, and often represented as a 'first flowering,' rather than a 'rebirth.'" While Johnson's chapter on the Harlem "Renaissance" presents a global dialogue in which Harlem intellectuals engaged across the world, Woolley's discussion about the Harlem period focuses on its position among other local "Renaissances." As "Renaissance" moves globally, it also moves in the other direction, namely, it becomes more local. While issues such as modernity, postcolonialism, and nationalism as well as cultural and linguistic revival preoccupied those intellectuals of the *Other Renaissances* at the national level, issues of race, identity formation and cultural diversity become the main concerns of these small-scale "Renaissances." In both directions, the "Renaissance" might seem to move further away from the European "Renaissance," but on the other hand, it might indeed move closer to that origin, namely, solely as an act of naming and as an analogy. To observe the push and pull that make the "Renaissance" a multidimensional world concept and to map the elliptical space that generates and reshapes various meanings of "Renaissance" not only sheds light on what a "Renaissance" is deemed to be but also on how a complicated cultural exchange network functions.

The awareness and acknowledgement of the "Renaissance" as an idea that travels as well as an idea that manifests itself differently in different geocultural contexts also helps reframe our understanding of world literature in world history. While expressing doubts about the validity of the broad uses of "Renaissance," Woolley nevertheless acknowledges the significance of the trope for producing scholarship and rethinking the landscape of American literary history. If each individual "Renaissance" in this collection designates a period as well as provides a narrative to rethink a national literary history, in what way can a volume like this one, *Other Renaissances*, help us rethink the landscape of world literature? The new paradigm regroups "Renaissances" as the boundaries and centers are questioned and redefined. By placing *Other Renaissances* in the front seat while gently nudging the European "Renaissance" into the back seat, the book aims to provide a comparative and transcultural reading of the "Renaissance" that is global and yet also local. It is a movement from center to periphery that takes the periphery as its new center.

The global circulation of the "Renaissance" has taken many forms. Indian and Chinese intellectuals explicitly adopted the Italian "Renaissance" as a model for the cultural changes in their countries in the late nineteenth and early twentieth centuries. Whether engineered or spontaneous, these shifts were characterized as marking moments of political, social, and cultural turmoil. As in the European "Renaissance," moreover, the reinvention of language played a prominent role, whether as recovery of an ancient culture in these and other cases, such as in the case of Sanskrit, Irish, or Hebrew, or as the embracing of the vernacular in the case of Chinese and Bengali, or the reestablishment of the old in new forms as with Hebrew and Celtic. The "Renaissance" was also used to describe other forms of self-reinvention, as in China and in the cultural flowering called the Harlem "Renaissance" in the United States and the long Maori "Renaissance" in New Zealand. By analyzing these *Other Renaissances* in light of each other, in light of the European "Renaissance," this book therefore provides an opportunity to link languages and cultures that usually are not to be found together.

It goes without saying that any project of this kind must be brutally selective. Readers are reminded that all the chapters in this volume do not mean to represent a field of inquiry or a survey but rather reveal or highlight individual voices of a collective project. To speak more specifically, each chapter is not supposed to give an encyclopedic account of how the term "Renaissance" was received in any given community, but rather to present a series of case studies that lay bare the process of assimilation, appropriation, reaction, and 'syncretism,' thus preparing a solid basis to address broader critical, historiographic, and theoretical issues. The issues at the core of this volume include the following:

How and to what political and ideological purpose was the term "Renaissance" appropriated in a particular cultural context?

In what way can examining these *Other Renaissances* lead to a reappraisal of the European "Renaissance"?

Because these *Other Renaissances* often involved major epistemological shifts connected to language, politics, social change, and cultural revolution, does "Renaissance" as a term describe an epistemology rather than a period, and what are the implications of these diverse uses of "Renaissance" as an epistemology to period divisions in history and literary studies?

How would a reappraisal of the uses of "Renaissance" be applied to an evaluation of the archeology of knowledge in the academy? Could a terminology for organizing literature that can be applied beyond predetermined European paradigms emerge from considering these *Other Renaissances*?

Does the existence of these *Other Renaissances* suggest that literary history can also be arranged non-chronologically, in which case premodern, early modern, modern, and so on actually describe cultural shifts at particular and sometimes repeated moments in history? Is literary history therefore recursive rather than teleological?

Other than Other

Some thoughts are appropriate on the naming of this project, especially what "Other" means in this context. Ever since Michel Foucault gave a special prominence to the concept of "subject," "other" also became a concept so mediated that it can only be understood in the elliptical refraction of power theory.

> A power relationship can only be articulated on the basis of two elements which are each indispensable if it is really to be a power relationship: that "the other" (the one over whom power is exercised) be thoroughly recognized and maintained to the very end as a person who acts; and that, faced with a relationship of power, a whole field of responses, reactions, results, and possible inventions may open up. ("The Subject and Power")

This project acknowledges the imbalanced power relationship between the European "Renaissance" and "Other Renaissances," but the "Other" here is not used as a scarlet letter symbolizing repression, subversion, and redemption but rather conceived as a kind that can be constitutive of selfhood as such. As Paul Ricoeur suggests in his book *Oneself as Another* (The Gifford Lectures for 1990) the selfhood of oneself implies otherness to such an intimate degree that one cannot be thought of without the other. For Ricoeur, the "as" that connects the one and the other is not only that of a comparison (one similar to another) but also indeed that of an implication (oneself inasmuch as being other). This book of *Other Renaissances* is therefore not only a book about *other renaissances* but also about the European "Renaissance" being yet another "Renaissance." It is about the shaping of the idea of "Culture," "Europe," even "Civilization" through the appropriation of the ever-shifting idea of the "Renaissance."

The European "Renaissance" and "Other Renaissances": Reframing the "Renaissance"

In his recent book *The European Renaissance: Centers and Peripheries*, Peter Burke (1998) reframes the European "Renaissance" with an emphasis on "reception." The European "Renaissance" presented in his book is "decentered," and is a movement received in the sense of "an active process of assimilation and transformation, as opposed to a simple spread of classical or Italian ideas." As illustrated in his book, the consequence of such a reframing is "a focus on contexts; on the networks and locales in which the new forms and ideas were discussed and adapted; on the periphery of Europe; on the later 'Renaissance;' and finally on what might be called the 'quotidianization' or 'domestication' of the 'Renaissance.'" While renaissance scholars have attempted to reframe the renaissance by seeking different forms of *other renaissances* our present collection suggests its own way to reframe renaissance. Obviously, *Other Renaissances* is also about those active processes that transform and rewrite the European Renaissance, but not from the peripheries of Europe as in Burke's perspective, but from transglobal centers where intellectuals were and are engaged in transcultural imaginative practices. From Hu Shi, Sri Aurobindo, to Maori, Jewish and Tamil writers, to the intellectuals in the Arabic world, *Other Renaissances* proposes a genealogy of the renaissance that approaches renaissance as a transcultural phenomenon rather than a critical category that originated in and therefore is owned by the West. Burke's enterprise of decentering the European "Renaissance" brings about an emphasis on those "Other Renaissances" on the periphery neglected by the earlier studies of the "Renaissance."

In the opening essay of this volume, Walter Andrews asks, "When is a Renaissance not a Renaissance?" to which he answers, "When it is the Ottoman Renaissance!" Andrews' chapter calls into question some features of the employment and deployment of the term "Renaissance," which the author argues, is assumed to give birth to modernity, even though that is hardly the case of the European Renaissance, as we know it today. An Ottoman "Renaissance," Andrews shows, happened in the fifteenth and sixteenth centuries, a "Renaissance" that paralleled the

European "Renaissance" in significant ways, but the term "Ottoman Renaissance" is rarely used by anyone to describe that movement. The explanation Andrews provides lays bare some unchallenged notions about what a "Renaissance" is and does. He argues that the idea of an Ottoman "Renaissance" continues to be so stubbornly suppressed because the movement did not *appear* to culminate in modernity, a feature with which all "Other Renaissances" are often associated.

In "The People's Entertainments: Translation, Popular Fiction and the *Nahdah* in Egypt," Samah Selim examines how the story of *Nahdah* ("Renaissance," revival) in Egypt is entwined with the history of the Arabic novel. She argues that in Egypt, modern criticism and new quasi-official literary institutions suppressed a thriving contemporary field of popular fiction to construct a national novelistic canon. Thus, a *particular* version of modernity, a *particular Nahdah* to the exclusion of all others, came to determine Arabic literary history. Orit Bashkin continues the discussion of Arab "Renaissance" with her chapter on the revival movement that came into being in a colonial and postcolonial context, the Ba'th movement, in Iraq. She argues that *Ba'th*, meaning among other things, awakening, and "the day of Ba'th," referring to the Day of Judgment or the resurrection of the dead, is highly important to our understanding of "Renaissance" (s) and revolution. These definitions raise interesting questions as to the ways in which the Ba'th intellectuals reconciled the messianic concept of resurrection with a national awakening and how these concepts produced a new understanding of rise and decline that they translated into Iraq's cultural and political rebirth.

In Germany in the eighteenth century, the struggle for a Jewish identity became linked to the "rebirth" of Hebrew as a vernacular. It had been a religious language in Europe from the time of the Romans, but the idea of a cultural identity linked to rebirth of Hebrew was not the "Renaissance" of Jewish culture. Rather it was seen initially as the platform through which European Enlightenment thought could be spread. As Moshe Pelli shows, this "rebirth" becomes a "Renaissance" of a Jewish, national identity only through the rejection of the claims of the Enlightenment Hebraists. The "Hebrew Renaissance" is part of the late nineteenth-century move that saw national and linguistic identity as intertwined.

Turning further East or West, depending on which way we look, in "The Chinese Renaissance: A Transcultural Reading," Gang Zhou's chapter examines how Chinese intellectuals in the early twentieth century understood and appropriated the idea of European "Renaissance." She discusses Hu Shi, the most important intellectual leader in modern

China and the main architect of the Chinese vernacular movement. Hu's creative uses of the Italian "Renaissance" and his passionate promotion of a Chinese "Renaissance" reveal to us the performative magic of the word "Renaissance" and prompt us to wonder, "Indeed, what is a Renaissance?" Connecting the Chinese "Renaissance" to various *Other Renaissances* in the lands outside Europe, the author proposes a scholarly reconsideration of "Renaissance" as a transcultural phenomenon rather than as a critical category, originated and therefore owned by a certain culture.

Schildgen's chapter, "Sri Aurobindo: Renaissance in India and the Italian Renaissance," discusses a transformation that occurred in India from the late eighteenth century, one that is called, both by Indian and European writers, the Indian "Renaissance." Centered in Bengal, even while the Tamil "Renaissance" exploded to recover cultures long suppressed, the Indian "Renaissance," spanning almost a hundred years in Aurobindo's version, had several stages. Written in 1920, Aurobindo's little treatise, *The Renaissance in India*, reviewed India's long history to express his political and nationalist aspirations for India's renewal. Analyzing the various aspects of the Indian "Renaissance" in contrast to his idea of Italy's, Aurobindo emphasizes the syncretic and translated nature of the cultural development underway. Aurobindo's essay suggests that the term "Renaissance" could be made an "Indian" concept, and that it had been appropriated to characterize both an epistemological and political transformation, of which he was both a participant and observer.

In her chapter on the "Irish Renaissance," Kathleen Heininge considers the different connotations behind the various terms used to describe the cultural, social, and intellectual movements in late nineteenth-century Ireland. Each term for that period of time, "The Celtic Dawn," "The Revival," or "The Renaissance," invokes a different idea of how to look at what came before. The idea of "The Celtic Dawn" focuses on a shift toward modernity, involving as it does a reconsideration of the traditional to explore a new consciousness. The term "Revival" is more aligned with a nationalist agenda, relying upon the resuscitation of an originating past to breathe life into an independent Irish future; its focus also tends to be primarily on the literary. Only the term "Renaissance" seems to take into account the full range of political (including postcolonial) and social ramifications of the various movements of the time, movements that pertain to literature, language, sports, dance, music, economy, and politics.

In "The Long Maori Renaissance," Mark Williams sets out to show that early twentieth-century Maori revivalism represented first by the

Maori, Apirana Ngata, and that of the late twentieth century, better known "Renaissance" of the 1970s and 1980s, share important continuities. True, the recent movement asserted separatist and overtly political goals, but what links the authors is a compromise between accommodation and difference in regards to the colonial heritage. Williams shows that these continuities, between Ngata and those represented by writers like Witi Ihimaera, suggest that rather than one "Renaissance" beginning around the early 1970s and continuing into the 1990s, in fact, there is a long "Renaissance" going back to the late colonial period marked by periods of greater and lesser intensity. The distinguishing feature of this "Renaissance" has consistently been that cultural revival and the claim to economic self-determination have been inseparably linked.

The last three essays continue the transglobal conversation by linking the Americas to the literary reception, translation, and transformation of "Renaissance" as an idea. In "Globalizing the Harlem Renaissance: Irish, Mexican, and "Negro" Renaissance in *The Survey and Survey Graphic*," Robert Johnson places the Harlem "Renaissance" in a world-historical context by framing it as one among several global rearticulations of racial and national identity in the post–World War I era. The chapter compares the Harlem "Renaissance" with the elite, state-sponsored "Renaissance" of postrevolutionary Mexico and with the Gaelic literary "Renaissance" of the newly independent Ireland. Continuing the discussion of African-American cultural "Renaissances," in "Two Chicago Renaissances with Harlem Between Them," Lisa Woolley, focuses on the United States, arguing that in American literary history, "Renaissance" retains the sense of innovation, institutionalization of learning, and patronage of the arts associated with the European "Renaissance" but almost reverses the meaning of the term in other ways. Locating one of the central questions in this volume, Woolley asks, "What does this situation say about the use of 'Renaissance' in American literary studies, about the possibilities and limits of designating literary periods, and about the contradictions involved in studying place-based movements?"

In the final chapter, Jane Newman focuses on the widespread dissemination of allegedly definitive works on the European "Renaissance" in the United States during the Cold War. These included Jacob Burckhardt's *The Civilization of the Renaissance in Italy* (orig. 1860) and Cassirer's *The Individual and the Cosmos in Renaissance Philosophy* (orig. 1927), among others. The chapter examines images of the European "Renaissance" that were produced, both literally and figuratively, by a mid- twentieth-century United States academy struggling to find its place within the highly polarized rhetoric and reality of the Cold War. This academic "Renaissance," packaged as a Eurocentric version of a "usable past" for the United States and rooted in "the great achievements and lofty ideas" of the fifteenth and sixteenth centuries emerged as the target of and foil for "new approaches" to the period in the 1970s through 1990s. These "new approaches" raised questions about race, gender, and sexuality, as well as the place of popular culture and dissident movements in the European "Renaissance." The Cold War "Renaissance" was itself based, however, largely on translations of the work of émigré scholars like Hans Baron, Ernst Cassirer, Paul Oskar Kristeller, Erwin Panofsky, and others. The much critiqued "Europeanness" of the study of the "Renaissance" was thus itself in large part already a transplant, a displaced object and "othered" version of the period, with less than firm roots in its original scholarly soil. After all, as these émigré scholars were only too painfully aware, "Europe," as an exported civilizing ideal, had massively failed in the first half of the twentieth century for the whole world to witness.

In the Epilogue, Sander Gilman engages in a compelling dialogue with Peter Burke's approach to the modern "Renaissance." Gilman lists numerous incidents where "Renaissance" is used in seemingly familiar or unfamiliar ways. Certainly "Renaissance" has won its special place in the public imagination and every day cultural practices, which rightfully demands expanded awareness and research. He cites numerous occasions where the word "Renaissance" is used in seemingly familiar or unfamiliar ways, making it almost a free-floating signifier, that he links to the careless use of the word "Holocaust," making the latter lose any specific meaning except in the concrete world of human experience and memory. He emphasizes how the term "Renaissance" possesses an almost magical power in the public imagination and in common speech.

A genealogy of the "Renaissance" starts with the question "what is a Renaissance?" It is a question not raised as a commonsensical one that awaits an essentializing definition but as one that questions common sense and opens up further possibilities. Examining how the idea of "Renaissance" was born and has been reborn again and again in different geocultural contexts, a genealogy of the "Renaissance" attempts to understand "Renaissance" not as an ontological autonomous subject that existed in the remote past, but as an accumulation of various readings and appropriations that is both transnational and transcultural. After all, it is hard to imagine that a great idea would be fixed and defined (dead?) at its birth; it is only natural that the idea would grow and be enriched, blossoming in other places and at other times with new, even contradictory inflections.

A genealogy of the "Renaissance" deals with meanings and interpretations of the "Renaissance"; it also explores how the concept of the "Renaissance" functions in concrete historical instances. Where is the "Renaissance" to be found? How does it get produced and regulated? What are its social effects? And finally, a genealogy of "Renaissance" centers on circulation and transmission of the term as well as on the idea initially encapsulated within it. Rather than asserting the will to truthfully represent the "Renaissance," such an approach invites rethinking the possibilities of the "Renaissance." While this volume examines how the "Renaissance" functions in specific locales responding to specific systems of reference, it also concerns itself with how such a concept contributes to a global cultural network.

Without doubt, the powerful position that western culture assumed granted the term "Renaissance" a certain aura that most ideas generated from marginal spaces do not have. But our attention to these creative uses of the term "Renaissance" in various geopolitical contexts should not be confined to the hierarchical relation enforced by the power of western culture. The circulation of the "Renaissance" beyond its historical origin shows the fluidity and mobility of the idea. It also reveals the power structure that directs the traffic in ideas, and it celebrates the transcultural imagination exercised by the people who participated in complicated networks of literary and cultural exchange.

Together the chapters in this volume promote a new emerging "Renaissance" that includes both the European "Renaissance" and *Other Renaissances*, a concept in the making that demands recognition. The fact that little attention has been dedicated to these *Other Renaissances* only suggests a scholarly narrowness that we attempt to correct. Issues such as modernity, anticolonialism, nationalism, and postcolonialism, as well as cultural and linguistic revival have preoccupied *Other Renaissance* intellectuals at the national level. In local or regional cultural "Renaissances," issues of cultural heritage and integrity, of race, of identity repression and formation, and of the right to self-determination, often become the main concerns of marginalized, racialized, or otherwise dominated people. Yet both national and regional "Renaissances" share a tendency to describe forms of self-reinvention.

Still other versions of "Renaissance," such as those deployed by nineteenth-century writers, for example, used the term to indicate developments traditionally associated with the "Enlightenment" or "modernization," because they applied it to describe social and political aspirations and reforms thought to advance the cause of reason against tradition and custom. When cultural issues like language, recovery of ancient texts, and religious reform predominate, such enterprises clearly inherited and appropriated what has come to be called the European "Renaissance." When the term "Renaissance" becomes (both explicitly and implicitly) a tool to construct a theory of history, as a way to describe a gap between the present and past and to question and reconfigure past traditions (whether of society, religion, or politics), however, the focus clearly has more in common with the European "Enlightenment." Examining these transcultural practices that make use of "Renaissance" as an idea underscores how European period distinctions like Medieval, Renaissance, Enlightenment, and even Modernism, for example, fade away or become transcoded as *Other Renaissances* engage in substantial programs of cultural, social, and political change that question the entrenched period distinctions borrowed or exported to other cultural settings.

The idea of "Renaissance" and its multiple uses and interpretations across the world leads us to propose that the word possesses a malleable meaning, open to change, to being redefined and revised, and to being appropriated in widely different cultural contexts. By examining how this idea of "Renaissance" circulated in different ways on various occasions in world cultural history, we argue that debating to what degree these *Other Renaissances* are similar to or different from the European "Renaissance" does not merely enrich our understanding and definition of what constitutes a "Renaissance." Rather, an evaluation of these *Other Renaissances* highlights how the European "Renaissance" and *Other Renaissances* belong to a complicated network of world literary exchange.

CHAPTER 1

Suppressed Renaissance

Q: When Is a Renaissance Not a Renaissance? A: When It Is the Ottoman Renaissance!

Walter G. Andrews

During the long sixteenth century, from approximately 1453 to 1625, Ottoman Turkish culture burgeoned spectacularly, paralleling the broader burgeoning of culture(s) in Europe commonly called "the Renaissance." In very general terms, many of the social and material conditions—everything from economics, agriculture, and labor, to modes of rule, demographics, trade, climate, and public health—that made the European Renaissance possible also existed in the Ottoman Empire and had very similar social and cultural consequences.[1] It is reasonable to conclude from evidence of this kind that there was a distinctly Ottoman Renaissance and this, in turn, raises a significant issue subsumed in the question: Why has the term "Ottoman Renaissance" *never* been used to any noticeable degree by anyone—Ottomans, Turks, non-Turks—in talking about the history of Ottoman culture?

Renaissances abound in our scholarly world. Exceedingly rare is the culture that does not claim a renaissance at one time or another. So why is the Ottoman Empire, arguably the largest and most powerful empire of the early modern world, without a renaissance of its own? The answer to this question underscores some features of the employment and deployment of the term "renaissance" that seem especially relevant to the concerns of this volume.

It is has long been generally accepted that the Ottomans did have a *golden age*, usually confined to the reign (1520–1566) of Sultan Süleyman (the Magnificent to Europeans, the Lawgiver to the Ottomans). But even though the golden age is itself a Renaissance concept,[2] in reference to the Ottomans, the golden age has always implied—sometimes unintentionally—that no matter how dull and unworthy Ottoman culture was in general, it did have a period in which it was more lively, more productive, and more brilliant than the (Ottoman) cultural norm. In part, this is a consequence of the notion that the Ottomans could not have had a *rebirth* of culture because Ottoman culture represented the dying days of traditional Islamic culture. A moment of deathbed lucidity is hardly a rebirth!

Before going on to explore how the Ottomans ended up with a golden age but no renaissance, it is necessary to point out that the whole notion of renaissance is embedded in a broader biological metaphor that has long been used for describing cultural change. The idea that cultures progress from birth to youthful exuberance to mature productivity to senescence and death is no longer even recognizable as a metaphor in many discourses and is commonly taken as just another concrete description of how the world works. The idea of renaissance represents a tweaking of the cultural-biology metaphor to account for the natural history of modernity in a way that preserves the continuity of an ethnic-cultural story. That is to say that the underlying premise assumes that a culture can avoid death by being reborn in a newly youthful culture with the implication that for the rebirth to be real (and not a golden age or golden moment in the midst of decline) it must culminate in modernity, a modernity that, in turn, is equivalent to the eternal youth or constant renewal of culture (and hence, to the "end of history"). This is why non-European renaissances are often associated with the nationalist, modernizing, and westernizing movements of the nineteenth and twentieth centuries and, in part, why the idea of an Ottoman Renaissance continues to be so stubbornly suppressed. Whatever happened during the golden age of Ottoman culture, it did not *appear* to culminate in an Ottoman modernity and, thus, to term this age a renaissance would call into question some cherished notions about what a renaissance is and does.

In order to examine the suppression of Ottoman Renaissance, we must begin from an epistemological issue. The state of knowledge about Ottoman culture (or of retrospectives on Ottoman culture) is characterized by a history of the continuing subterranean survival of widely discredited theories about culture, race, sociology, and even history itself.

Let us take, as our example, the case of Ottoman literature and especially of Ottoman poetry, which was the major art form of the culture of the Ottoman elites. Near the end of the nineteenth century, the British Ottomanist E. J. W. Gibb began the task of writing his monumental and vastly influential *History of Ottoman Poetry*, which would be published in six volumes from 1900–1909, all but the first volume edited after Gibb's death (in 1901) by his friend, the Persianist E. G. Browne. Gibb was an amateur scholar of independent means who became the preeminent expert in his field, having collected an impressive private library of Ottoman works. He is said to have loved the Turks and to have been loved by them and he regularly sheltered traveling Turkish intellectuals in his London home. Gibb's *History* is awesome in its erudition. His translations of Ottoman poetry achieved a wide readership in the English-speaking world at the turn of the twentieth century. Even his Turkish contemporaries were fulsome in their praise of his knowledge of Ottoman language and culture. In the ensuing one hundred years, no other work on Ottoman literature has supplanted or has had the enduring impact of Gibb's *History*.

Gibb loved Ottoman poetry and devoted his life to studying it. He also loved the Turks and saw himself as their friend. Yet the *History of Ottoman Poetry*, with its monumental display of erudition, is without doubt among the prime reasons why the Ottoman Renaissance became an unthinkable concept. We need look no farther than the introduction to Gibb's *History* to see how his general perspective poisons the whole project of characterizing Ottoman poetry. We will give a few examples of the consequences of this perspective, not with the purpose of exposing anything new about British orientalist thought, but to indicate how extreme the notions are that have passed into the realm of "what everyone knows" about Ottoman culture.

First of all, Gibb's perspective is fundamentally racist. In his introduction he says:

> That great race to which the Ottomans belong, that race which includes not only the Turks both Western and Eastern, but also the so-called Tartars and Turkmans as well as the Mongols, has never produced any religion, philosophy or literature which bears the stamp of its individual genius. This is because the true genius of that race lies in action, not in speculation. The Turks and their kinsfolk are before all things soldiers.[3]

He goes on to introduce a subsequent paragraph by saying:

> Though unable to originate any literature which should give expression to the true genius of their race . . .[4]

In Gibb's formulation, this fundamental genetic (racial) inability of
Turks to produce their own literature together with their soldierly inclination toward obedience and subservience made them the willing thralls
of Persian masters for some six hundred years of prolific literary production. Not only were the Turks unable to create their own literature, they
were incapable even of thinking their own thoughts or feeling their own
feelings. As Gibb put it

> in the spheres of science, philosophy and literature they acknowledged
> only too freely their deficiency; and there they went to school with the
> Persian, intent not merely on acquiring his methods, but on entering into
> his spirit, thinking his thoughts and feeling his feelings.[5]

Thus, everything that the Turks did in the area of culture was hopelessly
derivative. When we come to the so-called "golden age" of the sixteenth
century, we find there is really no escaping this genetic destiny:

> The poetry of this brilliant era is marked by no essential change from that
> which goes before; it proceeds along the old Persian lines, keeping in view
> the same old goal, and circumscribed by the same old limitations; its
> progress is that of development rather than of transformation. It arises
> from the nature of the case that this development runs almost entirely
> upon technical lines, the principal object of this School of Poetry being, as
> we well know, not so much the expression of true feeling as grace of dic-
> tion and faultless manipulation of language. It therefore follows that such
> development as it is capable of will naturally proceed in that direction.
> And so we find in the Suleymanic age a great improvement in the style of
> poetry viewed simply as an art, without any corresponding advance in its
> substance.[6]

Gibb moves through four volumes, recording the dismal history of an
irredeemably belated culture in Olympian self-affirmations: "as we will
know," "It therefore follows". However, the fifth volume opens with a
chapter entitled "The Dawn of a New Era" (whether this is Gibb's title
or Browne's is unclear) that begins on an ecstatically hopeful note:

> We have now to tell the story of a great awakening. We have traced the
> course of poetic literature amongst the Ottoman Turks during five cen-
> turies and a half. We have learned how, throughout this long period, no
> voice has ever reached it from outside the narrow school where it was
> reared; how, Persian in its inception, Persian in substance it has remained
> down to the very end, driven back after a blind struggle to win free,

baffled and helpless into the stagnant swamp of a dead culture. But now all is on the verge of change; Asia is on the point of giving place to Europe, and the tradition of ages is about to become a memory of the past. A voice from the Western world rings through the Orient skies like the trumpet-blast of Isráfíl; and lo, the muse of Turkey wakes from her death-like trance, and all the land is jubilant with life and song, for a new heaven and a new earth are made visible before the eyes of men.[7]

Following close on this paean to westernization, we find the long-awaited term. "The time is not come," Gibb says, "when it is possible fully and adequately to write the history of this *Renascence*."[8] Renascence/Renaissance finally the Turks have discovered a path of radical change that leads to western modernity and, at that point, to Gibb's mind they become worthy of a renaissance of their own. Of course the Turks go on being what they are and, "with that genius for assimilation which, as we have so often noticed, is characteristic of the race, this new revelation is made part and parcel of the intellectual life."[9] Still incapable of self-creation or authenticity, the poor Turks find themselves another more powerful and successful master and even Gibb's suggestion that this final rejection of a moribund tradition might be a renaissance falls flat.

Colleagues who study other non-western cultures will immediately recognize in Gibb's formulation a kind of naive, run-of-the-mill nineteenth century orientalism, the flaws and fallacies of which have been so thoroughly exposed in many contexts that they are immediately visible even to bright undergraduates. Consequently, one might ask why so many words have been expended here on something so patently absurd. The response is to point out that Gibb's basic premises have *never* been successfully critiqued, that they continue to be "the truth" about Ottoman literary culture, that the first volume of Gibb's work was even translated into Turkish without significant comment on its fundamental racism, that there is no major work in Turkish and only a few in other languages refuting Gibb's assertions, and that Gibb's conclusions about Ottoman literature continue to be reproduced in many forms and to ground the dominant modern literary historical tradition as regards the Ottomans.

Although some Ottomanists have attempted to point out the absurdity of Gibb's conclusions and to argue for beginning anew to assess the character and value of Ottoman literature, their efforts have been to little or no avail.[10] Gibb's pronouncements have even seeped into the great surveys of Islamic history where they continue their poisonous work. For example, in his influential three volume *The Venture of Islam: Conscience and History in a World Civilization*, which was published in several developing versions between 1958 and 1974, the late Marshal Hodgson located the fifteenth and sixteenth century "flowering" of Islamic culture in the "Persianate" culture of the short-lived court of Hüseyin Baykara in Herat (in present-day Afghanistan), in the Uzbek court in Bokhara, and in the Shiite revolution under the Safavids in Iran.[11] Of the Ottomans, whose literary and artistic production far surpassed all of the abovementioned, he says only, "Though in the fifteenth century they had still formed rather a 'frontier' area, in the sixteenth century the Ottomans also participated, if perhaps rather less creatively except in the field of architecture."[12] Later, in a chapter on the Ottomans, he depicts them as exemplary of the "problem" that Islamic civilization had in grappling with the possibilities of transformations in social and economic conditions, arguing that "These limitations are nowhere more visible, at least to our hindsight, than in the Ottoman empire."[13] He then introduces the Italian Renaissance, states that the Ottomans could not possibly have entered into this Renaissance because it was an "Occidental" movement, and finally makes the astonishing (and spectacularly erroneous) assertion that "it seems to be true that the Ottomans, for all their proximity, showed no more alertness to what was happening in the Occident, and possibly even less, than the Timurîs of India."[14] Yet Hodgson, for all his confidence, knows nothing first hand about Ottoman literature and culture and cites only two works on the topic: Gibb's *History of Ottoman Poetry* and the French translation of the Italian Alessio Bombaci's *Storia della letteratura Turca*, a historical survey of the literatures of Turkic peoples which devotes only 103 pages out of 398 to the Ottomans and cites Gibb's history as one of two works that make it possible "to trace, with all certainty, a literary panorama."[15] One could go on for some time multiplying examples of nearly identical views, expressed with similar confidence.

Of course, when faced with the certainty expressed by Gibb and those who followed him, the first response of a reasonable person without special knowledge would be to assume that the experts and giants of the field were accurate in their assessments. It seems inconceivable that a person who knew Ottoman literature as well as Gibb clearly did or a person as erudite as Hodgson could make confident and sweeping generalizations about the Ottomans that were in many cases entirely wrong and in almost all cases were open to serious question. How could such a thing happen?

The whole story is the topic of a large book and not an essay, but the short version is this: Gibb never experienced Ottoman or Turkish culture firsthand. He read everything but he never traveled to the Ottoman Empire. When it came to understanding how Ottoman poetry existed in its context he relied on Turkish friends, acquaintances, and correspondents. Most of his Turkish informants were cultured elites involved to some extent in the modernizing and westernizing movements of the latter half of the nineteenth century. They were glad to talk about the abstract theosophical content of Ottoman poetry, about its relations to Persian poetry (which enjoyed a considerable vogue in England during the nineteenth century),[16] and about its deficiencies in relation to the revolutionary new literature they championed. But they were not able to talk (immodestly) to a Victorian (and Christian) foreigner about the parties, the drinking, the taverns, coffeehouses, and baths, the entertainment culture, the beloved boys and women, the relations between sexuality and spirituality, between love and the sharing of power, between courtiers and patrons that made Ottoman lyric poetry lively and meaningful in its context. Read out of context, without reference to its vocation in the actual world, with an eye only to how it might reflect Persian poetry (which Gibb read extensively with his friend Browne) or how it compared to the ideals of late British romanticism, Ottoman poetry did not come off well. No early-modern poetry would or could have under such circumstances.

It is important to our exploration of this suppressed Renaissance to note that Gibb's narrative of Ottoman cultural ineptitude would never have been as overwhelmingly influential had it not dovetailed quite nicely with other significant literary, cultural, and political historical narratives that tell the story of the "rebirth" of national cultures in the modern Middle East. For example, the story of Arab cultural Renaissance (*nahda*: reawakening, renaissance) identifies a period of "decline" (*inhitat*) that usually begins in the eleventh century, which is—not accidentally—the time of the first major wave of invasions of the Middle East by Turkic peoples from Central Asia. The *nahda* itself comes in the nineteenth century simultaneously with the ebbing of Ottoman cultural and political hegemony over much of the Arabic-speaking world and a movement by Ottoman intellectuals toward engagement with European literature.[17] Likewise, the classical ages of Persian literature are seen as culminating in the poetry of Jami, who dies (1492) in the spring of the great burgeoning of Ottoman culture. Persian poetry finds itself again only when *empire* (represented by the Ottomans) gives way to the idea of *nation* in the nineteenth century. From the perspective (or retrospective) of Arab and Persian nationalism, the period of Ottoman ascendancy is a dark age in which the power center of the Islamic world began to speak Turkish and the former dominant cultures were repressed or obscured.

The West too had a huge stake in Arab and Persian nationalism and modernism, both of which concepts implied (to the West, at least) ideological westernization, and the hegemony of western notions of culture—which, in turn, contributed to legitimizing western colonizing intrusions in the Middle East. By assigning the six hundred years of Ottoman influence to the peripheries of the story and presenting Ottoman culture as nothing but the pale and moribund imitation of worthier cultures, the West, in the guise of scholarship and, at times, with the best of intentions, was able to marginalize an imperial and colonial rival and to turn the allegiances of important ethnic groups in the Middle East away from the dominant (if failing) Islamic power and toward the secular West.

Nonetheless, the narrative of Ottoman cultural ineptitude would not have survived so powerfully into the present had an emerging Turkish nationalism not been similarly inclined to marginalize Ottoman culture in favor of a modern, national (and westernized) culture. Early attempts, in the nineteenth century, to recreate Ottoman culture—the culture of a multiethnic empire—on modern, western models had faltered. With the catastrophic collapse of the empire following World War I and subsequent attempts by the West to dismember the remnants and parcel them out to various ethnic claimants, the Turks, under the inspired leadership of Mustafa Kemal Atatürk, carved out for themselves a national homeland in Anatolia and Europe. In a stunning series of profound transformations, the central lands of the Ottoman Empire became a secular national state firmly aligned with western ideals and ideologies, in many ways liberating itself from Ottomanism as thoroughly as did Eastern Europe and the Arabic-speaking parts of the empire. At the heart of these transformations was a radical cultural revolution in which the Arabic-script alphabet was discarded in favor of a Latin letter alphabet and the language itself was altered by the official replacement of Arabic and Persian vocabulary by words of Turkish origin or coined from Turkish roots. For the great majority of Turks, within a generation, Ottoman books became unreadable unless transcribed, the Ottoman language became obscure unless translated, and Ottoman literary culture became foreign to its own heirs. Subsequently, the Turkish Republic engaged in a delicate balancing act with regard to Ottoman culture. The past culture was privileged as a historical artifact and the object of study and preservation but only in the context of a narrative that at its roots did not challenge Gibb's. The degree of national pride and nostalgia with regard to the past was held below the level of dangerous counterrevolutionary fervor by reminders of the essential inadequacy of Ottoman culture as evidenced by the collapse of the empire it served and the "discovery" (or invention) of a purely Turkish (non-Ottoman) culture that had supposedly lived in parallel to the dominant culture and emerged to form the basis (and history) of modern Turkish culture. More than anything else, modern Turkish rejection of Ottoman literary culture has stood in the way of telling a more reasonable, less racially biased, and more positive story.

For the present generation of Turks, the situation seems to be changing. Although conservative religious elements still use Ottoman culture as a nostalgic emblem of the glories of an idealistically recalled "Islamic" past, and some of their progressive opponents still favor a negative evaluation of Ottoman culture, the Ottomans and their culture have increasingly become objects of interest for people holding a broad spectrum of political views.[18] It remains to be seen, however, whether or not enough Turkish cultural policy-makers, intellectuals, and scholars will be prepared to risk providing ammunition to those clamoring for an "Islamic state" and be willing to complicate their own identifications with Europe in order to challenge seriously the ethnocentrism and distortions of the prevailing assessment of Ottoman culture.

Returning to the notion of a long sixteenth-century Ottoman Renaissance, we can now begin to examine some of the challenges this notion presents to the narrative of modernity, which traces a distinct path from the Renaissance (and subsequent Renaissances) to the modern. Contrary to the views of Gibb and Hodgson (and many others), the Ottoman Renaissance was a period of intense and creative cultural and artistic activity. Significant monuments of architectural merit were arising everywhere, and the ateliers of miniaturists were churning out magnificent illustrations. During this period, Ottoman thought is infused with a sense of historical destiny. Writing the history of the Ottomans begins in earnest during the reign of Bayezit II (1481–1512) and reaches a high point with the monumental sixteenth century histories: Kemalpaşazade's *Histories of the Ottoman Dynasty* (Tevarih-i Al-i Osman), Hoca Sa'deddin's *Crown of Histories* (Tacu't-Tevarih) and Mustafa 'Ali's *Essence of History* (Künhü'l-Ahbar). Ottoman sultans of this period also employed a chronicler (şahnameci) to record their deeds in the language (Persian) and style of the *Book of Kings* (Şahname), the legendary history of the ancient Persian rulers. The biographies of poets (tezkire-i şu'era), works that appeared suddenly in the sixteenth century had notices for hundreds of poets and constitute the anecdotal history of a lively and productive cultural life.[19] Ottoman littérateurs translated and appropriated the classics of the Arabic and Persian traditions and prided themselves on their abilities to write verses in all the languages of the Islamic tradition: Ottoman Turkish, Arabic, Persian, and Chagatai (the literary language of the eastern Turkic dialects). The Persian master poets (e.g., Hafez, Sa'di, Jami) still inspired Ottoman poets—in much the same way that Dante and Petrarch and the literary masterpieces of classical antiquity inspired sixteenth century European poets. But significant voices were raised in opposition to the slavish imitation of Persian models—a controversy reminiscent of the differences between the views of Pico della Mirandola and Bishop Bembo on the topic of adherence to classical models.

For example, close to the turn of the sixteenth century, the poet and courtier Tacızade Ca'fer Çelebi [pronounced Tadjızade Djafer Chelebee], in the introduction to his *Book of Desire* (Hevesname), tells (quite conventionally) that he was persuaded by his friends to write a romantic narrative in rhymed couplets (a *mesnevi*).[20] He then engages in a dialogue with his heart, which points out to him that the ancients (the Persians) spent a lot of time turning out wonderful narrative poems and that he could, if he wanted, take one of their poems and turn it into Turkish word for word. But (the heart admonishes) for someone with skill this would be easier than easy and also (in the heart's opinion) dumber than dumb. A real poet would create his own story, write it in his own style, and be indebted to no one and to nothing but his own talent. Ca'fer then goes on to write a unique first person narrative about a clandestine love affair carried on with a married woman while the two are camping in the spring at the popular vacation resort of Kağıthane on the outskirts of Istanbul. [So much for Hodgson's assertion that the Ottomans were too "Sharia-minded" to be anything but uncreative!]

Like Ca'fer Çelebi, sixteenth century Ottoman writers constantly complain that everyone (else) is copying the Persians, which might give the impression that they were indeed the feckless imitators that Gibb made them out to be. Yet in every case, the complainer is pointing out that *he*—unlike his less-skilled contemporaries—is *not* imitating. Replace "Petrarch" with the name of any canonical Persian poet and Sidney's famous lines could be a loose translation of what Ca'fer Çelebi and many other Ottoman poets wrote to admonish their fellows and highlight their own creative talents:

> You that poore Petrarch's long deceased woes,
> With new-borne sighes and denisend wit do sing;
> You take wrong waies, those far-fet helpes be such,
> As do bewray a want of inward tuch:[21]

Art and literature were everywhere in Renaissance Istanbul. Poets were lavishly patronized by the palace and wealthy administrators. The salons of the great were places from which a skilled poet or writer could launch a spectacular career. Also in this period women appear prominently as poets and participants in literary pursuits. They are recorded in the biographical works and are rewarded by the palace for their poetry. Religious orthodoxy was dramatically challenged by the proliferation, at all social levels, of participation in the dervish (mystical) confraternities. The charismatic, ecstatic rituals of the mystics provided a hot, emotional alternative to familiar rituals of the mosque. Mysticism was the religion of love and love poetry was its scripture, singing its passion for unity with the divine beloved. This explosion of popular mysticism (and not the rise of Shiism, as Hodgson claims) was in many ways the equivalent of the Protestant Reformation. The dervish orders provided a variety of avenues for the direct personal experience of divine power; they bypassed the control of the elite scholarly interpreters of the faith and translated the emotional essence of Islam into the (Turkish and Persian) vernaculars.

As will be mentioned in more detail below, although actual interactions between Ottomans and Italians did occur during the long sixteenth century, they have little relevance to the idea being suggested here of a uniquely Ottoman Renaissance. Nonetheless, it is impossible to entirely ignore Hodgson's strange impression that "it seems to be true that the Ottomans, for all their proximity, showed no more alertness to what was happening in the Occident, and possibly even less, than the Timurîs of India." Given how stunningly false this assertion is, one cannot even imagine how a competent scholar could have come up with such an idea. In fact, Ottoman contacts with Europe were many and varied. Europe was, in a sense, only a few hundred yards away from the Ottoman capital. A boat ride across the Golden Horn could and did take Ottomans to the European colonies in the suburb of Galata, where they interacted, often quite intimately, with Europeans. In the mid-fifteenth century, Mehmet (II) the Conqueror's patronage brought highly regarded Italian artists and artisans to Istanbul, clearly indicating that he was well aware of what was happening in the artistic world of Renaissance Italy. The *fonduchi* of Venice thronged with Turkish merchants.[22] The Ottoman sultans were intensely involved in European affairs. Christian Europeans even worked for them in many capacities. During the sixteenth century, in a climate of intense apocalyptic speculation, the Ottoman rulers saw themselves in competition with the princes and emperors of Europe for the role of the Universal Monarch whose ultimate victory would usher in the last days.[23]

A simple example of the kinds of personal interactions that did occur is found in the career and family of Andrea Gritti who became Doge of Venice in 1523. As a young man, Gritti spent years as a diplomat and merchant in Istanbul, where he was befriended by powerful Ottoman courtiers and fathered four of his five sons with local concubines. His favorite son, Alvise, after being educated in Venice, returned to Istanbul where he became the companion of the highest officials including the grand vizier Ibrahim Pasha. He subsequently entered into the sultan's service, and built himself an Ottoman-style palace where he lived an Ottoman life until he died fighting for the Turks in Transylvania in 1534.[24]

Such indications of mutual attention and cross-fertilization do not, however, presume that either the Ottoman or the Italian Renaissance was somehow dependent upon or to any degree a consequence of relations between the two. As has been suggested above, it seems more accurate and productive to see the Ottoman Renaissance as paralleling the Italian Renaissance for reasons that have nothing to do with direct influences in either direction. What is being "reborn" for Renaissance Ottoman elites is the power and glory *both* of Islam (as a spiritual, cultural, social, and governing entity) and of the great pre-Islamic empires of the Middle East. Their discursive universe is filled with references linking the Ottoman rulers to the ancient "world-conquerors"—for example, Alexander the Great, Chosroes (Husrev), Darius (Dara)—and to the Byzantine Empire at the height of its power. They do not see themselves as "imitating" the classical languages (Persian and Arabic) so much as revitalizing them with a new, Turkish creative impulse. They are, at the same time, nostalgic about the glories of the past and confident about a future in which their own Renaissance will dominate both Europe and the East. Given the circumstances, it is difficult to guess what kinds of "attentiveness" to events in the Occident could have been expected of the Ottomans. They certainly could not have been expected to foresee the consequences in the West, some hundreds of years later, of the so-called "spirit" of the European Renaissance and there was no significant indication during the sixteenth century that the Ottomans would ever be anything but a dominant power in both East and West.

The ultimate intent of the above remarks is not so much to point out the missteps of past scholars but to show how a fundamentally flawed narrative can become so firmly embedded in our general view that it is consistently repeated without intent or conscious thought. Hodgson is by no means alone in this kind of repetition. In fact, he is cited here because he was courageous enough to make his understanding clear and to draw inferences from it. In most other places, the dismissal of

Ottoman culture is treated as an established fact that can be passed on without comment or attribution. For example, in Ira Lapidus' *A History of Islamic Societies*, Ottoman culture of the most productive period is mentioned only in a very short (and dismissive) paragraph. The notes to this paragraph, entitled "On Turkish Art and Literature," cite three works on art and architecture, one on the history of theater and popular entertainments, two on miniature painting, and none whatsoever on literature.[25]

These examples are most relevant to the larger purpose of this chapter insofar as they underscore the role that the notions of renaissance and the politics of renaissance played in creating the dominant narrative of Ottoman culture. As was mentioned earlier, one use of the term *renaissance* is to locate and define periods of cultural change within a biological metaphor. In this context, the Renaissance represents a model of a culture (classical Greco-roman or "western" culture or civilization) that passed through youth and maturity into senescence, at which time it was reborn as the result of a mix of cultural, social, intellectual, and, ultimately, political transformations. Dissociated from the specific cultural transformations that occurred in Italy at a certain time and applied generally and without temporal specificity to western civilization as a whole, this notion of renaissance invites general application to other "civilizations." The biological metaphor requires that a cultural phenomenon or period be located along a birth-to-death continuum imagined as a line that over time rises on the axis of achievement to the point of maturity and from there descends to either death or rebirth. The continuum that describes the trajectory of Ottoman culture is embedded in the continuum of *Islamic civilization* and is traced on the declining part of the line. Therefore, the Ottomans cannot possibly represent a rebirth despite compelling evidence that Islamic civilization as a whole was profoundly transformed and revitalized by Ottoman culture, institutions, and influences. The story of Renaissance, because it implies the story of the origin of western modernity, does not allow even for considering a modernity emerging from the transformation over time of Ottoman culture.

It is important to keep in mind, when examining discourses of *renaissance*, that the Renaissance is a model with an often unacknowledged teleological and ideological component. From the perspective of non-western cultures, the notion of Renaissance is more than a metaphor for radical change, it represents a transformation that must eventually culminate in a modern, national, and, in some degree, westernized (or globalized) culture. The "western-ness" and ultimate modernity of renaissances are, in the end, among the features that make such rebirths comparable to *the* Renaissance. (For example, it would be highly unusual for someone in the West to use the term *renaissance* to describe the contemporary Iranian Islamic revolution, even though some Iranians and other conservative Muslims would see it as a significant rebirth of traditional culture and social organization.) In addition, the "westernizing/modernizing" renaissances of the nineteenth and twentieth centuries in the Middle East and elsewhere are assigned to the positive, growth end of a new continuum of "global culture." Accordingly, if we take "global culture" to imply the cultural hegemony of the West on a global scale, the term "renaissance" then comes to be a compliment paid to westernizing/modernizing movements, a reward for some degree of ideological alignment with the West.

From a postmodern perspective, which assumes that there is a position from which it is possible to critique the master narrative of modernity from without, the biological metaphor for cultural change that underlies general application of the term *renaissance* begins to appear less and less useful (unless, of course, one is interested in complimenting some cultures and implying disapproval of others). Culture is not, after all, a biological entity. A culture may manifest itself in different configurations over time but it is not actually born, nor does it age or die; it does not have "life stages" because it is not alive. A more value-neutral and descriptive metaphor for culture might be derived from the suggestion made by Deleuze and Guattari that assemblages of the kind we identify as culture can be imagined as planes of consistency on which phenomenal multiplicities are interconnected horizontally (non-hierarchically) in a manner analogous to the connections made by the rhizomes of certain grasses.[26] The plane of consistency (or field of rhizomes) provides a non-linear, non-hierarchical model for talking about cultural transformations that can be seen as shifts to new planes of consistency or plateaus. A plane or plateau could be talked about as a "period" without *requiring* that the period be located on a birth to death (or even roots to branches) continuum. Moreover, any comparison of cultures or cultural artifacts would accordingly need to be made overtly with the terms of comparison spelled out rather than implied by the underlying metaphor.

Although the term *renaissance* is a heuristic tool seriously flawed by its inherent ideological complications, *the Renaissance* can be seen as a plane of consistency that invites (or demands) comparisons to other similar phenomena occurring within the same approximate time frame.[27] As was mentioned at the beginning of this chapter, the Renaissance was not just a cultural phenomenon. Much recent work on the Renaissance acknowledges that extraordinary cultural activity was linked to a complex set of social, economic, political, demographic, meteorological, and other phenomena that created the conditions of possibility for cultural florescence in Europe. Many of these contributing phenomena extend beyond the West and seem to have similar impacts on culture in many places at approximately the same time: the Ottoman Empire, Timurid Central Asia, Safavid Iran, Mughal India, perhaps even extending as far as Japan in the early days of the Tokugawa (Edo) shogunate. Just as the Renaissance has expanded out of Italy and is now seen as a European period, so might it eventually be recognized as a global phenomenon without losing too much of its meaningful specificity.

In the context of a globalized notion of the Renaissance it becomes quite possible and indeed instructive to talk about the Ottoman Renaissance. Such a conversation would break down artificial barriers that separate East from West, Ottomans from Europeans, barriers constituted more by the structure of our present scholarly institutions than by actual conditions during the Renaissance. If this perspective becomes an antidote to the poison that infects the project of understanding Ottoman culture, Ottomanists will be pleased, and if it provides a more accurate picture of relations between the Ottomans and Europe, Europeanist scholars should be pleased as well.

Notes

1. An extended discussion of some features of the parallel development of the Ottoman and European "Renaissances" is found in Walter G. Andrews and Mehmet Kalpaklı. *The Age of Beloveds* (Durham, NC: Duke University Press, 2005).
2. Peter Burke, "Concepts of the 'Golden Age' in the Renaissance," in *Süleyman the Magnificent and His Age*. Eds. Metin Kunt and Christine Woodhead. (Harlow, Essex: Longman Group, 1995), pp. 154–63. See also, Cemal Kafadar, "The Myth of the Golden Age: Ottoman Historical Consciousness in the Post-Süleymânic Era," in *Süleymân the Second and His Time*. Eds. Halil İnalcık and Cemal Kafadar. (Istanbul: The Isis Press, 1993), pp. 37–48 and Walter G. Andrews, "Literary Art of The Golden Age," in *Süleymân the Second and His Time*. Eds. İnalcık and Kafadar. pp. 353–68.
3. E. J. W. Gibb, *A History of Ottoman Poetry* in 6 Vols. (London: Luzac and Company, 1900–1906), vol. 1: 6.
4. Ibid. 1: 7.
5. Ibid. 1: 13.
6. Ibid. 3: 2.
7. Ibid. 5: 3.
8. Ibid. 5: 4.

9. Ibid. 5: 6.
10. The most extensive overview of the orientalist grand narrative is found in Victoria Holbrook, *The Unreadable Shores of Love* (Austin, TX: University of Texas Press, 1994), pp. 1–31. See also Walter G. Andrews, *Poetry's Voice, Society's Song: Ottoman Lyric Poetry* (Seattle, WA: University of Washington Press, 1985), pp. 11–18.
11. It must be pointed out that Hodgson resists calling this "flowering" a "renaissance" and states forthrightly that "the most decisive contrast to the Italian Renaissance is that the Persianate flowering did not lead on into modernity." Marshall G. S. Hodgson, *The Venture of Islam: Conscience and History in a World Civilization* in 3 vols. Vol. 3: *The Gunpowder Empires and Modern Times* (Chicago, IL: University of Chicago Press, 1974), 3: 50.
12. Ibid. 3: 49–50.
13. Ibid. 3: 120.
14. Ibid. 3: 119–20.
15. Alessio Bombaci, *Histoire de la Littérature Turque*, trans. I. Melikoff (Paris: Librairie C. Klinksieck, 1968), p. 273.
16. The nineteenth and early twentieth-century-vogue for Persian poetry is attested to by numerous indications from the immense popularity of Fitzgerald's translation of the *Rubaiyat of Omar Khayyam*, which was thrust into popularity by the interest of poets such as Dante Gabriel Rossetti and Swinebume to the spoof of the Persian poetry craze in the short story "For the Duration of the War" by H. H. Munroe, who adopted the pen name, Saki (the wine-server of Persian and Ottoman poetry).
17. We must remember that the nahda itself had its roots in intellectual and literary movements initiated by Arab reformers who were themselves subjects of the Ottoman Empire, who were often educated in Ottoman higher educational institutions, and who were in close contact with similar reform ideologies popular among Turkish-speaking Ottomans.
18. See, for example, Walter Andrews, "Contested Mysteries and Mingled Dreams: Speaking for Ottoman Culture Today from Gencebay to Pamuk," in *Cultural Horizons: A Festschrift in Honor of Talat S. Halman*, Ed. Jayne Warner (Syracuse, NY: Syracuse University Press/Istanbul (wga): Yapı Kredi Yayınları, 2001), pp. 518–37 and "Stepping Aside: Ottoman Literature in Modern Turkey," *Journal of Turkish Literature* 1 (2004), pp. 9–32.
19. For a general overview of the Ottoman tezkires, see James Stewart-Robinson, "The Ottoman Biographies of Poets." *Journal of Near Eastern Studies* 24: 1 and 2 (January–April, 1965), pp. 57–73.
20. Unfortunately there is no available edition of the *Hevesname*. The Ottoman Texts Archive Project [http://courses.washington.edu/otap] has a text under preparation. The material referenced here is found in couplets 476–579. Information on Tacızade Ca'fer Çelebi can be found in the introduction to İsmail E. Erünsal, *The Life and Works of Tâcî-zâde Ca'fer Çelebi, with a Critical Edition of his Dîvân* (Istanbul: Edebiyat Fakültesi Basımevi, 1983).

21. Sir Philip Sidney in *The Poems of Sir Philip Sidney*, Ed. William A. Ringler, Jr. (Oxford: The Clarendon Press, 1962), 15:172.

22. For an overview of the influences on Italian art of trade with the Ottomans see, Rosamund E. Mack, *Bazaar to Piazza: Islamic Trade and Italian Art, 1300–1600* (Berkeley, CA: University of California Press, 2002).

23. See Cornell H. Fleischer, *A Mediterranean Apocalypse: Imperialism and Prophecy, 1453–1550* (Berkeley, CA: University of California Press), forthcoming. Gulru Necipoğlu, in her essay, "Süleymân the Magnificent and the Representation of Power in the Context of Ottoman-Hapsburg-Papal Rivalry," in *Süleymân the Second and His Time*. Eds. Inalcık and Kafadar, (Istanbul: The Isis Press, 1993), pp. 163–94. [Reprinted from *The Art Bulletin* 71 (1989)], pp. 401–427 describes the production of a magnificent crown in the European style, fashioned by Venetian artisans for Sultan Süleyman and adorned with symbols of Ottoman domination over the whole of the known world.

24. Lucette Valensi, *The Birth of the Despot: Venice and the Sublime Porte*, trans. Arthur Denner (Ithaca, NY: Cornell University Press, 1993), pp. 18–20.

25. See Ira M. Lapidus, *A History of Islamic Societies* (Cambridge: Cambridge University Press, 1988), pp. 319–20 and note 943.

26. On the rhizome, see Gilles Deleuze and Félix Guattari, *A Thousand Plateaus: Capitalism and Schizophrenia*. Trans. Brian Massumi (Minneapolis, MN: University of Minnesota Press, 1987), pp. 3–25.

27. Linda T. Darling, "The Renaissance and the Middle East," in *A Companion to the Worlds of the Renaissance*. Ed. Guido Ruggiero. (Oxford: Blackwell, 2002), pp. 55–69.

CHAPTER 2

The People's Entertainments: Translation, Popular Fiction, and the Nahdah in Egypt

Samah Selim

The *Nahdah* represents an ambivalent period in Middle Eastern Studies. Renaissance, Revival, Awakening, all approximate translations that have been used to describe this foundational historical moment and all of which evoke a quixotic gesture of rupture with and return to cultural foundations. Arab intellectuals began to use the term in the middle of the nineteenth century to describe the linguistic and cultural revival that spread from Egypt and Lebanon to the rest of the Arab world in the first decades of the twentieth. George Antonius' classic 1939 work, *The Arab Awakening*, explored and celebrated the emergent political processes that led to the struggle for independence from Ottoman rule in the years leading up to World War I. Contemporary European scholars used phrases like "Islamic modernism" (Gibb) and "Il Risorgimento Arabe" (Gabrielli) to describe the cultural ferment of the nineteenth and early twentieth century in the Middle East.

In one strand of conventional historiography, *Al-Nahdah* refers to a finite era that begins and ends with what Afaf Lutfi Al-Sayyid Marsot has called "the liberal experiment" in Arab culture and politics. But in another, broader sense, it is also coterminous with the whole of Arab modernity as a set of historical potentialities. The various subdisciplines within western Area Studies approach it from different angles, giving it slightly different time frames and geographical centers: Beirut in the

1860s, Damascus in the 1910s, Cairo in the 1920s. For Arab historians and intellectuals today, it is both a foundational paradigm and a dream of the future. For the most part however, the period has been almost exclusively constructed around the genealogy of a narrow, elite political and intellectual culture.

While the "end" of the *Nahdah* is open to debate, scholars commonly offer a very precise date for its origins; 1798, the year of Napoleon's dramatic invasion of Egypt. The twentyodd years between this foundational moment and the institutional reforms of the Muhammad 'Ali era are seen as a necessary period of gestation during which Arab intellectuals began, slowly but surely, to absorb the coming of the West, mainly through numerous educational missions to Europe and the concerted translation of European technical, military, and administrative knowledge. In mainstream western scholarship, World War II marks the death of "liberalism" (and hence, of the *Nahdawi* project) and the rise of ideology in the Arab world, mainly in the form of Islamic fundamentalism and Arab socialism.[1] For the most part, contemporary Arab nationalist thought shares this periodization, while instead identifying the end of the *Nahdah* with the rise of neo-liberalism in Egypt in the 1970s and the final collapse of the nationalist project that it signaled (for the Egyptian left of the 1960s however, this demise was understood to have taken place a good decade earlier.) In either case, the region's "enlightenment" (*tanwir*) is understood to have been initiated, for better or worse, by the colonial project.

Up until recently, the leveling force of social history had rarely been brought into methodological play. Scholars have begun to investigate the transformation of everyday institutions and practices (such as labor and book markets, education, medicine, prostitution, and penal systems) as they affected the lives of the middle and lower classes of the region during this seminal period.[2] Revisionist historiography, largely deriving from postcolonialist and Marxist positions, has challenged the basic assumptions of mainstream scholarship, which continues to be rooted in a Eurocentric and liberal teleology that is institutionally hostile to the very material realm of the social. In literary studies we find a similar situation. The story of the literary *Nahdah* is usually told through the writings and biographies of its luminaries and an unequivocal line can thus easily be traced from Rifa'a al-Tahtawi (1801–1874) to Taha Husayn almost one hundred years later. This literary "renaissance" teeters precariously between a fundamental nostalgia for a lost golden age of classical Islamic Civilization and a heady modernist impulse, shaped and constrained by the pressures of the colonial encounter. The Arabic novel emerges from this double sensibility, specifically, as a distended *bildungsroman* that regularly narrates the crisis of the modern bourgeois subject in a world of maddeningly conflicting tensions and possibilities. The thriving *fin de siècle* marketplace of popular fiction has been largely invisible in literary history. When it does appear, it is as a sign of the social and cultural decadence that the project of renaissance struggles against.

Literary history—and particularly the history of the novel—is thus a useful site from which to launch a critical study of the discursive practices that have constituted the *Nahdah* as a singular historical period in the domain of culture. Of all literary genres, the novel is treated as the one that best represents the achievements of European modernity. It is the very record of that modernity: a brilliant testimonial to the triumphant rise of the European bourgeoisie, and a prescient witness to its slow decline. As such, it is a peculiar product—amenable to export like other European technologies but somehow resistant to the will of its new owners, as though the ghosts of innumerable Julien Sorels and Emma Bovarys must invariably haunt and meddle with its ideal design. The story of the *Nahdah* is closely entwined with the history of the Arabic novel, which is for the most part conceived to have begun with the translation, adaptation and imitation of the European novel toward the end of the nineteenth century. In Orientalist literary criticism, the extent to which Arab writers were able to reproduce this idealized European genre became a kind of yardstick with which to measure the progress and value of the *Nahdah* as a whole. The "defective" or "immature" novels that are supposed to litter modern Arabic literary history until the middle of the twentieth century are thus treated as an inflexible sign of Arab subalterity. Naturally, national literary history tends to be much more generous and nuanced in its assessment of movements and individual works and authors since it is deeply implicated in the construction of a national canon. It nonetheless reproduces the same paradigm as the Orientalist one: the novel is a western literary genre imported by the East. The Arabic novel develops from the blueprint of the European novel.[3] It struggles through a period of imitation and immaturity until it finally arrives at the stage of its self-realization, as a mature and properly national genre, in 1913 (with the publication of Muhammad Husayn Haykal's *Zaynab*) or 1933 (Tawfiq al-Hakim's *The Return of the Spirit*) or 1956 (Naguib Mahfouz' *Palace Walk*) and so forth.

It is not my intention here to revisit the belabored question of the origins of the Arabic novel. As Sabry Hafez and Lennard Davis have both noted, the question and its answers are invariably steeped in ideological positions that obscure more than they illuminate. Both writers foreground what Hafez calls "dynamic intertextuality" as a more useful interpretive mechanism than the genealogical one and its search for ever-retreating origins.[4] Davis points to the importance of an investigation of reading practices, literary markets, and the semantic "subconscious" of the text at the historical threshold of a new genre in order to transform literary history into a history of "ruptures and transformations" rather than genealogical chains of cause and effect.[5] My project rather, is to try to understand how the dominant genealogical methodology in Arabic literary history has arrived at a modern novelistic canon that represents the fruits of a *particular* version of modernity, a particular *Nahdah* to the exclusion of all others. In this major version, an emergent literary genre (the novel) is harnessed to the disciplinary project of a middle-class in the process of constituting itself as a national bourgeoisie. On the margins of this process, there is another, discarded body of texts that offers a different set of possibilities, of windows into the novel as the textual site of the modern—one that joins the powerful, mythopoeic imagination of established modes of popular narrative to the polysemous codes of a new and hence, potentially democratic genre.

Viewed from below so to speak, from the vast and hybrid realm of popular fiction, the literary *Nahdah* in Egypt becomes a dynamic constitutive process in which the novel, itself a new genre, represented a contested site of emergent social and cultural productions. If we abandon the capitalization of the term, we can perhaps speak of two intertwined literary *nahdahs*—one that, looking backwards to an antediluvian "golden age," was invested in an act of genetic and linguistic recuperation (renaissance) and another that was strictly materialist in the play of its textual and social articulations. If the bourgeois novel in Egypt struggled to realize itself in the *bildungsroman*, popular fiction strove toward the social catharsis of melodrama, in the broad and fascinating sense defined by Peter Brooks. Translation was an intermediate zone, a contested site of the novelistic in this constitutive process. First *Nahdawi* and later nationalist intellectuals celebrated translation as the mechanism through which Arab societies achieved enlightenment and modernity. As such, it was a jealously guarded literary zone that relied on concepts of originality, transparency, and accuracy for the purity of its foundations. The popular fiction of the *Nahdah* was also invested in a project of translation but in a much looser and more ambiguous sense. The popular novel cared nothing for origins and genealogies. It raided, plagiarized, and fabricated its sources and invented an entirely new literary syntax that drew on heterogeneous—and indeed, it was supposed, mutually exclusive—narrative languages and frames of reference.

Focusing on the Arabic novel in Egypt, this paper argues that the construction of a properly national novelistic canon was predicated on the suppression (through modern literary criticism) and management (through new quasi-official literary institutions) of this thriving contemporary field of popular fiction. The strategic charge of cultural "illegitimacy" was one of the ways in which this suppression was accomplished, a charge that turned primarily on the trope of "translation" as a deeply ambivalent activity, and that was moreover rooted in the national intelligentsia's profound suspicion of popular culture and popular narrative languages. A survey of this prolific and fascinating body of fiction must lead us to question a number of the basic tenets on which the cultural discourse of *Nahdah* is built as well as the social hierarchies that inform literature as institution and as praxis.

There is nothing particularly unique about this antagonistic encounter between the *Nahdawi* project and contemporary popular culture. Literary modernisms in Europe were also defined by their basic hostility to mass culture and mass readerships.[6] What is interesting in the case of Egypt is that this process of suppression and management was heavily inflected by a colonial cultural dynamic built into the very structure of the *Nahdawi* imagination. Popular fiction—translated and otherwise—was censored precisely because it eluded the binary articulation of colonial modernity produced on both sides of the imperial divide. Both form *and* content were deemed to be essentially "western" *and* scandalously lowbrow, or "vulgar." Orientalist and nationalist literary criticism had varying degrees of trouble accommodating both of these categories in their definition of the novel or what Alexander Hamilton Gibb circuitously called "genuine literary productions of a certain literary value."[7] On the other hand, the national or "artistic novel" was required to reproduce an autochthonous, modernist aesthetic, whereby subjectivity was understood to be crucially shaped in and through the colonial drama. The *bildungsroman* in Egypt constructed an Arab subject perennially and fatefully trapped within the two poles of this singular dialectic. The emergent canon thus inscribed modernity in terms of the social and existential trauma of the alienated bourgeois subject.

Orientalism and Nationalism

Edward Said and Peter Gran have explored the ways in which Area Studies came to inherit the paradigmatic postures of nineteenth-century

Orientalism in the post-World War II American academy. Both disciplines share the same basic starting point in relation to the objects of their study—"the Middle East," formerly, "Islam," namely, a resolutely Hegelian dialectic, imperial in its scope and universalist in its application. Invariably, the Napoleonic invasion of Egypt in 1798 is offered as the dramatic historical rupture that rouses the Arab world from its centuries-old slumber and introduces it onto the stage of world history. Gran neatly sums up this shared paradigm: "Modernity is supposed to come to the Middle East from the West and not from developments within the Middle East itself."[8] Related to this stunning absence of agency is the idea of the region's exceptionalism. In the Orientalist imagination, "Islam" is Europe's antithesis and can never be truly assimilated into Europe's expansive modernity.[9] For the most part, *Nahdawi* intellectuals, fascinated and repelled by the overpowering effects of colonial power, reproduced the basic paradox inherent in this paradigm. In nationalist thought, as in fundamentalist polemic, an ethic of identity— still articulated in binary terms—serves as the essential building block of a bifurcated Arab modernity. Selective reformism was the only way out of this impasse. Contemporary intellectuals insisted that it was both possible and necessary to maintain the familiar Manichean structures of identity (East/West; Orient/Occident; Europe/Islam) while at the same time attempting to produce a selective and harmonious synthesis between them. The deep anxieties provoked by this dilemma are partly responsible for the way in which both Orientalism and Nationalist thought approached the question of Arab modernity as crisis.

Reformism was, if not doomed to outright failure, constantly and essentially beleaguered by the ambivalent "duality of [its] method."[10] This, at least, is the position of Alexander Hamilton Gibb, the most prolific and influential British Orientalist of the first half of the twentieth century. Writing in 1929 on modern Arabic literature (or what he called "neo-Arabic literature", the neologism itself suggesting an impossible doubling), he has this to say about the essential problem of Arab modernity:

> Its roots lie in the methods of education adopted in Egypt and elsewhere, the twist so given to the minds of the literate classes and their consequent capacity, or lack of capacity, either to adhere to the orthodox Muslim worldview or to assimilate the intellectual basis of Western thought and literature. It is obvious that the imitation of Western models initiated by the violent impact of Western life on the East remained and must remain sterile until such assimilation can issue in a community of intellectual method and aim. The earlier literature of the nineteenth century, swaying between a lifeless reproduction of medieval Arabic models, and an imitation

of Western models without sufficient intellectual preparation, could not but be feeble and unfruitful. The whole intellectual life of the people was thrown into confusion by the contradiction in principle between the old system of thought with its dogmatic basis and the intellectual freedom of Western scientific method.[11]

Gibb's "community of intellectual method and aim" is clearly written as a deferred utopia. In the meantime, neither "the orthodox Muslim worldview" nor "western scientific thought" can offer a solution. What we are left with is an ontological absence at the center. Between "lifeless reproduction" and "imitation" lies impotence—a historical deadend. Edward Said notes, correctly I think, that Gibb's anxiety over the dialectical boundaries between "Europe" and "Islam" lead to his profound pessimism about Arab modernity and modernist intellectuals "whose ideas everywhere reveal hopelessness; ideas unsuited to the modern world."[12]

Marxist and postcolonial critics meanwhile propose a secular, analytic version of the old metaphysical "duality"—that of "form" versus "content"—as an explanation of the central problematic of colonial societies. Samir Amin identifies the "provincialist reaction" to Eurocentrism as a potential (and actual) fundamentalism at the heart of *Nahdawi* thought. While "the *Nahdah* was a movement that brought with it the possibility of the total re-examination of the prevailing ideology,"[13] Amin judges this opportunity to have been missed because modernist intellectuals were unable for the most part to extricate themselves from the grip of the dialectic described by Gibb, plunging headlong instead into the trap of "nationalist culturalisms": "In every case it seems to me that nationalist culturalist retreat proceeds from the same method, the method of Eurocentrism: the affirmation of irreducible 'unique traits' that determine the course of history, or more exactly the course of individual, incommensurable histories."[14] Partha Chatterjee offers a similar insight into the articulation of national sovereignty in colonial societies. The modern national identities produced by colonial thought hinge on a binary structuring (outer/inner; material/spiritual) of social institutions and practices.

The material is the domain of the "outside," of the economy and statecraft, of science and technology, a domain where the West had proved its superiority and the East had succumbed. In this domain then, western superiority had to be acknowledged and its accomplishments carefully studied and replicated. The spiritual on the other hand, is an "inner" domain bearing the "essential" marks of cultural identity. The greater one's success in imitating western skills in the material domain, therefore, the greater the need to preserve the distinctness of one's spiritual culture.[15]

In an important sense then, the nationalist culturalisms of which Amin speaks only served to reinforce the Orientalist narrative on culture and modernity in the Arab world. The new cultural products of Arab modernity, like the novel, hence came to be perceived as intensely ambivalent social artifacts. In the case of the novel for example, the form was judged to be *ipso facto* European (and that, in the most undifferentiated and idealized way); yet another fully integrated "technology" traveling in a one-way direction from West to East. Never mind that the roots of at least one important strand of the genre in Europe are surely linked to the medieval narrative traditions of Arab-Muslim Mediterranean culture (here I am thinking of Boccaccio and Cervantes). Never mind again, that at least one strain of the eighteenth century European novel—Gothic, for example—was permeated through and through, in terms of both structure and content, by the obsessive encounter with "Oriental" landscapes and literatures,[16] or that the "political unconscious," to use Frederic Jameson's famous expression, of the French and English novel is literally rooted in the soil of the colonial subject. Never mind that even by the end of the twentieth century, critics still cannot decide on what a novel really is. Orientalists and nationalists agree: the novel arrived in Egypt and the Levant as yet another complete and exclusive product of European modernity. In the first decades of the twentieth century and especially after 1919, Arab writers were confronted with two choices: "imitation" or "nationalization," so to speak. The former could only lead, at best, to "feeble and unfruitful" results, at worst to a betrayal of the national project. The latter severely restricted the formal and thematic possibilities of fiction by privileging first, realism as the only narrative mode adequate to the needs of the emergent nation and second, a reified national character as the end of all modern stories.

The Age of Translation and Adaptation, 1870–1925

The history of the Arabic novel is supposed to begin with the various formal narrative experiments induced by the encounter with western fiction in the middle of the nineteenth century. This initial period of encounter is followed by a period of concerted and prolific translation during which Arab writers in Egypt and the Levant indiscriminately (and altogether poorly) translated and adapted European novels, regardless of literary merit, and moreover without the least scruple regarding faithfulness to the original text or to the legal and moral institutions of authorship and copyright. Though considered on the whole a necessary, if faintly disreputable stage in "the modernization of [Arab] imaginative literature,"[17] the period is usually placed at the margins of the genealogy that eventually leads to the "artistic" or properly speaking, national Egyptian/Arab novel in the second decade of the twentieth century (*al-riwayah al-fanniyyah*), and which represents a nascent Egyptian *bildungsroman*.[18] Perhaps the best summation of this position, and the most illustrative of the ways in which the Orientalist and the national paradigms of modern literary history intersect is the following claim made by Kawsar El-Beheiry, a professor of French at al-Azhar University:

les écrivains arabes, encore inexpérimentés dans l'art romanesque et n'ayant fait aucune étude dans ce domaine, ne savaient comment écrire eux-mêmes des romans, ni quel thème choisir et quelles règles suivre pour développer ce thème. Cela ne veut aucunement dire que l'étude de la technique du roman est indispensable a toute production romanesque; les grands maîtres du monde entier n'ont suivi à quelques exceptions près, que leurs aptitudes naturelles. Or, les romanciers arabes de l'époque ne possédaient pas ces aptitudes; cela est possiblement du a la longue période de décadence politique et sociale qui a alors frappé le monde arabe. Effectivement, si on consulte les journaux et les revues de la deuxième moitié du XIX siècle, on ne trouve que des traductions ou des adaptations de romans étrangers, français en majorité. *Il n'y a aucun roman, aucune nouvelle ni aucun conte purement arabe.*[19] (emphasis added)

The "natural" novelistic aptitudes of the world's grand masters can only be reproduced by the inept and decadent Arab author, and after long apprenticeship, as a form of mimicry. El-Beheiry's imperious language, her string of emphatic negatives and her final insistence on the ideal category of "purity" in relation to culture repeats the critical impasse created by the major *Nahdah* discourse. The simple fact of the matter is that much original fiction was produced during this period. More to the point, the scholarly obsession with the purity and transparency of chains of transmission masks a deep-seated fear of textual, and hence social, contamination. A process of displacement thus occurs whereby a rich and variegated corpus of fiction is contained within the stabilizing and minor category of "translation." This slippage occurs in most major modern literary histories of the period. By a strange sleight of hand, the two terms—"translation" and "popular fiction"—come to stand for each other, the implication of course being that the popular itself is foreign to national culture.

The "Age of Translation" genus elides multiple genre practices that certainly included, but were not limited to direct translation of European fiction. First, many translators, like the Palestinian Khalil

Baydas, often left out the title or the author of the original work, making it difficult, if not impossible to confirm textual itineraries. We know from a number of contemporary writers that original novels were occasionally passed off as translations in order to capitalize on the huge commercial success of foreign fictions. There is no reason to believe that this phenomenon was limited to the specific instances of pseudotranslation mentioned by Jurji Zaydan, for example.[20] The most comprehensive annotated bibliographies from the period (such as Henri Pérès 1937 bibliography of Arabic translations of French fiction) have failed to determine the European "origin" of the majority of popular Arabic adaptations published serially in the numerous turn-of-the-century periodicals devoted to fiction. Moreover, many of these serialized novels explicitly claimed original authorship. Yet the period is still historically defined as one that turned on simple translation/adaptation and hence on a crucial evocation of *difference*. In fact, the dominant paradigm of literary history depends on this evocation, and translation is its necessary topos.

Second, because it assumes that translation is a transparent and unmediated activity, the model can neither acknowledge nor adequately interpret the narrative and social function of "adaptation" and its related praxes—plagiarism and forgery—except as a series of moral judgments on originality and the sanctity of authorship and copyright. Because of this prejudice, there are literally thousands of works of popular Arabic fiction spanning a period of fifty years that have never been studied in any detail, and specifically as a body of novelistic fiction in its own right.[21] The "Age of Translation" model delegitimizes and marginalizes this literary production in its entirety, effectively precluding any serious investigation of the novel genre in Arabic other than in its dominant, bourgeois, and properly national form, and this in spite of the salient fact that, between 1880 and 1919 at least, popular Arabic fiction in Egypt, translated and otherwise, constituted by far the lion's share of a burgeoning book and periodical market.[22] Even as late as 1937, the readership for this type of fiction was so large that highbrow writers frequently made bitter complaints about its seemingly impervious and ill-deserved popularity.[23] Moreover, it was especially, if not exclusively, through the mundane exigencies of commercial translation that the Arabic language was gradually transformed into a supple language of the modern quotidian. While scholars acknowledge the link between popular turn-of-the-century fiction and the modern revolution in the Arabic language, none have ventured to study it in any depth.[24]

Now, the obvious question is "why"? Popular fiction—the Penny Dreadful and the *roman de feuilleton* for example—are recognized and studied as important fields of literary inquiry in the various European national traditions. Moreover, certain subgenres of the nineteenth-century novel (Gothic and neo-Gothic for example) traveled in time and text across the Middle East and Europe through Byzantine processes of translation and adaptation, and the inevitable plagiarisms and forgeries that follow in their wake.[25] In Europe at least, the last few decades of critical scholarship on popular fiction laid the groundwork for important interdisciplinary work in literary history and theory.[26] Why not accord the popular novel in Egypt the same kind of literary-historical importance and the same sustained theoretical attention as has been given to its counterpart in England, Italy, and France? I propose three related factors that contributed to this suppression and delegitimization of popular fiction in Arabic: first, the disciplinary social and cultural postures of both modernism and nationalism; second, the hegemony of the European liberal-juridical concept of the subject, with its related institutions of authorship and copyright in the literary domain; and third, the dialectical model of Arab modernity itself, with its systematic fetishization of *content* or identity.

Bad Books for Bad Readers: "The Novel of Entertainment and Leisure"

In his classic 1963 study of the Arabic novel in Egypt, Abd al-Muhsin Taha Badr argues that the tremendous commercial success of the popular novel between the last third of the nineteenth century and 1919, the date of the Egyptian uprising against the British, was rooted in the growth of mass education and the rise of a semiliterate readership bent on "escape" from the bitter political and social realities of colonialism.[27] Badr's project is ultimately a recuperative one. His introduction to the study is a magisterial attempt to explain Arab literary modernity in reference to the "decline" that preceded it. As such, it represents a definitive statement of *Nahdah* in the conservative sense invoked by Gilbert Durand. Badr explicitly links "the novel of entertainment and leisure" (*riwayah al-tasliyah wal-tarfih*) to the persistent resonance of medieval Arabic popular narrative amongst this modern mass readership. His analysis is characterized by the historical tension between "high" (classical-nationalist) and "low" (popular) culture. He attributes the decline of medieval Arab culture to its linguistic and literary "vernacularization," as exemplified by the flawed style and linguistic usage of medieval writers from Ibn Iyas to al-Jabarti, and more generally, by the growing cleavages within what he views as a unitary, canonical Arab cultural tradition:

> The most prominent aspect of the age's cultural life was first, the rupture between contemporary culture and the true intellectual and literary tradition of classical Arab civilization and second, the rupture between this tradition and [the culture of] the popular masses. . . . Consequently, most of the age's literary arts deteriorated into the realm of popular literature.[28]

According to Badr, Arabic literary culture in the nineteenth and early twentieth century inherits this literary decadence, though through the medium of a new genre. While "the didactic novel" (al-riwayah al-ta'limiyyah), however formally inadequate, at least sought to address the great political and philosophical issues of the day, the great majority of the novels produced during this period was made up of commercially profitable romances, adventure stories, crime fiction and the like, geared toward a popular audience, newly —and yet marginally—literate. This is what Sabry Hafez calls "the new reading public" of the late nineteenth and early twentieth centuries. Badr refers to this metamorphosed popular audience simply as "the semi-cultured" (ansaf al-muthaqqafin). The third and final stage of the novel described by Badr is "the artistic novel" (al-riwayah al-fanniyyah), which signals the triumphant emergence of the autonomous national subject in fiction, and which marks the beginning of the novelistic canon in Arabic.

The opprobrious attitude toward popular culture implicit in Badr's description is rooted in a long tradition of modernist and nationalist critical discourse. In turn-of-the-century Egypt, reformist intellectuals conceived of modern narrative as a kind of social cement. By educating and improving the collective character of the Egyptians, it would prepare them for citizenship in the modern nation-state. On the other hand, these intellectuals—who by and large shared a highly ambivalent attitude toward the Egyptian masses, urban and rural[29]—understood popular narrativity as the antithesis of modern narrative, repeatedly attacking the former as both a cause and a symptom of the corrupt state of these masses.[30] The social context of the café-based hakawati (storyteller) reinforced their slothful, vice-ridden habits, while the marvelous themes of the popular epic cycles (sira) and the folk tale (haddutah) contributed to their superstition and gullibility. This specific—and often quite fervid—prejudice against the dominant literary genres of popular culture was built into much of the early twentieth century critical discourse that contributed to the elaboration of fiction as a properly national narrative form. Like Badr, intellectuals and highbrow writers of this period saw a direct link between a disreputable medieval popular tradition and an equally problematic new genre. They openly and repeatedly complained about the fierce competition to a nascent corpus of legitimate narrative offered by the popular novel, condemning it as yet another sign of the lamentable state of Egyptian culture. They went from outright moral and political condemnation of the genre as a whole in the last two decades of the nineteenth century, to qualified support in the teens and twenties based on a more nuanced understanding of its didactic and artistic possibilities, couched in specifically national terms.

In the nineteenth century, the attack on fiction was morally but also politically based. Writing in 1899, Ahmad Fathi Zaghlul linked the social and political project of *nahdah* to a proper readerly education. Egypt's backwardness was due to the widespread dissemination of "tales and fantasies," "frivolous publications," and "clownish books and novels."[31] In 1882, the journal *al-Muqtataf* justified its initial refusal to publish fiction in an editorial that complained of its dangerous moral effects on the minds of impressionable youth of both sexes.[32] Some critics even blamed popular fiction for Egypt's colonial bondage to France and Britain![33] A couple of decades later, this moral argument was inflected by a highbrow modernist bias that masked a deep contempt for the vulgar culture of the masses. Mahmud Taymur—one of the founders of the "New School" of naturalist fiction in Egypt—linked popular fiction to the "inferior classes" of Egyptian society,[34] Zaki Mubarak described its authors as belonging to "the lowest class of literary writers,"[35] while Tawfiq al-Hakim cryptically stated that "the difference between literature (*al-adab*) and fiction (*al-qissah*) is like the difference between the higher regions of the body and all the rest."[36] In these first decades of the twentieth century, a set of emergent social hierarchies was embedded into the literary taxonomies being developed by national critics and writers, anxious to disassociate fiction from its louche Grub Street stronghold and appropriate it to a respectable bourgeois milieu and worldview; to nationalize it, so to speak. This is precisely why Badr chooses 1919 and Moosa, 1925 as the welcome end of "The Age of Translation." Both of these dates are landmarks in the historical narrative of national awakening in Egypt.

Certainly, this modernist anxiety also derived from the realities of the contemporary book market. In a 1918 article in the journal *al-Hilal*, Hasan al-Sharif complained that "serious" authors (like Muhammad Husayn Haykal) were unable to sell even their miniscule first editions, while detective novels like *The Honorable Thief* and *The Adventures of Carter* went into multiple editions of thousands of copies.[37] The sheer perversity of this anonymous and insatiable reading public is of course compounded by the fact that its preference for "translated books" tended, not to the great novelists of the West (the Balzacs, the Tolstoys and the Dickens), but to its pulp writers—the unhappy likes of Ponson du Terrail, Pierre Zaccone, Eugene Sue, and Arthur Conan Doyle—and moreover, rendered into bad Arabic by mediocre translators motivated at best by the pressures of serial publication, at worst by nothing less than crass greed—a case of bad books for bad readers.[38]

By 1963, the novelistic canon was more or less in place. But already much earlier, in the twenties and thirties, foundational Egyptian writers like Muhammad Husayn Haykal, Mahmud Taymur, and Salamah Musa were urgently attempting to ground the new genre in a properly national landscape. This new critical concept of "national literature" was a pivotal element in the later canonization of the novel genre in Egypt. Its three main distinguishing features were setting, character, and time: Egyptian landscapes and Egyptian characters, urban and rural, and an overarching sense of national history were identified as the necessary ingredients for a genuinely national novel. Realist time—or what Davis has called "the median past tense"—must develop a steady temporal progression of cause and effect, rooted in the telos of the emergent subject. The expansive and hegemonic interiority of this subject was a largely unprecedented feature in Arabic narrative before the end of the nineteenth century and its elaboration in fiction was inextricably bound to the linked ideologies of nationalism and romantic individualism as they emerged in Egypt roughly around the time of World War I and the 1919 revolution. Realism was the natural metaphor for this project. Its main theme was the crisis of the bourgeois subject in a world torn apart by the clash between "tradition" and "modernity."

On the other hand, the modernity constructed in popular fiction was political and social, rather than metaphysical or existential. Popular fiction was cosmopolitan, hyperrealist, and generically hybrid. The same novel offered a pastiche of different modes: *policier*, thriller, romance, and melodrama, most often set in the exotic drawing rooms and criminal streets of the modern metropolis—Paris, London, New York, Bombay, Cairo. A sampling of subtitles clearly points to this genetic instability and insouciance. Labib Abu Satit's novel *The Innocents* was subtitled "a literary, romantic *policier*"; Muhammad Ra'fat al-Jamali's *The Beauty's Sustenance (or The Sorrows of Two Lovers)* carried the subtitle, "an Egyptian historical, psychological romance" and Ahmad Hanafi's

The Beautiful Vendor was described as "a literary, historical, social, love-story."[39] Niqula Haddad's novel *The New Adam* (1914) is an elaborate philosophical melodrama of social illegitimacy and redemption set amongst the Levantine Christian bourgeoisie of Cairo in the 1890s. In this and other melodramas of the period, property and inheritance, rather than serving as the invisible bases of the hero's coming of age, unleash the descent into intrigue and crime. Niqula Rizqallah's 1906 pseudotranslation, *The Lovely Beggar* is a sly cross between political thriller and *roman à clef* that features a baroque corporation of enterprising thieves and confidence-men drawn from the sinister underworlds of Paris, London, and Chicago. The events of Abd al-Qadir Hamza's 1908 adaptation, *City of Darkness*, unfold between Paris and Buenos Aires against the corruption and intrigue of the international stock market. Hamza's "translator's" preface includes an impassioned polemic on socialism and a stinging condemnation of the modern institutions of finance capitalism in Egypt. Other novels explore the contemporary urban nightmares of gambling, alcoholism, and prostitution in intricate melodramatic detail.

Nahdawi writers and critics viewed these elaborate and cosmopolitan fictions as the antithesis of the modern novel, precisely because they eluded the nationalist conceptualization of subjectivity, time, and location. If the artistic novel was soberly rooted in the new disciplinary power of the emergent national subject (*al-dhat al-rawiyah*)—a kind of domestic composite of the authentic (native) Muslim, middle-class Egyptian—the popular novel wandered promiscuously amongst a vertiginous range of hyperbolic urban characters and capitals, and offered a seductive vision of the drama and corruption at the heart of the modern city. In an important sense, Paris *was* Cairo and vice versa. The popular novel thus committed the cardinal sin of bypassing entirely the colonial dialectic and of rehearsing an "escape from Egyptian reality." This then, is the source of the genetic slippage previously alluded to: in the *Nahdawi* literary taxonomy, the spurious popular novel came to be subsumed under the ambivalent and syncretic category of "translation."

The Scandals of Translation

The most common trope used by historians of modern Arabic literature to describe the technique of turn-of-the-century popular translation is that of "mutilation" (*tashwih*). Latif Zaytuni's recent study, *The Translation Movement in the Nahdah*, is shot through with this and other metaphors of textual violence and corruption. In Zaytuni's and earlier writers' accounts, popular translation is invariably cast as a kind of crime committed against the institutions of language and literature in general, and the original text in particular. It manipulates and bowdlerizes the text as it pleases. It lies, cheats, maims, and steals in order to achieve its ends. The popular translation is a literary bandit of sorts.

Turn of the century translation practices included a wide array of narrative and textual strategies. Adaptation or "arabization" relied on a complex mechanism of domesticating characters and locations, strategic explanatory asides, lexical substitutions or the addition and deletion of whole passages and chapters in order to emphasize or avoid certain social, political, or philosophical issues, or simply shortening or lengthening the novel according to the taste and practical judgment of the writer and the projected interest of the reader. Very often, the act of "translation" did not even involve a direct encounter with the original text. Mustafa al-Manfaluti, for example, who knew no European languages, rendered his friends' skeletal translations of French novels into mellifluous Arabic prose.[40] Khalil Baydas translated Russian versions of English, Italian, and German novels into Arabic,[41] while Ahmad Hasan al-Zayat worked from a French version of Goethe's *The Sorrows of Young Werther* and Khalil Mutran from a French version of Shakespeare.[42] Tanius 'Abduh, meanwhile, reportedly translated from memory. According to his disapproving contemporary Salim Sarkis, he "carried with him sheets of paper in one pocket and a French novel in the other. He would then read a few lines, put the novel back in his pocket, and begin to scratch in a fine script whatever he could remember of the few lines he had read. He wrote all day long without striking out a word or rereading a line"[43] —a truly prodigious feat for a man who published more than six hundred "translations" over the course of his career![44]

Plagiarism, forgery, and pseudotranslation were also common strategies in the production of popular fiction. Many writers did not provide the title or the author of the work supposedly translated (a practice that dates back to the official scientific and administrative translation institutions set up by Muhammad 'Ali) merely claiming that it had been "arabized" or "adapted" by the Arab author or offering it as a second hand account, with a short preface such as "a friend of mine who had recently returned from a trip to Europe told me this story" or simply, "it is told that."[45] On the other hand, writers anxious to be published and read deliberately claimed the status of translations for their original works, attributing the work to a real or fictional European author.

Finally, language was a hugely important tool through which translators appropriated the original text, while simultaneously forcing open the lexical and syntactic canons of classical Arabic. This was a major flashpoint in the nationalist critique of popular fiction from the teens through the sixties. Critics from Taha Husayn and Mustafa al-'Aqqad to Muhammad Yusuf Najm and Abd al-Muhsin Taha Badr deplored what they saw as the outrageous liberties that these popular translators and writers took with the Arabic language, from their deliberate slight to the rules of grammar to their casual and ubiquitous use of foreign loan-words and colloquial idioms. Writing in 1961, Najm puts this linguistic "feebleness" (*rakakah*) down to the limited capacities and needs of a semi-literate readership and the hectic publishing pressures of the periodical market: "Most readers were ignorant of the grammatical rules and rhetorical structure of the [Arabic] language. They did not notice errors; all they cared about was that the language be simple and understandable, and the story pleasurable and entertaining."[46]

By the middle of the nineteenth century, classical Arabic was in the throes of a momentous transformation. Journalism and fiction were the two most important media through which a highly formal and rigorously policed literary language was made to respond to the new technologies and subjectivities of the modern world. "Good" translation was reformist in its method. It upheld the strict architecture of the Arabic language while rendering it suppler in its diction and lexical derivations. The sparse, elegant translations of modernist authors and academy members like Hasan al-Zayyat, Taha Husayn, and Ibrahim al-Mazini ushered in this transition and smoothed its way. They scrupulously translated the great works of western fiction into a refined and correct modern Arabic idiom.[47] "Bad" translation on the other hand was entirely pragmatic in its method. Its aim was not to reify a newer version of the language (or a new world-literary heritage), but to achieve maximum communicability and pleasure. It did not hesitate to ignore the refined art of Arabic rhetoric, to spurn the rules of diction and grammar and to make copious use of the "vulgar" vernacular in order to achieve this aim. On the whole, bad translation was held responsible for impeding the modern renaissance of the Arabic language. In either case, the challenges faced by translators of any stripe were considerable, as indicated by the plaintive remarks of the translators themselves in their ubiquitous introductions.[48] Contemporary critics grudgingly acknowledge the contribution of the popular translators to the modernization of the Arabic language, even if this contribution is understood to be deeply problematic.

The *Nahdah*'s controversy over the revival of the Arabic language is a huge subject and can easily fill many volumes.[49] For the purposes of this essay, it is the *disciplinary* nature of this struggle that is most important. In another context, Faysal Darraj has singled out the *Nahdah*'s fetishization of language as a major strand in the modern rearticulation of the institutions of tyranny in the Arab world. This point acquires an additional clarity in relation to the production and suppression of the popular fiction of the period. In all the senses discussed above, popular fiction *in toto* was treated as a dangerous activity maddeningly beyond the pale of institutional constraint. Hasan al-Sharif's bitter assessment of, and solution to, what he saw as the crisis of the literary revival in Egypt in 1918 is rooted in this sense of outraged authority. As usual, al-Sharif blames this crisis as much on an ignorant and lazy readership as on the greed of unscrupulous hack writers who care more for their pockets than for "true literature." More interestingly, al-Sharif bemoans the lack of qualified critics in modern Egypt. He develops the idea, at great length, of the critic as a judge and criticism as a sort of disciplinary institution that can and must select, interpret, and administer a public body of circulating texts: "Literature must have an organization to supervise and control it." The critic then becomes "an individual who is superior to all others in the art of interpretation;" "a vigilant and jealous warden" who can "discipline the taste of the public." The metaphor that al-Sharif here develops finally leads to the ultimate trope of criticism as a regime of power: "Criticism is a government for literature. It protects it from anarchy and attends to its regulation, and critics, if they excel at their work, are at the head of this government, kings to be feared and obeyed."[50]

While there is nothing inherently unusual about the idea of the critic as a professional arbiter of public taste, Al-Sharif's language is nonetheless remarkable for its vehemence and for the naked institutional power he metaphorically harnesses to his polemic. In the early twentieth century Egyptian context, this was unusual language indeed. Prior to the middle of the nineteenth century clear social divisions hierarchically dominated the business of literature, and the book was more or less the preserve of a small and highly educated elite who happily left the masses to their wandering poets and storytellers. By 1918, the exponential growth of a mass reading public and the dizzying production and circulation of printed texts looked like sheer anarchy to the new bourgeois intelligentsia. Even worse, the majority of these printed texts were fictions, unbound from both the classical Arabic literary and language canons *and* the high conventions of the European genre that they appropriated and carnivalized. Again, translation was the strategic mechanism of this event, in both its strictly literary and its broadly social sense.

Lawrence Venuti has described translation as a project involving a series of power relations between dominant cultural institutions and the act of translation itself. Translation is thus a moment of power, a double-edged sword that can either serve to reproduce or challenge dominant cultural identities:

> The authority of any institution that relies on translations is susceptible to scandal because their somewhat unpredictable effects exceed the institutional controls that normally regulate textual interpretation, such as judgments of canonicity. Translations extend the possible uses of foreign texts among diverse audiences, institutionally based or not, producing results that may be both disruptive and serendipitous.[51]

Both Venuti and R. K. Ruthven focus on the Romantic ideology of authorship, "whose operative terms are solitary genius and unique texts"[52] as the key site of the anxieties produced by translation and its first cousins, pseudotranslation and forgery: "Given the reigning concept of authorship, translation provokes the fear of inauthenticity, distortion, contamination."[53] In the colonial context, where the dialectic of identity inevitably shapes the cultural encounter, this fear of inauthenticity operates in an additional sense to the one invoked by Venuti. Badr's insight into the generic kinship between "the novel of entertainment and leisure" in Egypt and popular medieval Arabic narrative genres is a case in point. Like the oral epic and folktale, popular translations act as more or less freely circulating narratives, largely unbound from the Romantic conventions of authorship that the *Nahdah* appropriated and celebrated.[54] Instead of being understood to emanate from the individual imagination of the unique Self, narrative in this popular oral sense represents a kind of common store of stories that circulate socially in a direct and democratic encounter between audience and narrator.[55] Popular translation provokes anxieties of textual and cultural contamination precisely because it represents a potentially unregulated source of cultural and linguistic transfer, occasioning "revelations that question the authority of dominant cultural values and institutions."[56] In this context, forgery and pseudotranslation are especially threatening. Under the guise of "legitimate" translation, these serve as a convenient means of introducing new ideas and a plurality of linguistic and narrative practices into a closed and hierarchical literary system, and moreover, in a manner designed to circumvent the moral and juridical rules of textual accountability. As such, they are essentially disruptive and anarchic literary acts that simultaneously carnivalize both the foreign and the domestic cultural norms and literary conventions through which they operate.

The great majority of self-proclaiming translations within the Egyptian turn-of-the-century popular fiction repertoire are, in this specific sense, spurious. Many "translators" affixed the bare initials of some imaginary author onto the volume's frontispiece. Many simply stated that the work had been adapted "from the French" or "from the English" original. Clearly, it is next to impossible to ascertain the truth or falsehood of these claims. The attempt itself is perhaps altogether beside the point. The novels in question are fascinating precisely because of the web of semantic and structural ambiguity that infuses the counterfeit text; the wild play of cultural and narrative codes plucked whimsically from a basket of diverse traditions and knit together so as to produce a new text that is familiar and exotic, playful and profound.

If we agree with Peter Brooks that the "literature of the masses" is itself the fertile source of the novel imagination, then a nuanced and theoretically sophisticated literary history of Arabic popular fiction becomes essential to a constructive rereading of the *Nahdah* as a whole. Such an endeavor would eschew the hierarchical limitations of national literature disciplines and ideally explore what Margaret Cohen has described as the basic "transportability" of the novel form through a study of popular genres *precisely as* open-ended translation projects—in both a strictly textual and a broad worldly sense—across national and cultural borders. By emphasizing the importance of the literary archive as both a context and a counterpoint to canonical, masterpiece-based history, this kind of postsructuralist approach to literary history would inevitably lead to a decentering of the dominant disciplinary constructions of the *Nahdah* as a kind of historical dead end. Moreover, in raising inevitable questions about conventional conceptions of national culture— the way a canon formulates and reproduces notions of "originality" and "imitation" for example—or about the complex morphologies and social circulation of literary genres, it would also question some of the most basic premises of established *Nahdah* discourse: the European origins of Arab modernity is one of these; the ideology of the national subject is another. Perhaps then it will also become possible to meaningfully approach the Arabic novel from a sustained and serious comparativist perspective, rather than as an offshoot of Area Studies and the "coming of the West" paradigm that this entails.

Notes

1. See for example the preface to the 1983 reissue of Albert Hourani's classic 1962 work, *Arabic Thought in the Liberal Age, 1798–1939* (New York: Cambridge University Press).

2. For example, Peter Gran, *Islamic Roots of Capitalism: Egypt, 1760–1840* (Cairo: the American University in Cairo Press, 1999); Nelly Hanna, *In Praise of Books: A Cultural History of Cairo's Middle Class, 16th to 18th century* (Syracuse, NY: Syracuse University Press, 2003); Khaled Fahmy, *All the Pasha's Men: Mehmed Ali, His Army and the Making of Modern Egypt* (Cambridge: Cambridge University Press, 1997).

3. Some critics have vigorously disputed this claim however, attempting instead to trace the Arabic novel to pre-Islamic and medieval Arabic narrative sources. For example, Faruq Khurshid, *Fi al-riwayah al-'arabiyyah fi 'asr al-tajmi'* (Cairo: Dar al-qalam, 1960). For a general discussion of this contentious issue of origins, see Sabry Hafez, *The Genesis of Arabic Narrative Discourse* (London: Saqi Books, 1993), pp. 17–36.

4. Ibid., p. 27.

5. Lennard Davis, *Factual Fictions: The Origins of the English Novel* (Philadelphia, PA: University of Pennsylvania Press, 1997), pp. 2, 8–9.

6. See Patrick Bratlinger, *The Reading Lesson: The Threat of Mass Literacy in Nineteenth Century Britain* (Bloomington, IN: Indiana University Press, 1998); John Carey, *The Intellectuals and the Masses: Pride and Prejudice Among the Literary Intelligentsia, 1880–1939* (London: Faber and Faber, 1992).

7. H. A. R. Gibb, *Studies on the Civilization of Islam*, Eds. Stanford J. Shaw and William R. Polk (Princeton, NJ: Princeton University Press, 1982), p. 300.

8. Gran, *Islamic Roots of Capitalism*, p. xxvii.

9. Perhaps this is partly the reason why Arabic literature is rarely studied in comparative literature departments in the United States. On the other hand, Area Studies departments still offer modern Arabic literature courses as a window into "the Arab mind."

10. Gibb, *Studies on the Civilization of Islam*, p. 259.

11. Ibid., pp. 258–9.

12. Edward Said, *Orientalism* (New York: Vintage Books, 1979), p. 281.

13. Samir Amin, *Eurocentrism*, trans. Russell Moore (New York: Monthly Review Press, 1989), p. 129.

14. Ibid., p. 135.

15. Partha Chatterjee, *The Nation and Its Fragments: Colonial and Postcolonial Histories* (Princeton, NJ: Princeton University Press, 1993), p. 6.

16. Honoré de Balzac refers generally to this influence and particularly in relation to his own fiction in a letter to Hippolyte Castille: "How can one get across such a fresco [the *Comédie Humaine*] without the resources of the Arabian tale, without the aid of buried titans?" As cited in Peter Brooks, *The Melodramatic Imagination* (New Haven, CT: Yale University Press, 1995), p. 118.

17. Matti Moosa, *The Origins of Modern Arabic Fiction* (Boulder, CO: Lynne Rienner, 1997), p. 6.

18. The dates Matti Moosa gives for his "Age of Translation" in Egypt and the Levant are 1870–1925, 1925 being the year when "the New School" of writers in Egypt published their modernist manifesto in the first issue of their

short-lived journal, *al-Fajr*. Pierre Cachia uses 1834–1914 instead, 1914 being the date of publication of Muhammad Husayn Haykal's foundational novel *Zaynab*. For a discussion of the importance of "the New School" and for a more detailed morphology of popular versus national fiction in mid-century Egyptian literary criticism, see my essay "The Narrative Craft: Realism and Fiction in the Arabic Canon," *Edebiyat*, 14: 1 and 2 (May–Nov, 2003), pp. 109–28.

19. Kawsar El Beheiry, *L'influence de la littérature francaise sur le roman arabe* (Sherbrooke, QC: Naaman, 1980), p. 121.

20. See Abd al-Muhsin Taha Badr, *Tattawur al-riwayah al-arabiyyah al-hadithah fi misr* (Cairo: Dar al-Ma'arif, 1992), p. 144.

21. All of the extent bibliographies of these works of fiction are partial at best. See Henri Peres, "Le Roman, le conte et la nouvelle dans la littérature arabe moderne," *Annales de l'institut d'études orientales*, Tome III, Faculté des lettres de l'université d'alger, 1937, pp. 266–337; Muhammad Yusuf Najm, *Al-Qissah, fi al-adab al-arabi al-hadith* (Beirut: Manshurat al-maktabah al-ahliyyah, 1961), pp. 13–21; Badr, *Tatawwur al-riwayah al-arabiyyah al-hadithah fi misr*, pp. 413–30; Latif al-Zaytuni, *Harakah al-tarjamah fi 'asr al-nahdah* (Beirut: Dar al-nahar, 1994), pp. 163–71. See also Latifa Al-Zayyat's unpublished dissertation, *Harakah al-tarjamah al-adabiyyah min al-injiliziyyah ila al-'arabiyyah*, Cairo University, 1957 and Jak Tajir, *Harakah al-tarjamah fi misr khilal al-qarn al-tasi' 'asharah*, Cairo: Dar al-Ma'arif, 1946.

22. Hafez, *The Genesis of Arabic Narrative Discourse*, pp. 56, 85; Hasan al-Sharif, "Nahdah al-adab fi misr," *al-Hilal*, 1, (October 1918), p. 68; Gibb, *Studies on the Civilization of Islam*, p. 300.

23. Najm, *Al-Qissah fi al-adab al-arabi al-hadith*, p. 25.

24. An exception to this is Latif Zaytuni's recent study, *Harakah al-tarjamah fi 'asr al-nahdah* (The Translation Movement in the *Nahdah*). Zaytuni's book includes an appendix of newly coined and "arabized" words from the nineteenth century.

25. The marvelous itinerary of *The Arabian Nights* offers a fascinating example of this process. From pre-Islamic Persian to medieval Arabic and modern Indian translations/recensions, the "text" of the *Nights* travels across eighteenth- and nineteenth-century Europe, through a variety of adaptations, forgeries and rewritings, into the domain of contemporary fiction: Antoine Galland's 1717 forgery "Aladdin and the Magic Lamp"; Frances Sheridan's *The History of Nurjahad* (1767); William Beckford's *Vathek* (1787), for example. In his essay on Tarchetti's 1865 version of Mary Shelley's *Frankenstein*, Lawrence Venuti explores the intriguing politics of adaptation and plagiarism in the context of the nineteenth-century popular Italian novel, with its gothic, *feuilleton* and Orientalist sources. "I.U. Tarchetti's Politics of Translation; or A Plagiarism of Mary Shelley," in *Rethinking Translation: Discourse, Subjectivity, Ideology*, Ed. Lawrence Venuti (London: Routledge, 1992), pp. 196–230.

26. For example, Yves Olivier-Martin, *Histoire du roman populaire en France, 1840–1980* (Paris: Albin-Michel, 1980); Winifred Hughes, *The Maniac in*

the Cellar: Sensation Novels of the 1860s (Princeton, NJ: Princeton University Press, 1980); Anne-Marie Thiesse, *Le roman de quotidien: lecteurs et lectures populaires à la Belle Epoque* (Paris: Chemin Vert, 1984); Jean Radford, *The Progress of Romance: The Politics of Popular Fiction* (London: Routledge Press, 1986); Nicholas Daly, *Modernism, Romance and the Fin de Siècle: Popular Fiction and British Culture, 1880–1914* (New York: Cambridge University Press, 1999).

27. Badr, *Tatawwur al-riwayah al-arabiyah al-hadithah fi misr*, p. 121.

28. Ibid., p. 19.

29. For a discussion of these attitudes, see Timothy Mitchell, *Colonising Egypt* (Berkeley, CA: University of California Press, 1991); and Ahmad Zakariyyah Shalaq, *Ahmad Fathi Zaghlul wa qadiyyah al-taghrib* (Cairo: Maktabah madbuli, 1966).

30. Muhammad 'Umar—a turn of the century intellectual and social reformer—strongly denounced the decadence of popular narrative in his writing. *Hadir al-misriyyin wa sirr ta'akhkhurihim* (Cairo: Dar misr al-mahrusah, 2002).

31. As cited in Badr, *Tatawwur al-riwayah al-arabiyyah al-hadithah fi misr*, p. 123.

32. Hafez, *The Genesis of Arabic Narrative Discourse*, p. 85.

33. Zaytuni, *Harakah al-tarjamah fi 'asr al-nahdah*, p. 142.

34. As cited in Badr, *Tatawwur al-riwayah al-arabiyyah al-hadithah fi misr*, p. 45.

35. As cited in Gibb, *Studies on the Civilization of Islam*, p. 297.

36. As cited in Najm, *Al-Qissah fi al-adab al-arabi al-hadith*, p. 25, 1ff.

37. Al-Sharif, "Nahdah al-adab fi misr," p. 38.

38. El Beheiry, *L'influence de la littérature francaise sur le roman arabe*, p. 126; Gibb, *Studies on the Civilization of Islam*, p. 281; Moosa, *The Origins of Modern Arabic Fiction*, p.105; Najm, *Al-Qissah fi al-adab al-arabi al-hadith*, p. 23. Sir Hamilton Gibb lamented the characteristic Arab attraction to "particular currents in French literature" which included Rousseau, De Vigny, De Musset, Victor Hugo and Anatole France—cynics and pessimists all—and expressed the wish that Arab translators would pursue "the propagation of healthier and more constructive elements in Western thought," *Studies on the Civilization of Islam*, pp. 280–1.

39. Badr, *Tatawwur al-riwayah al-arabiyyah al-hadithah fi misr*, pp. 175–80.

40. Manfaluti rendered the following French novels into Arabic: Dumas fils' *La dame aux camelias*, Chateaubriand's *Atala et René* and *Le dernier Abencérage*, Alphonse Karr's *Sous les tilleuls*, Edmond Rostand's *Cyrano de Bergerac*, Francois Coppée's *Pour la couronne* and Bernardin de Saint Pierre's *Paul et Virginie*.

41. The authors translated by Baydas from Russian versions into Arabic are Marie Corelli, Emilio Salgari, and L. Mühlbach.

42. Moosa, *The Origins of Modern Arabic Fiction*, p. 102.

43. As cited in Ibid., p. 107.

44. Zaytuni, *Harakah al-tarjamah fi 'asr al-nahdah*, p. 125.

45. Ibid., pp. 121–2.

46. Najm, *Al-Qissah fi al-adab al-arabi al-hadith*, p. 23.

47. Between the two World Wars, the quasi-official Committee for Writing, Translation, and Publication (*Lajnat al-ta'lif wal-tarjamah wal-nashr*) oversaw the translation of a number of prominent Victorian and modernist European authors such as Charles Dickens, H. G. Wells, Thomas Hardy, and Oscar Wilde. This work was continued after World War I by The Egyptian Writer Publishing House (*Dar al-katib al-misri*), under the aegis of Taha Husayn. The publisher contributed works by Voltaire, Huxley, Gide, Stendhal, and Mérimée to the growing corpus of sanctioned literary translations. Moosa, *The Origins of Modern Arabic Fiction*, pp. 117–19.

48. See for example, Farah Anton's introduction to his 1908 translation of Chateaubriand's *Atala*, sections of which are cited in Zaytuni, *Harakah al-tarjamah fi 'asr al-nahdah*, pp. 25–6.

49. For one such study, see Nafusa Zakariyyah Sa'id, *Tarikh al-da'wa ila al-'ammiyyah wa athariha fi misr* (Cairo: Dar qasr al-thaqafah bi al-iskindiriyyah, 1964).

50. Al-Sharif, "Nahdah al-adab fi misr," pp. 69–70.

51. Lawrence Venuti, *The Scandals of Translation: Towards an Ethic of Difference* (London: Routledge Press, 1998), p. 68.

52. R.K. Ruthven, *Faking Literature* (Cambridge: Cambridge University Press, 2001), p. 91.

53. Venuti, *The Scandals of Translation*, p. 31.

54. Abdelfattah Kilito's fascinating study, *L'Auteur et ses doubles*, (Paris: Seuil, 1985) explores the fluidity of notions of originality and authorship in the classical and medieval Arabic canon. Kilito shows how the literary strategies that we now classify and expel as forgery and plagiarism formed part of a playful and highly evolved Arabic tradition.

55. Zaytuni relates an interesting anecdote in this context: In the introduction to his translation of Michel Zévaco's *Les Pardaillan*, Tanius 'Abduh claimed that his impatient readers would telephone him in between installments in order to find out the imminent fate of the characters. *Harakah al-tarjamah fi 'asr al-nahdah*, pp. 133–4.

56. Venuti, *The Scandals of Translation*, p. 1.

CHAPTER 3

Looking Forward to the Past: Nahda, Revolution, and the Early Ba'th in Iraq

Orit Bashkin

A favorite slogan of neoconservatives prior to the present Gulf War was de-Ba'thization. While debating and redebating the repercussions of a post-Ba'thi Iraq, little attention was devoted to the Ba'th itself, or to the narratives, histories, and periodizations articulated by its ideologues.

The Ba'th is a revival movement that came into being in a colonial and postcolonial context and is crucial to our understanding of renaissance(s) and revolution.[1] The modern Arabic-Arabic Dictionary *al-Munjid* elucidates in its entry on the verb *b-'-th* that the noun *Ba'th* means, among other things, awakening, while "the day of Ba'th" refers to the Day of Judgment or the resurrection of the dead.[2] These definitions raise interesting questions as to the ways in which Ba'th intellectuals reconciled the messianic concept of resurrection with a national awakening and how these concepts produced a new understanding of rise and decline. The texts written by early Ba'thists further underscore the tensions between an awakening of a past and a revolutionary future. The founder of the Ba'th party, Michel 'Aflaq, aptly summarized these dilemmas in his famous query: "How should our *reviving, modern awakening* (*nahda*) and *Arab revolution* come to be realized?" (emphasis added).[3] This question kindled another set of questions: How can the revival of a past be modern? How can an awakening be revolutionized? And, most significantly, should the Ba'th seek inspiration in the past or in the future?

Ba'th ideologues perceptively contextualized their comprehension of revival in a colonial context, confessing that the articulation of a theory that called for Arab unity, freedom, and socialism in a period when the majority of the world was colonized required a new definition of time. Ba'th intellectual production, in other words, was conceived as a response to the enormous difficulties facing "the awakening (*nahda*) of our nation."[4] The nature of the national past that needed to be revived was often ambiguously defined. Arab nationalists had a variety of "pasts" to resurrect anew: the pre-Islamic, Semitic world; the heroic battles of Muhammad and the four righteous Caliphs; and the golden age of the 'Abbasid Caliphate. As this chapter will demonstrate, the decision of the Ba'th to revive a particular period was predicated on historical narratives already in existence in the Arab world. Similarly, their definition of the period of "decline" was highly intricate. Dipesh Chakrabarty identified the process by which British colonizers represented a variety of pasts "through a homogenizing narrative of transition from a medieval period to modernity."[5] The Ba'th's thinkers both critiqued and appropriated a similar narrative by underscoring the decline of the Arab Middle East yet conversely arguing that the colonizers had done much to perpetuate this state of decline. Furthermore, thinkers like Michel 'Aflaq also asserted that the Islamic "Middle Ages" was not a pre- or antimodern era as it was in the European case, but rather a period of renewal and revival.

The association created by the *Iraqi* Ba'th between revolution and renaissance should be understood as responding to narratives that were widespread during the Iraqi monarchy period (1921–1958). The interpretation of Iraq's past rested on the concept of the Arab *nahda*. The word *nahda* itself means "awakening," "revival," and "renaissance."[6] The *nahda* involved linguistic movements that produced new dictionaries and encyclopedias in Arabic, written mostly by Syrian Christians; literary movements championing the adoption of new genres in Arabic literature; religious and theological reform movements, which reinterpreted the Qur'ān and the sacred prophetic traditions; and scientific currents that took inspiration from European scientism, social Darwinism and materialism. The *nahda* in Arabic literature is depicted as beginning in the early nineteenth century and evolving throughout the century. The *nahda*'s relationship to the state's modernization efforts was emphasized by historians like Albert Hourani and was thus associated with an endeavor to legitimize military, scientific, and educational imports from the West.[7]

The *nahda* may be perceived as the end result of western military and economic challenges, as the fruits of intellectual pursuit of Arab thinkers and littérateurs, or as a state-run project aimed at instilling new modes of education and conscription, but in all cases, it is generally linked to the Arab national enterprise.[8] Ba'th ideology, as I hope to demonstrate, sought to both appropriate and revolutionize certain elements in the conceptualization of the *nahda*. In doing so, early Iraqi Ba'thists highlighted their commitment to concepts of revival, on the one hand, yet used the same ideas to underline the fact that the monarchy had failed to bring about revival and renaissance, on the other.

This essay, therefore, examines the early writings of the Ba'thists in order to comprehend their notion of time and renaissance in relation to the projects of nationalism, colonialism, and language. In the first part, I examine concepts of time expressed by Ba'thi Syrian thinkers. In the second part, I consider why the Ba'thi political platform attracted young Iraqi nationalists during the early 1950s. I have chosen to focus on the early stages of the Ba'th in Iraq as a way of historicizing the party's appeal within the context of the interwar period and the 1950s, rather than in the context of the military coups of the 1960s. The perception of time as articulated by the Syrian founders, I argue, corresponded to local needs of Iraqi nationalists and to their critique of the state's national narratives. The Ba'th, in other words, corresponded to discourses already dominant in the Iraqi public sphere: pan-Arabism, unity, and empire. Iraqi nationalists were closely familiar with the Ba'th's founding texts (produced in Syria), as well as concepts of cultural renaissance, revival of ancient Semitic empires, and the unity of Arabic-speaking peoples.

Two introductory remarks are in order. Deciphering Ba'th concepts poses a challenge even to its ostensibly savvy critics. On the one hand, the critic wishes to avoid the obsessive interest in etymology that was characteristic of older generations of Orientalist scholars. Edward Said discussed the etymology of the word "revolution" (*thawra*) and pointedly demonstrated that this kind of essentialism reduced revolution to nothing more than the "rising of a camel," without paying heed to the "innumerable people [that] have an active commitment to it."[9]

The Ba'th, whose intellectuals called for freedom from colonial domination and complete independence (both economic and political), had much in common with other modern, anticolonial movements in the era of decolonization. Nonetheless, Ba'thi writers constantly preoccupied themselves with words and etymologies. Zakī al-Arsūzī, in particular, relentlessly examined Arabic terms and idioms: their histories, roots, and sounds. Michel 'Aflaq, moreover, often referred to the role of Islam as a living example for modern revolutionaries. The critic, then, is faced with the difficult task of remaining faithful to the modern, colonial context of the Ba'th, on the one hand, and the necessity to reflect on the history of the word *Ba'th*, its relation to Islam, and the ways in which the Ba'thists negotiated words and their meanings, on the other.

The second question is that of hybridity. Homi Bhabha formulated the concept of colonial hybridity as a way of describing the variety of strategies through which the process of colonial domination was reversed. The ambivalent space of hybridity rendered impossible the representation of the symmetry between self and other and consequently unsettled colonial rules of recognition and the visibility of colonial authority.[10] As noted by other postcolonial critics, colonized intellectuals often constructed narratives reflecting the interests of indigenous nationalism in the language of the western metropolis to substantiate their claim for appropriating the civilizing mission from the colonizers.[11] Ba'thi intellectual production was exceedingly hybrid. It incorporated readings of western metaphysics in order to understand Arab philology, appropriated the binary Aryan/Semitic in the service of Arab nationalism, and intertwined socialist secularism into historical narratives that expressed admiration for the Prophet Muhammad while presenting the prophet as a role model for both Christian and Muslim Arabs. As a result, any attempt to consider the Ba'th merely as a counterimage to the colonial politics of the British (in Iraq) and the French (in Syria) or as a mere continuation of the early works composed by theorists of pan-Arab nationalism like Sāti' al-Husrī, misses the hybrid components of the Ba'thi national dialectics and the political implications of this hybridity.

The Syrian Ideologues—'Aflaq and Arsūzī

The Ba'th party was founded by two Syrian schoolteachers; Michel 'Aflaq, an Orthodox Christian (born 1910) and Salāh al-Dīnal-Bītār, a Sunni (born 1912). The former taught history, the latter science. They were later joined by Zakī al-Arsūzī, a philosophy teacher and an 'Alawī (born 1900). All three studied in Paris. Bītār and 'Aflaq read Nietzsche, Mazzini, Andre Gide, Romain Rolland, Marx, and Lenin, whereas Arsūzī was influenced by the psychology of Georges Dumas (1866– 1946), the translations of Plato into French by Emil Brehier (1876– 1952), and the philosophy of Leon Brunsching (1869–1944). He was also inspired by the writings of Johan Gottlieb Fichte on the racial features of nations, the role of language and history in nationalist thought, and Fichte's delineation of the attempts to unite all German-speaking peoples. The slogan of the new party that merged socialism and pan-Arab nationalism was "One Arab Nation with an Eternal Mission." In April 1947, members officially established a political party in Damascus in a convention that brought together delegates from Syria as well as from several other Arab countries.[12] Below I address the conceptualizations of Michel 'Aflaq— the most important Ba'thist ideologue and founder of the party—and of the lesser-known, though no less significant Zakī Arsūzī, concerning revival, nationalism, and perceptions of time.

Michel 'Aflaq was conscious of the fact that the theories of the Ba'th, and their conceptions of time, were conceived in "a dynamic context" that was in a state of flux, and in which the presence of both the past and the future was highly significant.[13]

> When the party came into being, most the lands (*aqtār*) of our nation were occupied and colonized. The conditions of our people were diverse. How, then, was it possible to announce in such a time that we are one nation and that we have a human mission to the entire world? This meant that without [having a definite] horizon, without situating this spiritual and moral horizon to our struggle within our revolution, we could never have overcome the difficulties, harsh circumstances and powerful enemies that fought against us and against our awakening (*nahda*).[14]

The Ba'thi future was intimately linked to the past and diametrically opposed to the present. However, the present would be the power to inspire the coming revolution once it was juxtaposed with the Arab glorious past.[15] To 'Aflaq, revival can only emerge from decline and therefore Arabs should revive the present in order to deny its existence and to allow the future to emerge as a separate entity.[16]

The Arab public needed to believe in the authenticity of their nation and the possibility of pan-Arab unity. To facilitate the imagination of pan-Arab unity, the Ba'th needed to construct a novel perception of the future and of the past. 'Aflaq called on his followers to free themselves from conventions and to rise above the problems of the day.

> By revolution we understand the true awakening which is no longer possible to deny or to doubt, the awakening of the Arab spirit at a decisive stage in human history. The reality of the revolution lies in this awakening, the awakening of the spirit which had been weighed down by stationary and vitiated conditions which, for a long time, prevented it from rising.[17]

'Aflaq indicated that it was important to resurrect many elements of the past; in particular the spirit of the nation, an entity which transcends both time and space. He highlighted the fact that the past is always present in the life of the nation, as the period in which the Arab soul realized itself. As a result, any struggle for the near and long-term future must be directly inspired by the past, which becomes the guide to the future. The past, however, can never reoccur, and thus Arabs must not bemoan the passing of the golden era. Rather they "must march toward it [the past], onward in a progressive spirit. We must ascend to it."[18]

> We have turned to both the future and to the past with the same power, the same motivation and the same depth in our conceptualizations. We viewed the future and the difficulties of its realization and its distance from our present. We likewise saw the past as faraway from our present. Thus we looked in the past for the new and the alive, and we looked in the future for the authentic (*asīl*) and the original.[19]

'Aflaq was careful to distinguish the Ba'th from the communists who refused to reconfigure the past into their theorization, viewing it only as a symbol of a reactionary tradition. The Ba'th, in contrast, recognized that history, language, and culture were located in the past, though they were careful not to enslave the present to the norms of the past.[20] 'Aflaq did, however, incorporate certain Marxist elements into his thinking such as the belief that the march of progress is unstoppable; that the present colonialist-capitalist regime created the very conditions that would bring about its downfall, and that the revolution should be organized by a radical intellectual cadre. In other words, although the communists denigrated Ba'thi romanticism, kitsch, and obsessions with morbidity, 'Aflaq's own ideas conveyed the communist notion that the Arabs have "nothing to lose but their chains."[21] What rendered the Ba'th's mission unique was the vision that the revolutionary future incorporates elements from the nation's past.

The Ba'thists, however, felt that they were obliged to accentuate the fact that their visions of the future related to universal processes of progress and were located in the same linear progression as western history. The Ba'th, wrote 'Aflaq, was forced to position itself "within the framework of the grand historical revolutions that did not occur solely for saving one people, but for saving humanity."[22] He thus repeatedly argued that the Ba'th identified with the progression of historical events that marked the beginning of a new era in the history of humanity. These arguments hinted that 'Aflaq covertly criticized Europe for turning its back on its own enlightened past by denying Arabs their own demands for freedom, unity, and self-rule.

For 'Aflaq, a new revolutionary era meant a period devoid of colonialism and exploitation, and a time where the Arabs could disseminate their civilization upon the entire world.[23] The struggle against colonialism thus had universal importance. "Our theory was a piercing look into the human spirit, into human history, into our own history, and the formation of our nation," he clarified.[24] Presenting the Arab national struggle as universal, and indicating that this struggle has potential for future success, fulfilled the dual role of legitimizing pan-Arab nationalism using the western idiom, and, concurrently, of assuring Arab audiences that their movement would be able to effectively attain its goals.

Many essays affirm the colonial context in which the Ba'th operated. 'Aflaq believed that no national or revolutionary movement faced the difficulties experienced by Arab nationalism, most brutally seen in the case of Palestine. Hailing the Ba'th's uniqueness and national commitment, he argued that the pre-Ba'thi Arab national movements were superficial in that they formalized their nationalism as a response to western allegations. For example, when the Arabs were reproached that their culture did not treasure freedom or equality, they rushed to validate that these same values did, in fact, exist in their ethos. The search for such values, then, was not intrinsic to the national movement itself, but rather imposed on it by the demands of the West. 'Aflaq believed that only a revival based on both past and future would rescue the Arabs from blind mimicry of western norms. At the present, however, the encroachment of western culture was risky precisely because it caused the Arabs to question their authentic contribution to history and culture.[25]

Socialism was also formulated as an anticolonial mode. 'Aflaq asserted that the liberal capitalist regime, with its relations and economic associations with the colonizing West brought about class differentiation and exploitation.[26] He explained that the present discourse carried out by politicians about the need for *gradual* reform was intended to mask the reluctance of the feudal elite to relinquish their lands to the peasants.[27] A regime based on socialism, however, could grant equality and justice to Arab subjects. Salāh al-Dīn al-Bītār further emphasized that the formation of the Ba'th was a response to the Syrian bourgeoisie comprador political leadership that collaborated with the French mandate to allow the foreigners to come to power, in return for many personal benefits.[28]

Renaissance, then, meant reviving the past in order to generate a struggle for socialism, freedom from colonialism, and revolution. The revival of the past dictated a new assessment of Islam. 'Aflaq, a Christian, defined Islam as an Arab and human religion that had formed Arab nationalism

> [n]ot just with respect to the past, but in respect to *any time* when the Arab nation remained in this world. Islam is the spiritual heritage, the cause of the Arab nation, its mystical source, and the ideal revolutionary movement in the eyes of the Baʿth.[29]

When asked how the Baʿth reconciled its praise of religion with its secular, socialist nature, ʿAflaq replied that individuals who believe that Arab nationalism should disregard religiosity are adopting a superficial stance that does not recognize the profound historical bonds between Arabism and Islam. Moreover, such views echoed the voices of "the foreign western colonizer" who expected the Arabs to succumb to secular nationalism.[30] Arab nationalism ought to embrace Islam, based on the vision that "Islam was our history, heroism, language, philosophy, and outlook to many beings and things."[31] Secularism, however, was seen as the realm of "constitution and laws." In legal affairs, relating to rights of citizens, Islam fulfilled no part, yet in the national domain, it was "an ethical, ideological and social revolution in the history of mankind."[32]

ʿAflaq's writings on Muhammad most lucidly reflect the ways in which he wanted to represent Arab nationalism as an Islamic Renaissance. The persona of "The Arab Prophet," Muhammad, signified a moral and national revival. The period most cherished by ʿAflaq was the first twenty years of Muhammad's prophetic mission (*Baʿtha*) since in this period the Arabs reformed their souls. To him, Islam was a belief system that revolutionized the debased socioeconomic conditions of the pre-Islamic era, a moment of linguistic triumph signified by the deliverance of the Arabic Qurʾān, a victorious polity that resulted in a thriving state, and an occasion in the history of humanity when the combination of national revival and a religious mission spread truth and justice in the world. ʿAflaq underscored the fact that the life of the prophet could be revived by contemporary Arabs as a way of attaining a new cultural revitalization. Europe, moreover, feared the power of Islam precisely because it recognized its importance as a national, cultural, and political vehicle.[33]

The Islamic past to be revived was positioned between the pre-Islamic past and the years of the disintegration of the Arab Empire in the tenth century. ʿAflaq felt that prior to the arrival of Islam, the Arabs were limited by their narrow loyalties to tribal traditions, whereas the tenth century represented a brutal quest for power, weakness, despotism, and foreign intervention in Arab affairs.[34] It is obvious that this reading, which underscored the successes of Islam in breaking down tribal and local affiliation, challenging foreign intervention, and creating a new culture, must have sounded extremely topical to contemporary Syrian, Palestinian, and Iraqi readers. It consequently seemed inevitable to revive this secularized Islamic past which contained so many remedies for the contemporary Arab nation-state.

The Ba'th continued the tradition of many an Arab nationalist in its attempt to secularize and nationalize Islam, while representing Islam as a mark of national authenticity. It is helpful to consider Partha Chatterjee's definition of the spiritual and material domains in order to appreciate the construction of Islam in 'Aflaq's prose. Chatterjee maintained that the world of colonial social institutions was divided into two domains: material and spiritual. The material domain encompassed financial systems, science and technology in which the West had proved its superiority. The spiritual domain, on the other hand, was the inner realm of cultural identity, in which the colonial state had no place.[35] In 'Aflaq's view, the realm of law belonged to the material domain in which Islam played no role. This language of nationalism treated sectarianism and religiosity as obstacles in the path to modernity.[36] Islam, however, also belonged to the spiritual sphere as a signifier of Arab authenticity and national identity. As such, it was crucial for the future revival.

While 'Aflaq was somewhat aware of the contradictions in his theory, and therefore made a genuine effort to clarify them to the public, Zakī al-Arasuzī made no such attempt. A student of metaphysics, and a translator of Plato into Arabic, Arsūzī developed a complex theory of Arab nationalism and Arab linguistics. He left future scholars a monumental corpus of texts that included many new words that he had invented.

Arsūzī challenged the assertion, heard often by contemporary politicians, that "our awakening (nahda) was delayed." According to Ofra Bengio, Arsūzī clearly differentiated between the functions of the European Renaissance, which had revived the Greek tradition, and the more significant roles of a nationalist revolution that awakens the ancient cultural and linguistic heritage of a particular nation.[37] For Arsūzī, our understanding of time is closely connected to our grasp of both nationalism and civilization. Life, he wrote, is lived independently by every generation and by individuals, yet eventually it becomes a history of a nation and the expression of the cultural progressions that occurred in a certain age. The members of the nation, in other words, experience historical events as a collective. The age of a nation, nevertheless, should not be measured by the number of years that passed since its birth, but rather by the consciousness of its members.[38] The question of whether a nation is ancient or new is, therefore, not merely the outcome of the passage of time, but of the awareness of the nation's members and the words they invent to describe the changes in their consciousness. The nation, moreover, is constantly changing through the activities of heroes and reformers, which in the Semitic world were identified with prophets.[39]

Arsūzī identified continuities between various phases in the history of the Arab nation. He refused to acknowledge a break between the pre-Islamic and the Islamic periods,[40] professing that both represented the life of the same nation. The Semitic non-monotheistic religions had a pioneering role in the development of civilization. Contrary to European allegations, the Arab mentality had always avoided stagnation. The Semites, who came to appreciate heroism and bravery,[41] gave the world eternal thought, monotheism, which was the direct product of the cultures of the premonotheist era.[42] The Arab nation, however, was not only typified by evolution, but also by revolution, as each stage revolutionized the preceding era.[43]

To Arsūzī, all nations and their languages evolved from a primitive state in which the nation spontaneously came into being, into a stage when institutions like language, ethics, religion, and arts were formed.[44] The Arabs made groundbreaking contributions to all such institutions. If one was to categorize (tasnīf) nations by their values and regimes, the Arabs emerged as a nation combining mercy and mission, a people that cherished justice and bestowed upon the world prophets/reformers, who innovated archaic social norms.[45]

Arsūzī was interested in time and its relationship to language, which was more important to him than space.[46] Although he believed that language is an institution like religion or the arts, his theories shifted between the belief that language includes the *essential* features of a nation that do not change over time and the conviction that language is constantly developing and changing. Therefore, one needed to find, and define, the essence in order to revive the Arabic language.

Arsūzī claimed that the historical course of Arabic was different to that of the Indo-European languages. Aryan languages progressed in a mechanical form, in which words were signs that reflected meanings. In Arabic, conversely, words were structures. Unlike European languages, in which words were signs by which consciousness described things, each word in Arabic reflected ideals, nature, and history. Arsūzī endeavored to confirm that Arabic retained its primordial originality (*fitra*). He contended that words in Arabic had managed to retain a harmony between their meanings, sounds, and forms even though they had been created in various time periods and contexts.[47]

The link between the Arabic language and natural phenomena was manifested, in Arsūzī's view, in primary forms of Arabic words, which imitated sounds found in nature. He attempted to authenticate this theory by examining the derivation of new words from old Arabic roots (*ishtiqāq*), and neologisms based on old Arabic articles. Everything about the Arabic language—vocabulary, syntax, phonemes, and grammar—revealed to him the link between language and the national thought of the Arabs.[48] The relationship between nation and family, for example, was expressed etymologically in the common root of the word nation (*umma*) and the word mother (*umm*); just as the mother is the source of the family, the nation is the source of brotherhood in the society. Nevertheless, the fact that Arabic was also a dynamic language, which functioned in a dynamic context, engendered the hope that the Arab nation as a whole would also avoid stagnation and immobility.[49] Arsūzī's linguistic efforts represented a desire to contribute to national revival by understanding the uniqueness of Arabic and its potentials.

Although ousted from Ba'thi leadership due to internal party politics,[50] Arsūzī's ideas were similar to those of 'Aflaq in that both secularized religion, yet concurrently made the nature of Arab nationalism more religious. To them, prophets (especially Muhammad in 'Aflaq's writings) were reformers that changed society. To both Arsūzī and 'Aflaq, the notions of mercy, sympathy, and love among the members of the community were highly important as the nation came to represent a large family.

Arsūzī's writing likewise reflected the extent to which Syrian intellectuals borrowed paradigms from the colonizers and adjusted them to their particular national needs. Although not mentioned by name, the theories of Renan and Fichte resonate in his texts. His theories, however, also reflect views in interwar pan-Arab thinking. Ernest Dawn demonstrated the prominence of what he termed "the Semito-Arab nation" in the writings of interwar Syrian, Iraqi, and Palestinian intellectuals. "All authors highlighted the movement of Arabs such as the Ghassandis, the Lahkmids, and the Nabataeans into the Fertile Crescent . . . They pushed the Arab migration . . . to the times of Narim Sin, Hammurabi, the Amalikites, and the Hyksos."[51] Their writings dwelled on the conflicts between Arabs and Persians and, more generally, between East and West. Dawn hypothesized that these images incorporated ideas found in Breasted's *Ancient Times*[52] that emphasized the perpetual conflicts between Asia and Europe, Aryans and Semites.[53] Arsūzī manipulated the Semitic-Aryan binary to turn it on its head: he agreed that there were fundamental differences between Semite and Aryan but he accentuated the positive, essential qualities of the Semitic-Arab nation that had already existed in antiquity and needed to be revived. His Ba'thi perception of nationalism seems to be a mixture of diverse elements—modern and ancient, Arab and European—fused to support a new historical narrative, a new notion of time, and a modern political unit: the nation-state.

The ideas of both thinkers are articulated in the Baʻthi constitution that stresses the eternal mission of the Arab nation. The dialectic conceptualization of past-present-future is underlined in the statement that "the mission [of the Arab nation] reveals itself in ever new and related forms *through the different stages of history*. It aims at the renewal of human values, the quickening of human progress, at increasing harmony and mutual help."[54] This assertion reveals both a linear perception of time as well as the assumption of a national essence which manifests itself throughout history. The constitution also identifies "colonialism and all that goes with it" as "a criminal enterprise" which the Arabs must resist, just like "all [other] peoples are fighting for their freedom."[55]

Scholars point to the lack of originality in Baʻthi ideology, to the inner contradictions in 'Aflaq's ideas, to the ultimate commitment to the nation that is articulated in Baʻthist texts, and, at certain times, to their antidemocratic nature.[56] Yet Baʻthi ideology must be taken seriously; neither Arsūzī nor 'Aflaq were simply modifiers of random anticolonial theories produced in the West. Rather, they were thinkers whose works shed significant light on colonialism and Arab nationalism. As an anticolonial movement, the Baʻth nationalized the concept of the Islamic awakening that came to signify the revival of the national spirit. The Baʻth was both a revolution and a revival movement looking at the past and at the future for inspiration. The Baʻthi notion of time illuminates various aspects of Benedict Anderson's conceptualization of time.[57] It does not signify the simple transformation from an imperial, religious, and cosmological time to a national time. The early Baʻthists formulated their conception of time-progression in opposition to the periodizations formulated in Europe: while Europe identified Islam with stagnation and decay, Baʻthists claimed that Islam represented movement and change and an era of Semitic glory. The Baʻthist theorists also believed that if the Arabs could capitalize on their national heritage, they could once again emerge as a large, united entity. As 'Aflaq noted, the mere articulation of such an anticolonial vision during the colonial era was a revolutionary act in itself.

Early Baʻthism in Iraq

The Baʻth was a small Iraqi movement. Even after seizing power in 1968, the Iraqi Baʻthists did not enjoy popular support. Their most serious rivals were the communists, who competed with them for hegemony in the cultural field. Although both vied for the backing of the educated youth, the communists were far more influential in the ranks of the intelligentsia and the student body.[58]

The Ba'thi platform was propagated in Iraq by Syrian students: Fā'iz Ismā'īl, who studied law in Baghdad, and Wasfī al-Ghānim, who studied at the Teachers' Training College. The movement attracted some Iraqi students and gained supporters in Nāsiriyya, Basra, and Najaf. Initially, the Iraqi Ba'th was led by 'Abd al-Rahmān al-Dāmin. In 1951, however, Fu'ād al-Rikābī, a Shiite engineer, took over the leadership of what Hanna Batatu termed "the embryonic Ba'th." In 1952 an official branch of the Ba'th was opened in Iraq. Whereas in 1950 the party numbered about fifty members, in 1955 it already included some 289 members (excluding supporters). Members were mostly Muslims (the party included only five Christians). A hundred and two members were students, twelve were peasants, and eight were government officials. The other members included a lawyer, a union activist, and a telephone operator. Let us now explore the reasons that made a small number of students and educated professionals turn to the Ba'th in the early 1950s.[59]

Certain elements in Ba'thism were similar to popular elements in Iraqi nationalism such as the concept of *nahda* and pan-Arab unity as the signifier of the *nahda*. As we have seen, 'Aflaq's vision of a revolutionary future and an Arab awakening were to be realized in a united Arab nation-state. Pan-Arabism was not unpopular in Iraq, and in fact, had been enthusiastically adopted by many of Iraq's intellectuals in the 1930s and 1940s. Iraqi pan-Arabism, however, assumed numerous, often conflicting meanings.[60]

Pan-Arabism played a vital role in the education system since many intellectuals active in the Ministry of Education (directors, ministers, supervisors, teachers, and professors) sought to take advantage of this disciplinary institution to instill a pan-Arab national spirit among young audiences. Iraqi intellectuals who served as bureaucrats and policymakers, like Sāti' al-Husrī, Fādhil al-Jamālī, and Sāmī Shawkat, frequently wrote on the nature of pan-Arabism. Sāmī Shawkat, for example, asserted that the history of the region was the history of ancient Semitic empires like Assyria, Carthage, and Himyar.[61] In the writings of both Husrī and Shawkat, Islam was understood to be a social formulation (*nizām ijtimā'ī*), rather than a spiritual creed.[62] These views were very similar to the postulations of Arsūzī, who also evoked the Semitic heritage of the Arab peoples and their grand imperial pasts, and to 'Aflaq's secular understanding of Muhammad's prophetic mission.

The significance of pan-Arabism was manifested in the public sphere in the activities of clubs and societies. As Albert Hourani observed:

> New media of expression were creating a universe of discourse, which united educated Arabs. . . . The publishing houses of Cairo and Beirut produced textbooks for the increasing numbers of students, and also poetry, novels, and works of popular science and history which circulated *wherever Arabic was read.*[63] (emphasis added)

Iraqi intellectuals belonged to a world in which the Arabic print culture transcended the boundaries of a particular nation-state. Iraqi writers and intellectuals admired the works of fellow Arab writers from other countries and were eager for their approval as well, since all shared similar cultural, political, and social concerns. Prominent Egyptian, Lebanese, and Syrian writers were frequent visitors to Baghdad, and their visits were considered major cultural events that appeared in the pages of both the Iraqi and Arab press. Despite censorship and limitations on the freedom of speech in monarchic Iraq, Iraqi intellectuals were exposed to a variety of ideas in the Arab intellectual marketplace of books and journals.[64]

Within the discourse of pan-Arab unity, a special place was reserved for Syria as the emblem of Arab unity. Union with Syria was cherished more than with any other Arab country because of the significant role Syria had played in the Iraqi monarchy. The Iraqi royal household, the Hashemite, legitimized its rule by emphasizing the participation of Iraq's first monarch, Faysal ibn al-Husayn (1921–1933), in the Arab Revolt against the Ottoman Empire.[65] Syria was the place of Faysal's first Arab government, formed after the end of World War I, and many of the Sherifians (officers who participated in the Arab Revolt) came to Iraq from Syria with Faysal to become the political elite of the newly established state. The Iraqi press was full of accounts of visits of Iraqi students, intellectuals, and officials to Syria as well as stories about Syria's heroic battle against the French colonizers. Syrian teachers were imported to Iraq because of their educational expertise and to strengthen Sunni pan-Arab affinities.[66] Therefore, when Syrian Ba'thists advocated a close, harmonious relationship between all Arab countries, and in particular between Syria and Iraq, they were recapturing elements already present in the Iraqi national discourse.

Nevertheless, despite the similarities of some Ba'thi national ideals to those advocated by the Hashemites, the Ba'thi endorsement of revolution and its linking of renaissance to revolution was in *radical opposition* to the national narratives promoted by the monarchy. The Hashemites manipulated the *nahda* narratives to legitimize their rule. Faysal I and the Sherifians perceived the Arab Revolt as the climax of a cultural *nahda* that began in the Levant during the nineteenth century. Faysal, however, lamented the fact that the Iraqi nation, once a center of science, civilization, and knowledge, had declined into a state of anarchy and thus was unable to experience a *nahda*. The *nahda*, subsequently, legitimized the rule of the monarchy in a sophisticated manner. On the one hand, Faysal used the *nahda* to highlight the great achievements of the Arab Revolt. In this narrative, it was a successful movement that had led to the construction of the Iraqi nation-state. On the other hand, the *nahda* also signified a process of modernization. As such, it was an incomplete procedure since Iraq was not fully modernized and thus needed a strong leadership, embodied in the Hashemite monarchy, to ensure that this process would come to a successful conclusion.[67]

The Hashemite understanding of the *nahda*, however, was constantly challenged. The occupation of the Middle East by the British and the French, the fact that none of the new Arab countries enjoyed even formal independence until the 1930s and 1940s, and the growing influence of the Zionists in Palestine, all generated growing doubts concerning the *nahda*'s future success.

These uncertainties typified the Iraqi debate, in which writers went as far as doubting the existence of the *nahda*. The Iraqi poet, Ma'rūf al-Rusāfī negated the fact that "there existed a *nahda* in [Arab] politics, although I hear Egypt has experienced something of that sort." The construction of a map of "nation-states" was by no means the fruits of national revival but of foreign intervention, which had molded the East according to colonial interests. Rusāfī, however, was more optimistic with respect to a cultural *nahda* since he believed that spiritual, religious, and cultural reform was feasible even without political sovereignty. He used the example of the Jews who had managed to make progress and to bring about reform both in the East and in the West without having political sovereignty.[68] Thus although Rusāfī did envision a chance for Arab cultural revival, he saw no potential for political change.

Colonialism, as a result, turned *nahda* into a dilemma that begged for a solution and reflected the impossibility of an Arab revival—with its attendant concepts of civilization and progress—while the Arabs were still being occupied and exploited. The daily *Rāfidān* summarized this view:

> Some people claim that we are in a period of light, of knowledge, of high civilization. However, if we give this matter some thought, we quickly realize that our period is an era during which most of humanity is

tortured. . . . *Our period is no different from the Middle Ages.* Politics today means exploiting nations. This is the period of oppression and darkness.[69] [emphasis added]

Even after the termination of the mandate and the beginning of official Iraqi independence in 1932, intellectuals noted that the *nahda* had yet to materialize. Iraq's social democratic party *al-Ahālī* claimed that no regime could lay claim to true revival until it adopted democracy. The Iraqi *nahda* was unsuccessful since it had no positive effect on the lives of the majority of Iraqis.[70] A complete *nahda* represented a revolution (*thawra*) against tyranny[71] and social renewal (*tajdīd*). Yet, precisely because Iraq was not democratic or fully independent as its economy was still dominated by British interests, it was questionable whether the processes occurring in Iraq signified an awakening of any sort.[72]

The communists were even more radical in their assessment of the failure of revival. The leader of the Iraqi communist party, Yūsuf Salmān Yūsuf (Fahd) (hanged in 1949), dated the beginning of the *nahda* in the late Ottoman era when the national Arab movement started to aspire to a cultural and a political revival.[73] Nevertheless, after World War I, Iraq came to be controlled by groups of feudal *shaykh*s as well as urban merchants who wished to preserve their ties with foreign companies and were critical of any form of violence that might challenge their economic and social power. Even worse, the "men of the Arab Revolt" relied on British help to preserve their political hegemony.[74] This historical periodization denied the hypothesis that the Iraqi state was the manifestation of the Arab *nahda*. The monarchy, the Sherifians, and the tribal *shaykh*s were held accountable for the failure of the national movement. In the 1940s, Fahd presented the Arab and Iraqi *nahda* as "passive revolutions," that is, modifications creating a new political order, without changing structural social relations.[75] A state created by colonizers and sustained by a comprador leadership could not be accounted as responsible for any kind of revival.

The ideas of the Ba'th resonated with certain concerns of the young generation of Iraqis. The Iraqi Ba'th acknowledged the failure of the Hashemites to obtain a true revival of Arab culture, a view shared by the social democrats and the communists. They believed in pan-Arabism and felt that the Hashemite leadership, which was supported by Britain and was mostly loyal to interests of landowners and tribal *shaykh*s, was entirely incapable of realizing pan-Arab ideology. While the Hashemite narrative accentuated pan-Arabism to legitimate their rule, their lack of commitment to the same pan-Arab ideal brought about their demise.

The failure of the Iraqi state to commit to a pan-Arab, anticolonial agenda became ever more apparent in 1948, with the Palestinian *nakba* and the suppression of the widespread Iraqi protests against the pro-British policies of the Iraqi government (*wathba*). Iraq's national leadership, according to the opposition members of the educated elites, had failed in its mission to instigate true revival. Ba'thi ideology, then, began to appeal to Iraqis who felt the urgent need to adopt more radical means to protect Arab nationalism. The socialist component of Ba'thi ideology allowed them to respond to the communist critique of Iraq's economic affairs, in particular the necessity for land reform and redistribution of wealth.[76] Their allegiance to the idea of Arab unity permitted the Ba'thists to position themselves as more committed to Arab nationalism than the communists, and to present (often unfairly) the communists' critique of the pan-Arab language disingenuously employed by the Iraqi political elite as a betrayal of the very ideas of pan-Arabism.

The recently published memoirs of Fa'īz Ismā'īl, the Syrian Ba'thist who was active in Iraq, reveal much about the dilemmas facing the Ba'th during its early stages. The memoirs include excerpts of letters exchanged between Iraqi Ba'thists and their Syrian colleagues, which echoed the initial difficulties of the movement in Iraq.[77] Iraqi Ba'thists, such as the Syrian Michel 'Aflaq, deemed the "present" hopelessly corrupt. They realized that their beliefs were not shared by other Iraqis or were at least unknown to them and were worried about their general lack of influence in Iraq. 'Abd al-Rahmān al-Dāmin conveyed similar anxieties when lamenting the fact that the party had not engendered much support among the people. He remarked, nevertheless, that the youth was conscious and attentive to the Arab problem. He therefore highlighted the need for both unified as well as regional Arab action.[78] The Ba'thists, then, were able to recognize the national frustration of the youth, and hoped that the theories of their Syrian brethren would offer a solution to the failed project of the Iraqi *nahda*.

'Aflaq's appeal to set a new horizon for the future in which Arab unity would overcome colonial barriers seemed a useful way for young Iraqis to contend with present realities. Physician 'Abd Allah al-Samarā'ī confessed that "here we are in Iraq, in our horrific present, in the worst possible condition. . . . Everything in the country *marches backwards*, and it is surprising that we, in this land, in its capital, know nothing about the problems of [our] country" (emphasis added). The only solution to the Ba'thists' state of despair was Arab unity, which held out a shining hope for a better future, a revolution, and a meaningful life.[79] 'Abd al-Rahmān al-Dāmin took great pride in a map designed by the Ba'thists that ignored the borders between the Arab states and recognized only a united Arab nation. This map was far superior to contemporary maps that "acknowledged these despicable divisions of the Arab nation." The Baʿthists hoped to popularize the map, particularly in schools, so that people could learn more about the Arab nation as a whole, its geography and economics as well as the social and political formulations that distinguish this nation.[80] Iraqi nationalists often faulted Britain for creating a system of what John Noyes calls "nodal points." According to Noyes, colonization captures space by establishing boundaries and limiting passage across them. The establishing of privileged points of transformation allowed colonizers to classify spaces through the creation of conditions of passage between them.[81] Dāmin called for the unification of Arabic-speaking peoples or for the creation of a national space, as methods of challenging the construction of these artificial points of transformation.

The Syrian Baʿth, in consequence, proposed ideas to Iraqi youth that resonated with discourses already prevalent in Iraq, in particular the appeal for Arab unity. A variety of elements in Iraqi society were already questioning and criticizing the comprador nature of Iraq's political elite, particularly under the leadership of Nūrī al-Saʿīd, and the failure of the Hashemite monarchy to attain a revival or an awakening, despite the monarchy's legitimizing narratives and its raison d'être. This general dissatisfaction left a gap that called for a new definition of a revolution and an awakening. The Iraqi Baʿth was able to fill that void, although the movement was still in its embryonic stages during the early 1950s.

Fuʾād Rikābī's reflections on the Iraqi Baʿth in its pre-1958 formation likewise mirror a reflection of the Baʿth through Iraqi lenses. Rikābī viewed the Baʿth in historical perspective and believed that every historical event affected the future, whether profoundly or superficially. Revolution was *the* historical moment that linked the present to the future. In the Arab context, revolution was a much-needed social, political, and ethical act to respond to a process of perpetual decline that culminated in the 1950s. In the 1950s, however, Arab aspirations for unity and opposition to feudal regimes, decadent social systems, and political oppression inspired a political struggle as Arabs came to realize that only a unified effort would assure true liberation from colonialism and comprador regimes. The grim present, then, inspired a hope for a revolution and for a better future. Palestine was an example of the ways in which tragic political outcomes served to revolutionize Arab audiences. The idea to create a Zionist state in Palestine was nothing novel, argued Rikābī, and, in fact, appeared on the colonial agenda before World War I. Yet the failure to rescue Palestine forced the Arabs to become aware of the impotence of their own reactionary regimes. Rikābī narrated this event as a moment of bitter failure and dismay from which a new revival would begin to emerge. Iraq's history was told along similar lines. Iraq was colonized, directly and indirectly, under the Hashemite regime. In Rikābī's opinion, the negotiations surrounding the Baghdad Pact made it clear that colonialists would always resort to subterfuges to maintain their influence in Iraq. Interests in Iraqi oil began in the latter part of the nineteenth century and expanded in 1933 when British and American oil companies infiltrated the Gulf States. Events turned increasingly bleaker at the end of World War II, when programs to transport Iraqi oil from Kirkuk to the Mediterranean reconfigured Iraq's position in the new colonial order. The colonization of Iraq, and its exploitation, however, led to the demise of the Hashemite regime.[82] Thus, in a similar way to 'Aflaq, the accentuation of the bleak present inspired a new, and better, revolutionary future.

The fact that Rikābī was a Shi'i may indicate that the language of modernity and nationalism sometimes transcended religious and ethnic boundaries. In Iraq, Shi'ites and Sunnis alike were reading works of Arab nationalists and were preoccupied with the question of sect in relation to other themes such as nation, revival, and time. Although the post-1958 era is beyond the scope of this paper, it is important to note that Rikābī's revival was mostly understood in concrete terms of placing greater emphasis on military revolution rather than on romanticized notions of the past. Rikābī's views, however, underline the compatibility of 'Aflaq's Ba'thi ideas to the Iraqi milieu and demonstrate how the notion of the Renaissance, conceptualized in the 1940s, was transplanted in the early 1950s to re-explicate new realities. It is perhaps the eclecticism of the Ba'th that allowed it to respond to different needs at different times, and concurrently, retain a certain loyalty to its core concepts of unity and resistance to colonialism.

Epilogue

The end of the Ba'thi story in Iraq is quite famous. In June 1955, after protesting against the Baghdad Pact, twenty-two members were arrested including Rikābī. The Ba'thists supported the antimonarchic revolution of 'Abd al-Karīm Qāsim (1958), and Rikābī even participated in Qāsim's first cabinet. However, the Ba'thists were disenchanted by Qāsim's apparent support of the Iraqi communist party (the Ba'th's bitter rivals), and also by Qāsim's emphasis on an Iraqi, rather than a pan-Arab or Nasserite, agenda. This hostility between the Ba'thists and Qāsim resulted in a failed attempt of the Ba'th to assassinate him (1959).[83] One of the participants in this assassination attempt was the young Saddām Husayn. Despite the harsh retaliatory measures that were taken against Ba'th members, the party was able to collaborate in the successful overthrow of the regime in February 1963. Only nine months after assumption of power, internal fragmentation led to Ba'thi expulsion from power. In July 1968, Ba'thists Hasan Bakr and Saddām Husayn managed to reorganize the party, achieve the support of the army, and take control over the state. The Ba'th remained in power until very recently.

The nature of the Ba'thi regime, although a matter of topical debate, is not within the scope of this chapter. Suffice it to say that the regime of Saddām Husayn— whose networks of sociopolitical support relied on immediate family, kin, tribe, town, and a close circle of friends and supporters— was a drastic departure from the pan-Arab ideology of the Ba'thi founders. Although 'Aflaq resided in Baghdad until his death in 1989, he was only a legitimizing icon and devoid of actual political authority. The regime's hostility to the Ba'thist Syria,[84] and the provincial nature of its elite differed from both the educated Iraqis that supported the Ba'th in its first stages and from their ideas.[85] I believe I can claim with confidence that Saddām Husayn ventured into neither the particularities of Arsūzī's metaphysics nor his linguistic articulations.

It is therefore also vital to view the Iraqi Ba'th of the interwar period and the 1950s, as a movement reflecting on revival and Renaissance within a colonial and postcolonial context. The Ba'thi notion of Renaissance was conceived at a time when another conception of an awakening, the *nahda*, was already in existence. In Syria, thinkers like 'Aflaq and Arsūzī synthesized and hybridized a concept of renaissance that contained interlacing motifs from Marxist and Arab-national theory as well as contemporary philosophy. This Renaissance nationalized Islam and turned it into an emblem of the ability of the Arab to reform his soul and to revolt against the present in the promise for a better future.

The Iraqi monarchy, like other regimes in the Middle East during the interwar period, asserted that it embodied the longed-for Arab revival. Nevertheless, rival narratives of renaissance and revival challenged the Hashemite story from the very inception of the Iraqi state. The communists, in particular, highlighted the fact that the Iraqi state was created as a colonial tutelage and contested the Hashemite narrative to offer other timelines of rebirth and revival inspired by Marxism. The embryonic Ba'th of the early 1950s had played into, and manipulated, this mélange of historical periodizations. The Ba'th integrated into its ideology familiar national mythologies of the interwar period—such as tales about the

Semitic world and the power of the Prophet Muhammad—thus constructing a past to be revitalized. Simultaneously, however, the Ba'th also joined in criticism of the regime and claimed that the feeble political leadership had failed in bringing about both national independence and unity, and thus could not be considered as the realization of the *nahda*. The Ba'th platform also contained a socialist component that emphasized the failures of the regime in providing a just social system to the members of the community. This socialist component also served to counter the communists' claim as the sole representatives of the working classes and the only power capable of generating a revolution. For this reason, as Batatu notes, although "by 1957, . . . the Syrian Ba'th had become a babel of conflicting ideological currents . . . in Iraq the faithful would, for the next half decade, continue to seek guidance in the pages of 'Aflaq: in their eyes 'Aflaq and orthodox Ba'thism were inseparable."[86]

The Ba'thists, then, recognized the discrepancies between the language of revival, as employed by the Hashemites, and their own realities. These reflections upon the meanings of the Renaissance disclosed the impossibility, for both Arab intellectuals and for historians of Arab intellectual history, to conceptualize a single periodization of Arab *nahda* or a distinct interpretation of the term Ba'th. The multifaceted narratives of the revival imply that it is preferable to explore both the *nahda* and its intellectual offspring, the Ba'th, as an ethos, as movements of ideas concurrently emanating from diverse centers, differently interpreted according to interests of local elites and evoking simultaneously universal notions of time, inspired by European periodizations, yet attempting to capitalize on the multiplicity of the Arab and Islamic pasts.[87]

Notes

1. On the Ba'th see John F. Devlin, "The Baath Party: Rise and Metamorphosis," *The American Historical Review* 96, no. 5 (1991), pp. 1396–1407; John F. Devlin, *The Ba'th Party: A History from Its Origins to 1966* (Stanford, CA: Hoover, 1966); Kamel Abu Jaber, *The Arab Ba'th Party, History, Ideology and Organization* (Syracuse, NY: Syracuse University Press, 1966); Hanna Batatu, *The Old Social Classes and the Revolutionary Movements of Iraq* (Princeton, NJ: Princeton University Press, 1978), pp. 722–1110; Adeed Darwisha, *Arab Nationalism in the Twentieth Century—From Triumph to Despair* (Princeton, NJ: Princeton University Press, 2003), pp. 3–4, 124–8, 194–5, 153–9, 237–41, 221–4, 287–9, 302–3; Sylvia Haim, *Arab Nationalism: An Anthology* (Berkeley, CA: University of California Press, 1976), pp. 61–71 (Haim's text is an anthology of translations on Arab nationalism, yet in her influential introduction Haim debates some aspects of the Ba'th thinking); Albert Hourani,

Arabic Thought in the Liberal Age (Cambridge: Cambridge University Press, 1962), pp. 356–8; Leonard Binder, *The Ideological Revolutions in the Middle East* (New York: John Wiley and Sons, 1964), pp. 154–97; Raymond A. Hinnebusch, *Authoritarian Power and State Formation in Ba'thist Syria: Army, Party and Peasant* (Boulder, CO: Westview, 1990); Marion Farouk-Sluglett and Peter Sluglett, *Iraq since 1958: From Revolution to Dictatorship* (London: I. B. Tauris, 2001) (2nd edition), pp. 87–96.

2. Lewis Ma'lūf (ed.), *Al-Munjid fī'l lugha wa'l A'lām* (33rd edition) (Beirut: Dār al-Mashriq, 1992), Vol 1, p. 42.

3. Michel 'Aflaq, *Al-Ba'th wa'l turāth*, (Baghdad, Dār al-Hurriyya, 1976), p. 36.

4. Ibid., p. 14.

5. Dipesh Chakrabarty, *Provincializing Europe* (Princeton, NJ: Princeton University Press, 2000), 32.

6. Unlike "The [Arab] *Nahda*," a "*Nahda*" was used to signify various European revival movements: mostly the Renaissance (al-nahda al-urūbiyya), but sometimes the European Enlightenment, the Meiji Restorations (Japan) and in fact every nation that experienced cultural or national renaissance. The term "Awakening" also featured prominently in one of the most important texts on the history of Arab nationalism, *The Arab Awakening* by George Antonius. The title of the work was inspired by a verse, written by the poet Ibrāhīm al-Yāzijī, "Arise, ye Arabs and awake." "An ode of Arab patriotism" the verse "sang of the achievements of the Arab race" and assumed a wide circulation since it echoed national "sentiments unconsciously felt." See George Antonius, *The Arab Awakening: the Story of the Arab National Movement* (New York: Capricorn, 1965), 54–5.

7. A. Haywood, *Modern Arabic Literature 1800–1970* (London: Lund Humphries, 1971); Hourani, *Arabic Thought in the Liberal Age*, p. 67; John W. Livingstone, "Western Science and Education Reform in the Thought of Shakyh Rifa'a al-Tahtawi," *International Journal of Middle Eastern Studies* 28, no. 4 (1996), pp. 543–64.

8. Saree Makdisi, "Postcolonial Literature in a Neocolonial World: Modern Arabic Culture and the End of Modernity," *Boundary* 22, no.1 (1995), pp. 85–115.

9. Edward W. Said, *Orientalism* (New York: Vintage Books, 1979), p. 315.

10. Homi K.Bhabha, "Signs Taken for Wonders: Questions of Ambivalence and Authority under a Tree Outside Delhi, May 1817," in *The Location of Culture*. Ed. Homi. K. Bhabha (London and New York: Routledge, 1994), pp. 102–22.

11. See Partha Chatterjee, *The Nation and Its Fragments: Colonial and Postcolonial Histories* (Princeton, NJ: Princeton University Press, 1993) (esp. pp. 55–9). In the Middle Eastern context, see the analysis of modes employed by Egyptian intellectuals that adopted European disciplinary institutions in Timothy Mitchell, *Colonising Egypt* (Berkeley, CA: University of California Press, 1988), especially in the chapters "Enframing" (pp. 34–63), "The Appearance of Order" (pp. 63–95) and "After We Have Captured their

Bodies" (pp. 95–128); and Mitchell's recent *Rule of Experts, Egypt, Techno-Politics, Modernity* (Berkeley, CA: University of California Press, 1995).

12. On 'Aflaq's biography, early ideas and the intellectual currents that informed his philosophy, see Abu Jaber, *The Arab Ba'th Party*, pp. 10–14; Batatu, *The Old Social Classes*, pp. 724—8, pp. 730–41. Batatu believes that 'Aflaq was highly influenced by Herder (ibid., p.733). On Arsūzī's biography and ideals, see Batatu, pp. 722–4. See also Keith D. Watenpaugh's thoughtful article " 'Creating Phantoms:' Zaki al-Arsuzi, the Alexandretta Crisis, and the Formation of Modern Arab Nationalism in Syria," *International Journal of Middle East Studies* 28, no. 3. (1996), pp. 363–89. On the three founding fathers, 'Aflaq, Bītār and Arsūzī, see Devlin, pp. 7–20, on their ideas see ibid., pp. 24–46.

13. 'Aflaq, *Al-Ba'th wa'l turāth*, p. 36.

14. Ibid., pp. 14–15.

15. 'Aflaq, "The Ba'th as a Historical Movement,", (originally published in 1950) in *Fī Sabīl al-Ba'th*. Ed. Michel 'Aflaq (Baghdad: Dār al-Hurrīya lil-Tibā'a, 1959), pp. 37–9.

16. 'Aflaq, "The New Generation" (1944), ibid., pp. 153–9.

17. Michel 'Aflaq, "Nationalism and Revolution," (originally published in 1940), trans. Sylvia Haim, *Arab Nationalism*, p. 22.

18. Ibid., p. 247.

19. 'Aflaq, *Al-Ba'th wa'l turāth*, p. 36.

20. 'Aflaq, "The bond between Arabism and the Revolutionary Movement," (1950), *Fī sabīl*, pp. 78–83.

21. 'Aflaq, "The relationship between organization and revolutionary actions," (1957), *Fī Sabīl al-Ba'th*, pp. 93–8; "On the Arab Mission," (1946), *Fī Sabīl al-Ba'th.*, pp. 101–8.

22. 'Aflaq, *Al-Ba'th wa'l turāth*, p. 15.

23. Ibid., p. 17.

24. Ibid., p. 21.

25. 'Aflaq, "Revolutionary Organization" (1950), *Fī sabīl*, 71–4; 'Aflaq, "Ba'th is Revolution," (1950), *Fī Sabīl al-Ba'th*, pp. 65–70; 'Aflaq, "New thinking," (1943), *Fī sabīl*, pp. 139–8.

26. 'Aflaq, *Al-Ba'th wa'l turāth*, p. 25.

27. 'Aflaq, "Time and the Revolutionary Movement," (1950) *Fī sabīl*, pp. 75–7.

28. Salah al-Din al-Bitar, "The Major Deviation of the Ba'th is Having Renounced Democracy," an interview with Marie-Christine Aulas; Eric Hooglund; Jim Paul, *MERIP Reports*, 110 (Syria's Troubles), (1982): pp. 21–3. Nevertheless, as Bītār asserted, "the Ba'th, born in a colonized country, could not at first express a social ideology, but only a national one. National independence preoccupied everybody's thought at the time" and thus nationalism was privileged over socialism, although both were the result of the colonial order. Bassam Tibbi had therefore concluded that although "the notion of Arab socialism first took root thanks to Michel 'Aflaq," the Ba'th, as an "ideology, like the later counter-ideology of

Nasserist Arab socialism, is distinctly populist and sees itself as being first and foremost nationalistic." Bassam Tibi, "Islam and Modern European Ideologies," *International Journal of Middle East Studies* 18, no. 1. (1986), p. 23. On the role of socialism in the Ba'th see also Abu Jaber's monograph.

29. 'Aflaq, *Al-Ba'th wa'l turāth*, p. 21.
30. Ibid., p. 27.
31. Ibid., p. 28.
32. Ibid.
33. 'Aflaq, "In the Memory of The Arab Prophet," (1943), *Fī sabīl*, pp. 131–8; "On Theory of Religion," (1956), *Fī sabīl*, pp. 201–7.
34. 'Aflaq, "On the Arab mission," (1946), *Fī sabīl*, pp. 101–8.
35. Chatterjee, p. 6.
36. On sects and modernity, see Ussama Makdisi, *The Culture of Sectarianism: Community, History, and Violence in Nineteenth-Century Ottoman Lebanon* (Berkeley, CA: University of California Press, 2000); On sectarianism in Iraq, see Sami Zubaida, "The Fragments Imagine the Nation: The Case of Iraq," *International Journal of Middle Eastern Studies* 32, no. 2 (2002), pp. 205–15.
37. Ofra Bengio, *Saddām's Word—Political Discourse in Iraq* (New York: Oxford University Press, 1998), p. 34.
38. Zakī al-Arsūzī, *al-Mu'allafāt al-Kāmila* (Damascus: Matbābi' al-idāra al-siyāsiyya lī'l jaysh wa'l quwwāt al-musallaha, 1973–1976), Vol. 2, p. 36.
39. Arsūzī, like 'Aflaq, highlighted the role of religiosity from a secular perspective, indicating that prophets had a social function, as individuals generating social and political change. See Arsūzī, ibid., 1: 59–60.
40. Arsūzī, 2: 102.
41. Ibid., 2: 91.
42. Ibid., 2: 221.
43. Ibid., 2: 221.
44. Ibid., 2: 59.
45. On Arsūzī's readings of Plato, see: Zakī al-Arsūzī, *al-Jumhūriyya al-muthlā* (Damascus: Dār al-Yaqza al-'Arabiyya, 1965).
46. Arsūzī, *al-Mu'allafāt*, I: 59.
47. Ibid., 1: 337–9.
48. Ibid., 1: 71–81, 91.
49. Ibid., 1: 91.
50. Devlin, *The Ba'th Party, A History*, pp. 10–11. Devlin, however, notes that after Arsūzī's death in 1969, the Syrian government established a scholarship in his name. Devlin, *The Ba'th Party, A History*, p. 21, footnote 19.
51. Ernest C, Dawn, "The Formation of Pan-Arab Ideology in the Inter-war Years," *International Journal of Middle Eastern Studies* 20, no. 1 (1988), p. 69.
52. James Henry Breasted (1865–1935), *Ancient Times, a History of the Early World: An Introduction to the Study of Ancient History and the Career of Early Man* (Boston, MA: Ginn and Company, 1916).
53. Dawn, 72.

54. "Constitution—The Party of the Arab Ba'th" translated by Sylvia Haim. See Haim, *Arab Nationalism*, pp. 233–4.
55. Ibid., p. 234.
56. Devlin notes that Arsūzī, many years after resigning from political activity, asserted that 'Aflaq supported the Axis powers, while claiming to hold progressive ideas (Devlin, *The Ba'th Party—A History*, p. 10). Arsūzī, however, presented a translation of a segment from *Mein Kampf* in his essay about "Trends in Modern Culture." The segment, nonetheless, was used as a way of comparing Nazism to other regimes, and Arsūzī's essay thus included other texts, such as The American Constitution and the Magna Carta on the one hand, and segments by Stalin on dialectics, on the other (Arsūzī, *Mu'allafāt*, 2: 53–67). Adeed Darwisha maintained that the

> custodians of Ba'thist ideology focused their intellectual energies on "Arab unity" and the "anti-imperialist struggle," but said little about democratic institutions. While the constitution of the Bath party did assert the principle of the people's sovereignty and Ba'thist support for constitutional elective system, it also gave the Party and the ensuing Ba'thist state the central role in determining the scope and extent of political freedom.

While discussing the "misfortunes of liberal democracy" in the Arab world, Darwisha believed that in the Ba'th's thinking

> freedom on the whole would be associated with the struggle against imperialism rather than with individual liberty. The illiberal orientation would be reinforced during the Party's flirtation with political power in the 1950s and early 1960s, so that the party's Sixth National Congress in 1963 would reject the notion of liberal parliaments, espousing instead the Soviet concept of democratic centralism. (Darwisha, pp. 302–3)

Sylvia Haim had likewise referred to 'Aflaq's ideas, as manifesting Arab nationalism's "emphasis on the state as the regulator of private and public life, . . . deprecation of private loyalties at the expense of the public." She reads 'Aflaq's statement "nationalism is love before anything else" as an "uncompromising vision of a superhuman and transformed life as the end of political action" (Haim, pp. 71–2). For a theory identifying pan-Arabism, the Iraqi Ba'th, and Fascism, see Samir al-Khalil (Kanan Makiya), *Republic of Fear* (New York: Pantheon Books, 1990), pp. 147–258. Albert Hourani, on the other hand, believed that the Ba'th "stood in principle for a constitutional democracy. But in the years leading to the creation of the United Arab Republic it linked itself closely with the military regime in Egypt" (357–8). Batatu mentioned that "the theoretical commitment of the Ba'th to a 'democratic' state is unambiguous" (p. 734), yet some of its principles, especially the "dominant tendency in 'Aflaq . . . towards restricting freedom" to a national individual, strongly detracted from the Ba'th's democratic approach (pp. 234–736). As we have seen, 'Aflaq, despite his devotion to the state, supported constitutionalism and rule of law. For a general criticism of Haim and Kedourie's approach to Arab nationalism, see Rashid Khalidi, "Arab Nationalism: Historical Problems in the Literature," *The American Historical Review* 96, no. 5. (1991), pp. 1363–73; Israel Gershoni, "Rethinking the Formation of Arab Nationalism in the Middle East, 1920–1945: Old and New Narratives," in *Rethinking Nationalisms in Middle East.* Eds. Israel Gershoni and James Jankowski (New York: Columbia University Press, 1997), 3–25.

57. On Anderson's approach to the change in the concept of time between empire and nation, see Benedict Anderson, *Imagined Communities, Reflections on the Origin and Spread of Nationalism* (London: Verso, 1983).

58. On the cultural hegemony of the left, see Abdul-Salaam Yousif, "The Struggle for Cultural Hegemony during the Iraqi Revolution," in *The Iraqi Revolution of 1958—The Old Social Classes Revisited* Ed., Robert A. Fernea and William Roger Louis, (London: I.B. Tauris, 1991), pp. 172–96. As demonstrated by Marion Farouk-Sluglett and Peter Sluglett, 'Abd al-Karīm Qāsim's regime (1958–1963) enjoyed popular support until its very last moments. Furthermore, the violent massacre of communists upon the Ba'th's seizure of control in 1963, tarnished the image of the Ba'th in the eyes of many Iraqi intellectuals. The welfare policies the Ba'th adopted from 1968 onwards were seen by these scholars as responding to the party's initial unpopularity. See Sluglett, pp. 82–7; pp. 227–9.

59. Batatu, *The Old Social Classes*, pp. 740–8.

60. On Iraqi pan-Arab nationalism see Liora Lukitz, *Iraq: The Search for National Identity* (London: Frank Cass, 1994); Phebe Marr, "The Development of Nationalist Ideology in Iraq, 1921–1941," *The Muslim World* 75, no. 2 (1985): pp. 85–101; Reeva Simon, *Iraq between Two World Wars: the Creation and Implementation of a Nationalist Ideology* (New-York: Columbia University Press, 1986); Michael Eppel, *The Palestine Conflict in the History of Modern Iraq: the Dynamics of Involvement, 1928–1948* (London: Frank Cass, 1994); William L. Cleveland, *The Making of an Arab Nationalist; Ottomanism and Arabism in the Life and Thought of Sati' al-Husri* (Princeton, NJ: Princeton University Press, 1971); on the views of the left, see Muzaffar 'Abd Allāh al-Amīn, *Jamā'at al-Ahālī: munshu'hā, 'aqīdatuhā, wa-dawruhā fi'l siyāsa al-'Irāqīyya, 1932–1946* (Beirut: al-Mu'assasa al-'Arabīyya li'l dirāsāt wa'l nashr; Amman: Dār al-fāris, 2001); Su'ād Khayrī, *Fahd wa-al-nahj al-Mārkisī al-Līnīnī fi qadāyā al-thawra* (Beirut, Dār al-Farābī, 1974)

61. Sāmī Shawkat, *Hadhihi Ahdāfunā* (Baghdad: Majjalat al-Mu'allim al-Jadīd, 1939), pp. 11, 33, 63.

62. Shawkat, *Hadhihi Ahdāfunā*, pp. 11, 21, 47, 60, 110; On Husrī's view of Islam, see Cleveland, pp. 158–9.

63. Albert Hourani, *A History of the Arab Peoples* (London: Faber and Faber, 1991), pp. 338–9.

64. On Egyptians, Syrians and Palestinians in Iraq, see Zakī Mubārak, *Laylā al-marīda fī'l 'Irāq: ta'rīikh yufassil waqā'i Laylā bayna al-Qāhira wa-Baghdād min sanat 1926 ila sanat 1938* (Beirut: al-Maktaba al-'asrīya, 1976) and his *Malāmih al-mujtamā' al-'Irāqī: ktiāb yusawwiru al-'Irāq fī madhāhibih al-adabiyya wa'l qawmiyya wa'l ijtimā'iyiya* (Cairo: Matba'at Amīn 'Abd al-Rahmān, 1942); 'Abd al-Wahhāb 'Azzām, *Rahalāt* (Cairo: Matba'at al-Risāla, 1950–1951); Anīs al-Nusūlī, *'Ishtu wa-shāhadtu* (Beirut Dār al-Kashshāf, 1951); Akram Zu'aytar, *Min mudhakkirāt Akram Zu'aytir* (Beirut: al-Mu'assasa al-'Arabīyya, 1994); Amīn al-Rihānī, (1876–1940), *Qalb al-'Iraq* (Beirut: Matba'at Sādir, 1935).

65. On the formation of the Iraqi state, see Toby Dodge, *Inventing Iraq: The Failure of Nation Building and a History Denied* (New York: Columbia University Press, 2003); Eliezer Tauber, *The Emergence of the Arab Movements* (London and Portland, OR: F. Cass, 1993).

66. See for example: Shawkat, "In Damascus," *Ahādafunā*, 100–1; "Farewell Syria," pp. 103–4; Husrī, "Had Faysal Remained in Syria," *Safahāt min al-mādī al-qarīb* (Beirut: Dār al-'ilm, 1947), p. 24. See also: Reeva S. Simon, "The Hashemite 'Conspiracy': Hashemite Unity Attempts, 1921–1958," *International Journal of Middle East Studies* 5, no. 3 (1974): pp. 314–27.

67. Faysal ibn al-Husayn (King Faysal I), *Faysal ibn al-Husayn fī khutubihi wa aqwāli* (Baghdad: Mudīriyat al-di'ayāt al-'āmma, 1946), pp. 261–5; pp. 236–41.

68. Rusafi published as response as part of a series in which al-Hilāl's editors asked Arab intellectuals to define *nahda* and its prospects of success. See: *Al-Hilāl* Part 10, Vol. 31, July 1,1921.

69. *Rāfidān*, June 6, 1922, no. 103, pp. 1–2, an essay by Muhammad Kāmil.

70. *Ahālī* January 3, 1932, no. 2, p. 2.

71. Ibid., no. 3, p. 1.

72. *Ahālī* February 14, 1932 no. 28, p. 1. On Kāmil Chādirchī's views of democracy, see Husayn Jamīl, *Al-Hayāt al-niyābīyya fī'l 'Irāq, 1925–1946: mawāqif jamā'at al-Ahālī minhā* (Baghdad: Maktabat al-Muthannā, 1983), p. 225.

73. Yūsuf Salmān Yūsuf (Fahd), *Kitābāt al-Rafīq Fahd* (Baghdad: al-(arīq al-jadīd, 1976), pp. 223, 328–9.

74. Ibid., pp. 329–30.

75. Antonio Gramsci, *The Gramsci Reader: Selected Writings*, 1916–1935, (New York: New York University Press, 2000), pp. 263–7; see also David Forgacs' comments on Gramsci's perception of "passive revolution," in Ibid., p. 428.

76. On the communists' ideas concerning land reform, see Rony Gabbay, *Communism and Agrarian Reform in Iraq* (London: Croom Helm, 1978). On the youth in Iraq during the 1950s, see Michael Eppel, "The Elite, the Effendiyya, and the Growth of Nationalism and Pan-Arabism in

Hashemite Iraq, 1921–1958," *International Journal of Middle Eastern Studies* 30, no. 2 (1998), pp. 227–50; and his "The Fadhil Al-Jamali Government in Iraq, 1953–54," *Journal of Contemporary History* 34, no. 3 (1999), pp. 417–42.

77. Fā'iz Ismā'īl, *Bidāyāt al-Hizb al-Ba'th al-'Arabī fī'l 'Irāq: 1944–1950, 1950–1953* (Damascus: Markaz al-Sha'lān/F. Ismā'īl, 1997).

78. Letters from 'Abd al-Rahmān al-Dāmin to Fā'iz Ismā'īl (November 12,1950; November 20,1950; November 24, 1950) quoted in *Bidāyāt al-Hizb al-Ba'th*, pp. 278–87.

79. A letter from 'Abd al-Rahmān al-Samarā'ī in Baghdad to Fā'iz Ismā'īl (November 28, 1949) *Bidāyāt al-Hizb al-Ba'th*, p. 231.

80. A letter from 'Abd al-Rahmān al-Dāmin to Fā'iz Ismā'īl (January 4, 1951) *Bidāyāt al-Hizb al-Ba'th*, pp. 293–4.

81. John Noyes, *Colonial Space: Spatiality in the Discourse of German South West Africa 1884–1915* (Chur, Switzerland and Philadelphia, PA: Harwood, 1992), pp. 106, 122–3.

82. Fu'ad Rikābī, *'Ala Tarīq al-Thawra* (Cairo: al-Dār al-Qawmiyya li'l Tibā'a wa'l nashr, 1963), See also: Fu'ad Rikābī, *Fī Sabīl al-Thawra* (Cairo: al-Dār al-Qawmīyah lil-tibā'a wa'l-nashr, 1963).

83. Sluglett, p. 57.

84. John F. Devlin, "The Baath Party: Rise and Metamorphosis," p. 1396.

85. On the nature of Saddām's elite and the regime's relation to tribalism, see Amatzia Baram, "Neo-Tribalism in Iraq: Saddām Husayn's Tribal Policies 1991–96," *International Journal of Middle East Studies* 29 no. 1 (1997), pp. 1–31; Amatzia Baram, "The Ruling Political Elite in Bathi Iraq, 1968–1986: The Changing Features of a Collective Profile," *International Journal of Middle East Studies* 21 no. 4 (1989): pp. 447–93. See also Marion Farouk-Sluglett and Peter Sluglett's analysis of the regime's approach to the Arab-Israeli conflict: Sluglett, pp. 123, 132–4, 176–7 and in particular pp. 261–2. They also add that "it is of course absurd to analyze the struggle that accompanied the rise of Saddam Hessian to power in ideological terms [. . .] this characterization obscures rather than clarifies the real nature of what was taking place." Ibid., p. 134.

86. Batatu, *The Old Social Classes*, p. 730.

87. On ethos and time, see Michel Foucault, "What Is Enlightenment?" in *The Foucault Reader*, Ed. Paul Rabinow, pp. 32–51 (New York: Pantheon, 1984).

CHAPTER 4

How a Cultural Renaissance Preceded a National Renaissance: The Revival of Hebrew and the Rejuvenation of the Jewish People

Moshe Pelli

The modern Renaissance of Hebrew writing, as well as of the language itself, began about one hundred years before it was given the label in Hebrew, *Hatehiyah* (Revival, Renaissance, Rejuvenation) at the end of the nineteenth century. The "Renaissance" of Hebrew culture has its roots in the Hebrew Haskalah (Enlightenment), which marked a turning point in the modern history of the Jewish people, its culture, and letters. Its beginning can be traced to Prussia in the 1780s when a group of aspiring, young Hebrew writers undertook a new and daring mission—to revitalize the Jewish people by reviving the Hebrew language and Jewish culture. As part of their program, they began publishing a modern, up-to-date monthly journal in the Hebrew language named *Hame'asef* (The Gatherer). The periodical, published during the years 1783–1797 and 1808–1811, was more than just a literary journal patterned after contemporary German literary publications such as *Berlinische Montasschrift* and *Magazin für die Deutsche Sprache.*[1] The journal became the ideological mouthpiece of a literary and cultural movement that began a concerted effort to affect a cultural revolution among Jews in Prussia and elsewhere in Europe. It also served as an organ for publishing the literary works produced by its circle of writers.

4

Through their literary endeavor, these writers ushered in modern times in Jewish history and modern trends in Hebrew letters.[2]

This renewal or revival was initiated by a group of young Maskilim (Hebrew enlighteners) who were prompted by the German and the European Enlightenment movements to follow suit and establish their own version of the Enlightenment. Did these Maskilim have any thought of creating a "Renaissance?" While they did not expressly mention the Renaissance, they were aware of the innovative aspects of their activities and their thoughts, as attested in their writings.

The editors of *Hame'asef* wrote a prospectus, *Nahal Habesor* (The Brook Besor, or Good Tidings) in which they proclaimed the emergence of a new age by saying, "And behold wisdom now cries aloud outside." While employing a paraphrase from Proverbs 1:20, the statement highlighted three important concepts relevant to the new components of change during the Enlightenment: the concept of time ("now"), the principle of wisdom, and the dichotomy between "inside" and "outside." A call for immediate action followed: "Hurry up to call her in, hasten to bring her indoors."[3] The use of the biblical idiom and the parallelism between the two components of the statement intensified the message and suggested the image of a bridge, leading from the outside world into Jewish society.

These statements are indicative of a profound awareness of metamorphosis possibly leading into modernism. The editors accompanied these phrases by demands that their fellow Jews follow in the footsteps of the European Enlightenment and adopt its new ideology. The Maskilim believed that the times demanded a change from the traditional Jewish way of life, to a more updated (and, perhaps, "modern") course. Many of these statements heralded the dawn of the new Age of Reason in Europe, constituting the litmus test for discerning the emerging modernism. They were euphoric, hopeful, highflown, and naive. However, they certainly formed the literary and linguistic expression of the awareness of the changing times that students of the Haskalah are trying to identify.

The quotation, "And behold wisdom now cries aloud outside," cited above, is a paraphrase from the book of Proverbs, which served, like some other similar pronouncements, as a source of slogans for promoting and inaugurating the new age. The use of the sacral biblical idiom to present a new, contemporary concept, related to the new times, is of special interest. It signaled the accepted method, during the early (and the late) Haskalah, of employing "the holy tongue" to express secular concepts. The Hebrew language itself—the revived vehicle for communication—subtly reflected, in its sensitivity, the complex transition to modernity. Modernism was exemplified by the use of Hebrew, the traditional "holy tongue," *"leshon hakodesh,"* to express new, modern, and even secular notions. Thus, the study of the ideology of the Haskalah must focus on the problems of the resuscitated Hebrew language.[4]

The Haskalah writers sensed that a new age had emerged in Europe. They referred to it as "the days of the first fruits of knowledge and love in all the countries of Europe."[5] It is significant to note that the two concepts signifying the new epoch were "knowledge" and "love," namely, "tolerance," and that the two were connected. In other words, this phrase suggests that receptivity to happenings in the areas of culture and the humanities in Europe may impact the social level in human relations and in the attitude toward the Jews.

This feeling intensified in the early years of the publication of *Hame'asef*, as seen in the writings of the Maskilim. In the news section *"Toldot Hazman"* (Chronicles), published in the first volume in 1784, Hayim Keslin portrayed the new age with the familiar metaphors:

> Ever since the light of knowledge has shone among the nations, and ever since the veil of ignorance has been lifted from the face of the peoples among whom we dwell, God has remembered us as well and has made their leaders act in our favor . . . and they [now] consider us as brothers.[6]

Discerning the change in 1786, the Italian Maskil Eliyahu Morpurgo used a similar metaphor: "Now that the sun of wisdom has come out on the earth in this wise generation."[7] He highlighted this changing time by comparing it to the earlier period:

> Now it is unlike the early days for the remnants of this people, as the seed of peace has given its fruits, fig and vine have brought forth their crop— the crop of wisdom—and the tree of knowledge has given its fruits . . . and a clear spirit [wind] has passed throughout the world, a cloud will spread its lightening [light], and will saturate it under the entire heavens, and its light [will reign] over the corners of the earth.[8]

The Maskilim argued that recognizing the emerging changes on the (non-Jewish) European scene also necessitated that Jews pursue a course of action to implement those changes among themselves. They proclaimed:

> The age of knowledge has arrived among all the nations; day and night they do not cease teaching their children [both] language and book. And we, why should we sit idly by? Brethren, let us get up and revive [those] stones from the heaps of dust.[9]

The commitment to the mission that the Haskalah undertook upon itself and the strong sense of urgency to act permeate Shimon Baraz's poem *Ma'archei Lev* (Preparations of the Heart). The poem was published in 1785, on the first anniversary of the founding of the Society for the Seekers of the Hebrew Language, the umbrella organization of the Maskilim that published *Hame'asef*. This Hebrew writer used the seasonal revival of nature as the metaphor for the revival of the Jewish people and Jewish society. He emphasized the notion of the group working together for a unifying goal so as "to teach understanding to those who erred in spirit; enlightenment and knowledge to the impatient; and the earth should be full of knowledge as the water [covers the sea]."[10] The latter part is a partial biblical citation, based on Isaiah, purposefully omitting the name of God. Another Maskil, David Friedrichsfeld, summarized the goals of the Haskalah in this new age, expressing his wish in the form of a prayer: "May God make this community [of Maskilim] the teachers of knowledge and the clarifiers of good tidings, so that the children of Israel will walk in their light."[11]

It may be argued that these statements ought not to be taken as naive, innocent observations, authentically reflecting the current condition. However, even if these were attempts to disseminate propaganda, they represented a clear indication of the Maskilim's awareness of the changing times. To reiterate, this awareness of the ensuing change undoubtedly was coupled with the Maskilim's strong desire for such a change. It was part of their recognition that this change was possible and that they were committed to pursue it. These tendencies represented a new and innovative thrust, signaling a transition from a rather passive attitude toward Jewish existence to a more active one. The occurring change transformed a lofty slogan into an ideal that must be realized and into an enterprise that must be brought to fruition. Since its inception, and for some time to come, the Hebrew Haskalah literature was a tendentious literature, whose goal was to revive the Jewish people and its culture. Hebrew literature undertook a 'national' mission: to bring about a cultural revival for the ultimate rehabilitation of the Jewish people. Hebrew literature adopted a revolutionary goal and mobilized its resources to initiate action to affect the change. The clear signals of modernism that began to emerge from within the pages of *Hame'asef* were thus manifested by the awareness of the need for change, striving to define it, and struggling to execute it. These expressions of modernism, in its myriad, complex forms, continued to gain momentum. Even this awareness gained momentum, while leaving its cumulative impact on the beginning of modern times among the European Jews. It did not occur in one day nor in one place. Yet, the theme repeated itself like a leitmotif, indicative of this historical trend and attesting to the validity of these observations.

Undoubtedly, the editors of *Hame'asef* discerned that a momentous change was taking place in Europe. They advocated that their fellow European Jews partake in this process and reap its fruits. As the Haskalah progressed, their concerted efforts to introduce the ideas of the European Enlightenment started to bear fruit. In a long, continuous process, lasting over a century, they and their followers affected acute change in the attitude of modern Jews toward traditional Judaism. These Maskilim were cognizant of the innovative nature of their activities and of the fact that they had formed a new social and cultural framework. They were fully aware that they had created a new ideology which spoke on behalf of the new movement. As part of their plans, they established a new literary center, aiming to produce a new type of Hebrew literature, even if they did not name it at first "Haskalah." The Maskilim did not refer to this new orientation as the Haskalah literature, the Haskalah movement, or the Haskalah period.[12] However, the eighteenth-century Maskilim developed a full historical awareness, and it served them in shaping the self-consciousness of the period.[13]

Awareness such as this usually surfaced in public manifestoes, which targeted a certain audience and carried a social message. A writer of such a proclamation usually felt the need to cite the occurring change as the reason for implementing a reform, for he was arguing his position and advocating his cause. One such manifesto was published in *Hame'asef* in 1790 by Mendel Breslau, an editor of the periodical. Breslau called on contemporary rabbis to form a rabbinic assembly in order to alleviate the burden of religious ordinances.[14] He cited the new age as reason for his demand, arguing: "And who is too blind to see that the day of the Lord is coming, and in a short while wisdom and knowledge will become the faith of the times."[15] Breslau's phraseology was based on messianic hopes that were transformed and applied to the new age. In spite of the traditional metaphors, the reference to the proverbial Prophet Elijah, and the designation of the forthcoming great day as "the day of the Lord," Breslau was far from considering it a divine or heavenly phenomenon; rather, he deemed it an earthly one.

> You should pay attention to the splendid and awesome things that God has amazingly done in our times. And whosoever would not close his eyes in malice will indeed notice that it is God's hand . . . . And why are you indolent to arouse the heart of the people, who are seeking to benefit our

people in their toil, to reestablish the name of Jacob . . . ? My heart cries because of the evil that is happening in Israel. . . . Not so are the ways of the other peoples around us, for they are improving their ways, and remove falsehood from the truth. . . . Be ashamed, the house of Israel, for you have been doing the opposite, and truth is wanting.[16]

These words are charged with great emotional vigor and attest to the great excitement among the Hebrew Maskilim. Breslau's article was written against the background of the call by the English deist Joseph Priestly for the "return of the Jews," in his book *Letters to the Jews*.[17] Thus, Breslau's article was indicative of the awareness of the pending changes. Evidently, the Hebrew language was deceptive, playing a game of allusion and illusion, replete with sacred expressions and hope for a heavenly redemption. Nevertheless, the thrust of the article was completely secular, and its intent and tenor were mundane and earthly. The problem is that the author made use of the 'holy tongue,' with its religious and biblical allusions, in order to communicate with his contemporary readers. However, to read it naively and literally is incorrect.

From a historical perspective, Haskalah can be said to have emerged on the European scene as a reaction to both external and internal forces. Undoubtedly, it was a Jewish response to the new spirit generated by the European Enlightenment, yet it certainly was also an answer to a great need for change emanating from within Jewish society. It came in the wake of inner strife among Jews resulting from messianic movements, a breakdown in the structure of the Kehilah (the organized Jewish community), and a decline in the authority of the rabbinate.[18]

The ideas and ideals of Haskalah were not totally innovative nor even original. Drawing upon European Enlightenment on the one hand and upon medieval Jewish philosophy on the other, its ideology may be characterized as eclectic. Continuously in a state of formation, this ideology lacked a systematized code and its proponents did not have a single, unified view on how to implement their goal. Nevertheless, they were united in their aim to enlighten their Jewish brethren, leaning heavily on Moses Mendelssohn (1729–1786), his definition of Judaism, and its relations to the surrounding culture.[19] Haskalah's facets, factions, and voices were many, and they varied from the extreme enlighteners to the more moderate ones. Regardless of their position on the Enlightenment scale, the Hebrew enlighteners—as distinguished from the German-Jewish enlighteners, who in general were more radical—had one thing in common: a desire to introduce changes in Jewish culture that was coupled with loyalty to the Hebrew heritage.

Discussion of "modernism" is more often than not relegated to the notion of "secularism"—that creeping change that is said to have affected the thinking, *Weltanschauung*, and behavior of young Jewish intellectuals, the Maskilim. Both "modernism" and "secularism" in the context of this study are still subjects of continuous scholarly discussion, but they are yet to be defined satisfactorily. Nevertheless, the contribution of the Hebrew journal *Hame'asef* and its writers to the growth of modern Hebrew literature by promoting both modernity and secularism, has gained recognition in the past twenty-five years, as more scholars continue to produce critical assessments and analyses of literary works published by writers of the Berlin Haskalah.

It is in the activities of this group of young Hebraists, consisting of writers, educators, and even rabbis, that modern Hebrew writing was reborn and new trends of modern Hebrew letters were begun. This group and its writings represent the beginning of "modernism," which this writer identifies and defines as a strong awareness of the changing times, a desire to affect change, and a collaborative effort to disseminate ideas and establish tools for change. As modernism, this writer identifies the subtle, covert signals in the writings of the Maskilim, which are indicative of their sensitivities to the changes that were about to take place in Jewish society.[20]

The Maskilim's launching of the Hebrew journal *Hame'asef* was coupled with the formation of a new cultural institution, which manifested a great and innovative achievement: the establishment of a center for literary activities. No longer would the individual writer be completely isolated from his peers; rather, a group of individuals was now functioning both as individuals and as a group. At times they may have been isolated and geographically distant from each other; nevertheless, the established literary center in Prussia united them. They appeared to have a common goal and to share similar literary concepts. Despite their individuality, the Haskalah writers and thinkers continued to work together toward a common goal.

Such a center was established first in Königsberg in 1783 under the umbrella of "The Society for the Seekers of the Hebrew Language," as stated in the prospectus *Nahal Habesor*. This society for the promotion of the Hebrew language was later transferred to Berlin. This cultural society proved to be quite enterprising. It founded a publishing house with its own Hebrew and German typesetting and used the printing press of an established printer.[21] Thus, the new center for Hebrew literature was able to fulfill its cultural plans, promote its ideology, and disseminate its own books. Participating authors became independent of religious and traditional community leaders and were free to publish the literary works of Haskalah, including controversial books. One such book was Saul Berlin's *Besamim Rosh* (Incense of Spices), published in 1793. This was a pseudoepigraphical work in the responsa genre, which the author attributed to Rabbi Asher ben Yehiel of the thirteenth and fourteenth centuries.[22] The sum total of the cultural society's publishing enterprise is an impressive and diversified list of Hebrew books.[23]

The emphasis that the authors of *Nahal Habesor* placed on uniting the Hebrew writers as a group in an active center of Hebrew literature and a society for Hebrew language is striking. To disarm any possible rabbinic objection to their modern efforts by employing the traditional phrase "*Hadash asur min hatorah*" (the new [innovation] is forbidden by the Torah), the Maskilim themselves quoted from Hebraic sources the dictum that Torah may be studied only in groups.[24] Obviously, the group was not formed to study Torah in the traditional sense, even though the authors were initially very eager to describe themselves as educated both in Jewish and secular disciplines and as engaged in biblical commentary.[25]

In addition to cultivating the cultural agenda of Haskalah, the writers associated with this center and with *Hame'asef* addressed several important social issues related to Jewish existence, such as the attitude of Jews toward their host country and its citizens, their aspiration to become productive citizens of that country, and the like. Eventually they attempted to present an alternative to the existing structure of the Jewish Kehilah by establishing their own modern school and forming an "enlightened" burial society.[26]

This first, modest effort of the early Maskilim was followed during the second quarter of the 19th century by additional journals and scholarly periodicals devoted to literature and Haskalah. The second half of the nineteenth century saw the development of weekly publications, with a much greater impact on the dissemination of Haskalah. From its early start, Haskalah marks the end of passivity and the emergence of a concerted will to enact change in Jewish society and to fight for an enlightened ideology. Haskalah had to wage war on two fronts.

Externally, the Hebrew Haskalah defended Judaism in the face of the onslaught of European Deism against all revealed, positive religions. It attempted to portray Judaism, in contrast to Christianity, as a rationalistic religion, a religion of reason, befitting the Age of Enlightenment. Some of the Haskalah writings seemed to be apologetic, to be sure; others, however, were motivated by a profound allegiance to Jewish heritage and a strong belief in Judaism, as their authors perceived it.[27]

Internally, the Hebrew Maskilim desired to create a dialogue with the traditionalist rabbis in order to introduce some modernization into Judaism so as to make it contemporary and viable. They sought to prepare Judaism and Jews for the social and cultural trends that were current in Europe during the period of the Enlightenment. The end of passivity, which characterized the ideology of Haskalah, stemmed not only from the Maskilim's belief in the urgency of social emancipation for the Jews in Europe but, more importantly, from their striving for cultural emancipation as well.

The Maskilim rejected not so much the idea of Jewish exclusiveness but rather the notion of Jewish seclusiveness. They wanted to create a modern synthesis of Jewish and western culture while retaining their unique Jewish identity. This orientation does not mean that they desired to achieve assimilation as was advocated by some of the more extreme German Jewish enlighteners. The Hebrew Maskilim wished to free their fellow Jews from the ghetto mentality and to introduce them to the mainstream of European society and culture.

The Hebrew Haskalah envisioned a new social order in which the Jews were to be equal partners in European society, actively sharing in and contributing to its affairs. The Maskilim aspired to change the notion of Jewish anomaly that resulted from the *galut* (state of exile). They advocated broadening horizons for Jews and removing the shackles of a *galut* mentality, thus, reawakening in the people a yearning for the glories of the past.

Consequently, the Maskilim began to view the idea of *ge'ulah*, or redemption, in a more practical and mundane fashion. While not denying messianic hopes, the Maskilim advocated an end to passivity in this regard as well. They channeled the Jews' yearning for redemption into the sphere of humanism. The hope of national redemption outside of the European continent, namely, the return of the Jews to the Land Israel, was an idea that was yet to come. The Maskilim still endeavored to solve the Jewish problem within the European context.

All in all, this change of attitude and demand for action resulted in a self-scrutiny and a self-assessment on the part of the Maskilim. These tendencies were manifested by a critical view of the heritage of the past fortified by a search for a better future. The prevailing preoccupation in traditional Jewish circles with the corpus of past literature and its interpretation now began to shift to an outlook to the future, to the mundane, and to the practical.

It took much courage to demand an end to passivity, but it also took a great deal of naïveté to believe that both the Jews and Europe were ready for a major shift in values and customs, and in existing social and cultural practices.

The contribution of this group of writers to the rebirth of the Hebrew language and Hebrew culture at the beginning of Haskalah may be assessed in the context of several areas of endeavor, beginning with their use of the Hebrew language. In no other realm of their Enlightenment enterprise did the Maskilim face as difficult a task as in this area. They had to cope with the existing classical structures, forms, and idioms of historical Hebrew, which, prior to the period of the Enlightenment, were used continuously in rabbinic responsa, halachic writings, philosophical, historical, and grammatical treatises, as well as in *belles lettres*.

Interestingly enough, the Maskilim's determination to revive the Hebrew language was prompted, in part, by the general inclination of the *Aufklärung* (the German Enlightenment) to resort to the national language—German—in scholarly and literary periodicals and to eliminate the use of Latin. Following this trend of the *Aufklärung*, the Maskilim affirmed their interest in their own national language—Hebrew—and expressed a strong pride in it and in its aesthetic and innate qualities. Their mentor and guide, Moses Mendelssohn, elucidated the beauty of Hebrew poetry in the Bible in his *Be'ur*, the commentary and translation into German of the Pentateuch. In it, he stated his intention to "show that as the heavens are higher than earth so is the exalted state of religious poetry [in the Bible] over secular poetry. . . . Religious poetry [of the Bible] has an advantage and a tremendous value in splendor and beauty over any other poetry."[28]

Mendelssohn and Naphtali Herz Wessely (1725–1805), a poet, biblical commentator, grammarian, and one of the leading figures of the Hebrew Haskalah in Berlin, who shared similar views, followed Herder's dictum about the divine origin of the Hebrew language and poetry.[29] They further emphasized a strong belief in the potential of biblical Hebrew to be used for modern purposes. Thus, their followers, the young Maskilim, took it upon themselves to explore the modern linguistic capabilities inherent in that ancient language, which they still referred to by its traditional term *leshon hakodesh*, the holy tongue.[30]

In keeping with the prevailing notion that language is "the mirror of the soul" (as postulated by Leibnitz and others)[31] and that language affects thought and morality, the Maskilim rejected Yiddish, which they considered a "corrupted language." Instead, they preferred the "purity" of German for their vernacular and the revived form of Hebrew for their literary medium of expression.[32] Wessely, the poet laureate and linguist of Haskalah, asked the following question in his treatise on educational reform: "Why is the holy tongue used for matters of faith and Torah [the five books of Moses], and the German language used for discourse with other people and for secular studies?"[33]

The Maskilim rejected the contemporary rabbinical idiom because of its careless use of grammar, and its mixture of various layers of Hebrew with Aramaic. This rejection, however, was easier said than done. Many of them still resorted to the old rabbinic stylistic practices to which they were accustomed. Other writers rejected the rabbinic euphuism, a highly florid, turgid, and lofty use of Hebrew, for yet another type of euphuism, based on the Hebrew Bible.[34]

Indeed, the natural inclination of these young writers was to use biblical Hebrew, which they considered to be the pinnacle of linguistic purity. Although they could muster the biblical idiom in contemporary poetry and in poetic drama, it lacked the vocabulary and linguistic form adequate for philosophical or grammatical treatises. Nor was biblical Hebrew adequate for contemporary issues and modern ideas in secular subjects such as education, history, and the sciences. Trained in the medieval works of Jewish philosophy and theology (as autodidacts, to be sure), the Maskilim's natural inclination was to turn to medieval Hebrew for their nonbelletristic writings.

However, in search of additional sources for enrichment they reviewed some other literary traditions in the medieval Hebrew corpus, and many of these modern Hebrew writers rejected the *piyut* (liturgical poetry) and its high style of Hebrew. The Maskilim could not accept the *paytanim*'s (writers of liturgical poetry) excessive use of poetic license in innovating new forms in Hebrew solely for the need of a rhyme or for other aesthetic purposes. The *paytanim*'s linguistic freedom in coining new words, regardless of grammatical rules, was severely criticized by many Maskilim.

The literary and linguistic works of these Maskilim manifested the first major effort to search for ways to expand the Hebrew language so as to encompass all facets of modern Jewish life. Haskalah's experimentations with the Hebrew language facilitated its revival as a practical language for secular subjects, mundane matters, and scientific disciplines.

However, at this point, an ambivalent attitude toward the Hebrew language is noted: On the one hand, the Maskilim still referred to Hebrew, as mentioned above, as the holy tongue; they held a mystical concept of it as being endowed with unique traits and as carrying the innate values of the Hebrew *Geist* and Hebrew *Kultur*. On the other hand, they attempted to reduce the *sacred* aspect of the language and supplant it with a secular one. This ambivalence between the sacred and the secular continued to haunt the Maskilim on a grand scale, and characterized the tenets of early Haskalah.[35] The dominant feature of the Haskalah's use of Hebrew was its attempt to utilize language not only for lofty and scholarly purposes but also for the ephemeral, the temporal, and the immediate. Thus, they dealt with everyday practical concerns such as news, science, inventions, secular knowledge, and other useful information.[36]

This way, language served the purposes of disseminating Haskalah ideology, manifesting a this-worldly attitude and a mundane orientation. As resuscitated by the Maskilim, the Hebrew language was intended to be a practical tool of communication for a greater understanding of the modern world and for a better comprehension of the condition of the Jewish individual against the background of his Jewish and non-Jewish society.

Consequently, Haskalah literature initiated a long process, characterized by the continuous secularization of the Hebrew tongue, leading eventually to the linguistic versatility of Hebrew letters and to the transformation of the literary language into a vernacular. The use of the familiar idiom, taken from the sacred corpus of the Hebrew heritage, in modern contexts, assumed, at first, the form of *melitzah*, or euphuism. This highly florid style, although artificial and inappropriate for everyday use, enabled the writer to make a multidimensional use of language. The subtleties of the Hebrew language were thus developed, reflecting thereby the very problem of the duality of Jewish existence as a traditional culture in a modern, secular world.

The linguistic tension among biblical Hebrew, the talmudic idiom, and medieval usage continued to be felt throughout the Haskalah period. These strands were finally synthesized in the writings of Mendele Mocher Sfarim (Shalom Yaakov Abramowitz [1835/6–1917]) in the later period of Hebrew Enlightenment, toward the end of the nineteenth century. Simultaneous with its effort to revive the Hebrew language, the Haskalah launched a major drive to revive Hebrew culture and Hebrew literature. The literary endeavor was manifested in a number of areas of creativity that included publishing in both the classical and contemporary spheres. Some of these works appeared in *Hame'asef*, while others were issued as books by the Maskilim's publishing house.

A major characteristic of Haskalah as a modern, up-to-date literature was manifested by its writers experimenting with a variety of new or revived literary genres and modes of expression that they found in the classical Hebraic corpus and in the surrounding European literatures. It was the very [MP2]prolific and creative Maskil, Isaac Satanow [MP3]

(1732–1804) who undertook the task of reviving some classical Hebrew genres with a modern slant. He selected the genre of biblical wisdom writing as a model, and patterned his *Mishlei Asaf* (Proverbs of Asaf; 1789–1802) on this classical form.[37] To make his work more attractive, Satanow wrote that he had found an ancient text and attributed it to Asaf, a Levite of yore, thus the title, *The Proverbs of Asaf*. As Satanow stated, he just added his own commentaries below the text and published the book. In so doing, Satanow emulated the traditional façade of a canonical book in which a venerated biblical text is accompanied by a traditional commentary. He recreated the traditional two-tier structure of an 'ancient' text combined with a 'contemporary' commentary. This age-old practice in Jewish writing became a versatile literary device employed for the dissemination of the ideology of Haskalah. Satanow's contemporaries did not appreciate his inventiveness, and called him "a forger." Students of world literature, however, know many other such "forgers" who enriched world literature by utilizing similar artistic devices.[38]

Satanow also revived the medieval genre of religious disputation, based on the well-known historical Judeo-Christian disputations, and composed a contemporary story, *Divrei Rivot* (Words, or Matters of Dispute; ca. 1800).[39] Satanow patterned it on the classical work of Yehuda Halevi, *Hakuzari*, which he had published previously with commentary.[40]

Satanow's fictional neo-religious disputation is a drama-of-ideas. Following the dispute, Satanow's king proclaims religious tolerance, freedom of speech, freedom of thought, and freedom of religious practices throughout the land. He then proposes a plan to ameliorate the condition of the Jews by reforming Jewish education and making changes in the structure of the Jewish Kehilah and in the institution of the rabbinate. These reforms in Jewish education were similar to the ones advocated by Naphtali Herz Wessely in his educational treatise *Divrei Shalom Ve'emet*.

This renewed genre served to redefine Judaism in a fashion favorable to the Haskalah, defending the Jewish faith from the assaults of Deism and Atheism. This piece is also considered as a utopia in which the Hebrew author presents his wishes for a better society as a reality.[41] Satanow's dialogue promoted the ideas and ideals of Hebrew Enlightenment.

Another neo-classical genre was introduced by Saul Berlin (1740–1794), a traditionalist rabbi and a Maskil. He attempted a daring, and to some a deceitful, endeavor by composing a new *Shulhan Aruch* (Jewish code of law). Using a pseudonym to conceal his identity,

Saul Berlin attributed this halachic book of pseudoresponsa, *Besamim Rosh*, cited above, to the medieval authority on Halachah, Rabbi Asher ben Yehiel, known by the acronym of ROSH. Berlin said that he only added commentary to the manuscript that he had found in some old library.[42] The book advocated a new approach to Halachah and even hinted at religious reform.

This preoccupation with old formats, based on the heritage of past Jewish literature, is indicative that the Hebrew Maskilim did not desire a break with cultural tradition. Their plans to revive Hebrew letters were founded on a synthesis of their own culture and European culture.

As another means of bringing Hebrew literature up to date, writers of Hebrew Enlightenment emulated contemporary European literary genres and modes such as epistolary writing, travelogues, utopia, satire, biography, autobiography, and dialogues of the dead.[43]

Isaac Euchel (1756–1804), a prolific writer and editor of *Hame'asef*, is credited with introducing a number of European literary genres to Haskalah literature. Indeed, he was one of the literary innovators and a bridge builder between cultures. Following the pattern of Montesquieu's *Lettres Persanes* and similar such epistolary writings, he composed an original epistolary writing titled "Igrot Meshulam" (The Letters of Meshulam; 1790), which was published serially in *Hame'asef*. Not only is this an epistolary story and one of the early modern satiric pieces in Haskalah literature, but it may also be considered as utopian in its portrayal of an ideal picture of a Jewish society.

Similarly, Satanow's religious disputation piece, *Divrei Rivot*, which was mentioned above, also contains a section with a utopian element. In it the author envisions the righteous and enlightened king as helping to build an ideal Jewish society that, guided by the ideas and ideals of the Enlightenment, achieves both cultural and social emancipation.

Another Maskil, Saul Berlin, mentioned above, also wrote a satiric masterpiece, *Ktav Yosher* (An Epistle of Righteousness; 1795). He penned it in defense of Wessely, who was engaged in a dispute with traditional rabbis over educational reforms expressed in his book, *Divrei Shalom Ve'emet* (1782). Berlin's satire contains some of the most bitter and critical remarks about contemporary Judaism and Jews.

Borrowing a popular European literary genre, an editor of *Hame'asef*, Aaron Wolfssohn (1754–1835), introduced the dialogues of the dead to Hebrew literature. In his "Sihah Be'eretz Hahayim" (Dialogue in the Land of the Living [= Afterlife]; 1794–1797), he enlisted the figures of Maimonides and Mendelssohn to argue with a fanatic rabbi and to defend the ideals of Haskalah. This piece was serialized in *Hame'asef*.[44]

Another Hebrew Maskil, Tuvyah Feder (1760?–1817), used the genre of the dialogues of the dead in *Kol Mehazezim* (Voice of the Archers; published in 1853; written in 1813). This was an invective against another Haskalah writer, Menahem Mendel Lefin (1749–1826) for the latter's translation of Mishlei (Proverbs) into allegedly Yiddish-like German. I discussed this genre and Feder's book elsewhere. Many other writers published regular and didactic dialogues, the latter of which were used for educational purposes, as was customary at the time.[45]

Another European literary genre, the travelogue, enabled the Italian Maskil Shmuel Romanelli (1757–1814) to depict Morocco's Jewish society in the 1780s in his *Masa Ba'rav* (Travail in an Arab Land; 1793). This genre and Romanelli's book are the subject of a chapter in a previous book.[46] *Hame'asef* published a shorter travelogue by Euchel that described a trip back to his birthplace in Copenhagen.[47]

It was Euchel who contributed to the genre of modern biography in his book-length portrayal of Moses Mendelssohn, *Toldot Rabenu Hehachem Moshe Ben Menahem* (The Life Story of Our Rabbi the Sage Moshe son of Menahem [Mendelssohn]; 1789). This genre, too, served the goals of Haskalah, by promoting the figure of the "Jewish Socrates," as Mendelssohn was called.[48] *Hame'asef* serialized Euchel's biography of Mendelssohn. Other biographies of Jewish luminaries, such as Isaac Abravanel and Moses Maimonides, were also published in *Hame'asef*.[49] These personalities were selected for biographical sketches because their philosophies were thought to support Haskalah ideology. Their portrayal, too, served to exemplify the typology of enlightened and open-minded spiritual leaders who were loyal to Jewish tradition.

Resorting to another popular genre, the enlighteners published hundreds of fables, following both contemporary European trends as well as Jewish literary tradition. Two chapters are devoted to this genre in my cited books.[50] Concurrently, Hebrew writers also expressed their creative energy through other types of writings; some wrote allegorical dramas, biblical dramas, and biblical epics. The Hebrew novel is a phenomenon that would be introduced years later, in 1853, with the historical novel, *Ahavat Zion* (The Love of Zion), by Abraham Mapu (1808–1867). The short story, too, was to emerge in the second half of the nineteenth century, although some initial attempts can be found earlier.

In their efforts to revive Hebrew literature, the Maskilim assigned a unique role and mission to Hebrew literature as an educational medium. Literature was viewed by the Hebrew Maskilim along the lines of the literary aesthetics of European Enlightenment as combining the good and the beneficial. Literary boundaries were extended beyond sheer enhancement of beauty and aesthetic enjoyment. Paraphrasing the verse in Proverbs, a Hebrew Maskil summarized the aesthetics of Haskalah, saying: "Grace is deceptive, beauty is illusory, the good and the beneficial are to be praised."[51] It was literature's role to advocate the ideology of Haskalah and to promote its ideas. This was a didactic literature whose proponents endowed it with a mission: to educate and to teach the Jewish people in order to ameliorate their social, political, and cultural status in Europe.

The Maskilim were convinced that the only obstacle to their fellow Jews achieving equal rights was their failure to adjust to the European Enlightenment ideology that advocated cultural and social changes. Consequently, they made a concerted effort to introduce the ideology of Haskalah, promoting these changes via the medium of Hebrew literature. Changing Jewish society and its culture was part of their notion of "Renaissance."

This seemingly extraliterary concept of the role of Hebrew literature dominated the literary scene until the period of *Hatehiyah* (Revival, Renaissance, Rejuvenation) toward the end of the nineteenth century. Only through the efforts of such Hebrew critics as Abraham Uri Kovner (1842–1909) in the 1860s and David Frischmann (1862–1922) at the end of the nineteenth century and the beginning of the twentieth century, and others, did the Enlightenment concept of literature change. It was at times modified or discarded completely in favor of the pure aesthetic role of literature, namely, literature for literature's sake. It should be emphasized that aesthetics and the appreciation of beauty had also been evoked by the early Maskilim. For example, a study of poetry in *Hame'asef* reveals the Maskilim's emphasis on the aesthetic qualities and the sublime language of poetry.[52] However, beauty was regarded by many Haskalah writers to be intrinsically related to the beneficial and was pursued by them with this interpretation in mind.

The efforts of the early Hebrew Haskalah were also geared toward reviving Hebrew culture. The major thrust of its activities was reorienting modern Hebrew culture toward the secular and the mundane, highlighting the utilitarian and the practical, and emphasizing aesthetic values that were based on contemporary European standards. The revival of Hebrew was part of the Maskilim's attempt to revive the people itself and resuscitate Hebrew culture. There was no conflict with their German orientation. Their adherence to Hebrew culture exemplified their perception that their Jewish identity could be presented on terms acceptable to their fellow German enlighteners.

Education was deemed by the Haskalah to be the most important tool for enabling the individual Jew to improve himself, in accordance with the *Aufklärung* concept of *Bildung*—the individual's self-development, self-cultivation, and character-formation aiming to achieve moral and aesthetic refinement in order to fulfill one's spiritual potentials—and thus help change and improve Jewish society.[53] In their published essays on modern education, pedagogy, and curriculum, the Maskilim advocated introducing into Jewish education a modern secular curriculum and revised religious teaching. Toward this end, they published catechisms and numerous textbooks for use in Jewish schools. Informal education was also on their agenda, and they produced lengthy articles on world history, the history of other religions and cultures, science, nature, psychology, and ethics.

The Hebrew-language Haskalah in Prussia was short-lived. *Hame'asef* ceased publication in 1797 but reappeared in 1808–1809 only to shut down permanently three years later.[54] There had been great expectations upon its founding in 1783, and a bitter desperation at its end. It was Euchel who in 1800 bemoaned the changing times in his florid style:

> I have also tasted the dregs of the cup of reeling [the cup of poison], which came up on the nation of Judea and its enlighteners. The days of love have passed, gone are the days of the covenant between me [or between it, namely the Hebrew language] and the children of Israel. . . . They have run away, and they have gone![55]

However, the phenomenon of the German Haskalah was emulated as other centers of Hebrew literature came into being in Austria and in Eastern Europe. The early Haskalah in Prussia was a breakthrough in modern Jewish history and in the history of Hebrew literature. The Maskilim directed their creative and literary energies to establishing a new phase in Hebrew letters that we identify as modern Hebrew literature. In their search for new modes of expression, they initiated the beginning of modernism in Jewish culture and in Hebrew literature, thus leaving their literary legacy for a century of Hebrew writing.

The German Haskalah was equally short lived, and by 1811, with the final demise of the new *Hame'asef*, its Hebrew activities were curtailed and its ideals of reviving the Hebrew language and literature, discussed so far in detail, were transformed to another venue. In the 1820s and 1830s the Haskalah movement flourished in the Austro-Hungarian Empire, especially in Italy and Galicia, having the Hebrew journal

Bikurei Ha'itim (1820–1831), published in Vienna, as its main literary organ.

Subsequently, the Haskalah made headway further east in Russia, Poland, and Lithuania. Its ideological platform, as developed initially in Germany, had been modified to fit the needs and the circumstances of the Jews in Eastern Europe. This version of Haskalah continued to disseminate its cultural ideology among its expanding circle of new followers. Concurrently, Haskalah writers and poets continued to produce numerous creative works in prose and poetry, expressing their thoughts and feelings in various literary genres, and finally, as mentioned earlier, in mid-century (in 1853) also produced its first novel, titled *Ahavat Zion* (The Love of Zion) by Abraham Mapu.

The thrust of one hundred years of Haskalah, which had as its goal to revive the Jewish people in the Diaspora, generally aimed to integrate Jewish culture into the European "enlightened" culture. Thus, the Maskilim intended to solve "the Jewish problem" within the European setting, while creating a modern-day "renaissance" of Hebrew Enlightenment, wishing to uplift and invigorate the Jewish people by means of enlightenment, humanitarianism, and tolerance.

However, this trend came to a halt in 1881, mostly as a result of a series of pogroms that were perpetrated against the Jews in the south of Russia. A disillusionment from the mainstream Haskalah emerged as several groups of Maskilim mostly in Russia launched the "Love of Zion" movement, which began reorienting the Jews toward their ancient homeland in the land of Israel. Thus, the Jewish desire for a cultural Renaissance within the parameter of the Haskalah now transformed to a desire for a national Renaissance.

Prior to that there were several rabbinic interpretations of the notion of messianic redemption (*ge'ulah*), traditionally delegated to the divine, in human terms. They called for the establishment of Jewish nationalism in the Jewish historical homeland as the beginning of this human redemption. One was by Rabbi Yehudah Alkalai (1798–1878) who as early as 1834 advocated the building of Jewish colonies in the Holy Land in his booklet titled *Shema Yisrael* (Hear, O Israel). Another was Rabbi Zvi Hirsch Kalischer (1795–1874) who in 1836 presented the notion that "the beginning of the redemption should come through natural causes by human effort."[56] Both were considered to be the forerunners or precursors of Zionism, as the notion of divine redemption had been shifting to human spheres even among some traditional rabbis. A more secular approach to the same issue was that of Moses Hess (1812–1875), a journalist and a social activist and one of the thinkers of socialism, who in *Rome and Jerusalem* (1862) advocated the restoration of a Jewish state.[57]

It was the beginning of a national movement that emerged in the aftermath of the nationalistic trends in Europe in mid-century and the "Spring of Nations" in 1848. In Jewish circles, the national orientation promoted the idea of solving the 'Jewish question' not in Europe but in the land of Israel, which culminated in the emergence of Zionist ideology in the 1890s.

The change of heart in the attitude toward Haskalah permeated the literature ever since the 1870s as the idea of a national "Renaissance" had been slowly developing. In 1875, Peretz Smolenskin (1840/2–1885), the editor of the Hebrew monthly *Hashahar* (Dawn), and a prolific essayist and novelist, began to advocate the idea of "reviving" the people. He criticized the extreme exponents of early German Haskalah who, according to him, were responsible for the radical tendencies that led its followers away from the Hebrew culture and traditional Judaism.

Smolenskin was quite critical of the assimilation trends that came on the heels of the Berlin Haskalah, blaming Moses Mendelssohn and his followers for all the calamities that occurred to Judaism and the Jews in the nineteenth century. His main argument against Mendelssohn and the Berlin Haskalah was that they identified the Jews as belonging to one faith, thus eliminating any notion of Jewish peoplehood.[58] Smolenskin published his views in a series of articles titled "Et Lata'at" (Time to Plant), which to the literary historian Joseph Klausner signaled "the end of the Haskalah period and the beginning of the period of Nationalism and the Love of Zion."[59]

Smolenskin's attack on Mendelssohn and on the Berlin Haskalah was rejected by another prominent Maskil, Abraham Baer Gottlober (1811–1899). Gottlober defended both the German philosopher and his followers in a journal which he launched in 1876, *Haboker Or* ([First] Light of Morning), and argued that Smolenskin misread and misinterpreted Mendelssohn and the other Maskilim.[60]

As the criticism of Haskalah grew, another young writer, Eliezer Ben Yehuda, whose name would rise to the forefront of Hebrew culture in the following half century, entered into the national debate. He was to be considered later as the father of modern Hebrew, in effect one of the revivers of spoken Hebrew.

In an article that he published in Smolenskin's journal, *Hashahar*, in 1878, titled "She'elah Nichbadah" (A Venerable Question),[61] Ben Yehuda advocated the right and the necessity to resort to Jewish nationalism. Following the nationalistic trends that emerged in Europe earlier in that century, he argued for the legitimate adherence to a new form of Jewish nationalism. He examined the required attributes of a people, a discussion of which flourished at that time, such as a common language, common heritage, common religion, showing their applicability to the Jewish people.[62]

Ben Yehuda then argued that Hebrew literature till then did not affect the life of the Jewish people in any significant way. To him, it was a divisive force that rather than uniting the people under one flag and one goal shattered its unity. That literature, he wrote, looked at the past rather than face the future. Its aspiration to revive the Hebrew language while the Jewish people were dispersed in many countries was futile. Here Ben Yehuda suggested the solution that foreshadowed the national discussion for the next quarter century.[63] He argued that a center had to be created for the emerging nationalism, a center for the whole people, which would be the "heart" "from which the blood will flow in the veins of the people and will give it life," and this thing was "the settlement of the land of Israel."[64] Klausner considers Ben Yehuda's article "the first article for the new Love of Zion that was published in *Hashahar*."[65] Later Ahad Ha'am advocated the idea of creating a spiritual center in the land of Israel.

Other critics, such as Kovner and Frischmann, were critical of literary aspects of Haskalah. One of the main arguments against the literature of the Haskalah was that it did not reflect the actual life of the people nor did it address the issues related to the people. By the 1890s, one of the most vociferous opponents of Haskalah was Mordechai Ehrenpreis (1869–1951) who heralded the emergence of a new type of Hebrew literature, the literature known as "Hatehiyah," actually meaning revival or renaissance.

In a seminal article published in 1897 in the intellectual organ of Hebrew writers, *Hashiloah*, Ehrenpreis announced a revision in the attitude of the new breed of Hebrew writers toward their literature. He declared war against that kind of undertaking, which we call "Haskalah." The group of young writers did not purport to continue the literary work done in previous generations since the time of the Me'asfim, the writers active in the first Hebrew journal, *Hame'asef*, but intended to start a new kind of literature, new in its format and contents.[66] Ehrenpreis believed that the early Maskilim could not have created "a literary movement that was attuned to the life of the nation" because they were dilettantes. He further accused them of not being a product of their time and place, and that they did not relate to the cultural life of their time.[67]

In 1903, Ehrenpreis declared the younger generation's independence from the shackles of the past: "It is the uprising of the new generation in our Hatehiyah movement," he writes. "The new generation will not waste its strength on negative war; it wants a positive endeavor; it does not fight *against* the old, but *for* the new."[68] Ehrenpreis further pronounces the motto of this new generation, proclaiming its notion of renaissance:

> Here we came, men of freedom, full of faith! We freed ourselves of the shackles of sickly, rotting, dying tradition; a tradition that cannot live and does not want to die [. . .]. We freed ourselves of the extra spirituality of the *galut*, that spirituality that removed the Jew away from this world, that made our lives to be but a shadow of life. . . . We freed ourselves from the rabbinic culture, that encased us in a narrow cage of legal decrees, restrictions and prohibitions . . . we freed ourselves from that despair that characterized the Jewish street. . . . In as much as we removed ourselves from tradition, we also removed ourselves from its opponent, the Haskalah [. . .]. We freed ourselves from the yoke of superficial, fake and arid Haskalah.[69]

This was the new Renaissance that was sounded at the *fin de siècle*.

The major pundit of the national revival movement at the end of the nineteenth century and the first part of the twentieth century was Ahad Ha'am (pseudonym of Asher Ginsberg, 1856–1927). His interpretation of the idea of Zionism argued that prior to any physical revival of the people in the land of Israel, there should first be the preparation and the education of the individual Jew. "We should have dedicated our first actions to the revival of the hearts," he wrote, and by this he meant the preparation of the people for a united national goal.[70]

Consequently, Ginsberg fostered the idea of building a 'spiritual center' in the land of Israel. As compared to Theodor Herzl's concept of political Zionism, his was a spiritual Zionism. He argued that "the work of revival should not be limited just to establishing the material aspects . . . we have to create there a permanent and free center for our national culture: for science, art and literature."[71]

While this period was considered to be the "Hatehiyah period," by its own proponents' definition, literary scholars such as Shimon Halkin debunked this notion. He argued that the *desire* for "tehiyah" was confused with the "tehiyah" itself. Thus, he asserts that the period was not a Renaissance, but merely a desire for such. This Renaissance, he argued in 1920, was still pending.[72] Perhaps it came to fruition in the pre-State extraordinary development of Hebrew writing as well as the post–1948 revival of Jewish life, culture, and literature in the State of Israel.

Notes

1. Examples of contemporaneous German literary publications and their launching dates are *Berlinische Monatsschrift* (1783), *Magazin für die Deutsche Sprache* (1783), and *Der Deutsche Merkur* (1782).

2. See Moshe Pelli, "*Hame'asef*: Michtav Hadash Asher Aden Beyameinu Lo Hayah [*Hame'asef*: A New Publication Never Published Before], *Hebrew Studies*, 41(2000), pp. 119–46. The Hebrew periodical, *Hame'asef*, is discussed in detail in the introduction to Moshe Pelli, *Sha'ar Lahaskalah* [Gate to Haskalah], Annotated Index of *Hame'asef*, First Modern Periodical in Hebrew (1783–1811) (Jerusalem, 2000). A literary assessment of *Hame'asef* writers may be found in Moshe Pelli, *Dor Hame'asfim Beshahar Hahaskalah* [The Circle of *Hame'asef* Writers at the Dawn of Haskalah] (Israel: Hotsa' at ha-Kibuts ha-me' uhad, 2001). See also Moshe Pelli, "*Hame'asef* (1783–1811)— Peritzat Derech Baperiodica Ha'ivrit" [*Hame'asef* (1783–1811)—A Breakthrough in Hebrew Periodicals], *Hadoar* [Post], 79 (No. 19, August 25, 2000), pp. 18–2l; (No. 20, September 9, 2000), pp. 18–20; (No. 21, September 29, 2000), pp. 39–41. Additional discussion on the literary contribution of these writers will be found in Moshe Pelli, "When Did Haskalah Begin? Establishing the Beginning of Haskalah Literature and the Definition of 'Modernism,' " *Leo Baeck Institute Year Book* 44 (1999), pp. 55–96.

3. *Nahal Habesor* [The Brook Besor, or Good Tidings] bound with *Hame'asef* [The Gatherer], 1 (1783–1784), p. 3.

4. The subject of the revival of Hebrew language during the Haskalah is discussed in Moshe Pelli, "Tehiyat Halashon Hehelah Bahaskalah: *Hame'asef*,' Ketav Ha'et Ha'ivri Harishon, Kemachshir Lehidush Hasafah" [The Revival of Hebrew Began in Haskalah: "*Hame'asef*," the First Hebrew Periodical, as a Vehicle for the Rejuvenation of the Language], *Leshonenu La'am* [Our Language for the People], Series 50 (No. 2, January–March 1999 [5759]), pp. 59–75. See chapter 6 on the Hebrew language in Pelli, *Dor Hame'asfim Beshahar Hahaskalah*, pp. 177–95.

5. *Nahal Habesor*, p. 3.

6. H. K. (Hayim Keslin) in *Hame'asef*, 1 (1784), p. 111.

7. Eliyahu Morpurgo in *Hame'asef*, 3 (1786), p. 131.

8. Ibid., p. 68, based on Job 37: 11.

9. *Nahal Habesor*, p. 13.

10. Shimon Baraz, *Ma'archei Lev* [Preparations of the Heart] (Königsberg, 1785), based on verses from Isaiah 29: 24, 35: 4, 11: 9.

11. David Friedrichsfeld, "Hadlah Mimlitzat Yehudit Hatif'eret" [Glory Ceased from Jewish Rhetorics], *Hame'asef* 2 (1784–1785), p. 34.

12. Uzi Shavit, "Ha'haskalah' Mahi: Leverur Musag Ha'haskalah' Basifrut Ha'ivrit" [What Is Haskalah: Clarifying the Concept "Haskalah" in Hebrew Literature] *Mehkerei Yerushalayim Besifrut Ivrit* [Jerusalem Studies in Hebrew Literature], 12 (1990), p. 51. Shavit argues that the Maskilim were

not aware that they were "Maskilim." I tend to disagree with his notion if by this he meant that they did not consider themselves as Maskilim.

13. Shmuel Feiner, *Hahaskalah Beyahasah Lahistoriah—Hakarat He'avar Vetifkudo Bitnu'at Hahaskalah Hayehudit (1781–1881)* [Haskalah in Its Attitude to History—Cognition of the Past and Its Function in the Jewish Haskalah Movement 1781–1881], a doctoral dissertation (Jerusalem, 1990) in the introduction and chapter 1. Published as *Haskalah Vehistoriah* [Haskalah and History] (Jerusalem, 1995), which was translated into English, *The Jewish Enlightenment* (Philadelphia, PA: University of Pennsylvania Press, 2002).

14. Mendel Breslau, "El Rodfei Zedek Vedorshei Shelom Aheinu Bnei Yisra'el" [To the Seekers of Justice and the Searchers of Peace for Our Brethren the Children of Israel], *Hame'asef*, 6 (1790), pp. 301–14. See Moshe Pelli, *Bema'avkei Temurah* [Struggle for Change] (Tel Aviv: Mif'alim universitaiyim le-hotsaah le-or 1988), chapter 5, on Breslau, pp. 166–74.

15. *Hame'asef*, 6 (1790), p. 301.

16. Ibid., pp. 309, 313.

17. See Joseph Priestly, *Letters to the Jews* (New York: J. Harrison, 1794) [first edition: 1787]. See Pelli, *Bema'avkei Temurah*, pp. 166–74.

18. See the works by historians and social historians cited in Pelli, "When did Haskalah Begin?," pp. 55–96.

19. As delineated especially in his *Jerusalem* (1783); see an English edition, Moses Mendelssohn, *Jerusalem* (Hanover and London: University Press of New England, 1983), translation, Allan Arkush, introduction, Alexander Altmann.

20. The subject of modernism is discussed in Pelli, "When did Haskalah Begin?," pp. 55–96. See also an earlier, shorter version in Moshe Pelli, "Criteria of Modernism in Early Hebrew Haskalah Literature: Towards an Evaluation of the Modern Trends in Hebrew Literature," in *Jewish Education and Learning*, Eds. Glenda Abramson and Tudor Parfitt, published in honor of Dr. David Patterson (Switzerland: Harwood Academic Publishers, 1994), 129–142.

21. See, for example, the cover of *Hame'asef*, 1 (1783–1784): the printer was Daniel Christoph Kanter in Königsberg.

22. Saul Berlin, *Besamim Rosh* [Incense of Spices] (Berlin, 1793) published by "Defus Hevrat Hinuch Ne'arim" (The Press of the Society for Educating the Youths; in German: Im Verlag der Juedischen Freischule). On Saul Berlin, this book and his work see Moshe Pelli, *The Age of Haskalah* (Lanham, MD: University Press of America, 1979), chapter 9, pp. 171–89, and chapter 4, on Berlin, in Pelli, *Bema'avkei Temurah*, 140–165. On his satire, see Moshe Pelli, *Sugot Vesugyot Besifrut Hahaskalah Ha'ivrit* (Tel Aviv: Kibuts ha-me uhad, 1999).

23. A list of available books published from 1784 to 1796, with the exclusion of out-of-print titles, appeared at the end of Nahman Barash, *Ein Mishpat* [A Fountain of Justice] (Berlin: n.p., 1796).

24. *Nahal Habesor* [The Brook Besor, or Good Things], 4, bound in *Hame'asef*, 1 (1783). The phrase forbidding innovation, based on a biblical verse taken out of context, is attributed to Rabbi Moshe Sopher (1762–1839).

25. Ibid., p. 3.

26. See chapter 10, on Euchel, in Pelli, *The Age of Haskalah*, 190–230. Also Shmuel Feiner, "Yitzhak Euchel a Ha'yazam' Shel Tenu'at Hahaskalah Begermanyah" [Isaac Euchel—The "Initiator" of Haskalah Movement in Germany], *Zion*, 52 (No. 4, 1987), pp. 427–69.

27. See the chapter 1, on Deism, in Pelli, *The Age of Haskalah*, pp. 7–32.

28. Moses Mendelssohn, Ed., "Sefer Shmot" [Exodus], *Netivot Hashalom* [The Paths of Peace] (Berlin: Hotsaat ha-Kibuts ha-meuhad, 1783), 62b. See also Pelli, *Dor Hame'asfim Beshahar Hahaskalah*, p. 30.

29. Joh. Gottfried Herder, *Vom Geist der Ebräischen Poesie*, 2 (Gotha: Cotta, 1890), p. 24. See Moshe Pelli, "On the Role of Melitzah [Euphuism] in the Literature of Hebrew Enlightenment," chapter 4, in *Hebrew in Ashkenaz: A Language in Exile* (New York and Oxford: Oxford University Press, 1993), Ed., Lewis Glinert, pp. 99–110. See my article on the poetry in *Hame'asef* and the Maskilim's perception of language and poetry, " 'Lamenatze'ah Bineginot Maskil'—Melechet Hashir Vetofa'at Hashirah Be'hame'asef ', Ktav Ha'et Harishon Shel Hahaskalah Ha'ivrit" [Poetry and Poetic Theory in *Hame'asef*, the First Modern Periodical in Hebrew Haskalah], *Dappim Lemehkar Besifrut* [Dappim Research in Literature], 12 (1999–2000), pp. 65–116. See also Pelli, *Dor Hame'asfim Beshahar Hahaskalah*, chapter 1, on poetry, pp. 23–72, and my article " 'These Are the Words of the Great Pundit, Scholar and Poet Herder . . .' : Herder and the Hebrew Haskalah," *Hebräische Poesie und jüdischer Volksgeist: Die Wirungsgeschichte von Johann Gottfried Herder im Judentum Mittel- und Osteuropas* (Hildesheim, Zürich and New York: Olms, 2003), pp. 107–24.

30. See *The Age of Haskalah*, chapter 4, on the Hebrew language in Haskalah, pp. 73–90, and my article on the revival of Hebrew in Haskalah, "The Revival of Hebrew Began in Haskalah: Hame'asef, the First Hebrew Periodical, as a Vehicle for the Renewal of the Language," *Leshonenu La'am* [Our Language for the People], 50 (No. 2, 1999), pp. 59–75. See also, Pelli, *Dor Hame'asfim Beshahar Hahaskalah*, chapter 6, on Hebrew, pp. 175–95.

31. See E. A. Blackall, *The Emergence of German as a Literary Language 1700–1775* (Cambridge: Cambridge University Press, 1959), 4–5. See also ibid., 5, note 2, the English proverb: "Speech is the picture of the mind."

32. See Shmuel Werses, "Yad Yamin Dohah Yad Smol Mekarevet: Al Yahasam Shel Sofrei Hahaskalah Lileshon Yiddish" [Right Hand Rejects Left Hand Brings Close: On the Attitude of Haskalah Authors to the Yiddish Language], *Hulyot* [Links], 5 (Winter 1999), pp. 9–49.

33. N. H. Wessely, *Divrei Shalom Ve'emet* [Words of Peace and Truth] (Berlin: n.p., 1782), pp. 13a–b. Some scholars read this sentence differently, applying the question mark only to the first part while ignoring the conjunction which unites the clause to the main sentence. I disagree with this reading.

34. See Moshe Pelli, "On the Role of *Melitzah* [Euphuism] in the Literature of Hebrew Enlightenment," *Hebrew in Ashkenaz: A Language in Exile*, pp. 99–110.

35. See my studies on Hebrew in Haskalah cited in note 4.

36. See, for example, the various departments and items devoted to these matters in *Hame'asef*, and their description in the prospectus *Nahal Habesor*. See the index of *Hame'asef*, *Sha'ar Lahaskalah*, in the introduction.

37. More on Satanow and his work see the chapters devoted to him in Pelli, *The Age of Haskalah*, pp. 151–170, and Pelli, *Bema'avkei Temurah*, pp. 82–139.

38. Lessing published Reaimarus's controversial fragments anonymously; d'Hollbach published his *A Letter from Thrasybulus* saying that he had found it in a library. In Haskalah, Wolfssohn published his dialogue of the dead (see Pelli, *Sugot Vesugyot Besifrut Hahaskalah Ha'ivrit*, chapter 2a) anonymously, as did David Caro in his *Brit Emet* [Covenant of Truth] (Dessau:n.p., 1820). See *The Age of Haskalah*, p. 174, note 8.

39. I discuss the genre of religious disputation in detail in Pelli, *Sugot Vesugyot Besifrut Hahaskalah Ha'ivrit*, chapter 4, pp. 101–15.

40. See Pelli, *Bema'avkei Temurah*, pp. 129–39.

41. For a discussion about the genre of utopia, see Pelli, *Sugot Vesugyot Besifrut Hahaskalah Ha'ivrit*, chapter 10, pp. 291–327.

42. Saul Berlin's *Besamim Rosh* is discussed in my books: Pelli, *The Age of Haskalah*, chap. 9, pp. 171–89, and Pelli, *Bema'avkei Temurah*, chap. 4, pp. 145–65. See note 4 above.

43. These genres and the Maskilim cited here, Euchel, Satanow, Berlin, Wolfssohn, and Romanelli, are discussed in Pelli, *Sugot Vesugyot Besifrut Hahaskalah Ha'ivrit*, and *Dor Hame'asfim Beshahar Hahaskalah*.

44. Pelli, *Sugot Vesugyot Besifrut Hahaskalah Ha'ivrit*, chapter 2, pp. 48–72.

45. See chapters of Feder, the dialogues of the dead and the imaginary dialogue, in Pelli, *Sugot Vesugyot Besifrut Hahaskalah Ha'ivrit*.

46. See Pelli, *Sugot Vesugyot Besifrut Hahaskalah Ha'ivrit*.

47. "Igrot Yitzhak Eichel" [Isaac Euchel's Letters], *Hame'asef*, 2 (1785), pp. 116–21, pp. 137–42.

48. Cited in *Hame'asef*, 1 (1783–1784), 43: "The pundit of our generation, Socrates of our time." Mendelssohn was compared to Socrates by Ramler. See Altmann, *Moses Mendelssohn*, 742. Heinrich Heine, at a later date, referred to him as "the German Socrates" in *Religion and Philosophy in Germany* (Boston, MA: Beacon Press, 1959), p. 94. See chapter 8a, on biography, Pelli, *Sugot Vesugyot Besifrut Hahaskalah Ha'ivrit*, pp. 237–52.

49. *Hame'asef*, 4 (1788), pp. 113–44, pp. 177–208, pp. 337–68; 5 (1789), pp. 33–64. See Pelli, *Sugot Vesugyot Besifrut Hahaskalah Ha'ivrit*, chapter 8.

50. See Pelli, *Sugot Vesugyot Besifrut Hahaskalah Ha'ivrit* and *Dor Hame'asfim Beshahar Hahaskalah*.

51. *Hame'asef*, 1 (1783–1784), p. 132, by Joel Brill.

52. Pelli, *Dor Hame'asfim Beshahar Hahaskalah*, pp. 30–37.

53. On *Bildung* see George L. Mosse, *German Jews Beyond Judaism* (Bloomington, IN, Indiana University Press, 1985), pp. 1–11, 18–20, 41–3, and several articles in *The German-Jewish Dialogue Reconsidered*, Ed., Klaus L. Berghahn (New York: PeterLang, 1996), pp. 81–97, 125–32. See *Dor Hame'asfim Beshahar Hahaskalah*, 77, note 10.

54. The year according to the Hebrew calendar.

55. Shalom Hacohen, *Ktav Yosher* [An Epistle of Righteousness] (Vienna: n.p., 1820), pp. 95–6.

56. See Yehudah Alkalay, *Ketavim* [Writings] (Jerusalem, 1944); Zvi Kalischer, *Derishat Zion* [Search for Zion] (Torun: n.p., 1866); see also Arthur Hertzberg, *The Zionist Idea* (New York: Doubleday, 1984), pp. 101–14.

57. Moshe Hess, *Roma Virushalayim* [Rome and Jerusalem] (Warsaw, 1899); see also Hertzberg, Ibid, pp. 116–39.

58. Perez Smolenskin, *Maamarim* [Articles], 2 (Jerusalem: Hotsa at Keren Smolenski, 1925), pp. 8–17, 68, 75, 78.

59. Joseph Klausner, *Historiah Shel Hasifrut Ha'ivrit Hahadashah* [History of Modern Hebrew Literature], 2nd edn, Vol. 5 (Jerusalem: Ahiasaf, 1955), p. 104.

60. Abraham Baer Gottlober, "Et La'akor Natu'a" [Time to Uproot that which is Planted], *Haboker Or* [(First) Light of Morning], 1 (1, 1786), pp. 4–17; (2, 1786), pp. 77–86.

61. [Eliezer] Ben Yehuda, "She'elah Nichbadah" [A Venerable Question], *Hashahar*, 9 (1878), pp. 359–66.

62. Ibid., p. 362.

63. Ibid., p. 364.

64. Ibid., p. 365.

65. Klausner, *Historiah Shel Hasifrut Ha'ivrit Hahadashah*, 5, p. 104.

66. Mordechai Ehernpreis, "Le'an?" [Whither?], *Hashiloah*, 1 (1897), pp. 489–503.

67. Ibid., pp. 490–1.

68. Mordechai Ehernpreis, "Hashkafah Sifrutit" [Literary Outlook], *Hashiloah*, 11 (1903), pp. 186–92, the quotation on 186.

69. Ibid., p. 186.

70. Ahad Ha'am, "Lo Zeh Haderech" [This Is Not the Way], *Kol Kitvei Ahad Ha'am* [The Complete Writings of Ahad Ha'am] 5th edn, (Tel Aviv: Devir, 1956), pp. 11–14.

71. Ahad Ha'am, "Tehiyat Haru'ah" [Revival of the Spirit], *Kol Kitvei Ahad Ha'am*, pp. 173–86 esp. 181.

72. Shimon Halkin, "Tekufay Hatehiyah" [The Period of Tehiyah], *Derachim Vetzidei Derachim Basifrut* [Ways and Byways in Literature], 1 (1969), pp. 49–52; the article was written in 1920.

CHAPTER 5

The Chinese Renaissance: A Transcultural Reading

Gang Zhou

"To each eye, perhaps, the outlines of a given civilization present a different picture." Thus writes Jacob Burckhardt at the beginning of his influential work *The Civilization of the Renaissance in Italy*.[1] With these words, Burckhardt not only prepares his reader for the uniqueness of his vision of the Italian Renaissance but also negotiates a space for various kinds of interpretations to come. This chapter examines the ways in which the idea of renaissance was understood and appropriated by Chinese intellectuals in the early twentieth century. My discussion foregrounds Hu Shi, one of the most important intellectual leaders in modern China and the main architect of the May Fourth vernacular movement. I analyze his rewriting and reinvention of the European Renaissance as well as his declaration and presentation of the Chinese Renaissance in various contexts. Appropriating the linguistic shift that took place in the European Renaissance, Hu formed a brilliant narrative that facilitated the transformation of the vernacular in China from a vulgar tongue into the language of the nation and the language of the future. His creative uses of the Italian Renaissance and his passionate promotion of a Chinese Renaissance reveal the performative magic of the word *renaissance* and prompt us to ask what a renaissance is. As Edward Said comments, "Culture is never a matter of ownership, of borrowing and lending with absolute debtors and creditors, but rather of appropriations, common experiences, and interdependencies of all kinds among different cultures."[2]

The Renaissance: A Small Book

In June 1917, on his return trip to China from the United States, Hu Shi, who would soon become a major player in the Chinese literary scene, read a small book entitled *The Renaissance* by Edith Sichel. Sichel's book, priced at one dollar, was commissioned for the Home University Library and was intended to educate a mass audience. Sichel was an academic, and her approach to the Renaissance a product of centuries of knowledge transmission among elite thinkers, but her book targets the general public and is a good example of how ideas emerge from the academy and penetrate society.[3] When Hu encounters Sichel's book, however, the text meets a reader perhaps unanticipated by its producers. The meeting creates a "contact zone," a space where people geographically and culturally separated come into contact with each other and engage in meaning making.[4] What happened to the notion of renaissance in this contact zone; what did the term gain or lose? If the new possibilities of interpretation made the concept vulnerable, does this vulnerability also reveal the vitality of the idea itself?

Hu spent 1910 to 1917 as a student in the United States. He received his bachelor's degree in philosophy from Cornell University in 1914 and then studied at Columbia University under the guidance of John Dewey. His understanding of renaissance would undoubtedly have been influenced by his years of formal education in the United States and by intimate and lively contact with American ideas and institutions. Although it is impossible to reconstruct the hermeneutic process by which Hu took in information, we can trace perceptions of the European Renaissance in scholarship and in the American popular imagination at the time, both generally dominated by the Burckhardtian tradition. Peter Burke synthesizes Burckhardt's contribution to the popular and academic view of the Renaissance thus:

> with [Burckhardt] posterity associates the definition of the Renaissance in terms of the development of the individual and the discovery of the world and of man, and this is a fair verdict in the sense that it was [Burckhardt] who organized his whole essay around these ideas (together with that of "modernity") rather than around the more conventional concept of the revival of antiquity.[5]

In other words, Burckhardt brought about a paradigm shift and reshaped the conception of the Renaissance in Europe.[6] While renaissance had once been confined to a rebirth of arts or of letters, Burckhardt broadened the notion by adding to it what he regarded as the essence of the period: individualism and the discovery of the World and of Man. There is no evidence that Hu read Burckhardt during his years of study in the United States, but it is fairly safe to say that he would have received the Burckhardtian model by way of lectures and related reading. So, how does the Burckhardtian model play into Hu's reading of Sichel? One might expect individualism and modernity to dominate Hu's understanding of renaissance, but as we shall see, Hu perceived the vernacular movement to be the major feature of the European Renaissance and the strongest basis for his invention of the *Chinese* Renaissance.

Let us take a close look at Sichel's small book *The Renaissance*. Overall, the work follows the mainstream thought of the time, painting a Burckhardtian Renaissance slightly altered by John Addington Symonds' version. In fact, Symonds' *The Renaissance in Italy* is listed at the top of the recommended books on the back of Sichel's book. Symonds presented the Renaissance as an age of sharp contrasts, of highlights and deep shadows. He also termed the Renaissance as "the emancipation of the reason of the modern world," a claim Burckhardt would have hesitated to make.[7] Perhaps to make the Renaissance more visual and more graspable, Sichel's book opens with Michelangelo's great painting of Adam on the ceiling of the Sistine Chapel. The fresh image of Adam, "with a body naked and unashamed, and a strong arm, unimpaired by fasting, outstretched towards life and light," presents to the reader a dramatic and even exaggerated picture of youth and emancipation. Sichel then argues that "two main things there were which the Renaissance of Western Europe signified: it signified Emancipation and Expression."[8] While Burckhardt pays great attention to artistic expression, Sichel departs from him in emphasizing what she calls "a perfect passion for language." Following the humanistic interpretative tradition, Sichel's "passion for language" is nearly synonymous with "passion for the re-discovery of the classics, and for the unearthing of manuscripts." Only at the end of her account of this passion does she mention the vulgar tongue, "the growth of national speech and its gradual encroachment upon Latin."[9] However, it was this story of emerging vernaculars that captured Hu's imagination. As Hu wrote in his dairy on June 19, 1917,

> [W]e can see from Sichel's book, the national languages in Renaissance Europe all started as very small forces, but ended up having wide-reaching and powerful influences. Hence, we who advocate vernacular literature today ought to be confident about a promising future.[10]

In fact, Burckhardt never highlighted the problem of *volgare*, and neither was it Sichel's emphasis. But for Hu, who for years had been occupied with the question of language reform in China, the rise of vernacular languages became the episode that shone in the grand drama of the European Renaissance.

"Renaissance": Translation and Transculturation

Hu was not the only one in modern China passionate for the Renaissance. Irene Eber in "Thoughts on Renaissance in Modern China: Problems of Definition" discusses how the term *renaissance* was understood and interpreted by Chinese intellectuals from the late Qing period and the May Fourth period. Eber observes that earlier the notion of renaissance was loosely defined and that frequently flowery metaphors were used in place of actual analysis. Only after the May Fourth Movement in 1919 did the notion begin to crystallize; but there was still no agreement on its meaning. "Indeed, there was a variety of ideas: renaissance was free thinking and inquiry; renaissance was change in people's attitude; renaissance was overthrow of medievalism; and renaissance was new language and literature."[11] Eber's picture shows the volatility of the term as it moved across linguistic and cultural borders. As if opened up by the new circumstances, new needs and new interests, *renaissance* suddenly multiplied, attracting new meanings and shedding old ones. The translations of the term tell a story of transculturation.[12]

When *renaissance* first appeared in modern Chinese discourse, a number of almost identical phrases were used to translate the term, including *wenyi fuxing shidai, wenyi fuxing, guxue fuxing, wenxue fugu,* and *wenxue fuxing.* For instance, in his writing in 1904, the reformer Liang Qichao likens late Qing scholarship to the Renaissance in Europe. He goes on to say, "It is like a growing organism that has now reached its blossom, with a flourishing air of early spring. Hence I hold boundless hope for the future of our scholarship."[13] His use of *renaissance* is metaphoric, as was that of Vasari when he chose the term to describe the booming scene of fine arts in Italy. Liang uses *guxue fuxing* (restoration of antiquity) as the Chinese equivalent of *renaissance,* making no distinction between the European Renaissance and restoration of antiquity. Zhang Taiyan, another important thinker in the Late Qing period, also emphasizes restoration of antiquity in his translation of the concept: he uses *wenxue fugu* (revival of antiquity in literature), *wenxue fuxing* (restoration of antiquity in literature), *guxue fuxing* (restoration of antiquity) interchangeably in his rhetoric of the Renaissance. In a speech given in 1906 at a welcome party organized by Chinese overseas students in Tokyo, Zhang pairs the revival of Han learning with the restoration of antiquity that took place in the European Renaissance. He states, "If the revival of Han Learning can match what took place in *wenxue fugu de shihou* (the age of the revival of antiquity in literature), such a movement will certainly have the power to preserve the nation and the Han Chinese."[14] Here we actually see *renaissance* find its equivalent in spoken Chinese.

Both Liang and Zhang used *fuxing* (restoration) and *fugu* (the restoration of antiquity) in their representation of the Renaissance. In classical Chinese, *fuxing* means the restoration of something—a political order, a custom, a practice—that had fallen into disuse. Zhang's increasing interest in the European Renaissance was closely tied to his anti-Manchurian revolutionary cause, which championed returning to "authentically Chinese" and reviving Han learning. Similarly, Liang's use of *renaissance* in relation to the Qing scholarship implied that Qing scholars had a vital role in reviving the past and infusing it with new life for the present. For both, the European Renaissance by way of its Chinese translation, *fuxing, fugu*, provided a perfect model that looked to the future but at the same time harked back to the past, to an essential Chinese culture.

A considerable amount of resistance to the terms *fuxing, fugu* is visible in later generation intellectuals, many of whom sought a better phrase to capture their understanding of renaissance. Hu Shi noted in his diary that the title of Sichel's book *The Renaissance* should be translated as *zaisheng shidai* (the age of rebirth). He considered *wenyi fuxing* the Chinese equivalent of "a revival of literature and art."[15] By differentiating the Renaissance period and the revival of literature and art, Hu successfully debunked the equation that had been established in the Late Qing discourse of the Renaissance. In other words, according to Hu a revival of literature and art does not equate with the Renaissance. The European Renaissance is an age of rebirth, the beginning of the use of vernacular literature, which was reborn during that period. Thus, what a renaissance is and what is to be revived received a new definition in Hu's rhetoric: if anything is to be reborn, it is the vernacular, something far different from the essence of Chinese culture as perceived by Liang Qichao and Zhang Taiyan.

Other May Fourth thinkers preferred a more future-oriented word for the Chinese equivalent of *renaissance*. *Xinchao*, the Beijing University student magazine, began its publication in the winter of 1918, and *The Renaissance* was its English subtitle. Fu Sinian, one of the main editors, claimed unhesitatingly that *xinchao* (new tide) and renaissance were exact translations of each other. For Fu and others, the Renaissance was a return to free thinking and inquiry. The essence of the term *renaissance* was therefore not the mere revival of antiquity but rather *xinchan* (new birth), *xinchao* (new tide) by way of free thought. From restoration of antiquity to the age of rebirth and finally to new birth and new tide, *renaissance* moved further and further away from its original connection with antiquity as it was transformed into a symbol of newness and progress.

A Renaissance as a period of liberation, a period when individuals are freed from the bondage of tradition, echoed perfectly with the icono-clastic spirit of the New Cultural movement. In June 1919, one article spoke of the European Renaissance as an "emancipating movement," and pronounced the May Fourth Movement a first step in this direction: "We are going to change our attitude towards life and bring about a Chinese Renaissance, emancipating emotions, emancipating thought, and demanding human rights."[16] The author's assertion is made purely through analogy. Although what lies behind the analogy is unclear, the compelling and exciting sound of the rhetoric is perhaps what makes the idea of renaissance so readily adopted. Renaissance was a foreign term and concept not merely acquired by Chinese intellectuals but also sub-stantially revised and reimagined to serve different purposes. Those who transformed it engaged in the exact kind of practice of doing things with words that transculturation describes.[17]

As the above discussion illustrates, the search for the right Chinese word to translate *renaissance* was always accompanied by a group's or a cause's claim to be creating the Chinese counterpart of the European Renaissance. The connection between the European Renaissance and the May Fourth literary revolution was consciously cultivated by May Fourth intellectuals from the beginning. The two articles that launched the May Fourth literary revolution in 1917 used the European Renaissance as a reference point to discuss the contemporary Chinese lit-erary and cultural scene. While Hu's "Some Modest Suggestions for Literary Reform" ("Wenxue gailiang chuyi") drew on the linguistic tran-sition that took place in the European Renaissance, Chen Duxiu's "On literary revolution" ("Wenxue geming lun") emphasized the overall importance of the Renaissance period in the history of European civi-lization. Both declared that the literary revolution they called for paral-leled the European Renaissance and marked the starting point of a new nation, a new China that someday would be as awe-inspiring and bril-liant as its European counterparts.

A decade later, when writings of May Fourth intellectuals were can-onized and institutionalized, the similarity between the May Fourth lit-erary revolution and the European Renaissance was again consciously reemphasized. By then, *wenyi fuxing* (a revival of literature and art) had already become the standard Chinese equivalent of *renaissance*. Late Qing political reformers should have been happy that the word they chose remained in currency, but they would certainly be unhappy about what the term denoted in the new context. Restoration of antiquity was not in the picture, *wenyi fuxing* became an emblem of new birth and many forward-looking features of modernity and progress. It was with this utopian definition, not the definition used by Late Qing reformers, that May Fourth intellectuals reflected on their achievements in the first ten years. Their recapitulation was published in the 1930s as the *Compendium of Modern Chinese Literature*, a ten-volume anthology of critical theory, literary debates, fiction, poetry, familiar essays, and drama produced between 1917 and 1927. The following paragraph opens the preface of the *Compendium*:

> It has been almost two decades since the birth of the May Fourth literary movement, initiated in the 1917 *New Youth* magazine by Hu Shi and Chen Duxiu in Beijing. Compared to a four-thousand-year history of literature, two decades seem brief and not worthy of consideration. But in evaluating their significance for the future of Chinese culture, we realize the New Literature movement is just like the European Renaissance, ushering in a brand new age. Although what the movement has brought to the world may not be so miraculous and spectacular as what the European Renaissance produced, the adventurous spirit of these pioneers has provided a great model for our new youth, and the literary works they have created are immeasurable treasures in the history of the New Literature.[18]

While the *Compendium* authoritatively defines the New Literature through inclusion and exclusion, the preface defines the ways the New Literature should be read and interpreted through associations. Readers are taught to connect the European Renaissance and the May Fourth literary movement at the beginning of their reading and understanding. Here the term *renaissance* is not merely a neologism that signifies some foreign period in a foreign culture but rather a reinvented critical category used to legitimize and glorify certain literary values and practices.

The *Chinese* Renaissance: Two Important Essays

Transculturation goes beyond translation, and thus the term *renaissance* not only operates in a translingual context but also performs in various concrete processes of verbal communication. In other words, the individual thinkers who encountered *renaissance* constitute only part of the story. The idea of renaissance did not stay in the mind of an individual thinker or writer but rather it took certain concrete forms in a speech act or simply a specific text. Therefore, besides the thinker, who is the mediator, we should also consider the reader in the text as well as the concrete historical moment when the communication took place. The discussion about the reception of Renaissance in the context of modern China should not be confined to certain leading thinkers and writers. It should also include some contact zones that can only be delineated by the intriguing negotiation among addresser, addressee, and the historical situation. The "hero" is thus a relation or an interaction, rather than an individual who used the term *renaissance* in certain ways. Two of Hu Shi's essays, each written at a critical moment in the May Fourth literary revolution, provide points of departure to examine the middle ground where we may locate the reception of Renaissance at a particular moment in modern China.

The essay "Some modest suggestions for literary reform" marked the first time Hu championed vernacular literature in China as canonical. For almost two millennia China had maintained two written languages; classical Chinese was the prestigious literary language, and the vernacular was the medium for popular genres such as fiction and drama.[19] Vernacular literature was always kept outside the literary canon, but by the end of the nineteenth century, the language structure in China had been shaken. The development of modern print culture promoted the use of the vernacular in journalism and various other fields, challenging the previous monopoly of classical Chinese. Seeing the power of the vernacular to convey ideas and to influence people, Late Qing political reformers also enthusiastically promoted the change.[20] But even during this period, the conventional idea of language remained intact. The vernacular was still conceived as a vulgar tongue for uneducated masses, while the great literary tradition was always reserved for works written in classical Chinese. Hu Shi's essay was among the first attempts to bring dignity and literary importance to the vernacular. Ironically, Hu composed his essay in classical Chinese, the very language that he sought to overthrow.

That the essay was written in classical Chinese was by no means surprising since the classical language was still the common linguistic vehicle among literati. Even a progressive journal like *New Youth* would have to wait another year and a half to start publishing literary works written in the vernacular. Hu's essay discussed a serious matter and was aimed at well-educated intellectuals interested in literary reform: it was to them that Hu made his plea. The essay revolves around eight tenets: (1) avoid writing without substance; (2) do not imitate the ancients; (3) pay attention to grammar; (4) do not moan without an illness; (5) eliminate hackneyed and formulaic language; (6) do not use allusions; (7) avoid parallelism; and (8) do not avoid vulgar diction. These points were later termed the "eight don'ts" and commonly cited as the most important principles of the May Fourth literary revolution.[21]

The significance of Hu's essay and the linguistic shaky ground that it embodies remind us of Dante's *De Vulgari Eloquentia*, which, similarly, was composed in Latin, the classical language, and yet aimed to elevate the Florentine vernacular. In fact, near the end of his essay when explaining the last point of his eight don'ts—do not avoid vulgar diction—Hu offers Dante as a model for his countrymen. Recapitulating the development of Chinese literature, Hu argues that at the end of the Yuan Dynasty Chinese literature came closest to a union of spoken and written language and that the vernacular nearly became a literary language. "If this tendency had not been arrested, then a 'living literature' might have appeared in China and the great endeavor of Dante and Luther might have developed in old Cathay." To further clarify, Hu writes a long paragraph on the linguistic transition in the European Renaissance. Interestingly, the paragraph is in parentheses:

> (In the Middle Ages in Europe, each country had its own vulgar spoken language and Latin was the literary language. All written works used Latin, just as classical Chinese was used in China. Later, in Italy appeared Dante and other literary giants who first used their own vulgar language to write. Other countries followed suit, and national languages began to replace Latin. . . . Hence, all contemporary literature in the various European nations developed from the vulgar languages of the time. The rise of literary giants began with a 'living literature' replacing a dead literature in Latin.)[22]

Here Hu connects his cause of language reform with the European Renaissance. He implies that Europeans have set the example and that now it is time for China to follow suit—that in this universal path of progress, it is China's turn to march forward. In a way, it is only appropriate that a person like Hu, someone well versed in Chinese and European literary history, raises such a point. After negotiating back and forth with Chinese literary tradition and its scholarship (Hu cites an amazing number of traditional Chinese poets and works in this revolutionary piece), he distinguishes himself clearly as someone with access to foreign literary traditions. Again, he places the paragraph in parentheses; if there is a center and periphery in this essay, the European Renaissance is at the periphery, while the grand Chinese literary tradition occupies the center. *Renaissance* in this context is a word of low profile, a word of periphery, but also a word of subversion, of revolution. The author seems aware that some of his readers will be made uneasy by the association, some will be excited and will welcome it, some will be ambivalent, and some might feel the analogy completely out of place. But it is precisely in that unknown area, the territory where the authorial intention is tested, welcomed, defied, or revised that we locate the real reception of Renaissance. Here we see the modest debut of Renaissance on the May Fourth literary scene.

The second essay, "Toward a constructive theory of literary revolution" ("Jianshe de wenxue geming lun"), was published in April 1918, when the May Fourth literary revolution advanced to a new stage, the stage of construction. A number of things should be noted before we examine this text. First, the essay is written in the vernacular. To put its call for literary revolution into action, *New Youth* started to publish serious creative works and theoretical articles written in the vernacular, Hu's essay among them. Second, the essay was written as a systematic and constructive theoretical guideline for the vernacular movement. By then, Hu was a professor at Beijing University—the most prominent university in China—and was acknowledged as the most respected theorist in the circle of *New Youth*. The tone of the essay shows that the author was confident he would be treated seriously and embraced enthusiastically by the progressive youth. Third, the essay conveys a strong sense of being the "maker," the maker of the national language, the maker of a living literature, and ultimately the maker of a new, resurrected China. The author seems intoxicated with the significance of the movement and the future it will bring to China. His words successfully convey to the reader the differences that "we who promote the vernacular" can make in this exciting historical moment.

The essay begins with a preamble in which Hu repeats his famous eight *don'ts* and then says he intends to continue with more positive thoughts. He writes, "I hope that we who advocate the literary revolution will exert our energies constructively, so that within the next thirty or fifty years we may create for China a school of new Chinese living literature." But how to create a living literature? Hu Shi coins a slogan "a literature in the national language; a literary national language." The main argument in his second section is that a living literature has to be written in a living language, which is the vernacular. In the third section, he talks about how to create a national language, and here he repeats his story of the rise of national languages in the European Renaissance. This time the European Renaissance is placed at the very center of the essay, as a powerful model to be emulated. The story is provided with more detail, and the author is now confident about the symbolic value the model embodies. But the way he relates to the model he draws on becomes problematic.

Hu first claims that his argument is the result of many years' study of the history of European languages. Having established himself as an expert on the subject, he uses Italy and England as two main examples and stresses that the history of the Italian national language is especially instructive for China's current movement. According to Hu, Italy was the first country to enthrone the vernacular as the national language, and Dante was the first great master who elevated the Italian language to replace Latin. After Dante, Boccaccio and others also wrote literary works in the vernacular, and in less than one hundred years, the national language of Italy was firmly established. What is particularly striking here is the readiness with which Hu sees Italian as his model. A more factual account would show that it took much longer for the Florentine vernacular that Dante promoted to replace Latin as the dominant written language in Italy. During this long transition, the relation between the classical language and the vernacular was complicated.[23] I imagine it is Hu's wish for a sweeping victory of the vernacular language over classical Chinese that underlies his oversimplified narrative of the Italian literary scene. His assessment of the linguistic shift in the Italian Renaissance says more about his vision of Chinese literature than it does about its Italian model.

Hu's misrepresentation of the Renaissance story can also be seen in the negativity that he projects onto Dante's attitude toward Latin. Hu's Dante sees Latin as dead and the vernacular as surpassing Latin in its beauty. It does not seem to have occurred to Hu that, although Dante's promotion of the vernacular eventually led to its replacement of Latin, Dante would never have condemned Latin as a dead language in the way Hu and his fellow May Fourth writers condemned classical Chinese. Dante had great reverence for Latin and the Latin literary tradition. It is Vergil, after all, who is chosen by Dante as the great mentor to guide the pilgrim through the journey in *Inferno* and *Purgatory*. On the other hand, one is surprised that Dante says so little about the Latin language in his famous defense of the vernacular, *De Vulgari Eloquentia*. Instead of denigrating Latin, he separates the vernacular from Latin (the artificial language), building up the vernacular as a new authority, which ultimately counterbalances the old authority. In contrast, for Hu and his generation of intellectuals, the only way to establish the power of the vernacular was to dethrone and destroy classical Chinese. Hu's reinvention of Dante as an antiLatin hero therefore created a more fitting model for the Chinese vernacular movement, casting it as following a respected, universal model.

So how shall we address the significance of the concept of renaissance in this verbal instance? First, from its modest debut to this glorious staging, the European Renaissance was firmly established as a powerful model for the Chinese vernacular movement. Hu's position and intellectual influence, along with the symbolic value that was accorded any idea from the West, made *renaissance* an indispensable term. At the same time, the Renaissance narrative further consolidated Hu's role as a great visionary leader and reaffirmed the vernacular movement as a grand project in pursuit of modernity and progress. Later May Fourth discourses of language produced by participants such as Fu Sinian and Luo Jialun readily accepted the analogy, and it was also adopted to guide the reader through the *Compendium of Modern Chinese Literature* in the 1930s. Second, as we saw in "Some modest suggestions for literary reform" as also in "Toward a constructive theory of literary revolution," it is not a dictionary definition that tells us what a word signifies in a concrete historical verbal interaction but the social tone of a word as well as the contact zone a word indicates. V. N. Volosinov describes the phenomenon thus:

> in point of fact, word is a two-sided act. It is determined equally by whose word it is and for whom it is meant. As word, it is precisely the product of the reciprocal relationship between speaker and listener, addresser and addressee. . . . A word is a territory shared by both addresser and addressee, by the speaker and his interlocutor.[24]

The reception of the Renaissance in modern China may well be reconsidered in this sense.

The Chinese Renaissance: A Haskell Lecture Series

One might be amazed to see how the Renaissance was domesticated to serve local Chinese interests, but one will be even more amazed to see how the idea of renaissance was further defamiliarized when it was brought back to the United States by Hu in the 1930s.[25] In July 1933, Hu was invited as the Haskell Lecturer to give a series of talks at the University of Chicago. The original title of the series was "Cultural Trends in Present-day China." The lectures were put together and published later as a volume called *The Chinese Renaissance*. Chinese scholars have largely neglected the book since English is its linguistic medium. But, in my view, it provides us with a perfect case study to examine how renaissance geographically travels back and forth but semantically moves further away from what it originally meant.

The Chinese Renaissance embodies an intricate contact zone. Its anticipated addressee is an English speaker who seeks understanding about China, and Hu, the addresser, speaks for China as someone who knows the subject well and who is also a major player in an important historical drama. The foreword of the book, by A. Eustace Haydon, Head of the Department of Comparative Religion at the University of Chicago, describes a well-defined author-reader relationship. Haydon presents Hu as the perfect Haskell lecturer:

> Both as an interpreter of China's cultural renaissance and as an ambassador of interracial and intercultural understanding Professor Hu was an ideal Haskell lecturer. Culturally he belongs to both East and West. The vast changes in the cultural life of China are so recent as to fall within the span of his youthful age and in many of these movements he has been a pioneer and a trusted leader.

Indeed, how did this ideal Haskell lecturer present the Chinese Renaissance to his American audience, and what did *renaissance* mean in this specific verbal instance? A close look at Hu's own words in the preface is helpful:

> If I have any thesis to present, I want my readers to understand that cultural change[s] of tremendous significance have taken place and are taking place in China. . . . Slowly, quietly, but unmistakably, the Chinese Renaissance is becoming a reality. The product of this rebirth looks suspiciously occidental. But, scratch its surface and you will find that the stuff of which it is made is essentially the Chinese bedrock which much weathering and corrosion have only made stand out more clearly—the humanistic and rationalistic China resurrected by the touch of the scientific and democratic civilization of the new world.

Once again, *renaissance* is used to describe a cultural change of tremendous significance and to declare that something fascinating has taken and is taking place, although here the word is spoken to an audience not unfamiliar with what *renaissance* originally meant. Hu's American audience might have been excited about the set of images, vocabularies, ideas the trope conjures up, but they must also have wondered what Hu meant by *renaissance* as he talked about the "humanistic and rationalistic China resurrected by the touch of the scientific and democratic civilization of the new world." "Is this a real Renaissance?"

they might have asked. The term *renaissance* in Hu's lecture takes on a thematic dimension and becomes a creation beyond any correspondence with the "real" Renaissance they knew. Hu's text invites its audience to push the question one step further and ask, "But was the Renaissance I know a real Renaissance?" Perhaps what is real is a certain kind of theoretical practice that first took place in Europe and then emerged again and again in response to various circumstances. Perhaps the question of authenticity and realness should be replaced by the question of circulation and performativity.[26]

In fact, Hu is not interested in exploring the connection between the Chinese Renaissance and the European Renaissance, even though the third lecture, "The Chinese Renaissance," starts with a summary of three prominent features shared by the European Renaissance and the May Fourth literary revolution, which Hu terms the Chinese Renaissance: (1) both were conscious movements to replace classical literature with a new literature in the living language of the people; (2) both were movements of conscious protest against many established cultural ideas and institutions and of conscious emancipation of the individual from the bondage of tradition; and (3) both were humanist movements. One may well question whether these are prominent features of the European Renaissance or rather of Hu's representation. But either way Hu seems to care little, and he leaves the comparison hastily and moves on to his next argument: "there [have] been many periods of Chinese Renaissance"; first, the Tang-dynasty rise of the great poets and a new prose literature modeled after the classical style; second, the development of a secular neo-Confucianist philosophy in the Song Dynasty; third, the rise of the dramas in the thirteenth century and the rise of the great novels; fourth, the development in the last three hundred years of classical scholarship with its philological and historical approach; and fifth, the literary revolution just mentioned. If these are all Chinese Renaissances, then certainly the Chinese Renaissance bears little resemblance to the European one. Only the latest instance of the Chinese Renaissance was influenced by intimate contact with European culture. Hu's elaboration of the May Fourth literary revolution as a fully conscious and studied movement very different from earlier movements also frames it as the last phase of the Chinese Renaissance rather than the Chinese counterpart of the European Renaissance. Renaissance, in Hu's presentation, becomes a totally indigenous Chinese phenomenon, deeply rooted in the historical development of Chinese culture itself.

To avoid leaving the wrong impression, I mention that Hu's view of the literary revolution is still centered on the language problem. He defines the problem to which the literary revolution offers the solution as that of "finding a suitable language which could serve as an effective means of educating the vast millions of children and of illiterate adults."[27] He terms the mission of the Chinese Renaissance "a new language, a new literature, a new outlook on life and society, and a new scholarship."[28] However, the language shift that took place in the European Renaissance, which Hu Shi drew on in promoting the Chinese vernacular movement in 1918, is not highlighted in his narrative of the making of the national language in China. When he gives the account of his activities and contributions to the movement, he talks about his debates with his literary friends in the United States, his experimenting with the vernacular in poetry writing, and most important, his study of Chinese history and literature with a newly acquired scientific method. In a word, it is his pragmatism that he implies helped guide this vernacular movement, the Chinese Renaissance. He situates the rise of the vernacular in China in a world historical context, but in contrast to his essays of 1918, he mentions nothing about important Renaissance (or Medieval?) figures like Dante or Luther, who heroically promoted the vernacular, as he had done fifteen years earlier. What he offers is a scientific explanation that proves Mandarin Chinese has all the qualifications that a national language ought to possess. Perhaps these are the moments when Hu's American audience understands what "a touch by scientific method from the new world" means. *Renaissance* in Hu's rhetoric becomes a figure of speech that both pulls his audience along and pushes them back while the trope is contested and unsettled and the assumptions and opinions are defied and denied. Here *renaissance* functions as a conceit, a linguistic stretch that challenges the addressee's understanding and tolerance as the addresser totally reinvents the word and uses it in a new way. If fifteen years earlier Hu's conscious appropriation and manipulation of *renaissance* helped facilitate the transformation of the vernacular in China from a vulgar tongue to the national language, his reinvention and refashioning of *renaissance* in this particular context explores a unique space at the border between two cultures.

Renaissance As An Open Work

> Words resonate differently in the thoughts of every individual, and even the minutest difference quivers through language like an expanding ring on the water surface. All *understanding* is thus also a *non-understanding*, all agreement in thought and feeling also a divergence.[29]

At the end of this Chinese reading of the Renaissance, one wonders how the word *renaissance* resonated in other non-European contexts. David Kopf argues "The fact that the generalized concept of renaissance has been applied to their history and tradition by non-European peoples should be reason enough to abandon the older European-centered notion of the Renaissance."[30] Kopf's insights into a transcultural reading of the Renaissance not only frees *renaissance* from its European origin but also points to an understanding of *renaissance* as an idea that belongs to any culture. Perhaps it is time to rethink *renaissance* not as an onto-logically autonomous subject that existed in the remote past, but as an idea that is open-ended, that may change—indeed *must* change, when brought to different interpreters and different contexts. What may not change, however, is the dialogue that will go on and on. I believe that to get a fuller understanding of *renaissance* is about learning all the possible dialogues *renaissance* could generate, be they within Europe or outside Europe. It is in this sense we might say that *renaissance* may serve as an open work that allows mankind to hear voices from different cultures, different languages, and different people.

Notes

* This essay was supported in part by a grant from the University of California Pacific Rim Research Program. I thank Brenda Schildgen, Michelle Yeh, and Constance Anderson for their helpful comments and suggestions. A version of this essay was published in *PMLA* (May, 2005).

1. Jacob Burckhardt, *The Civilization of the Renaissance in Italy*, trans. S.G.C. Middlemore (London: Penguin Books, 1990).
2. Edward Said, *Culture and Imperialism* (New York: Knopf, 1993), p. 217.
3. My examination of Hu's encounter with Sichel's book benefits from Robert Darnton's illuminating study of bestsellers in pre-revolutionary France (Robert Darnton, *The Forbidden Best-Sellers of Pre-revolutionary France* [New York: W. W. Norton, 1995]), which showed that meanings do not come prepackaged in discourses but rather shaped by various circumstances. Darnton's work has made it easier for scholars to pay attention to popular genres and to explore the role of publishers and booksellers when discussing the reception of ideas.
4. In *Imperial Eyes: Travel Writing and Transculturation* (London: Routledge, 1992), Mary Louise Pratt uses "contact zones" to designate the social spaces where disparate cultures meet, clash, and grapple with each other. While I adopt the term, I do not emphasize the highly asymmetrical power relations of domination and subordination inherent in her study.
5. Peter Burke, "Introduction," in *The Civilization of the Renaissance in Italy* by Jacob Burckhardt (London: Penguin, 1990), p. 12.

6. Instead of uncovering an essence of the Renaissance, Burckhardt may have looked at the Renaissance with a particular horizon of expectation and found that some neglected aspects resonated with him.

7. See Wallace Ferguson, *The Renaissance in Historical Thought: Five Centuries of Interpretation* (Boston: Houghton Mifflin Company, 1948).

8. Edith Sichel, *The Renaissance* (New York: Henry Holt, 1914), p. 8.

9. Ibid., p. 13.

10. Hu Shi, *Hu Shi liuxue riji* (Hu Shi's Diary while Studying Abroad), Vol. 4 (Taipei: Commercial Press, 1959), p. 1155. Author's translation.

11. Irene Eber, "Thoughts on Renaissance in Modern China: Problems of Definition," in *Studia Asiatica: Essays in Asian Studies in Felicitation of the Seventy-fifth Anniversary of Professor Chen Shou-yi*, Ed. G. Thompson (San Francisco, CA: Chinese Materials Center, 1975), p. 216.

12. For more discussions on the problem of translation and translingual practice in modern China, see Lydia Liu, *Translingual Practice: Literature, National Culture, and Translated Modernity in China, 1900–37* (Stanford, CA: Stanford University Press, 1995).

13. Liang Qichao, "On the Recent Scholarship," *Xinmin cong-bao* (New Citizen Journal) 53–58 (1904), p. 103.

14. See Chen Pingyuan, *Zhongguo xiandai xueshu de jianli* (The Establishment of Modern Chinese Scholarship) (Beijing: Beijing University Press, 1998), p. 336.

15. See note 10 above.

16. Chow Tse-Tsung, *The May Fourth Movement* (Cambridge, MA: Harvard University Press, 1964), p. 338.

17. See the invention of the word *transculturation* in Fernando Ortiz, *Cuban Counterpoint: Tobacco and Sugar*, (Durham, NC: Duke University Press, 1995),

> the word *transculturation* better expresses the different phases of the process of transition from one culture to another because this does not consist merely in acquiring another culture, which is what the English word *acculturation* really implies, but the process also necessarily involves the loss or uprooting a previous culture, which could be defined as a deculturation. In addition it carries the idea of the consequent creation of new cultural phenomena, which could be called neoculturation, pp. 102–3.

18. Zhao Jiabi, "Preface" in *Zhongguo xinwenxue daxi* (Compendium of Modern Chinese Literature), Ed. Zhao Jiabi, Vol. 1 (Shanghai: Liangyou tushu gongsi, 1935).

19. For discussions of diglossia and pre-modern China as a diglossic community, see Charles Ferguson's seminal essay "Diglossia." Jerry Norman in his book *Chinese* also agrees with Ferguson's argument. Charles Ferguson, "Diglossia," *Word* 15 (1959) pp. 325–40; Jerry Norman, *Chinese* (Cambridge: Cambridge University Press, 1988).

20. See Milena Dolezelova-Velingerova for a detailed discussion of language reform in the late Qing period. Milena Dolezelova-Venlingerova, "The

Origins of Modern Chinese Literature," in *Modern Chinese Literature in the May Fourth Era*, Ed. Merle Goldman (Cambridge: Harvard University Press, 1977) pp. 17–35.

21. Hu's eight tenets called for a new literature that would replace the archaic and allusion-laden classical poetry and prose that dominated the Chinese literary scene at the time. For further discussions on the May Fourth literary revolution, see C. T. Hsia, *A History of Modern Chinese Fiction, 1917–1957* (New Haven, CT: Yale University Press, 1961); Michelle Yeh, *Modern Chinese Poetry: Theory and Practice since 1917* (New Haven, CT: Yale University Press, 1991); and Edward Gunn, *Rewriting Chinese: Style and Innovation in Twentieth-Century Chinese Prose* (Stanford, CA: Stanford University Press, 1991).

22. Kirk Denton, ed. *Modern Chinese Literary Thought: Writings on Literature, 1893–1945* (Stanford, CA: Stanford University Press, 1996), p. 138.

23. See Bruno Migliorini, *The Italian Language* (Boston, MA: Faber and Faber, 1984). The vernacular gained considerable ground in the fourteenth century, although the main contributions to the development of the vulgar tongue were made by Dante, Petrarch and Boccaccio, who drew strength from their knowledge of the classics in their efforts to give artistic nobility to Italian. In the early fifteenth century, the vernacular went through a crisis. The humanists' exaltation of Latin overshadowed the vernacular. However, in the last decades of the century, the humanists' search for a pure Latin only increased the uses of the vernacular in practical spheres. Between 1470 and 1550, printing made a decisive contribution to the stability and uniformity of language in Italy. The final codification of a standard written language occurred in the sixteenth century. The national language of Italy that Hu refers to did not even exist until a unified Italy was established in the nineteenth century.

24. V. N. Volosinov, "Verbal Interaction," in *Semiotics: An Introductory Anthology*, Ed. Robert Innis (Bloomington, IN: Indiana University Press, 1985), pp. 52–3.

25. It is tempting to approach Hu's appropriations of the Renaissance as instances of Occidentalism defined by Xiaomei Chen as "a discursive practice that, by constructing its Western Other, has allowed the Orient to participate actively and with indigenous creativity in the process of self-appropriation, even after being appropriated and constructed by Western Others" (p. 2). Xiaomei Chen, *Occidentalism: A Theory of Counter-discourse in Post-Mao China* (Oxford: Oxford University Press, 1994). The reason I am hesitant to do so is that Chen's Occidentalism is in a way a derivative of Orientalism, as Chen herself acknowledges: "Chinese Occidentalism is the product of Western Orientalism, even if its aims are largely and specifically Chinese" (p. 5). I am not denying that Hu's worldview is highly influenced by Western thought, but I do not think that should be considered a case study of Western world domination. On the other hand, the emphasis of my paper is certainly not on the workings of

power relationships. My choice not to focus on them is a response to the overarching domination of the theory of power. Sometimes one wonders whether obsessively talking about power merely reinforces power, verbally and in other ways. For this reason, I prefer a more neutral term such as *transculturation*.

26. Edward Said in his "Traveling Theory" discusses what happens to a theory when it is used in different circumstances and for new reasons. "Theory" writes Said, "in short, can never be complete . . . no system or theory exhausts the situation out of which it emerges or to which it is transported." Edward Said, "Traveling Theory," in *The Edward Said Reader*, Eds. Moustafa Bayoumi and Andrew Rubin (New York: Vintage, 2000) pp. 210–11. The idea of renaissance might well be perceived as a theory born in sixteenth-century Italy and reborn again and again in new contexts.

27. Hu Shi, *The Chinese Renaissance* (Chicago, IL: The University of Chicago Press, 1933), p. 48.

28. Ibid., p. 46.

29. A few years ago, Wolfgang Kubin, a well-known sinologist, gave a talk at University of California, Davis, titled "Only the Chinese can understand China: The Problem of East-West Understanding," which began with this paragraph by Wilhelm von Humboldt. Taking issue with the assumption that only the Chinese can understand China, Professor Kubin argues that a look at China from an outsider's perspective could be revealing. I believe no one has ever argued that only Europeans can understand the Renaissance, although this has been the assumption for centuries. Perhaps it is from here that we see the real crisis of Comparative Literature.

30. David Kopf, *British Orientalism and the Bengal Renaissance: the Dynamics of Indian Modernization 1773–1885* (Berkeley, CA: University of California Press, 1969), p. 282.

CHAPTER 6

Sri Aurobindo: Renaissance in India and the Italian Renaissance

Brenda Deen Schildgen

From the late eighteenth century on a cultural transformation was taking place in India that is called, both by Indian and European writers, the Indian Renaissance.[1] This movement was both the construction of English East India Company functionaries who became scholars of ancient India, and the work of Indians who came under the influence of the English "intelligentsia." Associated with intellectual figures like William Jones, who founded the Asiatic Society of Bengal in 1784, the movement sponsored various types of Indological scholarship.[2] Bengal came to prominence partly because the British had dominated the area longer, Calcutta was the capital of British India until 1911, and both the first printing press and the first Indian-English newspaper, *The Bengal Gazette*, appearing in 1816, began to operate in the region.[3]

The fact that initially this philological activity was the work of British scholars involved in the recovery of ancient Indian civilization testifies to the "hybrid," Homi Babha's word, nature of this development at its inception.[4] The work of Indian intellectuals active in this movement likewise demonstrates the syncretic and transcultural nature of the changes underway. *The Renaissance in India*, a little treatise written in 1920, by one of India's leading intellectuals of the last century, Aurobindo Ghose (1872–1950), undertakes an analysis of the developments of the nineteenth century. Transforming "renaissance" into a political-cultural tool, while adopting "essentializing" assumptions about India and Indian identity as his dominant approach, Aurobindo's treatise becomes a political and nationalist statement for India's "renewal."[5] As a Bengali, active in the Hindu and Sanskrit philosophy revival, Aurobindo represents how the Northern Indian and specifically Bengali notion of Renaissance came to dominate the discourse of "revival," a renewal that was simultaneously taking place in Southern India.

Seeing the Indian Renaissance as reaching its major turning point at the beginning of the twentieth century, Aurobindo distinguishes it from the European precursor while likening it to the reawakening occurring in Ireland at the same time as in India. Linking national awakening with cultural rediscovery, he writes:

> There is a first question, whether at all there is really a Renaissance in India. That depends a good deal on what we mean by the word; it depends also on the future, for the thing itself is only in its infancy and it is too early to say to what it may lead. The word carries the mind back to the turning-point of European culture to which it was first applied; that was not so much a reawakening as an overturn and reversal, a seizure of Christianized, Teutonized, feudalized Europe by the old Graeco-Latin spirit and form with all the complex and momentous results which came from it. That is certainly not a type of renaissance that is at all possible in India. There is a closer resemblance to the recent Celtic movement in Ireland, the attempt of a reawakened national spirit to find a new impulse of self-expression which shall give the spiritual force for a great reshaping and rebuilding; in Ireland this was discovered by a return to the Celtic spirit and culture after a long period of eclipsing English influence, and in India something of the same kind of movement is appearing and has especially taken a pronounced turn since the political outburst of 1905 (*Renaissance in India*, pp. 2–3).

Aurobindo defines the European Renaissance as the rebirth of humanism, the recovery of the Greco-Roman "spirit" as he reads the events as the overthrow of Christian, Germanic, and feudal Europe. He sees this as radically different to the events taking place in India, and indeed, emphasizing difference, he finds the European developments inappropriate to describe what might occur in India. Clearly, for Aurobindo, renaissance, though inspired by its European origins, has become a term to describe "renewal" divorced from its European cultural matrix: "the attempt of a reawakened national spirit to find a new impulse of self-expression which shall give the spiritual force for a great reshaping and rebuilding" (*Renaissance in India*, p. 3).

Allegedly Rammohan Roy (1772–1833) first used the word "renaissance" about this Indian movement in the early nineteenth century, about the same time as it had first been applied to the European Renaissance by the French scholar, Jules Michelet (1798–1874). When Rammohan Roy said, "I began to think that something similar to the European Renaissance might have taken place here in India,"[6] he was describing the early nineteenth century in Bengal. The Bengali novelist Bankim Chandra Chatterji (1838–1894), in fact, often used the term renaissance to talk about the language and literature debates and production in Bengal in his contemporary nineteenth-century region. And at the end of the century, Aurobindo, in his essays on Bankim Chandra Chatterji, called the writer's period the Bengali Renaissance.[7]

Aurobindo's *The Renaissance in India* elaborated on what defined and distinguished the Indian Renaissance. This work examines the various aspects of the Indian Renaissance in contrast to Aurobindo's idea of Italy's, but he is primarily interested in defining what would constitute a uniquely Indian Renaissance. In this respect, before Antonio Gramsci had even developed his theory of cultural coercion, Aurobindo was expounding the idea that culture was a means for making, defining, and reenforcing "national identity," whether economic, cultural, or political.[8]

In Bengal, particularly, where the Indian movement began, the "Renaissance" originally involved debates and disputes about language and education; earnest efforts to recover ancient Indian culture (i.e. Vedic and Sanskrit); and the encounter with the new—in this case, European ideas, education, and culture. The introduction of printing presses and new universities and curriculum in the early nineteenth century in Bengal contributed to an astounding cultural transformation, all of which ironically prepared the way for the independence movement from the colonial powers. Together these spurred an unprecedented explosion of literary, philosophical, and intellectual production. However, I would argue that the Indian political struggle against the British Empire came to direct the intellectual passions and shape the positions adopted. In fact, in this regard a regional culture writ large (Bengali) unwittingly came to marginalize all the other regions of India.

The Bengali Renaissance, usually labeled the Indian Renaissance, contrasts with the Southern Indian Tamil Renaissance that began during the second half of the nineteenth century. While both regions shared a resurgence of interest in the recovery of ancient texts, where the Bengali Renaissance was strongly nationalist and its supporters intent on defining an all "Indian" identity, the Tamil Renaissance "encouraged the view that the Tamil-speaking people had a separate national identity." This even led some to espouse a separate "Dravidanad for Dravidians" movement.[9] Dravidian, a word found in Sanskrit texts, was deployed to describe the non-Brahmin Movement comprising Telegu, Kannada, Mayalayam, and Tamil speakers, whose culture was deemed independent of Sanskrit.[10] While many Indian historians see similarities between the Indian and the Italian Renaissance, they also recognize that both share the same problems of dating and characterization. Are these cultural, political, or social movements? When are the beginning and end dates? Just as the controversies surrounding dating the Italian Renaissance, spanning almost two hundred years, the Indian Renaissance spans from 1772 all the way to the late nineteenth century without clear dividing lines, because dates depend on a clear definition of what constitutes this Renaissance. Herein, of course, as Aurobindo recognizes, lies the difficulty of imposing the term "renaissance" on the specific "rebirth" that was taking place. But the most evident discourse about Renaissance in the adoption of the term emphasizes the "transcultural" or syncretic nature of the cultural developments in India.

The Italian and Indian Renaissances do share traits, the most important of which would be the recovery of classical or ancient culture. But, the nineteenth-century European intellectual efforts in India applied the methods of German philology to approach Sanskrit culture in a pattern that paralleled their interest in Greco-Roman and medieval culture. This intellectual activity began before the Northern Indians began to explore and study their own cultural roots following these same objective academic methods of the European Enlightenment. Like the Italian Renaissance, the Tamil Renaissance also had an important philological dimension, for the discovery of Tamil classics that began during the second half of the nineteenth century actually initiated the Tamil Renaissance. The cultural and political consequences are very different to those that characterize what is usually called the Indian Renaissance. For example, when U. V. Swaminatha Aiyar (1855–1942) recovered the palm-leaf manuscripts of the great Tamil epics, he contributed to building a cultural identity for the Tamil people. Like the recovery of *Beowulf* in England and the creation of an Anglo-Saxon identity or the link between Hebrew/Zionist national identity and the resurrection of ancient Hebrew in the nineteenth century, the resurfacing of the Tamil classics that demonstrated a brilliant Dravidian ancient civilization arguably separate and distinct from Sanskrit contributed to advancing the idea of a Dravidian identity, with a unique history and culture.

However, both the Southern and Northern Indian Renaissances were radically different from the Italian period because the Italian had no commercial or political component directed by an external colonial power, although European colonial expansion did occur during this period. The Italian writers and intellectuals during the Renaissance were not engaged in an anti-colonial struggle. Thus, in Italy, the Renaissance was an elite movement, spurred by innovators in the arts, letters, and philosophy. In India, partly because the movement began in Bengal, a center for Hinduism, Hindu intellectuals dominated the movement, and since the Muslim population did not participate, it is difficult to characterize it as a pan-Indian movement. The Tamil Renaissance coincided with the nationalist movement that was loyal to the idea of one-India but at the same time promoted the unique cultural identity of Tamil literature and language.[11] In actual fact, many Indian intellectuals in the period saw more similarity politically with Italy in the nineteenth century when Garibaldi struggled to unify Italy and overcome regionalism and foreign domination.[12]

Others have argued that if the Italian Renaissance is understood as a cultural phenomenon, its link to the Indian "reawakening" or Renaissance becomes even more tenuous. India underwent a transformation under the impact of Europe, but its Renaissance did not involve any imitation of Victorian English culture or ancient Greco-Roman culture, unlike the Italian version where resurrection of "authentic" Greco-Roman culture was one of the goals; furthermore, the Italian movement, which was regional at the inception, did not result in a nation or a definition of Italian identity, whereas the Indian movement, which also began in a region, had nation-building and identity-formation as its primary motives.[13]

Earlier studies of the Bengali Renaissance have discussed how the "idea" of the Italian Renaissance period was applied during this literary movement. There are obvious structural similarities between what was taking place in Bengal and had transpired in Italy: both cultures (Italian and Indian) have direct lines to ancient civilizations and were recovering that past; both upheld the language of their ancient civilization (Latin and Sanskrit or Tamil) as the language of religion and of revered literary traditions; both were engaged in establishing the vernacular language as the medium for literature and culture (the Florentine vernacular and Bengali). But, colonialism and the British occupation render the Indian situation radically different to the Italian.

Culture is of necessity interrelated with political and social developments, as Gramsci and others have reminded us.[14] Certainly, it cannot be denied that political and economic ideologies have played important parts in forging cultural developments, just as shifts in culture have affected politics and economics. Gauri Viswanathan's *Masks of Conquest: Literary Study and British Rule in India*[15] has persuasively demonstrated how the British as economic, military, and cultural occupants of India directed the education, religion, and morals of their new territories and occupied people. She has shown, to the surprise of many, that the canon of English literature was initially developed to "colonize the Indian mind." Although the British imposed a foreign curriculum to help conquer India culturally, it was ironically the colonizers themselves who promoted the recovery of ancient Sanskrit culture, which then became a central feature of the Bengali Renaissance, both a political and cultural endeavor.

Initially the work of English "intellectuals" living in Bengal, once adopted by Indian intellectuals, this Sanskrit recovery became a primary means to create a national ideology of the Indian people, with ancient roots, an ancient religion, and a tradition of political autonomy. Both the British and the Indians were involved in creating a "golden age" when Aryan Indians had ruled India. This narrow ideological construction of an ancient Aryan golden age excluded the role and contribution of the traditional (tribal) peoples, of Southern India with its equally ancient Tamil civilization, and of Buddhist, Jain, Sikh, Christian, Parsi, or the Islamic contribution to India's culture and history.

For the Indian intellectuals, produced by the Bengali movement, who dominated the cultural discourse of India, in this earlier time India had possessed ideological unity. Indian decline had led to the Islamic and later European colonial rule, both of which were held responsible for a multitude of ills, including the oppression of women. Aurobindo remarks that European scholars, who note the continuity in Indian civilization, wonder whether the term "renaissance" applies to India at all, since "it has always been awake and has no need for reawakening." But, Aurobindo argues that India's "children," among whom he counts himself, recognize "the great decline which came to a head in the eighteenth and nineteenth centuries" (*Renaissance in India*, pp. 4–5).

But, if we bracket the political aspects of the movement, central as they were to the period, perhaps it is possible to ascertain more particularly how this cultural reconfiguring intersected with the "idea" of the Italian Renaissance. Also, dividing the cultural from the political and social helps to identify distinctions between what we might view, using European terms, as Renaissance in contrast to the Enlightenment aspects of the developments. For example, figures like Raja Rammohan Roy, Henry Derozio (1809–1831) and the Young Bengal Movement, composed of teachers at the Hindu college, started by Hindu citizens in

Calcutta in 1817 to teach a "modern curriculum," and Chandra Vidyasagar (1820–1891) focused on social and political issues that in the West are more characteristic of the Enlightenment or nineteenth-century *risorgimento*. These primarily include issues of reform and independence from customs and social structures associated with the past. For India, issues of social caste and stratification as well as women's issues (particularly the elimination of *sati* [widow self-immolation] and other varieties of ill-treatment of widows), officially prohibited in 1829,[16] a particular focus of Rammohan Roy, came to the foreground as did educational reform, political and economic modernization, and liberation from the colonial powers. The writers adored "reason" above all. Thus, Derozio could write, "He who will not reason is a bigot; he who cannot is a fool, and he who does not is a slave."[17] One of the Young Bengals, Kissory Chand Mitra, wrote of Derozio:

> He felt it his duty as such to teach not only words but things to touch not only the head but the heart. He sought not to cram the mind but to inoculate it with large and liberal ideas. Acting on his principle, he opened the eyes of his pupils' understanding. He taught them to think, and to throw off the fetters of that antiquated bigotry which still clung to their countrymen. He possessed a profound knowledge of mental and moral philosophy and imparted it to them. Gifted with great penetration, he led them through the pages of Locke and Reid, Stuart and Brown.[18]

Products of a liberal, rationalist, Enlightenment tradition, these early figures of the Indian Renaissance focused on India and its liberation from age-old customs and servitude. For example, Vidyasagar, wrote, "The Brahmo Samaj [a movement initiated by Rammohan Roy] helped to emancipate India from medieval feudalism to national democracy, from blind faith and anti-social customs to knowledge and science, in a three-fold emancipation: intellectual and religious, social and moral, and political."[19] These attitudes show the influence of European education and a combination of Reformation and Enlightenment ideologies that have been transformed into an Indian idiom. For Aurobindo, writing about these developments almost a hundred years later, this period witnessed "a nadir of setting energy, the evening-time from which according to the Indian idea of the cycles a new age has to start. It was that moment and the pressure of a superimposed European culture which followed it that made the reawakening necessary" (*Renaissance in India*, p. 5).

Nonetheless, while the Hindu University, under the influence of Vidyasagar and Rammohan, wanted education designed along a European Enlightenment model, with European Math, History,

Sociology, Physics, and Chemistry the primary subjects, and Sanskrit was left out of the curriculum, the British orientalists were fascinated by India's past. Discovering that India had books and poetry as old or older than Ancient Greece contributed to constructing a "Renaissance" along the lines of the European humanist recovery of ancient Greece and Rome. It is an ironic detail of the Indian Renaissance of classical Sanskrit that the revival of Indian classical studies came to Indians as a reaction to their western university curriculum.[20] When we look more strictly at the cultural dimensions of this time, however, we will see why the writers saw themselves as part of a movement that they called "renaissance." Like Petrarch, looking at the past with a sense of historical rupture, Rabindranath Tagore would write of India before its "renaissance," "India was in a death-like sleep. Her life was dried up, and it showed all those dead and forgotten customs, superstitions, all the ignorance and fear, all feuds, all bitterness and separateness."[21] In 1892, Tagore wrote about Chatterji:

> Standing at a point where two ages met we could instantaneously realize what went before and what we had afterwards. Whither departed that darkness, that confusion, that somnolence . . . whence appeared so much light, so much hope, so much music, so much color.[22]

While it is clear that the Bengali Renaissance was strongly nationalist politically, it was nonetheless internationalist culturally. Although it opposed the West politically and economically, it was open to the West culturally. At the same time, it searched anew its own ancient Sanskrit traditions for a golden age of origins that would reestablish Indian cultural foundations; it embraced the Bengali language, revered classical Sanskrit as the access to the past, and recognized English as a *lingua franca* that was necessary socially, politically, and also culturally. Thus, like the writers of the Italian Renaissance (and here clearly Renaissance reaches back to the beginning of the fourteenth century, for these Indian writers include Dante in their discussions), the Bengali writers embraced the possibilities of their own vernacular for literary production that was regional, but when they thought about their role as international writers, they demurred to the power of the international language, in this case English. Like their Italian precursors, they reconstructed the ancient world, but the Bengali writers were more particularly interested in the rupture from their ancient religious culture created by the impact of Europe and Islam. The advent of the European encounter had ushered in alienation from the past normally associated with modernism. Like

Petrarch, Valla, Erasmus, and other humanists who imagined early Christianity as a pristine form of the religion in contrast to its contemporary corruption, Vivekananda, Aurobindo, and Tagore saw in ancient "Hinduism" a way to overcome the descent into empty pieties and cruel customs to which they felt their ancient religion had descended. The rediscovery and to some degree the invention of Hinduism as a religion along the lines of Christianity and Judaism[23] was a cultural means to counter the impact of Christian missionaries who highlighted the failures of contemporary Hindu practice.

Sri Aurobindo's treatise sets out to define an Indian identity, a unique "Indianness," as he argues for an Indian nation conceptualized in European terms. Clearly a "hybrid" cultural and political situation, it is, nonetheless, a "hybridity" that is a direct result of the colonial experience. This syncretism resulted both from conscious adoption and reaction to an imposed external culture. The transcultural environment did not replace a "pure" Indian culture (that never had existed); rather it developed from the multiple Indian cultures that themselves possessed many diverse and syncretist features. The term "renaissance" describes the phenomenology of this transcultural situation in which Indian intellectuals during the colonial period tried to define themselves and their moment in history.

Aurobindo, in some ways typical of the Northern Indian intellectual of the period, was the child of a Bengali Anglophile, and had been raised speaking English and educated in a Catholic convent school in India. His father, eager to ensure his son's Englishness, sent him to England to continue his studies at Manchester Grammar School and then at St. Paul's in London. Later, at Cambridge, this outstanding student won the Greek and Latin prize. In training for the Indian Civil Service, he had already developed strong anti-British colonialism convictions even before he left St. Paul's, but at Cambridge he nonetheless continued to follow the course for his intended career as a British-Indian civil servant despite the fact that he was bored by the studies and found Indian Civil Service students uncultivated mediocrities. Ironically, he never took his degree at Cambridge because he failed the riding test that was required for the ICS credential. He had begun to write poetry in English while a teenager in England. Immersed in European literary traditions from the ancient to the modern periods, he was multilingual in European languages and knew European poetry as his own tradition. He taught himself Italian to read Dante in the original. K. K. Sharma wrote of Aurobindo's poetics:

> In short, Sri Aurobindo's poetics is the natural corollary of his strikingly original creative mind plus variegated influences that his receptive mind

felt from time to time in India as well as abroad. Thus on his aesthetic vision can be perceived the impact of Homer, Aristophanes, Dante, Goethe, French poets, Shakespeare, the *Upanishads*, the *Gita*, the *Ramayana*, the *Mahabharata*, Kalidasa, Bhavbhuti, Rabindranath Tagore, Ramkrishna Paramhansa, Vivekanand, the Indian aesthetic tradition, the Greco-Latin and French traditions, and above all, the Indian spiritual tradition and his own spiritual and intellectual experiences.[24]

Global before "globalism" was a buzzword, Aurobindo's aesthetic and philosophical canon testifies to his multicultural intellectual formation. Despite his immersion in European culture, when Aurobindo returned to India in 1893, he set about learning Bengali and Sanskrit, languages he had only studied at Cambridge while training for the Indian Civil Service, as part of the necessary training of an Indian civil servant.[25] In Bengal, in the midst of the Swadeshi Movement (a boycott of British goods movement) in the early part of the twentieth century, he became passionately engaged in the political movement that he hoped would lead to Indian independence from England. He was a revolutionary organizer, political journalist, and one of the leaders of the nationalist party labeled by history the "Extremists."[26] But he faced radical failure in the political sphere, which eventually sent him to prison. That experience, however, led to a spiritual quest that sent Aurobindo back to the literary roots of the Hindu traditions. When he was in prison he had one of many mystical experiences, the consequences of which were to turn him toward the spiritual traditions of his birthplace and to study Sanskrit and Hindu spiritual writings. This led to his commitment to philosophy, to Indian spiritual traditions, and to literature.

One of the features of Indian Renaissances that particularly distinguish them from the Italian Renaissance is what might be labeled "the search for identity," for just as the quest for deeper knowledge of the ancient civilization is underway, and India's political and social status is scrutinized in this period, so too are these efforts accompanied by an interrogation of Indian identity, both in the Tamil Renaissance and the Bengali Renaissance. This is, in fact, the primary topic of Aurobindo's treatise on the *Renaissance in India*. Written at least a hundred years after the height of what was labeled the Indian Renaissance, and in the middle of what would lead to India's independence from Britain, Aurobindo probes India's identity in the context of cultural and political reawakening.

A number of essays or books dealing with renaissance in India appeared in the early twentieth century. Written by British Indologists including Charles Freer Andrews and James H. Cousins, they referred to an "Indian awakening," conceptualizing India as a single unified culture, along the lines of the "imagined communities" of the United Kingdom or France. In addition, and importantly, it was Indian intellectuals who often saw the awakening as an escape from darkness to light, as in the passage from Tagore quoted above. The Europeans, who were immersed in classical Indian studies rejected the notion that India was rediscovering its spiritual roots, arguing that India had never abandoned its ancient traditions.[27] In this respect, these British indologists followed a typical western approach to "literary canons" which, as Aijaz Ahmad puts it, is held together by a

> preference for religion and metaphysics, so that it is said to exude, transhistorically, some essential Indianness in the form of an abiding spiritual ethos. This privileging of antiquity and preponderant citation of Sanskrit classics as the unique repertoire of "Indian Literature,"

Ahmad argues, is found not only in German orientalists like Friedrich Schlegel but is also celebrated by Indians, the most eminent of whom is Sri Aurobindo.[28] Aurobindo took the position that the reawakening was necessary because the British had both imposed a European view of culture on India and then defined what was characteristic of India. Thus Aurobindo would write,

> What was this ancient spirit and characteristic soul of India? European writers, struck by the general metaphysical bent of the Indian mind, by its strong religious instincts and religious idealism, by its other-worldliness, are inclined to write as if this is the Indian spirit. An abstract, metaphysical, religious mind overpowered by the sense of the infinite, not apt for life, dreamy, impractical, turning away from life and action as Maya, and this, they say, is India; and for a time Indians in this as in other matters submissively echoed their new Western teachers and masters (*Renaissance in India*, p. 7).

This "not apt for life, dreamy, impractical, turning away from life" Indian identity, of course, looks like an invitation for a disciplined army to appear and take on the practical management of life. In other words, the English cultural definition of India and Indianness provides a rationale for the colonial adventure. Aurobindo, nonetheless, sets out to redirect this characterization of the "Indian identity" both against the European definition of India and in keeping with his own "essentialist" spiritual reading of India's cultural history.

In *The Renaissance in India*, Aurobindo describes a brilliant ancient India where "spirituality," "the sense of the infinite," was "the master-key of the Indian mind" (*Renaissance in India*, p. 9). The ages of the Vedas, of the dharma, and of the Upanishads undergird this scintillating and defining past (*Renaissance in India*, pp. 9–22). But, he writes, "Undoubtedly there was a period, a brief but very disastrous period of the dwindling of that great fire of life, even a moment of incipient disintegration, marked politically by the anarchy which gave European adventure its chance, inwardly by an increasing torpor of the creative spirit in religion and art, science and philosophy and intellectual knowledge had long been dead" (*Renaissance in India*, p. 5). He sees this moment of European adventure as the rationale for the Indian Renaissance (*Renaissance in India*, p. 5).

For Aurobindo, India's Renaissance was a new age of an old culture transformed, not an affiliation of a newborn civilization to one that is old and dead, but a true rebirth, a renascence. Its three dimensions and stages included: (1) the reception of European contact leading to a radical rejection of India's past; the followers welcomed the modernization of India, and while patriotic in spirit "they were denationalized in their mental attitude" (*Renaissance in India*, p. 36); (2) then followed the reaction of what Aurobindo called "the Indian spirit" against the European influence and an unflinching reassertion of "Indian" values; and (3) as Aurobindo put it,

> only now beginning or recently begun, is rather a process of new creation in which the spiritual power of the Indian mind remains supreme, recovers its truths, accepts whatever it finds sound or true, useful or inevitable of the modern idea and form, but so transmutes and indianises it, so absorbs and so transforms it entirely into itself that its foreign character disappears and it becomes another harmonious element in the characteristic working of the ancient goddess, the Shakti of India mastering and taking possession of modern influence, no longer possessed or overcome by it" (*Renaissance in India*, pp. 32–3).

The three stages represent a "subtle assimilation and fusing" that recovered the old without overriding the new critical perspective (*The Renaissance in India*, p. 42).

This is a very revealing description for a number of reasons. First, Aurobindo recognized that a rebirth had been occurring in India beginning with the reception of Europe and rejection of certain features of Indian cultural practices. This was followed by an intellectual rebellion against European culture, and finally a new culture was emerging that had absorbed European culture, recovered India's cultural origins, and "indianised" (his word) what could be learned from Europe. It is the third element that he links to India's Renaissance. Recognizing the political meaning of these developments, Aurobindo described this development as follows:

> All that is as yet clear is that the first period of a superficial assimilation and aping of European political ideas and methods is over. Another political spirit has awakened in the people under the shock of the movement of the last decade, which, vehemently national in its motive, proclaimed a religion of Indian patriotism, applied the notions of the ancient religion and philosophy to politics, expressed the cult of the country as mother and Shakti and attempted to base the idea of democracy firmly on the spiritual thought and impulses native to the Indian mind (*The Renaissance in India*, pp. 60–1).

Here he refers to the Swadeshi Movement that both he and Tagore rejected on the grounds that it imitated violent European political nationalist movements even though it was spurred by Indian nationalism and incorporated Indian traditions. Aurobindo adheres to an almost rigid, essentialized definition of what it is to be a "reawakened" Indian. Following a Manichaean, Fanon-like dichotomy between Europe and the other, he also reflects Said's "orientalist" notion, the rigid divide between East and West, with India always the location of a deeper spirituality, that becomes the foundation for self-definition of the Indian nation and the Indian mind.[29] Furthermore, Aurobindo's engagement in this intellectual imaginary project also reflects Said's argument about the complicity of intellectuals in political plans: here, of course, we see "orientalism" promoted by an Indian intellectual, even though Aurobindo sees this "essentialized" and "indianized" psychology as a source of political strength,[30] the place to apply a critical interrogation of the "superimposed European culture." "We have now," he writes,

> in emergence an increasing sense of the necessity of a renovation of social ideas and expressive forms by the spirit of the nation awaking to the deeper yet unexpressed implications of its own culture, but as yet no sufficient will or means of execution. It is probable that only with the beginning of a freer national life will the power of the renaissance take effective hold of the social mind and action of the awakened people (*Renaissance in India*, pp. 62–3).

Thus, although clearly an Indian nationalist, Aurobindo is nonetheless arguing for nation in the European mode and seeing this emerging "nation" as the result of a renaissance. As Benedict Anderson puts it in describing nation-making in general, what we see played out in the case of Aurobindo, is "the objective modernity of nations to the historian's eyes", but "the subjective antiquity in the eyes of nationalists."[31] Aurobindo is in the process of imagining an Indian nation along very specific lines, and thus reflects Anderson's idea that "Nationalism is not the awakening of nations to self-consciousness; it invents nations where they do not exist."[32] Also, in terms of "identity" formation, we have to view Aurobindo's Fanon-like dichotomy critically, as indeed argued by Homi Bhabha, "Such binary, two-part, identities function in a kind of narcissistic reflection of the Other in the Other" because identity is never a fixed entity, nor as Bhabha suggests "a finished project."[33] Still, it must be recognized that Aurobindo's "orientalism" had anticolonialist purposes. We should be hesitant to criticize this nation-making ideology or this "orientalized" self-definition of a "spiritualized indianness," because we have to remember the colonial situation and anticolonial struggle in which these notions were germinating under the rubric of Indian Renaissance. His dominant language of "fusion," "transmutation," "absorption," "transformation," and "assimilation" reveal how aware he was of a turning "yuga" or age, in which long past and recent history were being played out in a present that brought many cultural and political developments together to serve the overriding purposes of awaking Indians to their "denationalized mental attitude," the direct result of the "superimposed European culture."

The term "Renaissance" is clearly very slippery, and not just in its European setting. Its use in this context highlights its plasticity and capacity to be reshaped for diverse cultural settings. The way some nineteenth-century Indian writers use it, it applies to what we normally characterize as Enlightenment or even modernism, suggesting that the division between medieval and renaissance has even less force than convention claims for it. Because these Indian cultural architects used it to describe social and political reforms and to advance the cause of reasonable understanding, it parallels developments in the eighteenth and nineteenth centuries in Europe. When they discuss cultural parallelisms, that is, issues of language, recovery of ancient texts and philosophy, and religious reform, they are clearly connecting their enterprise with Italian Renaissance, the Reformation, and Counter-Reformation. It is especially important to note that in this regard divisions between Dante, for example, and Petrarch are lost amidst the debate over the role of the mother language in Bengal, as the writers cite the developments of the Italian Renaissance when they believed (based of course on Dante's work) that the mother tongue was adopted for literature. Still, like the early Italian humanists, these writers are also interested in the purity of the ancient language and reestablishing its cultural status. Among the writers of the Bengali Renaissance, the term renaissance also most definitively refers to reckoning with the gap between present and past, and the questioning and reconfiguring of past traditions, whether of culture, society, religion, or politics.

In arguing for the overturning of superstitions and primitive customs, expanding educational opportunities, providing rights for women and untouchables, and debating the future of technology, and so on, the focus of Indian intellectuals has more in common with European Enlightenment than Renaissance. Even more importantly, the recovery of ancient Indian Sanskrit culture and the religion to which it belonged became a primary tool for redefining Indian identity in a nationalist, anticolonial struggle. The recovery of ancient Tamil culture, which is in the foreground of the Tamil Renaissance, on the other hand, introduced a powerful challenge to the hegemony of a Sanskrit-defined Indian identity, even while its architects still remained loyal to the one-India political and anticolonial position of the period. Thus, it is clear that the entire cultural, social, and political agenda covered by the term "renaissance" applied in India buries the European period distinctions between Medieval, Renaissance, and Enlightenment.

With this model, what happens to Frank Kermode's "transhistorical canons and historical periods"?[34] The European term, Renaissance, itself a convention based on one of what Kermode suggests are imaginative classifying structures, has been applied to wholly different sets of circumstances. The Indian model seems to follow Jacques Le Goff's idea of the Middle Ages, in which the ancient world ends with the collapse of the Roman Empire and the Middle Ages spans from then until the Industrial Revolution, and then the Modern period emerges.[35] Translated to India, this would make the age of the Vedas and Sanskrit and Tamil epics the ancient world, followed by a thousand or so intervening years that include Moghul and British domination, and the Modern period emerging in the early nineteenth century with the Bengali and Tamil Renaissances. The fact that the Indian movement evolved to become tightly linked to the intellectual struggle against the colonial powers also distinguishes it radically from the European or Italian Renaissance. Central features of the movement were social modernization, nation-building, and identity- formation, which would link the Indian Renaissance to similar movements in Ireland, Italy, and Egypt in the same period, for example.

Thus, terms like ancient, early modern, and modern as broad categories, indeed, may prove more useful both within the European and other cultural environments to describe cultural phenomena like the Indian Renaissance. "Renaissance" under these circumstances would become an epistemology rather than a period, for it would describe a cultural happening that could occur anywhere and anytime in contrast to its rigid and fixed use to describe what happened at a given moment in European cultural history. Such terms also provide a global model for talking about literature. In the case of formerly colonized countries, however, literary division must of necessity also follow a political model that includes precolonial, colonial, and postcolonial or neo-colonial periods, that no doubt coincide with the broader spectrum that divides ancient, early modern, modern, and now neo-modern.

Notes

1. Some of the points made in this essay about the Bengali Renaissance have already appeared in my essay, "Dante in India: Sri Aurobindo and *Savitri*," *Dante Studies* 120 (2002): 83–98. See David Kopf, *British Orientalism and the Bengal Renaissance: The Dynamics of Indian Modernization 1773–1835* (Berkeley, CA: University of California Press, 1969); David Kopf and Safiuddin Joarder, Eds. *Reflections on the Bengal Renaissance* (Dacca: Bangladesh Books, 1977); Kalyan Sengupta and Tirthanath Bandyopadhyay, Eds. *Nineteenth Century Thought in Bengal* (Jadavpur: Allied Publishers, 1998); B. R. Purkait, *Indian Renaissance and Education* (Calcutta: Firma KLM, 1992); Bijoy Bhattacharya, *Bengal Renaissance: A Study in the Progress of English Education (1800–1858)* (Calcutta: P. Sen, 1963).

2. Kopf, *British Orientalism and the Bengal Renaissance.*

3. N. Nambi Arooran, *Tamil Renaissance and Dravidian Nationalism* (Madurai: Koodal Publishers, 1980), pp. 2–4.

4. Homi Bhabha, *The Location of Culture* (London: Routledge, 1994).

5. Aurobindo Ghose, *The Renaissance in India* (Calcutta: Arya Publishing, 1920). Hereafter page number in text.

6. Quoted in G. Smith, *Life of Alexander Duff* (New York: A. C. Armstrong and Son, 1879), 1, p. 118.

7. Kopf, "Introduction," in *Reflections on the Bengal Renaissance*, p. 4.

8. Antonio Gramsci's *Gli Intellettuali e l'Organizzazione della Cultura* (Turin: Einaudi, 1955), written in 1930, develops this idea (p. 9). His notion was further expanded by Pierre Bourdieu, *L'Amore dell'Arte: I Musei d'arte europei e il loro pubblico* (Rimini: Guaraldi, 1972; orig. *L'amour de l'art: Les musées d'art européens et leur public* [Paris: Editions de Minuit, 1969]).

9. N. Nambi Arooran, *Tamil Renaissance and Dravidian Nationalism* p. 13.

10. Ibid., p. 35.

11. Ibid., p. 58.

12. D. P. Chattopadhyaya, "Raja Rammohun Roy: A New Appraisal," in *Nineteenth Century Thought in Bengal*, Eds. Kalyan Sengupta and Tirthanath Bandyopadhyay (Jadavpur: Allied Publishers, 1998), pp. 9–10.

13. Rajat Kanta Ray, *Exploring Emotional History: Gender, Mentality and Literature in the Indian Awakening* (Oxford: Oxford University Press, 2001), p. 33.

14. Gramsci, *Gli Intellettuali e l'Organizzazione della Cultura*; Edward Said, *Orientalism* (New York: Vintage Books, 1979); Edward Said, *Culture and Imperialism* (New York: Alfred Knopf, 1993); Benedict Anderson's *Imagined Communities* (London: Verso, 1983).

15. Gauri Viswanathan's *Masks of Conquest: Literary Study and British Rule in India* (Oxford: Oxford University Press, 1998).

16. Lata Mani, *Contentious Traditions: The Debate on Sati in Colonial India* (Berkeley, CA.: University of California Press, 1998).

17. Purkait, *Indian Renaissance*, p. 18.

18. As quoted in Bhabatosh Datta, *Resurgent Bengal: Rammohun, Bankimchandra, Rabindranath* (Calcutta: Minerva, 2000), p. 61.

19. Purkait, *Indian Renaissance*, p. 49.

20. Datta, *Resurgent Bengal*, pp. 62–3.

21. Purkait, *Indian Renaissance*, p. 47.

22. Rabindranath Tagore, *Rabindra Rachanavali* 10 (Calcutta: Government of West Bengal, 1984), p. 215.

23. For the creation of the term "Hinduism" to denote the religion of India, see Richard King, "The Modern Myth of 'Hinduism,' " *Orientalism and Religion: Postcolonial Theory, India and* "The *Mystic East*" (London: Routledge, 1999), pp. 96–117.

24. K. K. Sharma, "Poetry as 'The Mantra of the Real,' " in *Sri Aurobindo: Critical Considerations*, Ed. O. P. Mathur (Bara Bazar, Bareilly: Prakash Book Depot, 1997), pp. 65–80, esp. p. 66.

25. Peter Heehs, *Sri Aurobindo: A Brief Biography* (Delhi: Oxford University Press, 1989), pp. 14–17.

26. Heehs, *Sri Aurobindo*, pp. 38–50.

27. Ray, *Exploring Emotional History*, p. 31.

28. Aijaz Ahmad, *In Theory: Classes, Nations, Literatures* (London: Verso, 1992), p. 257.

29. Said, *Orientalism*, p. 150.

30. Ibid., p. 99. See also, Robert Young, *White Mythologies: Writing History and the West* (London: Routledge, 1990), pp. 126–40, for an interrogation of Said's unwillingness to offer an alternative to "orientalism."

31. Anderson, *Imagined Communities*, p. 5.

32. Anderson, *Imagined Communities*, p. 6.

33. Bhabha, *Location of Culture*, p. 51.

34. Frank Kermode, "Canon and Period," in *History and Value: The Clarendon Lectures and the Northcliffe Lectures* (Oxford: Clarendon, 1988), p. 109.

35. Jacques Le Goff, *Medieval Civilization*, trans. Julia Barrow (Oxford: Basil Blackwell, 1988).

CHAPTER 7

Irish Renaissance

Kathleen Heininge

Critics have several names for the movement that took place in Ireland at the turn of the twentieth century. Each name seems to suggest a different interpretation of the events at that time, and each interpretation, in turn, reflects a different idea of Ireland's relationship with the rest of the world. The Irish Revival, a term most often used to discuss the literary movement, implies that the greatness of a people can be resuscitated after it has been nearly lost, and is thus a term in keeping with a nationalist agenda. The Celtic Twilight, a term coined by W. B. Yeats, is a more sentimental and mystical rendering that suggests the illumination and reinterpretation of a previously underappreciated culture, and is a term in keeping with the transition from a romanticized concept of tradition to a modernist consciousness. The Irish Renaissance seems to be the term currently used most often, a term that appears to acknowledge the colonial (and postcolonial) implications of Irish history. Implying rebirth and renewal, a new beginning rather than a resuscitation, the term "renaissance" carries plenty of political resonance especially when deployed to refer to a movement that coincides with the various cultural elements of nationalism beyond literature. In fact, the use of "renaissance" seems to conflate the events that move from nationalism, through modernity, to postcolonialism. There is, then, a certain tension in the ways these terms are deployed, particularly when we examine the terms against each other and against the way "renaissance" is used traditionally.

The term "renaissance" is most often applied to the intellectual shift that characterizes a grossly oversimplified transition from the Middle

Ages to the modern world that took place between the fourteenth and the sixteenth century in Europe. This period is also often marked with an interest, sometimes bordering on obsession, with the classics, and a devaluation of national languages and culture. This aspect of "renaissance" thinking is fraught with tension because of the apparent paradox between the concerns with classic form and the desire for greater freedom of expression, a paradox that creates its own form of tyranny. This particular kind of tyranny is often at work in nationalist movements, where those who are involved in furthering nationalist agendas may become intolerant toward any ideas that may wend away from their own, a feature that characterizes the Reformation and the Counter-Reformation as well, both movements linked to nationalist agendas, particularly as they expressed themselves in England, Spain, Switzerland, and the Netherlands during the European Renaissance.

The very investment involved in choosing a term to describe what was taking place in Ireland indicates the kind of tension that is at work. Critical and historical interpretations of Irish history are, of course, guided by the motivations and positions of those doing the interpreting. A nationalist and literary perspective (which tends to prefer the term "Revival") is that past glory has been lost and is now returning, and that return can be hastened by embracing Irish thought and language. A modernist perspective (which tends to prefer the term "Celtic Twilight") is that there is and always has been a firm but undervalued national tradition, a tradition "of the people," albeit a tradition that benefits from a new perspective. A postcolonial perspective (which seems to align itself with the term "Renaissance") is that the glory has been previously usurped or quelled and is now being reclaimed and brought back to life; while still a nationalist perspective, this includes all aspects of Irish life, not just literary. The differences are subtle, but I do believe that they exist. Each term tells only part of the story about what happened in Ireland at the turn of the twentieth century, but "Renaissance," as rebirth, does seem to take into account a more comprehensive and political notion of what actually took place.

The tension that plays among these terms is best understood by looking at the discrepancies in critical evaluations of the events. Little agreement exists about when the nationalist movement really began (as there is little agreement about when or even if modernity arrived in Ireland). Some, including W. B. Yeats, believe that nationalism truly began after the huge political scandal of 1891, when the Church denounced Charles Stewart Parnell, the dynamic and influential leader of the Home Rule movement, for his affair with a married woman, Kitty O'Shea. Parnell's career effectively ended at its apex, with subsequent political rambling centered on the issue of Parnell's immorality rather than on the viability of Home Rule. The disappointment resulted in factionalism that remained at work throughout much of the twentieth century, a factionalism most famously illustrated in James Joyce's *A Portrait of the Artist as a Young Man* when an argument about Parnell destroys the family's Christmas dinner. While the Home Rule movement was indeed part of a nationalist movement already in place, the country became much more vocal and engaged after the Parnell scandal, when the issue expanded beyond the battle between England and Ireland to between Church and Nation.

Looking back on the events of that time, Yeats wrote in 1923:

> The modern literature of Ireland, and indeed all that stir of thought which prepared for the Anglo-Irish war, began when Parnell fell from power in 1891. A disillusioned and embittered Ireland turned from parliamentary politics; an event was conceived; and the race began, as I think, to be troubled by that event's long gestation. [1]

This is a stance that often includes seeing the Easter Rising of 1916 as the culmination of nationalism, and the events between that Rising and the Treaty of 1922 that separated Ireland into north and south as the failure of that nationalism. Yeats was not alone in this valuation, but although the sectarian split that came about as a result of Parnell's disgrace certainly added impetus to the nationalist movement, it did not cause the political upheaval that resulted in the Renaissance; the Renaissance was foreshadowed long before Parnell even rose to power.

Robert Fallis divides his book, *The Irish Renaissance,*[2] according to specific dates, and believes that the Renaissance began in 1880, and the Celtic Twilight in 1890, distinguishing between the two without examining the way the two movements overlap and without discussing the ways that nationalism intersects with these terms. Other critics believe that the nationalist movement began in "the mid-1880s, as a group of young, mostly Anglo-Irish cultural nationalists gathered around the aging revolutionary John O'Leary, and that it ended around the time of the establishment of the puritanical Irish Free State in 1922."[3] Some believe, acknowledging that Yeats was key to the idea of the Celtic Twilight, that the more specific date of 1885, when O'Leary and Yeats met, signifies the Literary Revival. The opinions seem to rely on which aspect of the Renaissance a critic wishes to address and often neglect to consider the fact that there was tremendous overlap in a multitude of events and arenas.

However, clear signs of a nationalist trend appear long before the end of the nineteenth century. The famine of the 1840s marked a change in thinking about Irishness and power; the certainty that England could not be relied upon for support was driven home to many, and autonomy was more desirable than ever. The nationalist magazine, *The Nation*, was published by Thomas Davis and Charles Gavan Duffy in 1842, and the Young Ireland movement began, although even that had its origins in Daniel O'Connell's push to repeal the 1800 Irish Act of Union with Great Britain and his achievement in 1829 to allow Catholics to sit in the United Kingdom Parliament. Davis believed, however, in uniting the literary, cultural, historical, and linguistic in a nondenominational nationalism, taking O'Connell's vision further than O'Connell had imagined. The recognition that Ireland needed to be able to stand alone, to rule itself, was gaining attention. Disagreement over how to bring that about prevented consensus, and tensions over secularism and the use of violence grew. Although Davis died in 1846 and O'Connell in 1847, those who followed, calling themselves the Young Irelanders, led a botched uprising in 1848, finally causing the group to disband. Many of the members later joined the Fenians.

The Irish Republican Brother (IRB) grew from the Fenian movement of the 1860s, focusing on active revolution. Their concern was to wrest control from the British and the Protestant landowners. The Sinn Fein movement centered on politics, intending to change the way industry, agriculture, and the constitution functioned in Ireland. The labor movement, led by James Connolly, attended to the workers, hoping to unite them to support Irish industry and change the Parliament. The claims that Connolly made for his Party are consistent with the desires of many leaders in the past, including Michael Davitt (leader of the Land League), Parnell, and Daniel O'Connell. Writing in 1896, Connolly exhorted:

> Fellow workers—the struggle for Irish freedom has two aspects: it is national and it is social. Its national ideal can never be realized until Ireland stands forth before the world, a nation free and independent. It is social and economic; because no matter what the form of government may be, as long as one class own as their private property the land and instruments of labor, from which all mankind derive their subsistence, that class will always have it in their power to plunder and enslave the remainder of their fellow creatures.[4]

The idea of a nationalism that extended to all facets of Irish life never quite died, however. Nationalism was no longer merely a political stance. Nonetheless, each organization was separatist in its goals and approaches, and intolerance became the rift that prevented true effectiveness.

In 1884, Michael Cusack founded the Gaelic Athletic Association (GAA) in an effort to promote Irish sports, fearing that the traditional games were being forgotten. Not only did he want to revive hurling and Gaelic football, but he also wanted to include the "man of the street" in athletics, promoting sports for those other than the leisure classes. While the first two objectives of the association were to organize Irish sports by Irish men and to set up official rules for Irish gaming, the third and final objective was much more inclusive: "To devise schemes of recreation for Irish people." With that objective, the GAA involved itself in much more than simply sports, producing literary and propagandist pamphlets, financing speakers, and encouraging both child and adult education about Irish music, dance, and language.

One of the coincident (and tyrannical) endeavors of the Renaissance was the revival of the Irish language. The Irish language had fallen into disuse for practical and economic reasons; leaders as far back as Daniel O'Connell insisted that the people could not succeed even within Ireland because the English held most of the real power, and the English did not understand (and had no intention of learning) Irish. In order to remain economically viable participants in their own country, to say nothing of the rest of the world, Irish citizens learned English. In colonial practice, the ruling people impose their language on the colonized, partly for fear of allowing communication (and subversive behavior) in a language that the colonizers cannot understand. By many accounts, children were punished for speaking Irish, and teachers were punished for teaching Irish, presumably ensuring that future generations would not be exposed to Irish. Documents such as Douglas Hyde's "The Necessity for De-Anglicising Ireland," published in 1894,[5] insist that the Irish people should "cultivate what they have rejected, and build up an Irish nation on Irish lines,"[6] in turn rejecting England and all things English. Supporting the foundation in 1893 of the Gaelic League, Hyde exhorted the Irish to revive the language that they had forsaken:

> We must teach ourselves to be less sensitive, we must teach ourselves not to be ashamed of ourselves, because the Gaelic people can never produce its best before the world as long as it remains tied to the apron-strings of another race and another island, waiting for *it* to move before it will venture to take any step itself.[7]

He foresaw that the advent of a new Irish education would be tied to the language itself, that a people's consciousness could be forged anew by thinking in a different language, and that ultimately the salvation of the Irish people would come about through a literature in the native language. His position was nonnegotiable, intolerant of any other points of view, and in his extremism he had difficulty convincing large numbers of people to his vision. The revival of the Irish language as a practical tool for everyday life has largely devolved into an academic exercise outside of certain parts of Ireland known as the Gaeltacht, where only Irish is spoken. It is suggested in many Irish language classrooms, however, that as an academic exercise, Irish is taught to more Irish people today than at any other time in history, as people study it all over the world. The argument is whether the language is living or dead, an argument that becomes that much more interesting when we consider again that many in renaissance movements value classical languages over idiomatic or national languages. Latin and Greek, both languages that were deader than Irish in the nineteenth century, were taught by the English-run schools, an irony that was not lost on the people of Ireland. If Irish is a dead language, does it become a "classic" language? Is it the national language if most of the people in the nation are not fluent in it? The majority of people who are thought to be central to the Renaissance had no Irish; were they, then, not really participating in a renaissance?

While the political, sporting, and linguistic threads of the nationalist movement were being woven, so was the artistic thread. While there were certainly Irish artists, such as Sir William Orpen, Walter Frederick Osborne, Paul Henry, and John Lavery, who were making names for themselves, they were often products of English or French art schools, and the influence showed. Their artwork had nothing especially Irish about it. Seán Keating, a student of Orpen, began to be drawn to Irish subjects somewhat, but his work at first tended to the realistic and the political. Jack Yeats, brother to William Butler Yeats, is the artist credited by many with having been the first truly "Irish" artist, depicting the life of rural, peasant Ireland in ways that no one had done before. His father, John Butler Yeats, painted portraits with a modicum of success, but Jack painted scenes of funerals, of horses, of swimming races on the Liffey (the river that runs through Dublin), of boxing matches, of people on the street. Bruce Arnold claims that Yeats saved Ireland "from nineteenth-century caricature and gave it an embodiment which was serious, and which lasted. It is within the purpose and the act of doing this that a substantial part of his greatness lies."[8] Later, artists such as Keating and Henry also began to draw from the west of Ireland for their subject matter, and the very idea of Irish painting changed.

The artistic vein clearly ran in the Yeats family, and although W. B. Yeats is the better-known brother for his contributions to the Revival, he does not represent the beginning of the literary nationalist movement. Much evidence exists to the contrary. In the late 1850s, Dion Boucicault wrote plays that began to support nationalist goals, rejecting the formulaic representations of the Irish that had been the tradition in plays written by the British and even in his own earlier plays. In the theater, the stage Irishman depicted a version of Irishness that the world consumed before the Irish had a say, most often portrayed in English drama as a figure of comedy, with his drinking and his "abuse" of the English language and his endless cheerfulness masking an underlying insidiousness. C. G. Duggan has quite thoroughly traced the history of the stage Irish figure in English-speaking drama (primarily that written by the British) from its earliest manifestations up through the first third of the twentieth century, giving the most complete analysis of who that figure is. Quoting a publication in 1913, Duggan tells us:

> The Stage Irishman habitually bears the general name of Pat, Paddy or Teague. He has an atrocious Irish brogue, perpetual jokes, blunders and bulls in speaking, and never fails to utter, by way of Hibernian seasoning, some wild screech or oath of Gaelic origin at every third word: he has an unsurpassable gift of blarney and cadges for tips and free drinks. His hair is of a fiery red: he is rosy-cheeked, massive, and whiskey loving. His face is one of simian bestiality with an expression of diabolical archness written all over it. He wears a tall felt hat (billicock or wideawake), with a cutty-clay pipe stuck in front, an open shirt collar, a three caped coat, knee breeches, worsted stockings, and cockaded brogue-shoes. In his right hand he brandishes a stout blackthorn, or a sprig of shillelagh, and threatens to belabour therewith the daring person who will tread on the tails of his coat. For his main characteristics (if there is any such thing as psychology in the Stage Irishman) are his swagger, his boisterousness and his pugnacity. He is always ready with a challenge, always anxious to back a quarrel, and peerless for cracking skulls at Donnybrook Fair. . . . The first stage representation of Irishmen was clearly drawn from the life.[9]

The fact that, as late as 1937, Duggan could think that this representation was true to life tells something about the pervasiveness of such representations, images which, it is important to point out, people other than the Irish were perpetrating. These are the versions of "Irishness" that the Irish, especially the cultural nationalists at the beginning of the twentieth century, were desperately trying to eradicate, recognizing as they did that audiences accorded an element of truth to these stage versions.

In response to such stereotypes, Boucicault wrote plays such as *Arrah-na-Pogue*, *The Shaughraun*, *The O'Dowd*, *Colleen Bawn*, and *Robert Emmet*, which were very popular in both Ireland and London, although

Boucicault's audiences rarely understood what he was trying to do, accustomed as they were to comic representations of the Irish. They had come to anticipate what an Irish character would be, a stage trope that required only a preconditioned and thoughtless response. In spite of Boucicault's attempts at recuperation of the stage Irish figure, audiences often laughed, regardless of what his characters might have been trying to do. Robert Hogan cites an anecdote related in Townsend Walsh's *The Career of Dion Boucicault*: "[Boucicault] acted in many roles, and even when he was attempting to play a great dramatic role, everyone thought he was hysterical because of his 'great Irish brogue'."

Once, however, he essayed the title role in his Louis XI, and the results were disastrous:

> At first the audience sat in dumb amazement; then came titters and giggles, and finally roars. Never did monarch receive less grave and reverent treatment. Boucicault's brogue came out thick and strong. . . . As the tragedy—or, more properly speaking, the tragic farce—progressed, John Brougham, who loved a good joke better than anything else in the world, began to exaggerate the unctuousness of his own fine, natural brogue. Next John Clayton, an Englishman and the son-in-law of Boucicault, who was playing Nemours, felt in duty bound to fall in with the others, and he too assumed a broad brogue. The rest of the company, either out of deviltry or catching the infection, became Gaelic instead of Gallic, degenerated into an orgy of Hibernian dialects. . . . People laughed till the tears ran down their cheeks.[10]

Recognizing the difficulty with trying to change stereotypes overnight, Boucicault included some familiar comic stage Irish figures, such as Conn in *The Shaughraun* and Myles-na-Coppaleen in *The Colleen Bawn*, but he begins to tweak these figures so that they have a subtle, sly power that they exert over the more powerful characters. He also includes Irish characters whose roles grow increasingly complex, while he explores themes that invite greater thought about the stereotypes that we accept, such as those in *London Assurance* and *The Octoroon*. Without Boucicault's work in redeeming "Irishness" as more than comedy, there would not have been a sympathetic audience for Standish O'Grady's 1878 work, *History of Ireland*, a literary retelling of the legends of ancient Ireland that is often pointed to as the beginning of the Celtic Twilight, as it led to a resurgence of interest in the old stories. O'Grady's seminal work, in turn, led the way for Lady Augusta Gregory and John Millington Synge as well as Jack Yeats to explore the lives and stories of the Irish rural population, especially in the west of

Ireland, resulting in plays, paintings and books that changed the way the rest of the world saw Ireland. Finally, without Boucicault, the work of the Irish Literary Theatre and then the Abbey Theatre would not have been possible.

The Irish Literary Theatre (ILT), the precursor to the Abbey Theatre (which is still Ireland's National Theatre), was created in 1899, and survived until 1901. Its aim was to raise the quality of drama being written and performed in Ireland, so that the stereotypes that even Boucicault perpetuated might be erased. Drawing from Hyde's doctrine, Yeats believed that an Irish Theatre, a national theater, would necessarily elevate the people through better representation, and when people began to see themselves in a better light, they would raise themselves as well. The Revivalists claimed as part of their project the reclamation of the stage Irish figure, insisting that they wanted a National Theatre that showed characters who were representative of the true Irish person and that they wanted to eradicate the figure of ridicule that was most often found on the Irish stage. Lady Gregory's often-cited statement upon the establishment of the "National Theatre," bears repeating:

> We will show that Ireland is not the home of buffoonery and of easy sentiment, as it has been represented, but the home of an ancient idealism. We are confident of the support of all Irish people, who are weary of misrepresentation, in carrying out a work that is outside all the political questions that divide us.[11]

The Abbey project was, as much of twentieth-century Irish drama has been, concerned with getting at the "truth" of the Irish character, showing to the world who the Irish really were, revealing some authenticity that has been clouded by the "misrepresentations" of the English, and indeed by the Irish themselves, Boucicault included. Their project was embraced by the audiences and critics as much as by the playwrights, and plays continued to be upbraided throughout the twentieth century because of their failure to succeed in presenting authentic Irishness. Adrian Frazier points out that it might seem absurd, to those for whom theater has never been central to a nationalist movement, to judge a play, a work of imagination, on whether it represents reality or not, on whether it remains true to the type of a particular people. However, since Yeats had assured his audiences that "he was going to show the Irish people who they really were,"[12] their judgment, according to Frazier, was fair: audiences and critics took umbrage at further "misrepresentation." Far from believing Oscar Wilde's exhortations that "Lying, the telling of beautiful untrue things, is the proper aim of Art,"[13] the Irish have traditionally demanded an element of truth to the characters who purportedly represent them on stage. With great fervor, critics have disparaged plays on the grounds that the characters that are represented are not truly Irish, that these "people" would never be found in Ireland, and that therefore they should not be presented on the stage, as though that stage were necessarily the site of performance for nationality, rather than for creative explorations of various intellectual or imaginative issues. The desire for "truth" and the fury at finding something portrayed that seemed untrue is arguably[14] at the base of the famous "riots" surrounding the performance of John Millington Synge's *The Playboy of the Western World* and *In the Shadow of the Glen*, but certainly does not stop there. Many other plays were attacked, albeit less spectacularly, on the same grounds. So while the ILT is often touted as the beginning of the Revival, it is clearly neither the beginning nor the end of nationalist concerns, nor is it the beginning of the Renaissance. Too much of the Renaissance way of thinking was already prevalent before the ILT ever began, but it certainly motivated the foundation of the ILT.

The point here is that none of these various crusades, literary, linguistic, social, or political, occurred by itself, without any influences or trends in other areas, and at the time that all of these events were occurring, none of them referred to itself as part of a Revival or a Renaissance; the term was largely applied after the fact. Each element contributes to a greater, somewhat convoluted picture, and that picture is the impulse toward nationalism and away from colonial submission, an impulse tending toward what becomes known as the Renaissance. The literary and social dimensions overlap each other in motivation and result. Inherent in each of these nationalist programs is the belief that something has been allowed to die, something which must be not only revived but renewed, reborn. Mythology and folklore were being retrieved from a nearly lost consciousness of the people, but being applied in new ways. Music, dance, and sports were being remembered as glorious forms of communication and connection and were to replace the "stilted" music, dance, and sports of the British. The reintroduction of the Irish language would result in the renewal of Irish thought, according to the reigning position.

What, however, is Irish thought? How does one define Irishness? The search for and the articulation of identity is at the heart of much of the nationalist movement, a fact which obliquely supports Declan Kiberd's theory that Ireland was not truly a nation before it became diasporic, and that it is only through being identified by non-Irish, by the "Other," that it actually came to recognize itself as a coalesced country, with traits that are common to many of its people.[15] Those diasporic Irish came to be identified as Irish by the same outsider who needed to categorize them, and without the perspective of the "Other," Ireland would not need to interrogate its own angst about identity and autonomy. The relationship with the "Other," however, is complicated by the question that remains at the heart of this discussion: who gets to be Irish? How can the "Other" be determined when "Irish" cannot? Indeed, lying behind many of the projects to define Irishness are the issues of emigration and exile: are those who no longer live in the country still considered Irish? The list of Irish dramatists who have written many of their works while living abroad is long and impressive, including George Bernard Shaw, James Joyce, Samuel Beckett, Sean O'Casey, Emma Donaghue, Thomas McGreevy, Padraic Colum, Austin Clarke, James Stephens, Paul Vincent Carroll, and Hugh Leonard. Who gets to wear this badge of Irishness? Who qualifies as the "dispossessed"? Does exile necessarily mean a forfeiture of national identity? When Boucicault writes plays about the Irish for London or American audiences, does he qualify as an Irish playwright? When James Connolly, the leader of the Irish Socialist Republican Party, is raised in Scotland by Irish parents but never actually settles in Ireland, does he qualify as an Irish leader? These questions are inherent to most of the discourse about Irishness. There are scholars now who have "splintered" off from discussing the Irish in Ireland alone, who are discussing art and literature and history and culture in terms of the Irish-Americans, the Anglo-Irish, the Irish in Australia, the Irish exile, the diaspora, and, in a move that is, curiously, only fairly recent, the Irish in England. The implicit assumption in these discussions is that these people are not "really" Irish, that somehow they have not earned or retained the privilege of being considered Irish.

In the 1910s, George Birmingham (a.k.a. Canon Hannay) wrote several books with titles such as *Irishmen All*, *The Lighter Side of Irish Life*, and *An Irishman Looks at His World*, all of which attempted to define who the Irish were and describe what they were about. Making some fascinating and sweeping generalizations to explain bemusing behavior of the Irish people, he created pictures for us of the various Irish types, including policemen, priests and ministers, farmers, publicans, officials, and servants. (Jack Yeats illustrated many of these "types" for us.) In Birmingham's work, the Irish type, as indicated by what position a person holds in society, that is, by what he or she does for a living and what class he or she belongs to, is somewhat different from the concept of type that came from England, where (as C. G. Duggan points out throughout his book on the stage Irishman) the type has more to do with personal traits and actions than with social position. Birmingham included in these works commentary on the Irishmen who came from various regions, particularly from the North or the South, noting differences between Belfast and Dublin men. His analysis allows for regional distinctions that were virtually ignored by non-Irish writing about the Irish, distinctions that indicated the need for the Irish to define themselves rather than allowing others to do so, since they demonstrated an awareness of differences that were otherwise missed. He claims that the Irish themselves prefer those who will conform to a particular Irish identity:

> Irishmen . . . dislike erratic personalities. We prefer men who are true to type. We recognize without resentment the existence of various types and we are on the whole fairly tolerant. In Ireland a man may be a Protestant or a Catholic, a Nationalist or a Unionist, without suffering any serious inconvenience. He may choose his fold, but he must be a sheep. We do not like wild animals. And, unfortunately, the man of letters is usually, the man of genius always, an eccentric creature who cannot be kept in an enclosure. He insists on looking at things from odd angles and seeing them not at all as other people see them. He keeps on describing things and drawing pictures of them, not as we know they are, nice and clear and flat, but as they appear to him through distorted glasses of his absurd temperament, all messed up with each other. We do not want people of that kind among us. It is far better for them to go away somewhere else, to London or to New York; which, indeed, is what such Irishmen generally do.[16]

Many people have participated in the project of identifying an Irish type. W. B. Yeats, Lady Gregory and John Millington Synge, Brendan Behan, Sean O'Casey, James Joyce, Seamus Heaney, George Bernard Shaw, Edna O'Brien, Lord Dunsany, Frank O'Connor, Eavan Boland, Austin Clarke, John B. Keane, Terry Eagleton, and Thomas Cahill have all attempted such books which try to illuminate Ireland and the Irish; some are written as tourist books, claiming that they will reveal the "truth" about what Ireland is like and often including pictures and bits of poetry or song; others are written as autobiographies that reveal the truth about what life is like in the "Emerald Isle." Some of them are comic, a wry look at the amusing quirks of a people and a place, and some are serious, purporting to set the record straight. A remarkable number of writers spend time discussing the Irish people, both explicating and defending, trying to express whatever it is that represents that kernel of being, that essence, that makes someone Irish.

Becoming the site of much more than play, the representation of the Irish in art turned into a kind of acclamation of identity and reclamation of a power that the Irish felt had been taken from them. This reclamation consisted of more, however, than just an establishment or creation of a positive Irish identity, as it included a repudiation of all things English as well and portrayal of Irish identity became grounds upon which the Irish would accuse each other of a lack of patriotism, faithlessness, and treason. It is interesting that, as Declan Kiberd says,

> Those peoples who *had* constructed themselves from within, the French for instance, never accused their bad citizens of being "unFrench": but throughout the nineteenth century delinquents were often called "unIrish", because Irish nationalism too often defined itself by what it was against.[17]

It became a political stance to consider oneself Irish, with all that might entail, from a hatred of all things English to a return to the Irish language and an insistence on buying only Irish-made products. Many mocked such efforts as fanatical, while others embraced them, and they became a source of contention among the Irish who could not agree on what it might mean to be Irish. The discussion surrounding the question of limiting Irish identity is at times absurd in its impossible goals:

> According to *Samhain* [Yeats' magazine published in 1904] what makes an Irish writer is not that he writes in Irish, pleads the national cause, expresses Irish morality, or creates typical Irish characters; not even that he is inspired by Irish literary traditions; certainly not that he executes in his plays the will of the people, or any will but his own. It becomes difficult to see what is left for a writer to do who wishes to be Irish. For Yeats, however, that person's wish should be to make himself not Irish but a writer. Do that and he would be Irish enough. Ultimately, Yeats says, only five or six people have the right to call themselves Irish, people who usually belong, he believes, to the leisured class (read Protestant population), whose thought is *harder* and *more masterful* than that of others; these have, he adds, an *essential nearness to reality*.[18]

The idea that there are only a few people who have earned the "right" to call themselves Irish, transcending any ethnic or native origins, birth, race, or even geography, seems ludicrous, but it is emblematic of the weight put (by the Irish themselves) on the labels that were being given and on the recognition that the labels received. The paradox is that while only the members of the leisured class get to call themselves Irish in Yeats's terms, because their thought is "harder" and "more masterful" than that of others, the characters portrayed in the practice of his "Irish" colleagues to represent the typical Irish were, almost invariably, members of the peasant class, as the Abbey Theatre produced primarily plays dealing with the rural, "simple" peasantry. Looking back from the perspective of the end of the century, a critic can see that,

> If England was urban, Ireland had to be rural. If England was industrial, Ireland had to [be] pastoral. Instead of looking clearly at Irish life in all its diversity, the new cultural movements tended to look for an Irishness that was defined in these ways, and that therefore excluded much of the reality of Irish urban life.[19]

The argument over how to look for Irishness continued throughout the life of Field Day, an influential theatrical organization in Derry that began in 1979, as Seamus Deane urged the Irish to try to get past the same old dissensions:

> The Irish character apologetically portrayed by the Banims, Griffin, Carleton, Mrs. Hall and a host of others has been received as the verdict passed by history upon the Celtic personality. That stereotyping has caused a long colonial concussion. It is about time we put aside the idea of essence—that hungry Hegelian ghost looking for a stereotype to live in. As Irishness or as Northernness he stimulates the provincial unhappiness we create and fly from, becoming virtuoso metropolitans to the exact degree that we have created an idea of Ireland as provincialism incarnate. These are worn oppositions. They used to be the parentheses in which the Irish destiny was isolated. That is no longer the case. Everything, including our politics and our literature, has to be rewritten—i.e. re-read. That will enable new writing, new politics, unblemished by Irishness, but securely Irish.[20]

Concerns about Irishness and its portrayal, its "Hegelian ghost," despite the "worn" character of the "oppositions," must be resolved before anything new can be written; yet the warning itself appears to reinscribe the same concerns that it supposedly seeks to mitigate. What does it mean to be "unblemished by Irishness" and yet still remain "securely Irish"? According to Foucault, "one of the main moral obligations for any subject is to know oneself, to tell the truth about oneself, and to constitute oneself as an object of knowledge both for other people and for oneself,"[21] and this is precisely what the Irish dramatists of the twentieth century were trying to do.

While for Boucicault attempts towards exonerating the stage Irish figure of ridicule may not have been overtly political, these attempts were certainly political for Yeats and those who are known as the Revivalists, contrary to their original claims. They asserted that they were not political, that their work was, again, "outside all the political questions that divide us,"[22] but the literary (and cultural) movement was inherently political. It was certainly more than just rhetorical. The politics at work here are the same politics behind whether the movement is called the Revival or the Celtic Twilight or the Renaissance. They wanted to unite all the different factions of nationalism under the aegis of drama. The schizophrenia of the Revivalist position is demonstrated by Yeats, who, as we saw earlier, ties the Revival to Parnell's downfall but at the same time insists that the Revivalist movement cannot be political, acknowledging that the political element would prevent their efforts from being purely Irish; he knew that the political nature of the GAA and of the Young Irelanders led those groups to the sectarian rifts to which they were subject, and he wished to unite Ireland rather than divide it. When the literary movement meets the revolutionary movement, despite equally nationalist beginnings, the completely different agendas are evident. While the two efforts may seem to be the same, the tension lay in the perceived desired results. The Revivalists were attempting to unite Ireland into one idealized culture, but not everyone had the same ideal; tensions remained not only because of sectarian differences, but also because of differences in class, education, and vision. The Theatre, for example, came into conflict with Hyde's position over the debate about language: shouldn't a national theater be in the national language? If so, what is that language? Again, the majority of the people involved in the theater had no Irish at all, including W. B. Yeats. The argument illustrates perfectly the conflict between nationalism and modernity: Does a Revival only harken back to a glorious past, without looking towards a successful future? Daniel Corkery, a later disciple of Douglas Hyde's, maintains the argument that the loss of the Irish language equates to a loss of Irish thought, insisting that there was a Golden Age to which Ireland could harken back, and that there is a language that, once recovered, would serve as the means for reclaiming Celtic glory.[23] The desire to return to that glorious past is in direct conflict with a world where the isolation of nationalism becomes increasingly undesirable.

Few people were unaware of the fact that English would take them much further in the world than Irish ever would. In 1900, W. B. Yeats wrote:

> Side by side with the spread of the Irish language, and with much writing in the Irish language, must go on much expression of Irish emotion and Irish thought, much writing about Irish things and people, in the English language, for no man can write well except in the language he has been

born and bred to, and no man, as I think, becomes perfectly cultivated except through the influence of that language; and this writing must for a long time to come be the chief influence in shaping the opinions and the emotions of the leisured classes in Ireland in so far as they are concerned with Irish things, and the more sincere it is, the more lofty it is, the more beautiful it is, the more will the general life of Ireland be sweetened by its influence, through its influence over a few governing minds.[24]

The differences between the various elements appear to be irresolvable. David Krause discusses the crucial flaw in the aggressive nationalist agenda, the determination to view literary independence as a threat to political independence, a misconception that can only be attributed to nationalist paranoia. That unfortunate collision between the principles of the Renaissance and the principles of the revolution illustrates why art and ideology are incompatible forces, not only in Ireland but in all countries exposed to excessive nationalism and rabid patriotism.[25]

Krause further summarizes F. S. Lyons, who believes that the conflict between what he saw as completely opposing forces, the political and the cultural, resulted in a necessary condition of anarchy.[26] Tracy Mishkin notes, "many community leaders were interested not in realistic representations but in idealized portraits because they wanted to enlist literature to fight prejudice. This clashed with the writer's desire for artistic freedom, which did not necessarily favor realism either."[27] It is the clash between nationalism and modernity, the Revivalists beckoning to the past and the revolutionaries looking toward the future. The literary became the political.

The Celtic Twilight, perhaps, is the embodiment of that tension. Thought by many to be the forerunner to the Revival, it is the part of the 1890s that romanticized all things Celtic as mystical and mysterious but did so in order to give a foundation to the concept of Ireland's future greatness. Truly the step-child of Standish O'Grady and the child of W. B. Yeats, the Twilight is the period during which the fairy world was given literary credence, and the old stories took on new sociological significance. The stories, some myth and some legend, gave the Irish a common past upon which to rest a confidence in a better future, according to many (especially Yeats). In his introduction to Lady Gregory's collection of Irish tales, Yeats explains:

the Irish stories make us understand why the Greeks call myths the activities of the daemons. The great virtues, the great joys, the great privations come in the myths, and, as it were, take mankind between their naked arms, and without putting off their divinity. Poets have taken their themes more often from stories that are all, or half, mythological, than from history or stories that give one the sensation of history, understanding, as I think, that the imagination which remembers the proportions of life is but a long wooing, and that it has to forget them before it becomes the torch and the marriage-bed.[28]

If, as Terry Eagleton explains, "Modernism springs from the estranging impact of modernizing forces on a still deeply traditionalist order, in a politically unstable context which opens up social hope as well as spiritual anxiety,"[29] then the Celtic Twilight is the modernist move at the end of the nineteenth century. In considering the sidhe (the fairy world) and the heroes (such as Cuchullain and Finn McCuill) as credible parts of Irish history and literature, the past is brought into contact with the future. The politically unstable context opens the space to allow such elements viability, in that the stories themselves provided hope for the future, samples of the ways that the Irish, in that mythic, originary past, attained and retained power and strength. The faeries, for example, while appearing magical and mystical, allowed for ways that the Irish could both explain a lack of control over their lives and imagine autonomy in both the past and the present. The Irish were also in a position of power because they alone had the understanding of the ways of the *daoine maithe*, the good people. The inexplicable, such as menopause, puberty, and uppity women, was always explained by blaming the faeries, and appeasing the faeries could mitigate such things.[30] Through looking at the past, one could see that the future could be both planned and preordained. The heroes function in much the same way, establishing a history of glory for Ireland, and by reexamining their stories, the Irish can be assured of future glories. In its use of the past to illuminate the present and to give hope for the future, the Celtic Twilight is in essence the beginning of the Modernist movement in Ireland.

Tensions also exist between the modernist and post-colonial perspectives. In a discussion that has most recently been debated in a collection of essays called *Ireland in Proximity: History, Gender and Space*,[31] both the modernist and the post-colonial approaches have been accused of being revisionist. Gregory Castle suggests that the "modernist dilemma," "the gap between experience and its representation," (and thus perhaps the gap between the political and the literary, the Celtic Twilight and the Revival) is actually part of the tension of post-colonialism, transforming "the revolutionary energies of the Revival into a reactionary nostalgia for 'archaic,' pre-colonial origins."[32] With this definition, however, modernity appears to be a subset of post-colonialism, cause and effect, in almost a fluid, albeit disruptive, transition from a secure culture to one that encounters dissonance and alienation, whether that dissonance be caused by industry, war, post-colonialism, or something else. What Castle calls "the uneasy relation of tradition to modernity in colonial Ireland"[33] complicates the idea of modernity because of the tensions between colonialism and nationalism in Ireland at the turn of the century. Where one aspect of European modernity is the struggle to define the individual subject in its relation to its own society, post-colonialism requires an assertion of the individual subject in relation to the dominant society, and can only work where nationalism is also at work. However, the nationalist movement tends to rely upon tradition, eschewing the idea of allowing new traditions to dominate for fear that those traditions are tainted by the colonizers. The tension between these terms is the same tension at work between the terms we have been discussing: Revival, Celtic Twilight, and Renaissance. The cultural, the political, the traditional, the modern, are all part of the arsenal deployed to forge a nation, but they are an uneasy complement to each other. If we consider the post-colonial situation in Ireland in terms of both the nationalist and modernist movements, we might be able to see what is gained by referring to this movement as a renaissance. Certainly the implicit belief is that there is something to be renewed, some mythic originary past to which to revert (Corkery's Golden Age of language, for example), and the assumption is that if we can only transcend whatever force is holding us down (whether it be external oppressors of culture and language or internal disconnection with history), we can return to a previously forsaken glory. The concept of renaissance incorporates many of the elements discussed here, in critical ways. As Krause notes, "The rebirth of a nation's literature . . . is not an immaculate conception. It is a painful process of renewal that grows out of attrition and contention, a civil war of violent words and conflicting aspirations."[34] Revival, in its concept of near-death, only goes so far, suggesting as it does that the culture had to be resuscitated; renaissance, in its acknowledgment of continuity with the past, seems to acknowledge the contentious nature of that rebirth and renewal, without ignoring the colonial influence that has been wrought. After all, the need for rebirth relies upon the past as well. Post-colonialism, in its awareness of two sides to the conflict, is a fuller interpretation of the Irish situation. The originary imagined past was disrupted by another force, and one cannot look beyond that influence to see what the originary past might have been; post-colonial theory supposes a kind of pre-authenticity that nationalism has yet to acknowledge, a sense that the true Irish nation has been interrupted and can be regained. The Revival behaves as though there is an accessible, authentic originary past, one that can be recaptured and celebrated by all who are Irish. The possibility of what Françoise Lionnet calls "transculturation,"[35] the inevitable crossing over of cultural elements that are unavoidable when two cultures rub against each other for any length of time, is unacceptable to Revivalists, who prefer to believe that all that has occurred during colonization can be wiped away by boycott. Colonialism is not one-way; the cultural slippage is on both the colonizer and the colonized. Whether England had ever achieved dominance in Ireland, the very proximity of the two countries would have caused some transculturation. As Lionnet points out, analyzing more specifically the consequences of French colonialism, " 'inferior' or subaltern elements contribute to the evolution and transformation of the hegemonic system by producing resistances and counterdiscourses,"[36] just as much as the hegemonic elements contribute to the subaltern cultures. The dream of an untainted Irish culture can never be more than a dream or an academic exercise.

With nationalism (and thus with the Revival), the assumption is that the glory must be reclaimed. With modernism (and thus with the Celtic Twilight), the assumption is that there is a firm tradition from which a new perspective arises. With post-colonialism (and thus with the Renaissance), the assumption is that the previous and potential glory has been usurped or quelled. Each term tells only part of the story about what happened in Ireland at the turn of the twentieth century, but the idea of "Renaissance" does seem to take into account more than just the literary or political or cultural movements that took place. Nonetheless, as one critic has said, "Renaissance is a beautiful word. We use it even when we are not sure what has been reborn."[37]

Notes

1. Tracy Mishkin, *The Harlem and Irish Renaissances* (Gainesville, FL: University Press of Florida, 1998), p. 35.
2. Robert Fallis, *The Irish Renaissance* (New York: Syracuse University Press, 1977).
3. Mishkin, xiv.
4. James Connolly, "To The Irish People," *Irish Socialist Republic*. 1896, 97–100.
5. Douglas Hyde, "The Necessity for De-Anglicising Ireland," *The Revival of Irish Literature* (London: T. Fisher Unwin, 1894), 115–161.
6. Ibid., p. 120.

7. Ibid., p. 161.
8. Bruce Arnold, *Jack Yeats* (New Haven, CT and London: Yale University Press, 1998), ix.
9. C. G. Duggan, *The Stage Irishman: A History of the Irish Play and Stage Characters from the Earliest Times* (New York and London: Benjamin Blom, 1937), p. 289.
10. Robert Hogan, *Dion Boucicault* (New York: Twayne, 1969), p. 39.
11. Lady Augusta Gregory, "Our Irish Theatre," *Modern Irish Drama*, Ed. John P. Harrington (New York and London: W. W. Norton, 1991), pp. 378–9.
12. Adrian Frazier, *Behind the Scenes: Yeats, Horniman, and the Struggle for the Abbey Theatre* (Berkeley and Los Angeles, CA and London: University of California Press, 1990), p. 7.
13. Oscar Wilde, "The Decay of Lying," *Dramatic Theory and Criticism: Greeks to Grotowski*, Ed. Bernard F. Dukore (New York and Chicago, IL: Holt, Rinehart and Winston, 1974), p.628.
14. G. J. Watson, *Irish Identity and Literary Revival* (London: Croom Helm, 1979), 71.
15. Declan Kiberd, *Inventing Ireland: The Literature of the Modern Nation* (Cambridge, MA: Harvard University Press, 1996).
16. George Birmingham, *An Irishman Looks at His World* (London, New York, and Toronto, ON: Hodder and Stoughton, 1919), p. 118.
17. Kiberd, *Inventing Ireland*, p. 141.
18. Frazier, *Behind the Scenes*, p. 105.
19. Fintan O'Toole, *The Ex-isle of Erin: Images of Global Ireland* (Dublin: New Island, 1996), p. 107.
20. Seamus Deane, "Heroic Styles: The Tradition of an Idea," *Ireland's Field Day* (London: Hutchinson, 1985), p. 58.
21. Michel Foucault, *Discipline and Punish: The Birth of the Prison*, trans. Alan Sheridan (New York: Random House Vintage Books, 1979), p. 177.
22. Gregory, "Our Irish Theatre," pp. 378–9.
23. Daniel Corkery, *The Fortunes of the Irish Language* (Cork: The Mercier Press, 1968).
24. W. B. Yeats, "Irish Language and Irish Literature," in *The Collected Works: Volume X: Later Articles and Reviews*, Ed. Colton Johnson (New York: Scribner, 2000), p. 47.
25. David Krause, *The Regeneration of Ireland: Renaissance and Revolution* (Bethesda, Dublin, and Oxford: Academia Press, 2001), xii.
26. Krause, *The Regeneration of Ireland*, p. 110.
27. Mishkin, *The Harlem and Irish Renaissances*, p. 14.
28. W. B. Yeats, "Cuchulain of Muirthemne," in *Explorations* (New York: The MacMillan Company, 1962), p. 10.
29. Gregory Castle, *Modernism and the Celtic Revival* (Cambridge: Cambridge University Press, 2001, p. 2.
30. Angela Bourke, *The Burning of Bridget Cleary* (London: Penguin Putnam, 2000).

31. Scott Brewster, *Ireland in Proximity: History, Gender and Space* (London: Routledge, 1999).
32. Castle, *Modernism and the Celtic Revival*, p. 36.
33. Ibid., p. 3.
34. Krause, *The Regeneration of Ireland: Renaissance and Revolution*, p. 45.
35. Françoise Lionnet, "'Logiques métisses': Cultural Appropriation and Postcolonial Representations," in *Postcolonial Subjects: Francophone Women Writers*, eds. Mary Jean Agreen (Minneapolis, MN: University of Minnesota Press, 1996), pp. 321–43.
36. Lionnet, p. 323.
37. Mishkin, *The Harlem and Irish Renaissances*, p. xiii.

CHAPTER 8

Globalizing the Harlem Renaissance: Irish, Mexican, and "Negro" Renaissances in *The Survey* and *Survey Graphic*

Robert Johnson

Alain Locke, dean of the Harlem Renaissance, claimed in *The New Negro* anthology that understanding the "Negro Renaissance" of the 1920s meant seeing it "in the perspective of" an emerging new world. In his opening remarks to that canonical text, a work typically considered to be the bible of the Harlem Renaissance, Locke explicitly connected this "resurgence of a people" in Harlem to the racial and national renaissances occurring "in India, in China, in Egypt, Ireland, Russia, Bohemia, Palestine, and Mexico." Claiming it as one of several "nascent movements of folk-expression and self-determination . . . playing a part in the world to-day," Locke placed the Harlem Renaissance in the context of a worldwide awakening of subject peoples across the globe. He explained that along with Europe, "seething in a dozen centers with emergent nationalities," and Palestine which was "full of a renascent Judaism," the Harlem Renaissance and the advent of the New Negro were part of a pattern in world events—an indigenous expression of the type of racial and national renaissances occurring abroad.[1]

The "Negro Renaissance" of the 1920s took shape not only within the crucible of national politics but within a world historical context.

Locke's words serve to recall us to that context, reminding us that the Harlem revival occurred synchronously with the rise of soviet communism in Russia, the birth of a new Ireland in northern Europe, the May Fourth movement in China, the advent of fascism in southern Europe, the quickening of Zionism in the Middle East and throughout the West, and the racial renaissance of the new Mexico. In framing the Harlem Renaissance as one among several global rearticulations of racial and national identity in the postwar period, Locke thus provides us with a starting point for reconstructing a perspective on the Harlem Renaissance that was world-historical in orientation. Such a perspective might help to supplement the strong body of transnational literature that already addresses the pan-Africanism that came out of that Renaissance.[2]

Alain Locke was not the only one at the time to see the Harlem Renaissance as part of a trend in world affairs. American progressives of the time perceived it to be a local instance of larger global forces. As the historian Alan Dawley has recently observed, many American progressives like Locke viewed the postwar world itself as a world in flux in which great social movements were recasting international relations and remaking modern peoples. It was to them, he tells us, a world alive with "African rhythms, Indian ragas, Chinese folk tunes, and the 'Communist Internationale.' "[3] While not all postwar progressives viewed the world or the events in Harlem in such an openly pluralist fashion, many did indeed struggle in the postwar period to formulate a pluralist and internationalist perspective for understanding relations among the world's races and nations. Such a perspective was nowhere more clearly developed than in the pages of the progressive journals that introduced the New Negro to a national audience, *The Survey* and *Survey Graphic*.[4]

The Harlem Renaissance was, in important respects, a textually constructed event that had its roots in the March 1, 1925 issue of *Survey Graphic*, "Harlem: Mecca of the New Negro."[5] It was in the pages of this unique issue that Alain Locke famously pronounced the birth of a New Negro and conscripted, with varying degrees of consent and dissent, the major African-American writers, intellectuals, and artists of the time into his version of that Renaissance. *Harlem: Mecca of the New Negro* consolidated in one publication the works of the major writers and artists of the Harlem Renaissance—among them, Langston Hughes, Jean Toomer, Walter White, Charles Johnson, James Weldon Johnson, Countee Cullen, W. E. B. Dubois, and Claude McKay; more important, the articles, poems, and editorials that comprised it became the basis of the aforementioned *New Negro* anthology published by Boni and Liveright the following year. Of course, Locke's pronouncement in 1925 of a "Negro Renaissance" would have landed on deaf ears had the intellectual, literary, and social groundwork not already been laid by African Americans in the preceding years, but the idea that a "renaissance" was in the air awaited just such a claim and institutional focus as that provided by *Harlem: Mecca of the New Negro* and its subsequent revision into *The New Negro* anthology.

To American progressives like Locke and those in *The Survey* community, the Harlem Renaissance was one act in a larger worldwide drama of racial and national awakening. That global drama, as seen by American progressives in the 1920s, can still be glimpsed in the unique series of annual issues of *The Survey* that were put out to celebrate the national and racial identities taking shape across the globe during the postwar years. Progressives who were introduced to the Harlem Renaissance in *The Survey* publication would also have read other remarkable issues on the making of the Irish and the new Ireland; the building of a new Russian identity in Soviet Russia; the reconstruction of Mexican identity in postrevolutionary Mexico; the shifting identities of "Orientals" throughout the Pacific Rim; and the emergence of a fascist nationalism in Italy after the Great War.[6] *The Survey* staff termed these annual issues of its magazine its Race Issues, although, as will be seen shortly, the idea of racial awakening, which gave focus to the series, was a metaphor for the multitude of ethnic, racial, and national renaissances of the postwar period. As a series, these issues provide a perspective on postwar political and intellectual life on something of a world-historical scale, and they place the Harlem Renaissance back within the context of other concurrent struggles to document, define, and remake races and nations in the postwar world.

This essay makes the case that recontextualizing the Harlem Renaissance in such a way has advantages over a more nation-centered approach. In order to begin to develop such a history of the Harlem Renaissance, it thus examines the publication of *Harlem: Mecca of the New Negro* in relation to the aforementioned series of Race Issues in *The Survey* of which that publication was a part and then looks more specifically at the Harlem Renaissance in relation to two of the more prominent of the other major Race Issues published by *The Survey* staff in the 1920s, the 1921 issue on the Irish Renaissance and the new Ireland, which included the work of such Irish intellectuals and activists as A. E. (George Russell), W. B. Yeats, Horace Plunkett, James Stephens, and Erskine Childers, and the 1924 issue on the Mexican Renaissance in postrevolutionary Mexico, which included the work of the major Mexican intellectuals and artists of that era, including Diego Rivera, José Vasconcelos, Manuel Gamio, and Felipe Carillo.

Recontextualizing the Harlem Renaissance in such a way has fairly straightforward heuristic advantages. First and most obviously, it draws the Harlem Renaissance into a world historical narrative in which it is one instance of a wider set of racial and national rearticulations of modern identity dating to the postwar period. Second, it puts African-American intellectuals like Alain Locke into something of a transnational conversation with intellectuals outside the United States who were sorting through similar questions of ethnic and racial identity in the 1920s, thus allowing us to consider both the extent to which such intellectuals shared a common discourse on the meaning of race and nation as well as the extent to which their separate histories drew on local ideas and circumstances. Finally, globalizing the Harlem Renaissance points us methodologically in the direction of world history both by highlighting the political and cultural *connections* that tie such events together and by casting those events in a *comparative* light so as to clarify the ways in which renaissances, such as the three we are considering here, were generic or unique. Of course, this chapter only provides one such perspective and, as such, is not more than a contribution to such inquiry.[7]

Racial and National Renaissance in Postwar Progressivism

The notion that the world was alive with renaissance can be felt throughout progressive writing in the postwar years. Important progressives with names such as Jane Addams, Emily Green Balch, Frank Tannenbaum, and John Collier were wholly convinced that theirs was a moment of renaissance characterized by, in Addams' words, a growing "world consciousness."[8] Seeking to imagine a postwar world rebuilt around pluralist principles, these progressives carried into the 1920s the earlier internationalist dream of a renewed global order that had dominated American rhetoric during World War I. Progressives at *The Survey* such as longtime editor-in-chief Paul U. Kellogg certainly believed such renewal was in the air. Kellogg's introduction to the Harlem Issue was just one example of the widespread sense of hope and millennialist optimism that permeated progressive writing in these years. Referring to the glacial speed at which the work of progressive reformers, artists, and activists typically progressed, Kellogg proclaimed triumphantly that times do finally come "when these forces that work so slowly and so delicately seem suddenly to flower" and "the curtain [lifts] on a new act in the drama of part or all of us." Such a "dramatic flowering," he said, was precisely what characterized the monumental events taking place in "the

New Ireland," in "the newly awakened Mexico," and in the very heart of America's largest city where "a new race spirit [wa]s taking place among American Negroes."[9]

This spirit of renaissance, be it in reference to Ireland, Mexico, Harlem, or elsewhere, was linked in postwar progressive thought to the notion of a revived racial spirit. Writing in the Harlem issue of *The Survey*, Alain Locke, for example, proclaimed that African Americans were in the midst of a profound "racial awakening" that had filled their lives with a "renewed race spirit" palpable to anyone who cared to notice. Writing in a similar vein in the 1924 Mexico issue of *The Survey*, the historian Frank Tannenbaum spoke of the unprecedented "racial revival" going on in that country which was likely to prove "the greatest Renaissance in the contemporary world." And after the same manner, Ireland's A. E. pronounced in the pathbreaking 1921 issue of *The Survey* devoted to the new Ireland that there were "great currents of energy and thought in Ireland" that foreshadowed the Gaelic race finally rising up to join the world's "other races of genius."[10] Similar pronouncements in *The Survey* referred to the making of a new German race out of the wreckage of the old dynasty, of a new Italian race emerging from Benito Mussolini's fascist state, and of a new Russian people forged out of the cultural and political experimentation of the early Soviet years.

Such proclamations of racial and national rebirth were structurally bound to two important influences on progressive thought that date to these years, pragmatism and cultural pluralism. Pragmatism, for its part, encouraged progressives to see the world as fungible and ripe for renaissance. By repudiating the sort of philosophical idealism that had long dominated western thought and replacing it with the claim that knowledge and truth were subjective phenomena, pragmatism urged progressives to reconceive the world as a world ultimately of their own making. Pragmatism, that is, pushed American progressives to reject the assumption that the world they inhabited was ordered by external forces or natural laws and to accept the fact that the world was fundamentally manmade. This turn to pragmatism in the progressive community generated, on the one hand, a new uncertainty about the direction the world should or would take (for it provided no infallible template for guidance), while, on the other, it had the positive effect of producing both a new openness toward experimentation and a revitalized tolerance for cultural difference. In important respects, pragmatism thus opened the way for interpreting the world as alive with endless renewal, rebirth, and renaissance.

This important shift in the infrastructure of progressive thought was complemented by a closely related shift in the progressive valuation of racial and ethnic difference that gained momentum after World War I. Amidst the fallout of a war that had shaken the foundations of western society, many progressives shed their earlier unexamined faith in unilinear progress and the virtues of western civilization. While earlier progressives had assumed that the less fortunate nations and races needed to be uplifted and assimilated into the liberal mainstream through western education, capitalism, and Christianity, important progressives in the postwar period began to argue for the validity and value of cultural diversity. Critical of a western model of civilization that had led to the catastrophes of World War I, such progressives turned outward toward the world's cultures for inspiration. In line with the sort of cultural pluralism being espoused by such well-known intellectuals as Alain Locke, Horace Kallen, John Collier, Randolph Bourne, and Franz Boas, influential progressives came to believe, if imperfectly, that the strength in humanity lay in its diverse peoples and cultures.[11] The growing influence of such cultural pluralism was the intellectual impetus behind *The Survey's* renaissance issues, each of which was an effort to survey the world's racial and cultural diversity.

The incorporation of pluralism into progressive thought was shaped moreover by a dramatic change in the progressives' understanding of the relationship between race and culture. While mainstream thought was still dominated by a misguided faith in eugenics and social Darwinism, which supposed that more or less immutable breeds of inferior peoples were polluting an otherwise healthy human gene pool, progressives like Franz Boas in anthropology and Robert E. Park in sociology were busily accumulating a body of evidence that pointed to the fact that differences in aptitude and behavior had their origin in culture and history rather than in biology or nature. This ultimately meant to progressives that racial, ethnic, and national identities were not simply *a priori* facts but rather processes of socialization. Such an intellectual reorientation worked to empower the progressive, providing intellectual justification for believing that the minds of men and women could remake the world and its peoples in the seemingly most essential of ways. In terms of collective identity, progressives were coming to see, if incompletely, that the races, ethnicities, and nations of the world were not stable facts but rather processes of becoming. From such a perspective, their perception of the renaissances of the 1920s might be understood as part of a deeper humanizing of the ontological and epistemological realms begun in western culture during the earlier Italian Renaissance.

But if the new intellectual foundations of progressive thought played a vital role in the making of renaissance in the progressive community, so too did older assumptions. The idea that the core of human identity was bound to one's racial and national life continued to play a constitutive role in progressive thought. The ideas of race and nation, that is, still frequently masqueraded as facts rather than collectively constructed fictions. There may have been a notable fluidity between and within the concepts of race and nation in progressive thought during these years. The Harlem Renaissance was, for instance, claimed as both a national and a racial awakening while the Mexican, Italian, and Irish cases were purported to be racial as well as national revivals. But the older belief that races and ethnicities embodied fairly stable strains of descent continued to exert an influence on progressivism into the mid-twentieth century. Indeed, one of the things that makes the racial and national renaissances of the post-war years so interesting is the marked strain we can see between the ideas of descent and consent that went into their making. For, on the one hand, the idea of renaissance always presumed that an already present but dormant group consciousness was waiting to be reborn, while, on the other, renaissance in these years frequently suggested that *new* nations and races could actually be called into being. The bold proclamations of a revived Gaelic, Negro, or Mexican spirit among renaissance writers were regularly accompanied by a sense of expectation and hesitancy at odds with such strident claims. A. E. referred to the *anticipation* of a new Irishman rather than a new Irishman; Locke to the *making of* a Negro race as much as he did the New Negro himself; and Tannenbaum to the *promise* of a new Mexican race rather than its *de facto* existence.[12] The pronouncements of a new Irishman, of a New Negro, or of a new Mexican were, in other words, always prophetic gestures as much as they were statements of fact.

There were, of course, very real political, economic, and social roots to each of these racial and national rebirths, but the idea that Ireland, Mexico, and Harlem (or Russia, Italy, and Germany, for that matter) were in the midst of renaissance was as much as anything else an act of the imagination, or what one historian has called, a "willed historical fiction."[13] Renaissance was, that is to say, a creative cultural act in each of these cases as much as it was the product of unconscious social forces. Compelling new collective identities issued forth in Ireland, Mexico, and Harlem from the pens and brushes of artists, intellectuals, and writers who willed these renaissances into being. Such renaissance writers and artists reimagined life in their respective societies; they rebuilt their worlds discursively; and they rewrote in powerful ways the meaning of racial and national identities. More than anyone else, they endowed the political tumult and the carnival of life around them with collective meaning. The impact of their work, whether in Ireland, Mexico, or Harlem, was especially enduring not only because such writers and artists provided compelling new narratives that reflected the politics and history of the societies from which they came but also because they proposed persuasive new ideas about the relationships among race, nation, and history that promised to bring into life more fulfilling and empowering expressions of identity. The significance of the new stories and the new subjectivities to which they gave life become clearer as we turn briefly, as progressives of the time did, to each of these renaissances.

Irish Renaissance: The Gaelic Revival and the Irish Free State

The 1921 issue of *The Survey* dedicated to the new Ireland, *Irish Anticipations*, was the prototype for the successive renaissance issues published annually over the course of the next decade by *The Survey* staff. It set the pattern for future issues of the magazine like *Harlem: Mecca of the New Negro* by documenting the type of aesthetic and political groundwork being done across the globe to remake races and nations. Although in some respects *Irish Anticipations* was a more effete publication than those to come, it contained the work of important Irish intellectuals, artists, and activists such as the influential philosopher and writer George Russell; the leading figure in rural reconstruction, Horace Plunkett; the dominant figure of the Irish Renaissance, W. B. Yeats; the nationalist poet and playwright James Stephens; a soon-to-be executed leader of the Irish resistance Erskine Childers; and such lesser known figures as Paul Henry and Padraic Colum. As a historical document, the publication *Irish Anticipations* thus provides us both with a contemporary perspective on the making of the new Ireland and the new Irishman and with evidence pointing to the fact that nation-building in the postwar period was a transnational affair in which public intellectuals in different parts of the world interpreted themselves across borders to an international progressive community.[14] In returning to *Irish Anticipations*, we return to, among other things, a transnational conversation that was taking place long before the rhetoric of globalization or the idea of a global village came into fashion.

By November 1921, when *Irish Anticipations* was published in the United States, the Irish Renaissance had seen its heyday. In that respect, the Irish case differs from the other two renaissances under consideration here, both of which reached their apex in the postwar decade. In Ireland, what was historically momentous in the postwar years was not the Irish

Renaissance itself so much as the political consequences of that Renaissance. In the 1910s and 1920s, the cultural nationalism of the Renaissance years had ceded the limelight to the political nationalism that produced an Irish Free State. In the years preceding the publication of *Irish Anticipations*, Irish nationalists, building on the momentum of a Young Ireland movement and the Gaelic Renaissance, staged the famous Easter Uprising of 1916 and conducted a war of resistance against the Royal Irish Constabulary and other symbols of the English occupation through 1921. Having solicited international support from Russia, Germany, and the United States during World War I (a war which at least the Allies claimed had been fought for national self-determination), Irish nationalists had declared independence from England, repudiated ties to the Union, abandoned the British Parliament in Westminster, and founded an alternative Irish Parliament in Dublin. In the years leading up to 1921, this parliament, the Dáil Eireann, along with a volunteer army of nationalists had come to manage Irish affairs and represent Ireland to the world. England had vacillated during these same years on the proper course for dealing with the assertion of independence from one of its colonies, but capitulated by 1921 to the court of world opinion and the impact of continued Irish resistance. Complete independence for Ireland did not come until 1948 when Ireland withdrew from the British Commonwealth, but in the months following November 1921, Ireland gained real legislative, executive, and judicial sovereignty over all but the Ulster provinces in the north. *Irish Anticipations* came out just as this Irish Free State was emerging on the world scene.[15]

In taking inventory of renaissances across the globe, *The Survey* chose a good starting point in Ireland. To the American progressive who believed in the possibility of reconstructing modernity and its subjects along new collective lines, Ireland in 1921 seemed proof that he or she was not chasing after phantoms. Events in Ireland seemed to testify to the fact that the slow work of cultural production mattered, that the work of artists, historians, and writers could over time recast the discursive infrastructure of racial and national identity and pave the way for new forms of solidarity and political action. Developments in Ireland confirmed, in other words, what American progressives like those writing for *The Survey* had been saying all along: politics and aesthetics were two sides of the same coin. Contemporary Irish history seemed to offer conclusive evidence that the revitalization of the political sphere and the remaking of citizens necessitated reconstructing consciousness through something like a national renaissance. Moreover, and just as important, Irish independence captured the attention of American progressives because it struck a strong note for racial and national distinctiveness that resonated with the progressives' growing affinity for a pluralist politics based on difference. Ireland claimed its rights to nation-state status on a particularist vision of a resurrected Gaelic self. Drawing on the work of renaissance writers and artists, Irish nationalists of this period envisioned a postcolonial state built upon the rebirth of a Gaelic nation/race that had been suppressed during centuries of English rule. Although there were always, of course, disagreements over precisely whom and what constituted the Gaelic self and the Irish nation, Irish nationalism in the early twentieth century, as the critic Seamus Deane has explained, centered in the main on three claims. The first was that Ireland was a culturally distinct nation; the second that Irish culture had "been mutilated beyond recognition by British colonialism"; and the third that Ireland's lost past could be recovered and given a political form suitable to life in the modern world.[16] The nationalists' claim to an independent postcolonial state thus drew its legitimacy from the idea that a distinctive Gaelic culture, buried beneath centuries of English rule, still resided in the bodies of a Celtic race that was waiting to be reborn in the twentieth century. Such claims by nationalists to racial and cultural difference produced an alternative to the accommodationist identity and civic ideas of an Irish people put forward by pro-Unionists and advocates of Home Rule.

The dominant ideal that emerged in this period was a racial vision of the nation-state as much as it was a purely cultural one. That is to say, while Irish nationalism was very much an affair of language, literature, and song, it was also entangled in a racialized history of descent. Promising to give rebirth to a Gaelic self, Irish nationalists summoned to life an unproblematic Gaelic body that had descended through time despite all efforts at eradication and assimilation. They imagined that it was from within this yet intact Gaelic body (which linked the nearly forgotten Gaelic past to a projected Gaelic future) that a distinctive and independent Irish nation might reemerge. This sometimes tacit and sometimes explicit narrative of descent behind Irish nationalism, which gave rhetorical power to Irish claims for independence, ultimately supposed a national ideal that was more exclusionary at root than the national ideals promoted in either the Harlem or Mexican Renaissances, both of which defined the nation-state along more racially complex lines.

In many respects, whether or not the Irish Renaissance was *primarily* racial is beside the point, for the references to a Gaelic or Celtic race, whenever they did turn up, as they did in *Irish Anticipations*, struck an emotional register far deeper than the less mystifying debates over the complex relations between Anglos and Celts, Protestants and Catholics, landlords and tenants that comprised the last several centuries of Ireland's history. Seen from this perspective, it is not surprising, for instance, that the philosopher, writer, and mystic, A. E. evoked a sort of racial sublime at the end of his otherwise tempered lead article for *The Survey*. Having explained to the American progressive in pedestrian prose that the political claims to an independent Irish homeland flowed from four concrete developments—from the simple and straightforward struggle for political liberty after the manner of the French and American Revolutions led by men like Michael Collins and Eamon de Valera; from the emergence of the agricultural cooperative movement headed by Horace Plunkett; from the claims of labor unions for control over production; and from the unprecedented revival of Gaelic thought and culture led by figures such as W. B. Yeats and Lady Gregory—A. E. discarded quotidian politics for a more mystical declaration of the great destiny awaiting the Gaelic race, a race which, he claimed, had begun among the gods in a time barely remembered:

I cannot believe that the legend of the Gael, which began among the gods, will die out in some petty peasant republic or dominion as a river which rose among the mountains might eddy at last in mud flats and the sewage of squalid cities. What began greatly I think will end greatly, and there will be some flare-up of genius before the torch of the Gael is extinguished and it becomes like the torch once held by the Greeks and other races of genius which are now but memories in the Eternal Mind.[17]

The 1921 issue of *The Survey* with poems by W. B. Yeats and the less well-known Irish poet Padraic Colum reinforced such racial pride. In "The Fair Hills of Eire O," Colum, for instance, told of Ireland's descent from "Eivir's race" in the hills of Ireland where a psychically (if not physically) displaced people yet survived longing for their return to homeland and kin. And a reproduction of Yeats's "To Ireland in the Coming Times" in this issue summoned for the American progressive a timeless Gaelic past that flowed beneath the mutilated Irish present. Yeats captured the spirit of renaissance in this famous poem which reclaimed for his contemporary Irishmen a moment long ago, an origin, during which Ireland's "heart beg[a]n to beat." Yeats told his fellow Irishmen that his moment had not yet passed, for "elemental beings" like "Davis, Mangan, and Ferguson" were yet moving about the air of the present like "flood and fire and clay and wind." Ireland was not an innovation in such renaissance works, rather it was the natural political manifestation of a race and a nation that had been in waiting since the "world's first blossoming age."[18] Poems such as those of Yeats and Colum endowed the

184 • Robert Johnson

Irish present with the fullness of an imagined Gaelic past that called into being a Gaelic self that had always already been. By naturalizing the events of the 1910s and 1920s and endowing them with the emotional and psychological substance of a racial awakening, poets like these gave an emotional substance to events that might otherwise have been cast as merely political.

The idea of renaissance in the 1920s implied the creative act of *remaking* a nation and its people, but in the Irish case it also contained (understandably, given the excesses of British colonization) an ideology of racial descent. An Ulster unionist, like the poet Richard Rowley who contributed an essay on "Ulster's Position" to *Irish Anticipations*, seized on such phantoms of racial purity as one of the primary lines of division separating the northeastern Ulster provinces from those that were to become the Irish Free State. Rowley, unlike other Ulster activists, remained optimistic about the potential for building a united Ireland around civic principles of tolerance and diversity rather than a racial nationalism, but, as he saw the state of affairs in 1921, racial antagonisms (in addition to well-known religious and economic tensions) divided the northeastern provinces from the rest of Ireland. The dominant "Celtic Irish," he claimed, bore a racial identity that distinguished them from an Ulster population that was "Saxon in blood" and retained "unmistakably the characteristics of the Saxon race." Such racial cleavages, Rowley asseverated, were moreover so thoroughly tied up in economic and religious conflicts that it was impossible to tell where the lines were to be drawn among religion, economics, and race. The long history of brutal colonization by Anglo-Protestants and their longstanding political ties to the British Empire meant, that despite intermixing of culture and blood, and a notable cultural hybridity that compromised lines of demarcation, unionists and nationalists alike both drew neat lines of division between Gaelic, Catholic, and economically disfranchised Irish separatists and Anglo, Protestant, and economically privileged unionists.[19] That is to say, the narrative of racial descent, legitimating Ireland's claims to nation-state status, was interwoven with other narratives of political, economic, and cultural conquest. In such a context, race served as an essentializing projection of this long history of class, cultural, and political conflict.

The dominant narrative of an imagined Ireland that we get from this period was neither pluralist nor syncretic, but Irish nationalists did, nonetheless, feel obliged to address themselves to the more cosmopolitan international community outside of Ireland.[20] In *Irish Anticipations*, the American progressive was introduced to two very different versions of

Ireland's role in that global community. The Irish poet, playwright, and nationalist James Stephens explained in his contribution to *The Survey* that the rebirth of Ireland would be followed by a period of defensive solitude wherein nationalists would set about "re-gaelicizing the nation" and "imposing the barrier of language" between themselves and the English. During such a time, Irishmen would, he said, abandon the "foreign tongue" for a Gaelic tongue more suitable to the "Irish mind" and pave the way for the rebirth of a Celtic race, the resurgence of Gaelic culture, and the "disappearance of Irish literature in the English tongue." As "Ireland returned to her fountains," Stephens explained, it would "retire from England . . . from the world, and, like some happy anchorite . . . live in contentment, unheard of, unminded, until the time comes for her to do whatever work the gods assign her." Stephens' real hope for Ireland was quite simply that it might remove itself from world affairs and perhaps even from modern times, so as to "never again have a history."[21]

The more cosmopolitan intellect A. E. supposed a different future for Ireland. Although markedly unsure of the tide of history, A. E. allowed himself to imagine that a future Ireland would not retire from the world, as Stephens hoped, but would take an active part in the course of modern world history. Quoting international authors as diverse as Walt Whitman and Laotze, A. E. linked the destiny of Ireland to the vision of a cosmopolitan world. While he agreed with Stephens that an independent Ireland would certainly reclaim its Gaelic heritage in order to replace the "characterless culture" of colonialism with a "civilization as distinct in character as the Japanese," he believed that the triumph of Gaelic civilization would "generate its own antitoxin" to the sort of provincialism and isolationism of a nativist like Stephens. A. E. imagined that rather than retire from the world and abandon the English language, great numbers of Irishmen would "ransack world literature and science for truth, and bring the aged and the new thought of the world into Ireland." Irish culture, A. E. hoped, would not retreat from world history but instead seek ways "to enrich it[self] and graft onto it those fundamental and universal ideas without which the intellectual life of a nation would be barren and its culture and literature provincial." More alert than Stephens to the sheer force of globalization at work in the world at large, A. E. projected Ireland into a global community that he imagined might be built on pluralist principles. A. E. did not go so far as to imagine Ireland itself along pluralist lines, but he did imagine the island as part of a world where small, postcolonial nations like itself would contribute their share to a larger pluralist world culture.[22]

The Gaelic revival and the type of nationalism it engendered were, like their counterparts elsewhere in the postwar world, products of the global modernizing process. However heavily they depended on archaic icons and promises of resurrection, awakenings like that of the Irish were not atavistic throwbacks but rather distinctly modern developments. As Deane has explained, the seemingly regressive and "archaizing impulse[s]" within events like the Gaelic Renaissance were an integral part of the larger "modernizing process," for it was precisely through the rhetoric of "rebirth, renaissance, and recovery" that modern nations like Ireland and modern races like the Irish gained their legitimacy and meaning. Such renaissances and such projects of recovery indeed give the world the sort of racial and national histories we continue to tell today. The conscription of a particular and exclusive past into the making of an Irish identity and a new Ireland was, in this respect, the manifestation of a more general structure of renaissance that informs modern subjectivity in the world at large.[23] The significance of modern renaissances like that of the Irish (and, as we will see, elsewhere) was, in other words, not that they gave *rebirth* to premodern identities but that they helped to naturalize what were fundamentally new racial and national imaginaries.

To the extent that modern Irish identity was fundamentally embedded in ideas of "rebirth, renaissance, and recovery," the Irish route into the modern world was structurally similar to that of African Americans in Harlem and Mexicans in postrevolutionary Mexico. Yet, while such postwar developments shared a common discourse of historical recovery, it is also true that the terms of renaissance in the Irish case differed markedly, as we will see shortly, from the terms that dominated the politics of the Mexican or "Negro" renaissances. While the best thinkers and writers of the Irish Renaissance, like James Joyce and J. M. Synge, offered a more complex representation of Irish identity in contrast to the more narrowly defined versions of an Irish person or the Irish nation in this period, it is also the case that the dominant narrative of race and nation adopted and propagated by postwar nationalists did not overly trouble itself with the sort of questions of hybridity and pluralism that characterized developments in Mexico and Harlem. This difference becomes clearer when we contrast the Irish case with the Mexican and "Negro" cases, the first of which pointedly celebrated the syncretic, or "mestizo," history of the Mexican nation and the second of which proposed an early version of the multicultural nation.

Mexican Renaissance: La Raza Cosmica and State-Sponsored Cultural Revival

The progressive journalist and historian Frank Tannenbaum began the 1924 issue of *The Survey* by asking American progressives "to stand humbly before a people come to life." Others writing for this special issue, *Mexico—A Promise*, claimed that Mexico was in the midst of "one of the most amazing political, cultural, and economic developments of the decade." This postwar revival, they said, had as its only parallel the "great prototype" of renaissances—the Italian Renaissance. "Just as Boccaccio, Leonardo, [and] Galileo voiced the spirit of the Italian Renaissance," American progressives claimed, "so do Rivera, Gamio, Vasconcelos, Atl and others . . . make articulate the promise of a new day in Mexico." Such progressives identified several major developments in postwar Mexico that seemed to justify the contention that the country was in the midst of an unprecedented historic revival. The emergence of a revolutionary new racial ideology that claimed the Mexican mestizo as the epitome of evolutionary development, the resuscitation of cooperative control of agriculture in the form of the *ejido*, and a cultural renaissance in the arts headed by the famous Mexican muralists—together, these seemed to American progressives clear indicators that the world was witnessing the rebirth of a nation and its people after several centuries of oppression and more than a decade of civil war. The history of Mexico in these years looks different to us than it did to progressives of the time, for we know today that Mexico would ultimately fail to live up to the hyperbolic rhetoric that surrounded its postwar reconstruction, but to American contemporaries writing in the 1920s, Mexico was in the midst of a renaissance of world-historical import.[24]

Mexico—A Promise, the special issue of *The Survey* dedicated to the Mexican Renaissance of the 1920s, is a rich and neglected source that provides us with one of the more interesting contemporary perspectives we have on this event. Carrying important articles both from prominent Mexican intellectuals and statesman and from influential American social reformers, it is evidence of a direct transnational dialogue between progressives in the United States and their counterparts south of the border.[25] Among the contributors to *Mexico—A Promise* were, for instance, such notables as Plutarco Elías Calles, the leading Mexican general who was soon to become Mexican president; José Vasconcelos, the Minister of Education and the public figure most responsible for the cultural revival in Mexico during these years; Manuel Gamio, Mexico's preeminent anthropologist and former student of the Columbia University anthropologist Franz Boas; Felipe Carillo Puerta, the recently deceased Mayan rebel, writer, and statesman; Ramon de Negri, Mexico's Secretary of Agriculture and the person in charge of the nation's rural reconstruction; and Gerardo Murillo, an influential Mexican ethnographer known as Dr. Atl and a founding figure in Mexico's cultural revival. The "Mexico Number" also included reproductions of Diego Rivera's murals and a series of drawings by the Bavarian portrait artist Winold Reiss that captured visually what others put into words. Finally, as important as any contribution to *Mexico—A Promise* was the lead article provided by the American social reformer Frank Tannenbaum, an emerging pioneer of Latin American Studies who had been commissioned by *The Survey* to edit this special issue.[26]

Published on May 1, 1924, *Mexico—A Promise* proved to be a timely look at Mexico. By the mid-1920s, Mexico had entered a period of cultural and economic reconstruction after more than ten years of civil war following the overthrow in 1910 of the neo-liberal dictatorship of Porforio Diaz. In these pivotal years, the revolutionary elite who came to power in the new administration launched out on a crusade to remake the nation culturally, economically, and politically.[27] The economic and political project of the postrevolutionary elite entailed an ambitious (if somewhat disappointing) program in agrarian and social reform which included the reintroduction of collective ownership of land in some villages as well as the adoption of a radical constitution that seemed to guarantee a number of sweeping improvements in labor relations and social welfare. But the success of political and economic reconstruction was viewed by the postrevolutionary elite to be dependent upon a parallel and complementary reconstruction of Mexican history, culture, and identity. In a country wracked by years of war and factionalism, postwar political and economic reconstruction seemed to hinge, in other words, on the rescripting of the racial and national imaginary of Mexico in such a way as to draw Mexico's various peoples, classes, and factions into a shared story of progress. To that end, substantial federal funds were allocated in this period to the cultural apparatus of the state in the hopes of summoning a national renaissance into being. The Mexican Renaissance that came of this was consequently at root a cultural revival sponsored by the state, led by state-funded teachers, researchers, artists, and bureaucrats, and reflective of the larger nation-building objectives of Mexico's postrevolutionary elite.

As in the Irish case, a rescripting of the relationship between race and nation was at the symbolic center of this Renaissance. Three figures whose work appeared in *Mexico—A Promise*, José Vasconcelos, Manuel Gamio, and Diego Rivera, all played especially important roles in articulating,the new narrative of race and nation that was to come out of Mexico in these years. The central figure in this respect was undoubtedly, José Vasconcelos, who as the new Minister of Education commissioned and oversaw the Mexican mural movement, the state's educational projects, and various other propaganda activities, and thus exerted an influence on the Mexican Renaissance that perhaps no other can claim. In this respect alone, Vasconcelos is a historically central figure, but his influence on postrevolutionary thought and culture extended beyond his administrative role. An intellectual of global stature, Vasconcelos also articulated the most important revision of race theory to come out of Latin America during the early twentieth century. In a bold and highly publicized challenge to the racist assumptions of northern social Darwinists on both sides of the Atlantic, Vasconcelos proposed in the 1920s a theory of racial evolution, which he termed *la raza cosmica*, that proclaimed Mexico's mestizo race to be at the forefront of human evolutionary development. Directly counter to the hegemonic claims of the world powers of the day, Vasconcelos declared that it was not the genetically pure and attenuated Anglo-Saxon race that would lead the world into the future but rather the more racially fluid and syncretic ones (created from the best traits of multiple races) like the Mexican mestizo that would do so. Although in 1924 Vasconcelos was still a year away from publishing his famous essay on the cosmic race, the ideological tenets behind *la raza cosmica* had by the postwar years already saturated the state's cultural project and come to function as something like an official creed of the new Mexico.[28]

In *Mexico—A Promise*, American progressives were introduced to Mexico's new racial creed by Manuel Gamio, head of the nation's Department of Anthropological Research and, after Vasconcelos, the country's second most important figure on matters of racial thought. Gamio played a central role in articulating and disseminating the new narrative of race and nation that came out of this period, and it is thus not surprising that American progressives first learned about Mexico's revolutionary racial ideals from him. In his contribution to the 1924 issue of *The Survey*, Gamio informed the American progressive that his nation had chosen to reject the principles of racial hierarchy that prevailed in the western world in favor of a revolutionary new "national synthesis" that celebrated the nation's racial hybridity. That new synthesis, which was to emerge from the "reciprocal contributions" of "Mexico's various racial groups," would eventuate, Gamio foresaw, in nothing less than a total "realignment of the [nation's] races." Moreover, the Mexican state's new commitment to "racial understanding," to "a fusion of different cultures," and to "linguistic unification," would ultimately have the effect of producing a new national and racial imaginary. As the nation's Indian and Creole races merged into a single mestizo ideal, Mexico would gain for the first time, Gamio said, a "coherent national consciousness, a true patria."[29] Rivera's murals gave visual expression to this new racial and national imaginary in *Mexico—A Promise*. Murals such as Rivera's "Sugar Refinery," a now-famous section from the larger mural on the walls of the Ministry of Education building, offered American progressives and Mexicans alike a new portrait of Mexico that incorporated the nation's indigenous peoples into the new narratives of racial and national progress advocated by the Mexican state.[30] The caption to *The Survey's* reproduction of the "Sugar Refinery" explained along these lines that Rivera's murals offered a new role for the Indian in the national imaginary. The "Sugar Refinery" along with other murals in the series reprinted in *The Survey* were, it was claimed, dramatic illustrations of the new role that the "native arts and industries" had within "the ideals of the new regime."[31] The mural itself illustrated just that point. It centered on a group of three Indian men, stirring liquid sugar in rhythm, their bodies arched in unison, left arms raised to the tip of a body-length puddling stick, right arms and hands tensed low on the stick to gain leverage in the stirring, the workers arranged in such a way as to downplay their individuality and reinforce the collective nature of their enterprise. (In the piece, each is dressed identically, white slacks and shirts drawn tight around muscular bodies, faces shielded from view.) In the foreground, five other indigenous laborers are methodically at work casting the sugar into a series of bowls, two pouring the liquid, three molding the sugar in a long series of casts. The "Sugar Refinery" gives the impression of an organic machine made up of indigenous bodies busily and comfortably working together on building a new Mexico, the collective and nonmechanized nature of their work suggesting a pace and quality of modernization peculiarly Mexican.[32]

"Sugar Refinery" like other murals reproduced in *Mexico—A Promise* functioned iconographically to represent the new narrative of the postrevolutionary Mexico—a narrative which combined the life of a Mexican past, with its human rhythms, its cooperative life, and its indigenous and syncretic history, with the promise of a modern future, with its assembly line work, its commercial character, and its industrial order. Such murals gave the impression that Mexico's indigenous peoples were deliberately, methodically, and even languorously, at work rebuilding a people and a nation that were as much of their own making as they were the creole's or the mestizo's. In an interview for *The Survey* conducted by the American writer Katherine Anne Porter, Rivera himself situated his own work at the intersection of race and nation. Rivera told Porter that Mexico was passing through a unique episode in its history wherein "a whole nation" was beginning to "evince the astounding fullness of genius." "Almost every such race," he claimed in a way not unlike his Irish counterpart George Russell, "experiences one such epoch of lofty intellectual and spiritual development . . . a culmination of centuries of preparation, centuries wherein the race grows gradually in the love and understanding of art and . . . the power of projection."[33] Rivera's own work was to be understood as one such expression of that burgeoning racial genius.

Rivera's murals, like Vasconcelos' theory of the cosmic race, repudiated the explicit racism of the creole-centered ideology that had dominated Mexican history and, as such, fundamentally changed the ways in which race would be discussed in Mexico thereafter, but the new narrative of race and nation that came out of this moment was, like its forebears and its Irish counterpart, a political vision that simplified racial matters for the sake of unity. *La Raza Cosmica* in its various incarnations reflected the goals of a nationalist elite that was opposed to the more radically pluralist racial thought espoused by many of Mexico's indigenous peoples. In many respects, the Mexican Renaissance that we learn about in *The Survey* was a conquest in the name of renaissance as much as it was a popular outpouring of "race spirit," to steal a phrase from Locke.

The title to Gamio's essay, "The New Conquest," said as much. In the eyes of nationalist architects like Gamio, "a coherent national consciousness" would mean among other things linguistic unification and economic development along a culturally specific trajectory of national progress. In practice, such a program would always be one-sided, as creole and mestizo missionaries went into Indian villages to enact a program of reeducation that included not merely lessons in reading and writing but, in Gamio's own words, lessons in "industry, commerce, agriculture, hygiene, morality, [and] civics." Such a renaissance may have aimed admirably at the ideal of national unity, but achieving that unity implied serious changes for the Mexican Indian who would be brought further into western market culture, who would be trained in new methods of farming, dressing, and behaving, and who would be educated into a western model of citizenship and western notions of morality.[34]

The Mexican Renaissance that American progressives applauded in the 1920s was thus a state-sponsored revival that promoted a hegemonic version of hybridity. The narrative of race and nation that emerged out of these years in Mexico was syncretic in rhetoric and aspiration but it did not reflect indigenous culture nearly as much as it did the culture of the mestizos and the Creoles who made up the ranks of the postrevolutionary elite during the Obregón administration. Racial rebirth would, if the new nationalists had their way, mean a radical revamping of Indian identity for the sake of national unity. Whatever the rhetoric and however sincere the intent of the revolutionary elite, their version of renaissance always reflected the goals and aspirations of those mestizo and creole nationalists who held positions of power in the metropole.

Renaissance in both the Irish and Mexican cases was a fundamental part of the process of nation-building and as such centered on a powerful rescripting of the narratives of race and nation that had legitimated the older political orders. Renaissance in the Mexican case served the purposes of legitimating the state's program for postwar reconstruction. A state-sponsored Renaissance, it was thus distinctly different in form and spirit from the subaltern Renaissance that gave birth to a postcolonial Ireland. The one, at least in its starkest form, imagined a racially homogenous nation-state in which the subaltern might recover his or her agency; the other introduced the ideal of a racially mixed state which celebrated diversity but threatened to subsume the subaltern into a hegemonic national imaginary crafted by those who thought they knew what was best for him or her. As we turn to Harlem, we get yet a different politics of renaissance. Harlem, as will be seen, was a subaltern renaissance directed not so much at nation-building as were the previous two renaissances but at reforming the discursive infrastructure of a white supremacist state that had seriously circumscribed the literal and symbolic terrain in which black Americans moved.

Harlem Renaissance: The Politics of the New Negro Narrative

As with the Mexican Renaissance, the Harlem Renaissance in the United States was a highly politicized affair that sought to redress the dominant narrative of race and nation in that country. Moreover, like that Renaissance, it was a cultural project shaped by an elite who had specific notions of the form the new racial self should take. It differed, however, from the Mexican Renaissance in important ways. Most notably, the Renaissance in Harlem stood in stark contrast to the cultural project of the Mexican elite in that it was, in ways similar to the subaltern Renaissance in Ireland, not endorsed by the state but rather in response to a state that was overtly antagonistic to its participants' aspirations. In contrast to Rivera, Vasconcelos, and Gamio who received both funding and ideological support from the federal government, African Americans who promoted the Harlem Renaissance in the United States found themselves in the 1920s relegated to a second-class status and hamstrung by state policies that protected Jim Crow segregation and a wide array of discriminatory practices in the North and South. Such conditions together with the reformist politics of its middle-class advocates gave to the Harlem Renaissance a different shape than either of its counterparts in Ireland or Mexico.

There is disagreement in the historical profession over the precise substance and meaning of the Harlem Renaissance, but certain features are clear. Its social origins lay in the new black communities of the northern United States that had come into being as the result of a large-scale internal migration of African Americans to northern manufacturing centers during and after World War I and the subsequent ghettoizing of such migrants in neighborhoods like Harlem. In historic terms, it began with the return of African-American troops during postwar demobilization and ended with the onset of an economic depression that struck African Americans harder than anyone else (taking shape amidst a reactionary political climate that included among other things, the federal seizure and deportation of immigrant radicals, the passage of draconian immigration restriction, the rise of a powerful second Ku Klux Klan, and the series of nativist race riots which struck the United States from Texas to Chicago). In terms of substance, it was an elite-driven cultural revival among urban African Americans who believed that the power of the written word might be used to undermine the prevailing structures of racism in the United States. A highly politicized cultural movement, it was, in the words of one of its less admiring scholars, "an arts and letters movement" for social justice, a sort of "cultural nationalism of the parlor" that aimed at gaining for African Americans social respect and civil rights through their participation in and contributions to western culture.[35]

Whatever historiographical disagreements there may be regarding the efficacy of its politics, the Harlem Renaissance plays a prominent role in American history. It does so primarily because, like the Irish and Mexican Renaissances, it proposed a compelling and dramatic new narrative of the relationship between race and nation. Locke's expositions of that narrative in *The Survey* and *The New Negro* anthology (a narrative which we might term simply the New Negro narrative) are among the most lucid and influential. An awakened black self, a "New Negro,"

Locke claimed, stood at the center of the Harlem Renaissance. In contrast to an Old Negro, which was imagined by Locke to be steeped in Uncle Tom-ism, the New Negro had broken off in three new directions: he repudiated the accommodationist tradition of conservative black elites like Booker T. Washington, the American race leader who urged deferring full racial equality for more immediate material uplift; he rejected the paternalistic race work of the older order of white liberals who frequently condescended to their subjects of interest and urged an assimilationist model of race relations; and he reclaimed for African Americans, in stark contrast to earlier efforts to downplay racial difference, a racially distinct culture rooted in historic and biological ties to Africa. This New Negro, in short, had a different orientation to the white world and a different sense of self-possession than his accommodationist or assimilationist precursors did. According to Locke, not only did he view himself as the psychological and intellectual equal of white Americans, he was newly alive to the racial origins of the rich and deep collective memory he carried within him.

The New Negro narrative was, as such, an explicit challenge to the dominant narratives of race and nation circulating in the early twentieth-century United States. Whereas the dominant narrative in the white community claimed blackness as a mark of inferiority and whereas the dominant narrative among black race leaders downplayed the relevance of race in order to promote an assimilationist agenda based on a western model of progress, Locke and the new generation for which he claimed to speak played up their racial difference, designating racial difference in general and blackness in particular to be the wellspring of their identity. Quite explicitly, Locke stressed the importance of race consciousness to the Harlem Renaissance project, claiming that the New Negro carried within him a "deep feeling of race" that was "the mainspring of Negro life" and that he was motivated by "the sense of a mission" to rehabilitate the black race "in world esteem."[36] Assertions of the centrality of race consciousness to African-American identity were reinforced by the work of several renaissance poets who sought to reclaim the notion of blackness in the Harlem number of *The Survey* by stressing the beauty of the black body. Langston Hughes, for instance, compared the coming of dusk to his own body, "Rest at pale evening,/A tall, slim tree,/Night coming tenderly/Black like me"; Angelina Grimke wrote in a similar vein that she had "just seen a most beautiful thing/Slim and still,/Against a gold, gold sky,/A straight black cypress,/Sensitive,/ Exquisite,/A black finger/Pointing upwards"; and Countee Cullen spoke adoringly of the beauty in a "brown girl's swagger" and of a "Dark Madonna" whom even Death found so "sweet."[37] Such pronouncements in prose and poetry were part of the broader project to reclaim, and resignify, the meaning of both blackness and black peoples in western culture.

The assertion of racial distinctiveness by Harlem Renaissance writers was not, however, the predicate to a separatist agenda. In contrast to the exclusionary tendencies in a case like that of the Irish, the New Negro narrative of race and nation explicitly disavowed the idea of racial separatism (at least in political matters) by proposing a racially pluralist version of the nation-state.[38] The reformist rhetoric of the New Negro emphasized in no uncertain terms that African Americans were reclaiming rather than rejecting a nation that was as much their own as any Anglo American's. Locke's sentiments were representative in his introduction to *Harlem: Mecca of the New Negro* where he explained to the American progressive that the New Negro reached out "to nothing but American wants, American ideas" and that the New Negro augured not the balkanization of the United States but rather "a new democracy in American culture."[39] Similarly, emphasizing that inclusion not separation was the objective of race politics among Harlem intellectuals and artists, the prominent African-American writer James Weldon Johnson explained, "Harlem talks American, reads American, thinks American."[40] And perhaps the most memorable expressions of this reformist message from these years came from the budding poet Langston Hughes, who began his famous poem "I, Too," reproduced in the Harlem number of *Survey Graphic*, with the memorable lines: "I, too, sing America/ I am the darker brother./They send me to eat in the kitchen/When company comes."; and ended with a patriotic appeal to an imagined American conscience: "Tomorrow . . . ./ . . . they'll see how beautiful I am/ And be ashamed,—/ I, too, sing America."[41]

By claiming a common national identity, Renaissance writers drew a shared bond with white America. But the real rhetorical strength of their writings centered on their claims to racial difference. Renaissance, in this respect, supposed a pluralist conception of the nation-state that valued diversity over homogeneity. Locke's version of a pluralist nation, which paralleled other pluralist conceptions of the state put forward by contemporary American writers like Randolph Bourne or Horace Kallen in the same period, supposed that the United States might gain in depth and spirit were it to give up its ethnocentric hopes for the assimilation of its minorities and reorient itself toward a cosmopolitan nationalism that protected and valued the distinct cultures, experiences, and psychologies of the nation's different races and ethnicities. The pluralism that came out of the Harlem Renaissance attempted to carve out, at least within the realm of discourse, just such a space for racial and ethnic difference.

Representing racial difference was, however, a delicate matter, and the Harlem Renaissance understandably produced no final consensus on this score. But many writers did venture, if cautiously, to sketch the contours of that difference. Locke, for his part, was especially tentative to sharpen his ideas of racial difference too finely, but he did claim in his opening remarks to *The Survey* that African Americans had a natural "humor, sentiment, imagination and tropic nonchalance" that both distinguished them in character from their white counterparts and might help to "leaven" out an otherwise materialistic, overworked, and spiritless nation.[42] Others who wrote in *Harlem: Mecca of the New Negro* like the West Indian writers W. A. Domingo and Claude McKay depicted such tropic nonchalance and imagination by claiming that peoples of African descent in the United States carried within themselves "palm fringed sea shores, murmuring streams, luxuriant hills and vales," as well as "[b]ananas ripe and green,/ . . . memories/Of fruit-trees laden by low-singing rills,/ . . . dewey dawns, and mystical blue skies."[43] And even a more classically trained poet like Countee Cullen or a modernist one like Langston Hughes ventured to claim that beneath the veneer of the alienated, assimilated, and overcivilized Americans they had become yet beat within their hearts, a more natural, simple, and rhythmic African self.[44] Such soft brushstrokes of racial difference were given less cautious formulation in the writings of the famous art collector Alfred Barnes, a white progressive who summed up in his contribution to *Harlem: Mecca of the New Negro* what he saw to be the racial differences that distinguished the African American from his white counterpart. As Barnes saw it, African Americans were "primitive," "natural," "naive," "spontaneous," "untutored," and in "harmony with nature," and were, moreover, "poet[s] by birth" who bore within their bodies "tremendous emotional endowment[s]" and "luxuriant and free imagination[s]."[45] Whether or not these in particular were the distinct racial gifts that the New Negro had to offer an American civilization, Renaissance writers like Locke did suppose, or at least said, that African Americans had histories and souls that distinguished them from other Americans.[46]

Such claims that Locke and other Renaissance writers made to racial distinctiveness cut against the grain of the more standard universalist ones that had long informed progressive politics, and as such their writings mark an important break with earlier conceptions of the relationship between race and nation that circulated in the United States. The most compelling ideal to emerge out of this Renaissance was the vision it offered of a pluralist nation-state wherein race remained the marker of difference among peoples (a difference which transcended the bounds of the nation) and nation remained the mark of their identity with one another. This pluralist ideal allowed Harlem writers like Locke to claim a realm of racial autonomy from white America without foreclosing on African-American claims to a shared national heritage and tradition. Rather than repudiate the pernicious idea of race itself, a strategy that seemed utopian and out of joint with the tenor of the times, Harlem writers like Locke chose to underscore the centrality of race by proposing a more or less naturalized narrative of racial identity.

This new variety of race consciousness and its claims to racial difference were, however, of course, something of a double-edged sword, for such claims to racial difference could in the hands of white and black writers alike easily reify into the sort of racial stereotypes that African Americans had long struggled to overcome. Moreover, to the extent that the resignifying of African-American identity in the Harlem Renaissance continued to promote an unproblematized genealogy of racial descent or a simplified notion of African-American identity, it remained in essential ways caught within the terms of the racist society from which it sprang. Nonetheless, the symbolic revaluations of racial difference by writers and artists of the 1920s still made the Harlem Renaissance a very real and potent assault on the reigning discourse of race and nation in the United States, and though its impact was not felt immediately, this Renaissance project did over time help both to transform the symbolic role of blackness in the American imaginary and to shift the discursive infrastructure of progressive thought towards the type of pluralist worldview that has become more fashionable since the 1960s.

The version of renaissance that Locke and other New Negro advocates espoused took on a different shape than the two cases we have thus far examined. Its rescripting of the narrative of race and nation reflected among other things the segregated society and demographic realities from which it emerged. The hostile racial climate of postwar America as well as the long legacy of a strictly imposed color line militated not only against the type of racial intermixture that was common in Latin America but even against the sort of *symbolic* syncretic ideals that might have produced an American version of *la raza cosmica*. Moreover, the demographic realities that African Americans faced as a minority group in the United States and the circumstances under which many of their ancestors had come to North America did not point very neatly toward the likelihood that they would acquire anything like a postcolonial nation-state as the Irish did. The New Negro narrative might thus be viewed as something of a political compromise, as a delicately balanced pluralist ideal that rescripted the symbolic infrastructure of racial discourse in the United States without threatening the American racial imaginary too completely. In this sense, the New Negro narrative can be understood as a bid to gain for African Americans an increased mobility, at least within the realm of symbols, than that which was offered under the terms of the previous discourses of race and nation, while the narrative it proposed was as importantly a careful rewriting of the relationship between race and nation that did not challenge in any fundamental way the prevailing idea in America that the races of the world were indeed different in essential ways.

Conclusion: The Harlem Renaissance in Global Perspective

This chapter proposed at the start that situating the Harlem Renaissance alongside the Irish and Mexican Renaissances might generate insights different from those likely to emerge through the study of any one of these alone. Let me conclude with three observations.

The first is that each of these renaissances was, as we have seen, fundamentally tied to a politically charged revision of the narrative of race and nation. Each put forward a different equation of the relationship between race and nation that reflected the unique context in which it arose. In the case of the Irish Renaissance, the dominant narrative deployed by Irish nationalists was that of a racial nationalism premised on both a real and imagined Gaelic past. In that narrative, the Irish Free State was imagined to be the political embodiment of a more or less homogeneous nation of peoples who had always already been Irish. This postcolonial Renaissance drew hard lines between the colonizer and colonized in an effort to legitimize the rights of Irishmen to their own nation-state. Race functioned, in this case, as an essentializing force that legitimized just such claims to postcolonial independence. In the case of the Mexican Renaissance, the narrative of race and nation crafted by the postrevolutionary elite and sponsored by the new Mexican state proposed a syncretic version of the nation-state, wherein the bodies of colonizer and colonized merged at least in theory to form a mestizo race quite unlike the more purifying tendencies of the Irish case. That version of a hybrid nation was, however, as we have seen, a hegemonic version that continued to privilege the European pole at the expense of the Indian. In the final analysis, the notion of *La Raza Cosmica* had the paradoxical effect of both opening up new possibilities for a revolutionary revaluation of Mexico's indigenous peoples, while simultaneously fore-closing on those possibilities in the pursuit of an imagined national unity. And finally, the Harlem Renaissance put forward a narrative of race and nation that differed from both of these in that it proposed neither a racially homogenous state nor a syncretic one but a nation-state built on an ideal of racial pluralism. In joining together an assertion of a racial difference that transcended the bounds of the state with the claim to a common national identity, Harlem writers and artists in the 1920s delicately balanced the equation of identity and difference in such a way as to revalue black culture without fundamentally threatening the race-based thinking so deeply engrained in American society. Whatever new possibilities this opened for the expression of African-American agency in the United States, there was an element of symbolic segregation in the New Negro narrative that reflected the political order from which it sprang.

If it is clear that these renaissances gave to the world three very different equations of the relationship between race and nation, it is also clear that each contributed to a larger transnational discourse that we might choose to label "progressive." This discourse was at least trans-Atlantic, if it was not fully global. The second conclusion I want to draw here is that each of these three revivals took part to some degree in a very direct transnational conversation that was discursively structured in good part both by a dominant western racial ideology that devalued non-Anglo Saxon peoples as well as by a more progressive pluralist discourse that was emerging in this period. On the one hand, we can see quite clearly that each was in its own way a direct response to a modern world order that denigrated the culture and race of its participants. In all three instances, the equation of race and nation proposed by Renaissance writers repudiated explicitly the dominant racial assumptions of early twentieth-century western thought. In different ways, each, publicly rejected the claims made by contemporary social Darwinists that there were inferior races to be found residing at the bottom of an evolutionary ladder. The Irish case, as we have seen, retrieved a glorious Celtic race from that narrative by imagining itself as an alternative to an homogenizing and racially biased British identity; the Mexican case rejected prevailing western ideas of racial evolution to place the mestizo, rather the pure-bred, at the forefront of human evolution; and the Harlem case proposed a pluralist model that denounced the very idea on which social evolutionary thought was premised, that there was a single standard by which one could rank races and cultures in the first place.

Furthermore, this transnational discourse was comprised of more than just a reaction to the racist thought of the day. It was also premised on a new appreciation of racial and cultural diversity among international progressives that stood in stark contrast to the imperializing and assimilationist tendencies of earlier progressive thought. Irish writers like A. E. attempted to imagine a global order which had room on its stage for the people of a minor postcolonial state like Ireland to play their part in world affairs without subjecting themselves to colonizing empires like that of Britain. Mexicanists like Tannenbaum, Rivera, and Gamio imagined a world order in which a mestizo nation like Mexico could claim global significance precisely because it challenged the racial strictures and prophesied the breakdown of a racial order propagated by world dominators like England and the United States. And African-American writers like Locke strove to imagine both a world order and a national order that did not devalue racial or cultural difference but rather resituated subaltern peoples and the contributions they had made, and might yet make, near the symbolic center of modern history.

Third and finally, globalizing the Harlem Renaissance serves to accentuate the political function that the rhetoric of renaissance performed both for American progressives and their counterparts in Ireland and Mexico. We have seen that renaissance, along with its synonyms, rebirth, revival, and awakening, captured the belief among American progressives like Locke that the world's peoples were deliberately remaking themselves and their societies through a conscious, collective engagement with the past. Renaissance in Harlem, Mexico, Ireland—but also too in China, Palestine, Russia, and Italy—suggested to such progressives that the postwar world was alight with creativity and purpose and that its people were marching towards a future of deliberate self-determination in politics and culture.

We have seen that renaissance thus functioned in this instance as the discursive means to integrating different political and cultural developments across the globe into a metanarrative of progressive change. While renaissance in each of the three cases we examined certainly opened up new expressions of communal purpose and collective identity in ways that conformed to a progressive worldview, ironically, it did so by closing off other political possibilities and compromising the pluralist worldview progressives were espousing. The rhetorical force of renaissance thus served to mask over the messier side of identity politics and political self-determination in the modern world. In globalizing the Harlem Renaissance, we thus draw closer to understanding the political and cultural machinations through which some races and nations—and not others—are reborn onto the modern world stage.

Notes

1. Alain Locke, Ed., *The New Negro* (New York: Atheneum, 1992), pp. xxvii, 7.
2. The argument developed here is meant to supplement rather than challenge the excellent transnational scholarship that has focused on the pan-Africanism of the Renaissance years. See, for instance, Sidney Lemelle and Robin Kelley, Eds., *Imagining Home: Class, Culture, and Nationalism in the African Diaspora* (New York: Verso, 1994).
3. Alan Dawley, *Changing the World: American Progressives in War and Revolution* (Princeton, NJ: Princeton, 2003), p. 220.
4. *The Survey* and *Survey Graphic* were staples of left-liberal journalism in the early twentieth century. *The Survey* was a weekly social reform magazine that had been in existence since 1912; *Survey Graphic* was a richly illustrated and more broadly distributed monthly issue of the magazine that began in 1921.
5. In *The Harlem Renaissance in Black and White* (Cambridge, MA: Harvard, 1995), George Hutchinson has developed this connection most fully, but the earlier histories told by David Levering Lewis and Nathan Huggins also accord *The Survey* an important role in the making of the Renaissance. See Nathan Huggins, *Harlem Renaissance* (New York: Oxford, 1973) and David Levering Lewis, *When Harlem Was in Vogue* (New York: Penguin, 1997). The University of Virginia has made the full text and illustrations of the March 1, 1925, issue of *Survey Graphic* electronically available at http://etext.lib.virginia.edu/harlem/contents.html.
6. This series of special issues of *Survey Graphic* included among other publications: *Irish Anticipations* (November 1921); *Russian Dreams, Russian Realities* (March 1923); *Mexico—A Promise* (May 1924); *Harlem: Mecca of the New Negro* (March 1925); *East–West* (May 1926); and *An American Look at Fascism* (March 1927).
7. I do not want to be overly naive in following early progressives who cast such disparate international events together under the heading of renaissances or awakenings. Lumping together, for instance, such historical developments as the Bolshevik takeover in Russia, the cultural movement in China, and the New Negro movement in such a way demands a certain caution and humility in considering what can be learned from such comparisons and what new distortions might emerge. An example of the incommensurability of which we should remain aware is the Harlem Renaissance, which while historically important both nationally and internationally, was not the political equivalent of the birth of either communism or fascism in Europe; the Harlem Renaissance was not a post-colonial independence movement in the manner that Irish nationalism was; and the Harlem Renaissance was not a state-sponsored renaissance in the way that the cultural revivals in Russia, Italy, or Mexico were.

Moreover, considering the Harlem Renaissance (or the Mexican and Irish renaissances for that matter) from the point of view of American progressives distorts to a degree the substance of those renaissances. In this chapter, for instance, Alain Locke, A.E. (George Russell), and Frank Tannenbaum, the major interpreters, respectively, of the Harlem, Irish, and Mexican renaissances to the American progressive public in the 1920s are accorded representative status. While each undoubtedly played a substantive role in articulating the meaning of those renaissances to the American public, it is important to note up-front that the Harlem, Mexican, and Irish renaissances were complex, negotiated events, each with its own host of political and cultural actors who worked, labored, and fought both alongside and with the aforementioned. This chapter does not mean to suppose those renaissances were other than that.

8. Dawley, *Changing the World*, p. 305.
9. Paul Kellogg, *Survey Graphic*, March 1, 1925, p. 627.
10. Alain Locke, "Introduction" and "Enter the New Negro," *Survey Graphic*, March 1, 1925, pp. 629–34; Frank Tannenbaum, "Mexico—A Promise," *Survey Graphic*, May 1, 1924, p. 129–132; A. E., "Irish Anticipations," *Survey Graphic*, November 26, 1921, pp. 291–4.
11. For further information on cultural pluralism and conceptions of race and culture in the early twentieth-century United States see Everett H Akam, *Transnational America: Cultural Pluralist Thought in the Twentieth Century* (Lanham, MD: Rowman and Littlefield, 2002); Hutchinson, *The Harlem Renaissance in Black and White*; and George W. Stocking, *Race, Culture, and Evolution: Essays in the History of Anthropology* (Chicago, IL: University of Chicago Press, 1982).
12. Locke, "Introduction" and "Enter the New Negro," p. 629–34; Tannenbaum, "Mexico—A Promise," pp. 129–32; A. E., "Irish Anticipations," pp. 291–4.
13. Huggins, *Harlem Renaissance*, p. 3. Fiction is not used in a derogatory way here to suggest that they were merely fantasies of the mind so much as it is used to emphasize the construction of historical events.
14. Jesus Velasco makes a similar argument for the relationship between Mexican intellectuals and the international progressive community. See Velasco, "Reading Mexico, Understanding the United States," *Journal of American History*, 86:2 (September 1999), 641–67.
15. Such independence was not easily won even after acceptance by the British government. Two years of civil war between Irish nationalists, separatists in the Irish Republican Army who objected to continuing ties to England and supporters of the new Irish state who saw the 1921 compromise to be a good first step, had to be fought before even a measure of peace descended on the new Ireland. See James Lydon, *The Making of Ireland: From Ancient Times to the Present* (New York: Routledge, 1998), especially chapters 12–14.
16. Seamus Deane, *Strange Country: Modernity and Nationhood in Irish Writing since 1790* (New York: Oxford, 1997), p. 53.
17. A. E., "Irish Anticipations," p. 294.
18. Padraic Colum, "The Fair Hills of Eiré O," and W. B. Yeats, "To Ireland in the Coming Times," *Survey Graphic*, November 26, 1921, p. 294, 304.
19. Richard Rowley, "Ulster's Position," *Survey Graphic*, November 26, 1921.

20. The high modernist fiction of the Irish Renaissance, such as the work of James Joyce or J. M. Synge explicitly complicated the portrait of Irish identity we are discussing here. Political nationalism in the Irish case, as in most cases, simplified Irish identity and history in its struggle for legitimacy and support. For a more thorough portrait of the Irish Renaissance, see Declan Kiberd, *Inventing Ireland* (Cambridge, MA: Harvard University Press, 1996).

21. James Stephens, "Ireland Returns to Her Fountains," *Survey Graphic*, November 26, 1921, p. 302–4.

22. A. E., "Irish Anticipations," pp. 291–4.

23. Deane, *Strange Country*, p. 51.

24. Press Release, "Mexico—A Promise," April 25, 1924, Box 195, Folder 1552, Survey Associates Records; "Editorials," *Survey Graphic*, May 1, 1924, p. 186. For a contemporary interpretation of the Mexican Renaissance focused exclusively on the art of the early twentieth century, see Mackinley Helm, *Mexican Painters: Rivera, Orozco, Siqueiros, and Other Artists of the Social Realist School* (New York: Dover, 1989).

25. Velasco, "Reading Mexico, Understanding the United States," p. 642–5.

26. Plutarco Elías Calles, "A Hundred Years of Revolution," pp. 133–4; José Vasconcelos, "Educational Aspirations," pp. 167–9; Manuel Gamio, "The New Conquest," pp. 143–6, pp. 192–4; Felipe Carrilla Puerta, "The New Yucatan," pp. 138–42; Ramon de Negri, "The Agrarian Problem," pp. 149–52; Elena Landazuri, "Why We Are Different," pp. 159–60; Dr. Atl, "Popular Arts of Mexico," pp. 161–4; Diego Rivera, "The Guild Spirit in Mexican Art," pp. 174–8 (including an interview with Katherine Anne Porter); and Frank Tannenbaum, "Mexico—A Promise," pp. 129–32. In *Survey Graphic*, May 1, 1924. For Tannenbaum's role as a pioneer of Mexican and Latin American Studies in the United States, see Charles Hale, "Frank Tannenbaum and the Mexican Revolution," *The Hispanic American Historical Review*, 75:2 (May 1995), pp. 215–46.

27. During these years, the Ministry of Education's José Vasconcelos, for instance, presided over a considerable expansion in federal funds for, what he termed, "the education of the masses," allocating substantial financial support for a legion of nationalist teachers (whom he termed missionaries) entrusted with bringing the revolution and its aims into the various corners of the nation. Likewise under government auspices, Manuel Gamio, head of the Anthropological Branch in the Department of Agriculture, began his comprehensive survey of the various peoples of Mexico in an anthropological enterprise that amounted to what *The Survey's* editors claimed to be "the most comprehensive project of [its] kind in the world." And the Mexican muralists of the period, also with substantial government support behind them, formed their famous art syndicates as they set out to rescript the nation's racial and national life on the walls and ceilings of the public sphere throughout Mexico. For the politics of the Mexican Renaissance, see Leonard Folgarait, *Mural Painting and Social Revolution in Mexico: Art of the New Order* (New York: Cambridge, 1998).

28. The historian Alan Knight has termed Mexico's racial ideology in this period, "revolutionary *indigenismo*." "Revolutionary indigenismo" in its various formulations was a nationalist ideology that sought to integrate the Mexican Indian, the mestizo, and the creole into a unified image of the Mexican nation. It was essentially a Mexican version of cultural syncretism supported and propagated both by the new Obregón regime and the regimes to follow. Knight explains that other more radical ideologies were also propagated at the time. "Indianism," for example, was an alternative, grassroots racial ideology that asserted the right to indigenous racial and political autonomy at the expense of national consolidation. See Knight, "Racism, Revolution, and *Indigenismo*: Mexico, 1910–1940," pp. 71–117. In Richard Graham, Ed., *The Idea of Race in Latin America, 1870–1940* (Austin, TX: University of Texas Press 1990).

29. Manuel Gamio, "The New Conquest," *Survey Graphic*, March 1, 1924, pp. 143–6.

30. Rivera's murals were the centerpiece of the larger renaissance project. In a nation with a high illiteracy rate and with a variety of indigenous peoples speaking a variety of languages, art played an essential role in communicating the vision of a racial-national revival. Mural-making was as such the most visible piece of the much broader government-sponsored "populist program of education" that also included sweeping educational reform, notable public works, and extensive anthropological research. See Folgarait, *Mural Painting and Social Revolution in Mexico*, pp. 18–19.

31. Diego Rivera, "Metal Workers," *Survey Graphic*, May 1, 1924, p. 128. It is interesting to note that the "Sugar Refinery" was mislabeled in this edition of *The Survey*, entitled instead "Metal Workers." Symbolically, sugar is one of the original staple commodities of the modern world order just as steel has long functioned metonymically for the modern age itself.

32. Rivera framed the mural as a receding series of rectangles that give the impression that this organic machine might go on forever in an endless cycle of productivity that is as long as Mexico's past.

33. Diego Rivera, interviewed by Katherine Anne Porter, "The Guild Spirit in Mexican Art," *Survey Graphic*, May 1, 1924, pp. 174–8.

34. Gamio, "The New Conquest," pp. 144–6, pp. 192–4.

35. Lewis, *When Harlem Was in Vogue*.

36. Locke, "Enter the New Negro," pp. 632–3.

37. Langston Hughes, "Dream Variation, *Survey Graphic*, March 1, 1925, p. 664; Angelina Grimke, "The Black Finger," *Survey Graphic*, March 1, 1925, p. 661. Grimke's poem had originally appeared in *Opportunity*.

38. There were, of course, major demographic differences between the Irish and African-American cases. The fact that African Americans were a demographic minority militated against any realistic claims they might have had to a post-colonial state in North America, just as the more homogeneous demographic situation in Ireland did not force nationalists to reckon with the notion of a multicultural state.

39. Locke, "Enter the New Negro," pp. 632–3.
40. James W. Johnson, "The Making of Harlem," *Survey Graphic*, March 1, 1925, p. 639.
41. Melville J. Herskovits, "The Dilemma of Social Pattern," *Survey Graphic*, March 1, 1925, p. 676.
42. Locke, "Enter the New Negro," p. 634.
43. W. A. Domingo, "The Tropics in New York," and C. McKay, "The Tropics in New York," *Survey Graphic*, March 1, 1925, pp. 648–50.
44. Countee Cullen, "Heritage," and Langston Hughes, "Poems," *Survey Graphic*, March 1, 1925, pp. 674–5.
45. C. Barnes, "Negro Art in America," *Survey Graphic*, March 1, 1925, pp. 668–70.
46. Locke, "Enter the New Negro," p. 634.

CHAPTER 9

The Long Maori Renaissance

Mark Williams

After his dramatic gesture of exile in 1902, James Joyce returned to Ireland twice in 1909, on the second occasion, in October, as agent for four Triestine businessmen whom he had talked into financing Dublin's first cinema. Joyce's entrepreneurial career was short-lived; the Volta Theatre at 45 Mary Street failed after a few months, having featured mainly Italian films.[1] Part of what Joyce had left behind in flying, first to Paris then to Trieste, was the claim of the Irish Renaissance—his speculative cinematic venture demonstrating (apart from a willingness, surprising in a socialist, to act on behalf of international capital) a resistance to the notion that the Irish people needed to consume images of Ireland. Yet Joyce's postexile fiction is so supersaturated in the material of his country that it has been subsumed over the course of a century into the iconography of literary (and cinematic) Ireland. Bloomsday is now a Dublin tourist event while phrases from *Ulysses* are printed on the upholstery of Aer Lingus planes. Even his abandonment has become part of national mythology.

A year before Joyce's ill-fated attempt to import an international art form into nationalist Ireland a Maori member of the New Zealand Parliament, Apirana Ngata, contributed a poem written in the high Victorian style to a small publication marking a Maori congress.[2] "A Scene from the Past," first written in 1898 while he was a student at Canterbury College in Christchurch, both mourns the loss of Maori tradition and reinvents it in the service of contemporary revivalism. In his elegiac rendition of Maori emotionality, color, and maladaption to modernity, Ngata constructs a far-flung version of the Celticism Joyce was determined to escape in Ireland. Ngata today occupies a place in Maori history as central—albeit as ambiguous—as Joyce does in Irish history. Both represented their colonized peoples to the world and both have been chosen by those peoples as favored interpreters. Both have been assimilated into nationalist programs they would not have supported. Both have become posterboys for the tribe, signifying its most exportable qualities: talkative, alcoholic Dublin; Maori success in spanning the opposed worlds of the rural and the urban, the archaic and the modern.

Ngata and Joyce raise difficult questions not only about the cultures they have come to represent but also about the meaning of the word "culture" applied to peoples struggling to disentangle their identities from those of colonizing powers, yet seemingly fated to conduct that struggle in terms borrowed from the colonizer. In bicultural New Zealand/Aotearoa Ngata's legacy has been caught up in debates about the appropriate strategies to adopt towards the dominant culture and the meaning of another problematic term, the "Maori Renaissance." The Maori Renaissance is usually assumed to begin in the early 1970s when books of fiction by Maori writers Witi Ihimaera and Patricia Grace first appeared. Ihimaera's *Pounamu Pounamu* (1972) was described by the publisher on the jacket as "the first collection of short stories by a Maori writer to be published."[3] There was a sense of beginnings and discovery, although Maori writing had a history longer than colonization if one includes the elaborate languages of carving and tattoo. Precontact Maori inhabited an oral world that was also inscribed with marks that preserved cultural memory, telling the narratives of ancestry, of place, of history, and of the gods. The arrival of Europeans and especially of missionaries from the early nineteenth century extended the written world of Maori. There was resistance to the written word,[4] yet interest in the Bible was strong and the Old Testament stories of a displaced tribal people and the stories of prophets rescuing their people from captivity provided potent analogies to the Maori situation. As well, the Bible contained a written system of verbal signs that could be accommodated to Maori purposes. By the late nineteenth century, Maori had not only developed a number of synthetic religions combining Biblical and Maori beliefs and symbols[5] but they were also contributing to the production of newspapers and bulletins in Maori and to translations of Maori lore.[6] From the 1960s, poems and stories by Maori were appearing in places like *Te Ao Hou*, the schools journal, and a major writer had appeared, the poet Hone Tuwhare.[7]

Maori literature did not, then, spring from nothing in the early 1970s. What was different about the writing by Maori that appeared then and which has issued since so plentifully and with such force that it came to be known as a Renaissance was first that so much of it appeared in book form and second the attention paid to it by non-Maori. There had been an expectation by the late 1960s among literary scholars that Maori voices would emerge to articulate an experience which had hitherto been conveyed in novels and stories mainly by Europeans.[8] W. H. Pearson, the most important of these scholars in initiating and developing knowledge of Maoritanga (Maori culture), surveys representations of the Maori in literature in a 1968 essay that moves from the colonial to the modern periods. Pearson begins by noting that "[t]he greater part of this essay must be concerned, because there is so much of it, with *Pakeha*[9] writing about Maori."[10] He concludes optimistically:

> In 1960, Bruce Mason predicted the appearance of a Maori novelist of outstanding talent. I like to share this hope, and am confident that Maori writing will be distinct in its passion, its lyricism and unforced celebration of living. . . . New Zealand life will be greatly enriched when we can learn to see ourselves and the country through the eyes of a number of Maori writers and it may well be that Maori can help us find ways we wouldn't have found for ourselves.[11]

Ihimaera's outburst of publications in the 1970s indicated that the period of waiting was over—and that the passion and lyricism Pearson had predicted would be amply provided. The publication in 1983 of Keri Hulme's *the bone people*, greeted in the *New Zealand Listener* as the book for which the whole nation had been "waiting,"[12] confirmed that the desire for a kind of writing that would show Pakeha to themselves in new postcolonial ways had also been fulfilled. Hulme's book somehow straddled the fashionable categories of the time: feminist, new age, Maori, and bicultural. Yet Hulme's increasing insistence on the priority of her Maori identity, in response particularly to C. K. Stead's denial that neither she nor her book was authentically Maori, consolidated its Maori status.[13] For the reading public, Maori literature had not simply arrived, it had transformed New Zealand literature generally. When *the bone people* won the Booker Prize local doubts about the novel's disturbing mixture of violence and optimism were swept aside; having carried its vision of New Zealand as wounded by history yet possessed of a special ethnic destiny, the novel became the defining document for the bicultural nationalism of the 1980s.

For Pakeha, the Renaissance of Maori culture was something to exhibit proudly to the world, extending a habit dating back to the colonial period of displaying their native race and their culture, but now with a postcolonial motive. Britain had joined the European Economic Union in 1973, and Pakeha were forced to come to terms with the cultural as well as the economic consequences of Britain's abandonment of its old settler colonies. They began looking with new anxiety for signs of validation, value, and distinctiveness in the world to hand. This produced an unconscious return to a narrative of difference and superiority locked into the country's early patterns of settlement: that the two races thus joined enjoyed a special relationship, unequalled in any other colonized state. Pride in the efflorescence of Maori writing in English in the 1970s and 1980s recalled colonial satisfaction in possessing an especially fine native race and having especially good intentions toward that race. Even the insistent voice of resistance and condemnation of the Pakeha in the new Maori literature in English did not dispel the exceptionalist myth: New Zealand was not just another settler colony adjusting to no longer being "on the fringe of the mother country's skirts"[14] but a land of utopian promise where, as the Australian writer Henry Lawson put it in a poem describing his romantic illusions on visiting New Zealand in the 1890s, "the last that were born of a noble race—when the page of the South was fair—/ The last of the conquered dwelt in peace with the last of the victors there."[15]

For Maori, however, the literary side of the Maori Renaissance was merely one expression of a new assertiveness and another adaptation of European tools to a long struggle against cultural disappearance conducted through written appeal, symbolic action,[16] and increasingly in the 1970s by direct protest. Crucial moments in the "cultural" assertiveness of the decade were not just the publication of books by Maori authors but the Land March, or *hikoi*, of 1975, in protest of the ongoing loss of Maori land even during the tenure of a sympathetic Labour government (1972–1975), and the later land occupations of Raglan and Bastion Point.[17] Ihimaera, in his 1986 novel, *The Matriarch*, addresses the reader regarding the hikoi of 1975, the most important statement of resistance by Maori people to the continued loss of Maori land in the modern period:

"The march promises to be one of the most significant events of the decade," Te Matakite[18] said,

and to the Maori people, it will be the climax of over 150 years of frustration and anger over the continuing alienation of their lands. Land means much more to the Maori people than it does to any other New Zealander. To them it has a deep spiritual value. You can realise then the frustration the Maori people have had over the last 150 years as they have seen their lands gradually fall out of their hands. Before the arrival of European settlers, the Maori had 66 million acres of land, today they have less than three million. Matakite is deeply concerned as it sees more acts brought in by Parliament which continue this process of alienation. These acts include the Town and Country Planning Act, the Public Works Act, the Rating Act and the Counties Amendment Act. Matakite wants to press for the abolition of monocultural laws pertaining to Maori land, and establish new laws for Maori land based on their own cultural values. Matakite wants to establish communal ownership of land within the tribe as legitimate title equal in status to the individual title.[19]

It would be mistaken, then, to see the political and cultural aspects of the Renaissance as distinct. Cultural revival meant the disengagement of the expressive, political, and economic modes of Maori life from the assimilationist program that had dominated governmental thought since the nineteenth century when the policy of amalgamation by intermarriage and education assumed that the race in its existing state would die out, giving way to an improved and unified hybrid race.

The Maori Renaissance of the 1970s and 1980s was conducted largely in separatist terms as an effort to distinguish Maori culture from that of the dominant Pakeha culture and to challenge the lingering effects of amalgamationist ideology. Apirana Ngata represents an older revivalism of the early twentieth century, less overtly antagonistic to assimilation, but which may also be seen as a "Renaissance." Ian Pool observes that Maori "despair" produced by the Land Wars of the 1860s had given way by the turn of the nineteenth century to what has been called a "Maori Renaissance."[20] In the early twentieth century distinguished Maori leaders including Ngata and Peter Buck (Te Rangi Hiroa) were urging a greater share in modernity for Maori, especially by measures to improve health, at the same time that they were encouraging a resurgence of traditional skills and knowledge.[21] The white writers of the late colonial period (dubbed the writers of "Maoriland") had dwelt not on the modernizing tendencies within Maoridom but on the ancient world of the Maori where warriors and maidens provided compensating images to the stresses and restrictions of Pakeha life. Against this background Ngata formulated a conception of Maori culture and of Maori themselves as agents of modernity, fully inhabiting the present without sacrificing their past. In the 1910s and 1920s Ngata provided models of both cultural revival and successful Maori farming and economic organization.[22] There are similarities and differences here to the better-known Renaissance of the 1970 and 1980s. The latter was more separatist, assertive and more overtly political than the former, but both involved a compromise between accommodation and the maintenance of difference.

The continuities between the early twentieth-century revivalism represented by Ngata and that of the late twentieth century, represented by writers like Witi Ihimaera, are sufficiently marked that I shall argue that there has been not one Renaissance beginning around the early 1970s and continuing into the 1990s but a long Renaissance going back to the late colonial period marked by periods of greater and lesser intensity. The two main phases of this "long Renaissance" are separated by the period from the 1940s through to the 1960s when Maori society shifted from a predominantly rural base to suburbs designed to accommodate a new industrial work force in the postwar years. At issue throughout this whole period has been the effort to revive the culture not by returning to its state before colonization but to assert the Maori claim over what came after colonization as well as what prevailed before. The distinguishing feature of this Renaissance has consistently been that cultural revival and the claim to economic self-determination have been inseparably linked. The career of Apirana Ngata illustrates this interdependence.

Ngata was born in 1874 into the Ngati-Porou tribe on the East Coast of the North Island, into a family prominent in the locality, and was marked early for leadership of his people. His birth was even attended by the fulfillment of a prophecy.[23] His isolated tribe had been able to retain much of its land, was Christian, and had supported the Crown during the land disputes of the 1860s. Ngati Porou had also seized the economic opportunities provided by the Pakeha, engaging in large scale farming during a period when other Maori communities languished. Ranginui Walker, Ngata's biographer, describes the world in which Ngata's father, Paratene, grew up:

> He witnessed the hapu of Ngati Porou growing wheat and corn at Waiapu, Tuparoa, Waipiro, Tokomaru, Uawa, Whangara and Turanga. Every arable acre on undulating country, even steep hillsides, was under cultivation. The profits from wheat were invested in coastal vessels to convey the produce, including pigs, to the Auckland market.[24]

By the mid-1870s, rather than leasing land to Pakeha farmers or working as shearers on land they had sold, Ngati Porou were involved in significant sheep farming on their own land and on their own account. But the following decades were marked by difficulties in Ngati Porou's economic activities that mirrored those of the Maori population generally. The government was hungry for land to satisfy settler demand and to continue the modernization of the pastoral economy. The success of refrigerated shipping from the late 1880s meant that farming sheep for meat export had become viable and the old Maori pattern of raising produce for urban markets in Auckland or Sydney was in conflict with an expanding economy which required ever more land for an industrialized pastoralism directed at the imperial market. The economic benefits of globalization in the late colonial period were reserved for Pakeha. As Joyce's father represented the decline of the Catholic middle class, so Ngata's father experienced the increasingly limited options for Maori economic independence in an increasingly confident and expansive settler society.

Like Joyce, Apirana received the most elite religious education available to his people. Te Aute College opened in 1854 with twelve pupils, supported by Government grants and with land gifted by Hawkes Bay chief, Te Hapuku. Initially the school aimed to provide its Maori pupils with a primary education to equip them with basic skills for non-professional jobs; in line with the aims of the Native School system, of which the school was part, the intention was to lift the race out of its threatened condition at a time when it was widely held to be dying. In 1878, however, John Thornton was appointed headmaster and the school embraced a more ambitious purpose. Thornton shifted the emphasis of the school to academic learning modeled on the English grammar schools, preparing Maori students not for jobs as shearers or domestic servants but for the professions.[25] His aim was to educate future leaders of the Maori race to be able to compete with Pakeha on their own terms.

Ngata became Thornton's most distinguished pupil. Te Aute not only prepared him for an exemplary career in law, politics, and scholarship, it encouraged in him the determination that he would dedicate his life to improving the condition of the Maori people. The Te Aute College Students' Association formed in 1897 was the basis of what became the Young Maori Party, a movement among young and educated Maori to bring Maori into the mainstream of New Zealand political, economic, and social life. There is some commonality between the Young Maori Party and the more radical youth movement modeled on Black activism in the United States that appeared in the 1970s, Nga Tamatoa. Both represented young Maori against older traditionalists at a time of crisis; both included educated and idealistic Maori activists seeking to advance the general interests of Maori and adopting what were seen at the time as radical policies by Maori elders. But the Young Maori Party was less separatist than Nga Tamatoa, although it is easy to overstress this. The aim of the earlier movement, which sought "a united Maori people, united for the maintenance of the best characteristics of the race, for its protections against well-meaning but cruel civilizations," employs the stilted language of the time but constitutes a defense of what the Maori radicals of the 1980s and 1990s understood by *tino rangitiratanga*— self-governance according to Maori protocols and traditions—as the powerbase of Maori life.[26]

That "well-meaning but cruel" civilization of the late nineteenth and early twentieth centuries was exemplified by the Liberal government of the 1890s and the first decade of the twentieth century responsible for some of the most advanced social legislation in the world at that time, notably the introduction of universal suffrage, a welfare system, and pro-labor laws. The Liberals also allowed individual sales of Maori land to speed the rate at which new land could be made available for Pakeha settlement.[27]

It was a time when the race was considered to be faced, like all indigenous peoples colonized by Europeans, with extinction. Ngata took the view that Maori must adapt to survive. They must apply modern methods of health, sanitation, and agriculture to Maori life. The state for its part must enact legislation that respected the communal ownership of Maori land, while Maori must use their land efficiently and profitably. Ngata wrote to his father seeking approval for his going to Canterbury College on matriculating from Te Aute in 1890: "Perhaps I will have a role in reviving the Maori people."[28] Walker recounts that, at the conclusion of his time at Canterbury, he declined the suggestion of Ernest Rutherford, a fellow graduate about to go to Cambridge and win fame as an atomic scientist, that he also should go to a prestigious European university. Ngata replied that he would "remain here to help the people."[29]

Ngata began his career by working for a law firm, having earned his LL.B in 1896 as the first Maori to complete a degree at a New Zealand university.[30] Returning to his family land Ngata dedicated himself to the improvement and modernization of farming methods. One of his improvements was the extension of an existing system of incorporation that allowed title to remain in tribal hands while facilitating farming in smaller and more viable units. The determination to find ways to retain tribal ownership while achieving modernization and greater production was a crucial element in Ngata's model for managing Maori economic activity. He wanted Maori generally, not just his own Ngati Porou people, to demonstrate that they could farm as efficiently as Pakeha.

In 1905, Ngata entered Parliament as the representative for Eastern Maori (an allocation of four parliamentary seats to Maori is still built into the New Zealand electoral system). Throughout his long and distinguished parliamentary career, Ngata worked tirelessly on behalf of Maori people by his part in drafting land legislation and by achieving in 1927 an inquiry into the confiscation of Maori land following the wars of the 1860s. At the same time, he encouraged Maori to participate fully in the larger society, actively supporting the 1914–1918 war effort, both encouraging Maori to enlist and promoting the formation of a separate Maori Battalion.

A modernizer, Ngata also spoke for the past and its preservation, encouraging a revival of Maori crafts and establishing a means of signifying, vivifying, and profiting from traditional culture without bastardizing or corrupting it. He encouraged not only traditional performance arts— haka and poi—but also decorative arts.[31] In 1927, a Maori school of arts was established in Rotorua with his support. Ngata's efforts to make tradition both correctly observed and marketable forms the basis of a discourse about culture in New Zealand that has either liberated or imprisoned generations of Maori, depending on your viewpoint. At a time when the major source of foreign income for a rapidly modernizing Japan was derived from the export of traditional crafts, Maori were also learning the value of the symbolic associations of the past when attached to commodified icons. The difference between the two peoples was that Maori as a colonized people did not have full control over that traditional symbolism. Both by way of exports of Japonoiserie and by fastening the disciplinary values of the Samurai tradition to modern industrial organization, Japan reinvented its past in the service of nation-making. The Maori past meanwhile was being conscripted by the nation-makers of settler society, eager to signal their distinctiveness by way of the myths and decorative features of a conquered and romantic race. Modernity and tradition, for Maori, were necessarily difficult terms to bring into alignment, but the reason for this was neither that they sought to return to the precontact past nor that they wished to accept the present wholly on settler terms; the terms were opposed because Pakeha culture excluded Maori from the modern, consigning them to a romantic version of the past. In Ngata's dealings with settler society, he steered carefully between the claims of tradition and modernity without sacrificing one to the other.

Like Joyce, Ngata occupies a contested place in the cultural history of his people; advocating strategic adaptation to the dominant culture, he is both a reproach to the vigorously separatist tendencies of Maori nationalism and a beloved and defining figure in Maori cultural and material history. He has, moreover, played a crucial role in the ongoing revival of Maori people throughout the twentieth century, the "long renaissance" that straddles both sides of the massive demographic shift of Maori from their rural to an urban base. His stance towards the Pakeha is less antagonistic than that of the Maori voices of the 1970s and 1980s, but he shares with them the determination to revivify Maori cultural traditions, to impress upon the dominant culture the urgency of Maori needs, and to preserve cultural memory while taking advantage of the opportunities presented by modernity.

When Witi Ihimaera in *The Matriarch*, nearly eighty years after Joyce's foray into cinema and Ngata's appointment to Cabinet,[32] compares a rural Maori meeting house, Rongopai, to the Sistine Chapel, he makes a grand statement not only about Maori culture in the world but also about what it means to apply the term renaissance to specific and very different cultural movements. What connects Renaissance Italy, turn-of-the-nineteenth-century Ireland, 1920s Harlem, and 1980s New Zealand/Aotearoa? Surely not as much as what separates them. The first is an expansive renaissance; the others are defensive renaissances. The Italian Renaissance reconfigures a past conceived as glorious and exemplary at moments of great confidence and new wealth. The Irish Renaissance—which is sometimes more tentatively called a "revival"— uses a past that has been invented as much as remembered to generate confidence in what might be achieved in a country neither prosperous nor self-determining. In doing so, it establishes the machinery of other postcolonial renaissances. Irishness is a national and unifying phenomenon that can be expressed as something complete and autochthonous within the imposed structure of an alien nation state. Similarly, the Harlem and Maori Renaissances arise within existing nations and within unifying ideologies against which they must assert not just their separateness but also their value. They do so ostensibly by drawing on the oral memory of a cultural plenitude prior to conquest or contact; in the process, they inevitably mythologize the past to make it usable in the present.

Renaissances are predicated upon a particular relation between a revered past and a fallen present. They aim to reenact this imagined past. They are not, then, merely acts of preservation, repetition or return but acts of imagination which convert the present into the shape of a supposedly superior past by an assertion of will. Ihimaera is quite aware of these acts of invention, as his description of Rongopai shows:

> Ah yes, Rongopai was a fantasy as well as a real world. It conjured up an
> Eden where the spirit and the flesh were integrated, where creatures of

light and creatures of darkness lived coincidentally with man in the one, single, universe. There were no barriers between the past and the present, the living and the dead, and the spirit and the flesh, for all were contained in that eternal continuum known as the Creation. And Rongopai itself was the healing place, the joining place for the Maori people, the place where the fingers interlocked in prayer and supplication as well as in union. And amid the profusion of plants, fabled creatures, men and exotic trees were the small symbols of the interlocking—the moko patterns of the young painters, the astrological signs, the nautical inscriptions, the whimsical patterns of playing cards, the signs of vivacity, of life, rather than death, of renewal rather than recession.[33]

Ihimaera knows very well that present and past are not continuous. He has spoken of the damage done to Maori cultural memory by colonization, so that at times only a few threads remained intact of the once sound rope.[34] Hence the building is a fantasy as well as reality, deriving from an imaginary reconstruction of the past as well as from memory and tradition. But this does not make it any less valuable as an act of renewal and restoration. It is part of a conscious process of encoding and protecting culture that connects the very earliest engagements of Maori with European missionaries and settlers to the most recent global projections of Maori culture in film, ethnographical display, and fiction.

In a 2001 book on the Maori struggle for tino rangitiratanga, Ranginui Walker describes the building of a chief's house, Te Hau-ki-Turanga, in 1842 carved by Rukupo, tohunga and master carver: "The philosophy underlying the design of the house aimed to conserve tribal history and whakapapa for the generations to come, who faced loss of cultural memory under the onslaught of Pakeha colonization."[35] Just two years after the founding document of the nation was signed as an agreement between Maori and the British Crown at Waitangi, Rukupo's building anticipates the cultural loss of memory that Maori people will suffer through the wars of the 1860s and the subsequent extension of Pakeha control over Maori by an endless series of laws, small and great, that would compromise the ability of Maori to govern their own lives and protect their treasures and resources. Yet the building also anticipates survival and continuity. For Ihimaera, the trick is to ensure survival not merely as the tribe faces settler nationalism but also as it deals with the worlds beyond that which the settlers are able to imagine. Like all those Irish writers throughout the twentieth century who skipped London en route from Dublin to New York or Europe, Ihimaera has a larger notion of what the Maori nation means and what it might attach itself to than that supplied merely by its historical relationship to empire. He has said in an interview that the Maori conception of reality does not stop when you leave New Zealand. As New Zealand consul in New York in the 1980s, he has claimed that he could look over the East River and see mythological figures drawn from his ancestral spiritual beliefs. Nicki Caro's film version of his fable *Whale Rider* has, in a sense, projected precisely those mythological figures away from their source to the world elsewhere, making New York, as he puts it, "a Maori world."[36]

What Ihimaera will not allow is that Maori reality need be circumscribed by the specifically national constraints of Pakeha New Zealand, and he makes the point extravagantly in *The Matriarch* by loading his epic tale of the Maori people since colonization with Italian reference, especially to Verdi's opera. Ihimaera's linking of Rongopai to an icon of the Italian Renaissance is a way of bypassing the British settler hierarchy of cultural valuation in which Maori carving and architecture, judged superior to that of other savage races, nevertheless fell short of the art and literature brought with empire. He makes a direct and dramatic leap to a universal highpoint and attaches the rural building to that transcendence. But he also makes another kind of link in the novel by way of Verdi's close identification with the Risorgimento. Nineteenth-century Italian nationalism becomes an analogy to that of the Maori people, and the expressive modes of one are linked sympathetically to those of the other. The cultural claim, then, is also a political claim, just as the identification with the Children of Israel by nineteenth-century Maori prophets was deeply political. Vertiginous transitions from small to great worlds characterize Ihimaera's method and the conceptual system that governs a novel in which nationalism is both the enabling condition of a protracted struggle for self-determination and a fatally limiting worldview imposed by a conquering group on others. What Maori people are fighting for includes the local and the universal, the world of a rural past and that of the Italian Renaissance, but the settler-nationalist forms of belonging that lie between these poles are inevitably disappointing and often squalid. The crucial point is that Maori have sought to remain the owners of the symbolic activities of culture. Whether transporting tourists to the Pink and White Terraces before their volcanic destruction in 1888, taking Maori concert parties on tours of Britain in the 1900s, or opening the Te Maori Exhibition in New York in the 1980s, Maori have shown a disposition actively to control the access to their culture and the display of its imagery. Culture is the way Maori represent themselves to the world as vitally as it is the way they represent themselves to themselves. With the emergence of a Maori cinema in the 1990s and with Maori arts and crafts now a branded and regulated industry, Maori have extended their ability to project themselves and their culture globally. Culture, then, is not simply an idealizing gesture, nor is it realized exclusively in the tribulations of daily life in an antagonistic social reality; increasingly, it is that which facilitates Maori economic and political survival and which shifts the terms of engagement with the other from the nation-state to the world. This might be seen as a departure or break with existing forms of engagement, but it also involves a return to colonial-period modes of Maori economic and cultural interaction, exporting not just goods to the markets of Auckland, Sydney, and even America but also cultural displays, artifacts, and images. For Chris Prentice, the effects of globalization are at odds with the nationalism of the Maori Renaissance of the 1970s and 1980s. The assertion of separate identity within the nation- state is in conflict with the marketing of Maori as an international brand. In terms of keeping definitions tight and discrete this is useful, but it assumes a conflict between Maori and capitalism. As Lydia Wevers has pointed out, Maori were routinely condemned for the charges they applied for access to iwi-controlled tourist attractions as far back as the 1880s.[37]

Prentice has demarcated the historical limits of the Maori Renaissance, looking back from a position in which its cultural revivalist energies are seen to have run into the counterforce of globalization:

> To ask, "What *was* the Maori Renaissance?" is to accept, at least provisionally, the assumptions built into the question's tense, and its positivistic and singular framing: that there was "a" Maori Renaissance that could be subsequently identified as a knowable phenomenon, from a perspective enabled by its completion and closure, a position from which to review and assess its meaning and significance. It quickly becomes clear that while a number of cultural and political commentators have been comfortable using the term "Maori Renaissance", they do so in varying ways, and its earliest usage—which might disclose the intention and implications encoded into it—remains obscure. Nevertheless, even a provisional acceptance of the Maori Renaissance enables an analysis of some important meanings attributed to Maori culture through the twentieth century, and of the transformations of these meanings, as culture is increasingly articulated through the processes of globalisation.[38]

Prentice reads the term Maori Renaissance in respect of its complex relations to other renaissances: its repetition of and difference from the Italian Renaissance and the Harlem Renaissance. She notes the definitional difficulties of the term, the obscurities of its origins, and its connections to long-established patterns of Maori history in the twentieth century. Nevertheless, she sees it as representing a break or rupture rather than continuity. The Renaissance of the 1970s to the 1990s is seen as a kind of Cultural Revolution involving the sharpening of difference from previous Maori political stances as well as from Pakeha society. Yet, as Pool's reference shows, the contemporary usage is not the first time the word Renaissance has been applied to Maori cultural resurgence.

The central question in how we delimit the Maori Renaissance rests less on dating than on definition, and the crucially disputed term is "culture." If the Maori Renaissance of the 1980s is different from the revival of the early twentieth century that is because the intellectual parameters of Pakeha ethnology have shifted, allowing Maori aspirations and Maori cultural practice to be interpreted in fundamentally different terms. In the late colonial period ethnology was largely amateur and drew heavily on contemporary ideas of Aryanism, crudely applied to Maori to demonstrate their superiority to other savage races and their consequent fitness for amalgamation with Europeans. Maori themselves have been susceptible to these narratives in which the British and Polynesian races travel through time and geography, supplanting lesser races, and settling at last into the fit resolution of the imperial moment.[39] In the late twentieth century, the tradition of idealism in the way both Pakeha and Maori commentators have interpreted Maori tradition has been countered by materialist and skeptical interpretations of culture. American anthropologist, Alan Hanson, caused a furor when he argued that Maori culture was an invention rather than the authentic revival of tradition.[40] Ruth Brown argued that the Pakeha association of Maori culture with supposedly authentic spiritual qualities was a convenient cover for ongoing acts of appropriation and marginalization.[41] Steven Webster in *Patrons of Maori Culture*, a recent anthropological study of the Renaissance, points out:

> since the 1960s most students of Maori culture (including many Maori themselves) have focused on traditional culture rather than everyday Maori society as they encounter it or live it. Although Maori are everywhere, Maori "culture" is assumed to occur elsewhere in some sense, even somehow outside history.[42]

For Webster, cultures are not discrete and self-contained but " 'whole ways of struggle' inseparable from a specific history of involvement with other societies and cultures."[43] This struggle is conducted chiefly at the level of economics, in the effort to maintain agency in daily life. Clearly, culture takes its meanings from its exchanges with other cultures, especially in a colonial country. However, the symbolic aspect of identity has more force than Webster allows, and it has a force in the way economic exchanges are managed. The symbolic and the material cannot be pried apart where the economic imperatives of colonization have been disguised in the process of manufacturing an image of national harmony and where both parties have become captivated by the chimaera thus conjured into existence. Maori have certainly been involved in an ongoing struggle with the colonizing culture; however, their relationship to capitalism—whether settler, nationalist, or global—has been characterized less by antagonism than by the desire to wrest a share of the opportunities for themselves. Self and other have never been absolutely separate at any point in the history of conflict and accommodation between Maori and Pakeha: each has continually been modified by the other intellectually, economically and spiritually;[44] each has fashioned identity out of the exchange with the other.

Webster notes the way cultural idealism imprisons Maori within their past, but his cultural materialism equally imprisons them in a condition of permanent opposition to economic power. The Maori struggle has not been to overthrow capitalism or to return to pre-European "primitive" socialism, but to protect the communal basis of their social organization while achieving not just economic sufficiency but economic advantage. In late nineteenth-century colonial discourse "Maori communism" was often noted as an attractive but doomed feature of a now nearly extinct race.[45] By "communism" the observers meant the traditional structure of Maori life in which land was owned communally. This occurred at a time when banks would not lend capital to Maori for development precisely because of the lack of individual title to Maori land and when the government was pressing for the breakup of communal ownership so that land might be purchased more easily. Maori, meanwhile, were eager to adapt the opportunities provided by technology and capital to their communal forms of life. It was settler protectionism that denied them access to loans for the development of tribal land, not the inherently "communistic" structure of their own society.

Turning to the late twentieth century, Webster sees the prominence given during the Renaissance to Maori in public institutions, specifically the university, as a form of cultural conscription by the larger program of capitalist restructuring. His question—"might the increasing enrolment, employment, and cultural prominence of Maori in the University be as much a part of the national capitalist 'restructuring' as it is a Renaissance of Maori culture?"—needs to be seen against an historical backdrop of Maori efforts to interact with capitalism and modernity. Just as Maori in the 1830s and 1840s assimilated and adapted new military technologies and Christianity to their own purposes and in the 1920s applied new methods of financial organization and agricultural technology to their farming practice, so in the 1980s and 1990s Maori negotiation with government over historical grievances and enterprise sought to provide a modern economic base for tribal independence, while Maori cultural activity, especially literature and film, carried images of Maori life to the world. Cultural revival has consistently meant not something at odds with material life but an extension of it, not an antagonism to contact with the worlds beyond tribe, people, and nation but an eagerness to explore and exploit such contact. The difference between the renewals of early and late twentieth century is not that one was rural one urban, one moderate one angry, but that the technologies available for projecting the culture have increased. Maori have resisted all those efforts to limit the worlds they are supposed to belong within, whether spiritual, pastoral, or traditional. It is not Maori but Pakeha who have determined that an unbridgeable gulf exists between Maori and modernity, and it is Pakeha who have protested whenever Maori have encroached on realms—especially economic ones—to which they believe they themselves hold exclusive title.

The long Maori Renaissance has involved a protracted effort neither to repudiate all that came as a consequence of colonization nor to return to some prior condition of wholeness but to reclaim title to Maoritanga. This has meant that, whether the rhetoric has been separatist or ameliorist, active engagement with the symbolic representations of Maori identity promulgated by Pakeha has been unavoidable. To establish a meaningful Maori difference is to decline to be included in the harmonious picture of the nation that was constructed in the late colonial period and survived in the benevolent clichés of politicians as late as the 1970s. If cultural nationalism is the desire to find or establish sources of cultural meaning peculiar to the culture being represented, not derived from elsewhere and not imposed by some other culture, then neither Maori nor settler society has achieved that desire. For each, the pursuit of definition has been complicated by the images of self constructed by the other. In New Zealand, cultural nationalism, as in all settler countries, has involved a struggle by the colonizing culture to free its means of self-representation from the cultural forms derived from the imperial source at the expense of the colonized. But in New Zealand, much more than in other similar societies this has also involved a habit by the colonizers of appropriating cultural signifiers from the colonized, even naming themselves in the language of other as "pakeha." This has meant that Maori culture has been filtered through Pakeha efforts not to understand Maori but to represent themselves to themselves. For Maori, the struggle has been to repossess those images of self not in order to retreat into separatist fantasy but so as to consolidate their hold both on the worlds they remember and those they have encountered: colonial, modern, national, and global. Their success thus far as part of a long Maori Renaissance shows no sign of diminishing.

Notes

1. See Richard Ellmann, *James Joyce* (New York: Oxford University Press, 1982), pp. 300–11. Joyce also returned a fourth time in 1912.
2. Hone Heke and A. T. Ngata, *Souvenir of Maori Congress, July, 1908: Scenes from the Past with Maori Versions of Popular English Songs*. What this congress was is unclear. It was probably associated with the system of Maori councils with which Ngata, now a Member of Parliament, was involved. For a full discussion of this poem see Jane Stafford and Mark Williams, "Victorian Poetry and the Indigenous Poet: Apirana Ngata's 'A Scene from the Past,' " *Journal of Commonwealth Literature* 39:1 (2004), pp. 29–42.
3. Witi Ihimaera, *Pounamu Pounamu* (Auckland: Heinemann, 1972).
4. Danny Keenan argues that, although the growth of Maori writing and literacy in the nineteenth century "has generally been considered in positive terms . . . Maori people were in fact severely disadvantaged by the developing power and dominance of the written word," "Aversion to Print? Maori Resistance to the Written Word," *A Book in the Hand: Essays on the History of the Book in New Zealand*, Eds. Penny Griffith, Peter Hughes, and Alan Loney (Auckland: Auckland University Press, 2000), p. 17. For an influential skeptical view of Maori adjustment to literacy see also D. F. McKenzie, *Oral Culture, Literacy and Print in Early New Zealand: The Treaty of Waitangi* (Wellington: Victoria University Press with the Alexander Turnbull Library Endowment Trust, 1985). However, Steven Webster points out reasonably that "[j]ust as Pakeha history is spoken as well as written, Maori history has long been written as well as spoken," Steven Webster, *Patrons of Maori Culture. Power, Theory and Ideology in the Maori Renaissance* (Auckland: Auckland University Press, 1998), p. 26.
5. See James Belich, *Making Peoples: A History of the New Zealanders: From Polynesian Settlement to the End of the Nineteenth Century* (Auckland: Allen Lane, 1996), pp. 217–23.
6. Most books in Maori until 1900 were translations by Pakeha, although Maori scholars and experts on tribal lore had an active role in producing some of these. Herbert W. Williams in *A Bibliography of Printed Maori to 1900: and Supplement* (Wellington: Government Printer, 1975) lists mainly missionary works, dictionaries, grammars, official government, and legal publications in Maori. But he also cites translated collections of popular Maori songs and of authors like Bunyan and Defoe. Phil Parkinson and Penny Griffith, *Books in Maori, 1815–1900* (Auckland: Reed, 2004) extend the work on nineteenth

century Maori writing in book form. Jane McRae observes that "[a] literature which represented Maori culture emerged from the written and printed forms of the oral tradition and from the political documents which Maori people produced in response to colonization," "Maori Literature: A Survey," in *The Oxford History of New Zealand Literature in English*, 2nd edn., Ed. Terry Sturm (Auckland: Oxford University Press, 1998), pp. 6–7.

7. The Maori poet, Hone Tuwhare's first book of poems, *No Ordinary Sun*, appeared in 1964. In 2003 he was awarded, with Janet Frame and Michael King, with the Prime Minister's Award for Literary Achievement.

8. Notable Pakeha writers on Maori themes were A. A Grace and O. E. Middleton and Roderick Finlayson.

9. "Pakeha" is the term for non-Maori New Zealanders, generally applied to British rather than other immigrants, which has been widely accepted by the Pakeha themselves as well as by Maori.

10. W. H. Pearson, "The Maori and Literature 1938–65," in *The Maori People in the 1960s: A Symposium*, Ed. Erik Schwimmer (Auckland: Longman Paul, 1968), p. 217.

11. Pearson, 'The Maori and Literature," p. 256.

12. Joy Cowley, rev. of *the bone people*, *New Zealand Listener*, May 12, 1984, p. 60.

13. Controversy remained. Stead in an essay much debated both inside New Zealand and in international post-colonial circles argued that as she had only one Maori great-grandparent Hulme was not entitled to the Pegasus Prize for Maori she had received and that the novel's Maoriness was "willed." See "Keri Hulme's *the bone people* and the Pegasus Award for Maori Literature," *Ariel* 16.4 (October 1985), pp. 101–8. For further discussion of Stead's position, see Margerie Fee's "Why C. K. Stead Didn't Like *the bone people*: Who Can Write As Other?" *Australian and New Zealand Studies in Canada* 1 (1989), pp. 11–32.

14. Daphne Marlatt, *Taken* (Concord, ON: Anansi, 1996), p. 7.

15. "The Writer's Dream," in *Henry Lawson: Collected Verse, Volume One 1885–1900*, Ed. Colin Roderick (Sydney: Angus and Robertson, 1967), p. 343.

16. By symbolic action I have in mind protests such as Hone Heke's cutting down of the British flagpole at Russell, Kororareka in 1845.

17. The Hikoi was by Whina Cooper who marched from the far north of the North Island to Wellington to present grievances to Parliament. On the other land protests see Aroha Harris, *Hikoi: Forty Years of Maori Protest* (Wellington: Huia, 2004).

18. Te Roopu o te Matakite ("the forseeing group") organized the 1975 Land March.

19. Ihimaera, *The Matriarch*, (Auckland: Picador, 1988), pp. 234–5.

20. D. Ian Pool, *The Maori Population of New Zealand, 1769–1971* (Auckland: Auckland University Press, Oxford University Press, 1977), p. 27.

21. Pool, *The Maori Population of New Zealand*.

22. Princess Te Puea provided a similar model in the Depression years from the late 1920s for Maori farming. Te Puea Herangi (1883–1952) was the granddaughter

of the Maori King Tawhiao. On her efforts to encourage the development of Maori land in the 1920s and 1930s see Michael King, *Te Puea: A Life*, new edition (Auckland: Hodder and Stoughton, 1977), pp. 148–59

23. Graham Butterworth, *Sir Apirana Ngata* (Wellington: A. H. and A. W. Reed, 1968), p. 3.

24. Ranginui Walker, *He Tipua: The Life and Times of Sir Apirana Ngata* (Auckland: Viking, 2001), p. 41.

25. Ibid., p. 63.

26. Butterworth, *Sir Apirana Ngata*, p. 8.

27. Webster, commenting on the 1993 Maori Affairs Bill, notes that "[w]hereas most Maori land law has since the 1860s been biased towards individualisation of title . . . the new legislation encouraged joint retention and utilisation by kin groups." *Patrons of Maori Culture*, p. 36.

28. Walker, *He Tipua*, p. 65.

29. Ibid., p. 67.

30. See M. P. K. Sorrenson's entry on Ngata in *The Dictionary of New Zealand Biography, Volume III, 1901–1920* (Auckland: Auckland University Press and Department of Internal Affairs, 1996), 359–63. I am indebted to Sorrenson for the following discussion of Ngata's career.

31. Haka is martial dance, poi is a choreographed performance using balls of flax on strings.

32. Ngata was appointed to Cabinet in the Liberal Government in 1909.

33. Ihimaera, *The Matriarch*, pp. 192–3.

34. Ihimaera uses the image of a 'rope of man' (Te Taura Tangata), originally used by John Rangihau, in an interview with Mark Williams in *In the Same Room: Interviews with New Zealand Writers*, edited by Elizabeth Alley and Mark Williams (Auckland: Auckland University Press, 1992), p. 222.

35. Walker, *He Tipua*, p. 43.

36. Witi Ihimaera interviewed by Mark Williams, *In the Same Room*, pp. 227

37. Lydia Wevers, *Country of Writing: Travel Writing in New Zealand 1809–1900* (Auckland: Auckland University Press, 2003), pp. 202–5. An iwi is a tribe.

38. Chris Prentice, "What Was the Maori Renaissance?," in *Writing at the Edge of the Universe: Essays Arising from the 'Creative Writing in New Zealand Conference*," University of Canterbury, 2003 (Christchurch: Canterbury University Press, 2004), p. 85.

39. See Edward Tregear, *The Aryan Maori* (Christchurch: Kiwi Publishers, 1995), p. 8.

40. Alan Hanson, "The Making of the Maori: Cultural Invention and Its Logic," *American Anthropologist* 91 (1989), pp. 890–902.

41. Ruth Brown, *Cultural Questions: New Zealand Identity in a Transnational Age* (London: Kakapo Books, 1997), pp. 10–12.

42. Webster, *Patrons of Maori Culture*, p. 8.

43. Ibid., p. 7.

44. "Spiritually" seems an idealizing and vague term. I use it to designate the important points of artistic and religious contact between Maori and

Pakeha, often realized by way of individuals from disenchanted missionaries to Maori prophets to late modernist Pakeha writers and artists who have crossed the borders between the two.

45. Certain colonial writers have exhausted their powers of ridicule—no very difficult task—upon what they inaccurately call Maori communism. But the system, in full working order, at least developed the finest race of savages the world has seen, and taught them barbaric virtues which have won from their White supplanters not only respect, but liking. The average colonist regards a Mongolian with repulsion, a Negro with contempt, and looks on an Australian black as very near to a wild beast; but he likes the Maoris, and is sorry that they are dying out, William Pember Reeves, *The Long White Cloud Ao-tea-roa* (London: Horace Marshall & Son, 1898), p. 57.

CHAPTER 10

Two Chicago Renaissances with Harlem between Them

Lisa Woolley

In American literary history "renaissance" retains the sense of innovation, institutionalization of learning, and patronage of the arts associated with the European Renaissance but almost reverses the meaning of the term in other ways. Movements such as the New York Little Renaissance, Southern Renaissance, Chicago Renaissance, and Harlem Renaissance were short-lived, limited to a small region or demographic group, sometimes involved only a few of the arts, and often represented a first flowering, rather than a "rebirth."[1] The use of "renaissance" in Chicago's literary history is further complicated by Robert Bone's landmark essay, "Richard Wright and the Chicago Renaissance," in which he argues that, if scholars of African-American literature are going to call the period from 1920 to 1935 the "Harlem Renaissance," then we must call the years from 1935 to 1950 the "Chicago Renaissance."[2] Following Bone, "Chicago Renaissance" now refers to two different periods, separated by a decade or less. One includes developments in American journalism, realism, naturalism, and the new poetry, and the other is thus far mainly the province of African-American literary study. What does this situation say about the use of "renaissance" in American literary studies, about the possibilities and limits of designating literary periods, and about the contradictions involved in studying place-based movements?

In the case of the Chicago and Harlem periods, "renaissance" asserts cultural independence but also relies on some other American literary period for its significance. Delineating these periods leaves out important authors but newly recognizes others as the boundaries and centers of periods are questioned and redefined. Place-based periods lead to disorderly definitions and become confused with mythologies about places. They also compel, however, investigations across traditional lines of scholarship, even as the authority of the term "renaissance" declines.

Chicago's First Renaissance

What has now become known as the first Chicago Renaissance was sparked by a new region of the country coming into prominence. Chicago's location on Lake Michigan and in the center of the continent made it the heart of transportation networks. As it hosted the 1893 World's Columbian Exposition, its rapid growth, heavy industry, and ethnic diversity made Chicago seem the city of the future. Chicago also became known for its social experiments and conflicts. The Haymarket Affair (1886) and the Pullman strike (1894) brought notoriety, while Jane Addams's and Ellen Gates Starr's founding of Hull House in 1889 produced both suspicion and admiration.

Chicago became a magnet for mid-western talent. Eugene Field, George Ade, Finley Peter Dunne, Carl Sandburg, Ben Hecht, Elia Peattie, and other writers raised outside of New England found outlets for their work in Chicago's newspapers. The African-American press, too, was becoming a national force, and Ida B. Wells brought her antilynching crusade to Chicago when she married Ferdinand Barnett. Although Theodore Dreiser had left the city by the early decades of the twentieth century, his success encouraged other mid-westerners. Literary journals, such as the *Dial, Poetry*, and the *Little Review*, published Carl Sandburg, Edgar Lee Masters, Vachel Lindsay, Fenton Johnson, and Sherwood Anderson alongside Wallace Stevens and Ezra Pound. The visibility of editors Harriet Monroe, Alice Corbin Henderson, Margaret Anderson, and Jane Heap encouraged women poets to try a wide range of styles. Experimental theaters, events at Hull House, and literary societies created a sense of intellectual community. Addams even became a minor character but a major force in novels by women. Their reforming heroines attempted to improve upon Addams' example as they explored careers, new housing arrangements, and solutions to urban problems.

The literature from the Midwest represented new experiences—the farming tragedies portrayed by Hamlin Garland or Frank Norris's scenes from the Chicago Board of Trade, for example—but these subjects also seemed indicative of what America had become. Both William Dean

Howells and H. L. Mencken noted the Americanness of this new literary development. Bernard Duffey, author of an early retrospective on the period, writes that the literary efforts originating in Chicago were "the working out within the city of creative forces common to the nation at that time."[3]

Early twentieth-century descriptions of Chicago's writers suggest that the American Renaissance serves as a model for proclaiming the city's literary activity a period or Renaissance. Just as Ralph Waldo Emerson called on Americans to stop imitating British and European artists, writers discussing Chicago called for independence from the American literary establishment in the east. As early as 1892, debate arose in the Chicago-based *Dial* as to whether the western half of the United States could or should have its own literary identity. The *Dial*, founded by Francis Fisher Browne and co-edited by William Morton Payne, covered national discussions about literature, the arts, publishing, libraries, and education and also reported on cultural events at home and developments at the University of Chicago. A letter to the editor signed only with initials and entitled "Who Reads a Chicago Book" complained, "[T]he average Chicago reader steers clear of a Chicago book, unless it chances to be written by a friend, or a man who has made his name and fame by Eastern success."[4] The writer rallies readers to support their own local authors, rather than turning elsewhere. Another reader, Stanley Waterloo, exuberantly praised the style of western writers and their subject matter, which captured "the swing of manhood. It will not be told in the soft, trig sentences of some distant essayist or laboring sonnet-writer."[5]

Like Emerson, these writers suggest that the time has come to reexamine American intellectual life, the loyalties it entails, and the means of representing it. The equation of manhood with cultural superiority in Waterloo's letter is consistent with the pattern Nina Baym identifies— truly American literature is defined in terms of its masculinity.[6]

The editors of the *Dial* rejected regional allegiances in an 1893 editorial, "The Literary West":

> Some composer of dialect doggerel, cheaply pathetic or sentimental, gains the ear of the public; his work has nothing more than novelty to recommend it, but the advent of a new poet is heralded, and we are told by Eastern critics that the literary West has at last found a voice. Some strong-lunged but untrained product of the prairies recounts the monotonous routine of life on the farm or in the country town, and is straightway hailed as the apostle of the newest and consequently the best realism. Some professional buffoon strikes a new note of bad taste in the columns

of the local newspaper, and the admiring East holds him up as the exemplar of the coming humor.[7]

While rejecting "local patriotism" and insisting that "[t]he same standards apply to all the literature written in the English language, whether produced in England or Australia, in Canada or the United States,"[8] the editorial maintains regional rivalries and the dynamics of the American Renaissance. Tellingly, the editors accuse eastern critics of stereotyping westerners, implying that these aesthetic powerbrokers undermine westerners' literary efforts through misplaced praise. The editorial begins with the following comparison:

> For many years past the attitude of Eastern writers towards literary activity in the West has been similar to that once assumed by Boston towards New York and by England towards the United States. It has been an attitude of condescension, of patronizing counsel, of mild surprise that a region so far removed from the centre of the intellectual system should venture to have such things as literary aspirations.[9]

In arguing against the notion of western literature, then, the editors nevertheless reinforce the idea that the west must throw off discouraging eastern dominance.

The label Chicago Renaissance can therefore be understood as an assertion of independence but this gesture is only meaningful within a pattern that includes the American Renaissance. F. O. Matthiessen writes that Emerson, Hawthorne, Thoreau, Melville, and Whitman "felt that it was incumbent upon their generation to give fulfillment to the potentialities freed by the Revolution, to provide a culture commensurate with America's political opportunity."[10] William Dean Howells says of the Chicago writers:

> This is the really valuable contribution of the West, and of that Chicago in which the West has come to its consciousness, toward that poor American condition of English literature which has long been trying so hard to be itself in the face of such sore temptations to be something else. The democracy which was the faith of New England became the life of the West, and now it is the Western voice in our literary art.[11]

The label Chicago Renaissance implies that the mid-western/western region has found its literary identity but simultaneously that the importance of that identity rests on its best representing American ideals.

The Harlem Renaissance

At almost the same time that Chicago was producing its celebrated burst of writing, Harlem was having its own surge of activity. A brief examination of this literary period is crucial in explaining why there are two Chicago Renaissances within half a century. After World War I, Harlem became the focal point of a national movement to highlight and encourage African-American achievement in the arts and letters. Alain Locke's *New Negro Anthology* gave a varied group of texts visibility, purpose, and a name. This period of publishing, conversation, and recognition was made possible by migration of southern African Americans to northern cities; increased access to education; an emerging African-American middle class; the militancy of returning black veterans; the founding of the Urban League, NAACP, African-American women's clubs and other civil rights organizations; anthropological interest in folklore and music; pseudo-Freudian glorifications of the "primitive"; and white patronage of the black arts, especially jazz. Prominent writers included James Weldon Johnson, W. E. B. DuBois, Jessie Fauset, Claude McKay, Countee Cullen, Langston Hughes, Jean Toomer, and Zora Neale Hurston.

Like the rhetoric surrounding the American Renaissance and the first Chicago Renaissance, the act of proclaiming an African-American Renaissance signals cultural independence from another place or entity. Locke titles the first section of his anthology "The Negro Renaissance" and in its opening essay asserts that he is witnessing a movement toward "group expression and self-determination." This trend is expressed both by African-American intellectuals and by uneducated southern migrants, whose mass departures from the South often force black professionals to follow their clients and congregations North.[12] Locke writes that "the Negro of the Northern centers has reached a stage where tutelage, even of the most interested and well-intentioned sort, must give place to new relationships, where positive self-direction must be reckoned with in ever increasing measure. The American mind must reckon with a fundamentally changed Negro."[13]

Locke resembles those writing about the first Chicago Renaissance when he emphasizes the American character of his movement's participants. Although African Americans will no longer conform to demeaning stereotypes of themselves, they are nevertheless seeking "none other than the ideals of American institutions and democracy."[14] He calls the new portrayals of African Americans in art and literature "an augury of a new democracy in American culture."[15] This emphasis on the consonance of American and African-American aspirations has led Nathan

Irvin Huggins to conclude:

> Locke's view of the New Negro was strikingly familiar, an iteration of very traditional values of self-sufficiency and self-help, as American as the Puritans and the 'self-reliance' of Ralph Waldo Emerson. Whatever else he was then, as Locke explained him, the New Negro was an assertion of America.[16]

If those observing Chicago concluded that the heart of America had moved West, those commenting on Harlem argued for a new image of what America looked like.

The Harlem Renaissance is the most Renaissance-like in that it also takes place in an international context. Locke argues that the developments he describes do not just affect the status of Americans but influence the perception of Africa throughout the world.[17] In explaining the importance of Harlem, Locke claims that it "has the same role to play for the New Negro as Dublin has had for the New Ireland or Prague for the New Czechoslovakia."[18]

Connections between New York and Chicago

Although it is a new kind of creature in American literary history, the second Chicago Renaissance shares the characteristics of other American Renaissances. Like the writers of the Harlem Renaissance, writers and artists in Depression-era Chicago looked beyond national borders. Because many of them were associated with the American Left, they would have had some international perspective, whether or not it appears in their writing. Although regional rivalry is not as pronounced as it is in the process of delineating the first Chicago Renaissance, a feminizing of the East and a bit of underdogism does creep into the discussion. One of the first to comment upon this nexus of activity, Arna Bontemps, wrote in 1950, "One way or the other, Harlem got its renaissance in the middle twenties, centering around the Opportunity contests and the Fifth Avenue Awards Dinners. Ten years later Chicago reenacted it on WPA without finger bowls but with increased power."[19] Above all, the imagining of a second Chicago Renaissance resembles the designation of the other periods in that it relies on a relationship to an earlier Renaissance for its full significance.

Instead of constituting a break with an earlier era, the second Chicago Renaissance is imagined as continued momentum under different circumstances and in a new location. Looking back at Bontemps's essay,

Bone concludes that "false periodization" has hidden the work of Chicago's African-American writers. He argues that "the flowering of Negro letters that took place in Chicago from approximately 1935 to 1950 was in all respects comparable to the more familiar Harlem Renaissance."[20] To make his case, Bone surveys the writers involved, including Richard Wright, Arna Bontemps, Frank Marshall Davis, Theodore Ward, Margaret Walker, Willard Motley, Frank Yerby, Gwendolyn Brooks, and white associates on the Illinois Writers' Project of the WPA, including Nelson Algren, Jack Conroy, Studs Terkel, and Saul Bellow.[21] Bone then provides context by discussing Chicago's role in the African-American migration.[22] He gives an overview of the department of Sociology at the University of Chicago and Wright's connection to it,[23] as well as a description of the kinds of projects funded by the Julius Rosenwald Fund.[24] The essay also discusses the importance of newspapers and leftist publications for this period.[25] Bone writes that African-American literary history has emphasized the Harlem Renaissance and the Black Arts Movement of the 1960s, but "our sense of the intervening years is at best vague and indistinct." He then claims that designating a Chicago Renaissance

> will force us to reconsider the current fragmentary view, and replace it with a perspective stressing continuities. The Harlem Renaissance will then seem less an isolated episode, and more a part of a larger movement unfolding in two phases, one based in Harlem and the other in Chicago. What these two literary outpourings have in common is that both are at bottom responses to the Great Migration. What differentiates them is the nature of the two responses to the basic phenomenon of urbanization.[26]

Scholars disagree about the nature of these responses, and different versions of the Harlem Renaissance therefore produce different versions of the Chicago Renaissance. Bone himself sees the Harlem Renaissance as being "diverted from its historic task [of responding to the Great Migration] by the myth of primitivism," a myth that was no longer tenable during the Depression era, when the second group of Chicago authors wrote.[27]

Debate about the differences between these two movements surfaced in a special issue of the *Langston Hughes Review* focusing on Frank Marshall Davis and the Chicago Renaissance. There Lawrence R. Rodgers argues that most writers of the Harlem Renaissance expressed little interest in the new arrivals from the South, even though the migrants in large part determined Harlem's identity,[28] whereas the writers in Chicago "put migration at the center, not the periphery, of its artistic imagination."[29] According to Rodgers, although both movements concentrate on cities, the writers focus on different aspects of urban life, its cosmopolitan possibilities in the one case and its poverty and violence in the other.[30] Cheryl Lester's response to Rodgers addresses the difference between the two periods, questioning, among other issues, whether "it was precisely the collision of middle-class and working-class black culture that produced the variety of effects we link with and trace to the Harlem Renaissance."[31] She proposes a number of possible ways of distinguishing between the periods and asks whether "the Harlem Renaissance represents a response *to* the arrival of working class migrant culture while the Chicago Renaissance represents a response *from* them."[32] In an essay in the same number of the *Langston Hughes Review*, Deborah Barnes writes that the authors of Harlem took the rural South of earlier generations as their subject matter, but the Chicago writers "looked ahead to a future of social, cultural, and economic parity and integration."[33] As the grounds for comparison between periods disappear in these conflicting accounts of the Harlem Renaissance, the two African-American movements and their relationship raise questions about the very concept of literary periods and the purposes they serve.

If the original intent of designating literary periods was to help us distinguish between changing literary styles, philosophies, and historical discourses, then having two back-to-back periods with the same name would seem to thwart that basic purpose. The repeated use of "renaissance" in twentieth-century American literary history has emptied the word of its original meaning. After all, can this many renaissances take place in one country in such a short time? Bone's reluctant use of the word and his choice of a moniker already referring to another period show that "renaissance" has become a cliché.[34] It just means "period," despite some of the similarities between this group of Chicago writers and other movements dubbed renaissances. In a time of highly specialized scholarship, delineating a second Chicago Renaissance could merely be a way to legitimate the study of the gap between the Harlem Renaissance and the Black Arts Movement.

A Second Renaissance in Chicago

What, then, are the possibilities opened up by this term? The second Chicago Renaissance constitutes a new use of "renaissance"—strictly as a convention. Although Bontemps implies that the stock market crash ends the Harlem Renaissance and that the New Deal helps produce the

Chicago Renaissance,[35] subsequent critics do not emphasize the narrative of death and rebirth or even first blooming, nor do they proclaim independence from some other tradition. Declaring a renaissance serves mainly as a prompt to further scholarship. This goal, though, has succeeded extravagantly. The outpouring of scholarship that Bone's essay has inspired takes place, of course, within the establishment of African-American literature as a field in its own right, complete with its own courses, anthologies, scholarly journals, and increasing number of literary periods. Although a renaissance may now just be a period (not even as large as an "era"), assigning a collective name to some writers challenges scholars to question standards for inclusion in the wake of feminist scholarship, new historicism, cultural studies, gender studies, racial- and ethnic-based approaches, Marxist criticism, and challenges to the canon.

As I have argued in the case of Fenton Johnson and Marita Bonner, organizing courses, anthologies, literary histories, and scholarly studies around periods leaves out writers significant in their own day when these authors do not fit neatly into one movement or another.[36] In addition, our periods in American literature are usually shorter than writers' careers, limiting our view of an author's oeuvre by emphasizing one phase at the expense of another. At the same time, disagreement about the center and boundaries of a period can prompt discussion of forgotten or misunderstood figures, as we see in the example of the second Chicago Renaissance.

The fiercest debate over this period concerns whether or not Richard Wright should be seen as the center, as Bone first posited. Carla Cappetti writes that "Bone's essay contains both an invitation to rethink the 'literary thirties' alongside the 'sociological thirties,' and an implicit suggestion that studying Wright's relationship with the Chicago sociologists can represent a first step in such a direction."[37] Cappetti accepts this invitation and suggestion, but her subsequent book, *Writing Chicago*, also includes white writers in this rethinking.[38] In the *Langston Hughes Review* devoted to the Chicago Renaissance, John Edgar Tidwell writes Frank Marshall Davis back into the canon of African-American poetry.[39] Rodgers sketches a period in which Richard Wright and Frank Marshall Davis represent different attitudes toward the city and different levels of adaptation to the experience of migration.[40] Barnes's essay examines Wright's influence on those around him and his "domination of the period."[41] In his response, Theodore O. Mason, Jr. describes Wright as "a writer in motion," whose writings are perhaps too varied to anchor a renaissance. "[A] study of Wright's career," he argues, "reveals as much about the sort of mapping we do as critics and theorists as it does about his work."[42] In *Popular Fronts: Chicago and African-American Cultural Politics, 1935–46*, Bill V. Mullen examines Wright's motives for conflating his separate departures from Chicago and the Communist Party in the *American Hunger* section of *Black Boy*. Mullen suggests that placing Wright at the center of the Chicago Renaissance is part of "the recurring attempt to erase the impact of political radicalism."[43] Removing Wright from the center allows Mullen to discuss many forgotten writers, editors, and activists, as well as to reread Gwendolyn Brooks.

In addition to questioning Wright's centrality to this recently christened movement, scholars have proposed alternative discursive centers to the Chicago School of Sociology. Joyce Russell-Robinson reexamines the period by including visual and performing artists, Communist activities in Chicago, and a discussion of working conditions in federal programs.[44] Mullen argues that

> what has been more famously labeled Chicago's cultural "renaissance" of the 1935 to 1950 period is better understood as the fruit of an extraordinary rapprochement between African-American and white members of the U.S. Left around debate and struggle for a new "American Negro" culture. Put another way . . . Chicago's late 1930s and 1940s "renaissance" was one of black and interracial cultural radicalism best described and understood as a revised if belated realization of the Communist Party's 1936 aspiration for a Negro People's Front.[45]

In addition to Mullen's and Russell-Robinson's rethinking of the period, Craig Werner looks at the beginnings of Leon Forrest's fiction and the work of the Association for the Advancement of Creative Musicians in the second Chicago Renaissance. He argues that "artists respond[ed] to W. E. B. DuBois's call for African Americans to merge the fragments of their 'double consciousness' into 'a better and truer self' incorporating African and European traditions."[46] Werner's essay extends the discussion of the Chicago Renaissance to imply a postrenaissance period that could be read alongside the Black Arts Movement.[47]

Why a Chicago Renaissance?

Calling this Chicago period a "renaissance," then, has been an impetus to scholarship discussing not only writers but also other discourses, art forms, and events. Naming this activity a "renaissance" has, in a sense, made it one. Confining our American Renaissances to a region or city, however, leads to a sloppiness that potentially undermines this way of grouping writers and other thinkers. Limiting the movement to those who live in a particular place for the entirety of the period seems overly constraining, but once that criterion is gone the regional designation seems meaningless. Mencken wrote of the first Chicago Renaissance,

> Find me a writer who is indubitably an American and who has something new and interesting to say, and who says it with an air, and nine times out of ten I will show you that he has some sort of connection with the abattoir by the lake—that he was bred there, or got his start there, or passed through there during the days when he was tender.[48]

"Some sort of connection" and "passed through there" seem hopelessly vague (especially for a railway hub), but in my own work on this period, I found myself proposing a similar definition.[49] Bone asks about his own categorizing, "How can a writer who left Chicago for New York in 1937 be regarded as the central figure in a 'Chicago School' whose dates are 1935–1950?" He answers his own question by saying, ". . . Wright's artistic imagination clung to its shaping-place long after he moved to New York."[50] One wonders why these place names need to be employed at all. If some sort of spirit, style, or political orientation unifies the period, then why not give that a name?

Naming periods for locations also risks confounding literature and mythologies about places. Although literature and images of places have a mutually constituting relationship, a popular understanding of a city or region can obscure the diversity of its people and literature. Sandburg's "tall bold slugger set vivid against the little soft cities"[51] and similar virile portrayals have long overshadowed other realities about Chicago and its writers, as Joseph Epstein[52] and Maxine Chernoff have pointed out.[53] Mullen argues that because of Wright's associating Chicago with his Communist past, "[O]ne of Wright's legacies to African-American cultural history is his successful appropriation *of* the city for the creation of a personal and political myth."[54] "How," Mullen asks, "can a time and place . . . be reduced to a scene in a novel?"[55] Images of places that have become stereotypes help to cloud our sense of who truly belongs to a region, captures its spirit, or deserves a spot in its local renaissance.

I would argue that, despite its vagueness, a regional designation can disrupt conventional ways of grouping writers. In response to absences from literary canons, scholars often have realigned writers according to gender, ethnicity, political affiliation, or other classifications that have traditionally excluded some writers from our study of a time and place.

Because of the way knowledge is built in the academy, approaching African-American literature as a distinct field, for instance, has increased our understanding of individual texts and of the traditions within which African-American writers write, as the example of the second Chicago Renaissance has shown. Yet, the delineation of a regional renaissance suggests that a particular set of circumstances, institutions, and events produces favorable conditions for writers in a certain area, and therefore the label invites us to examine how a variety of authors might benefit. When we think about the organization of anthologies and the survey courses that serve as many undergraduates' only exposure to literature and or critical thinking about American culture, we want them to see how men and women and writers of different ethnicities and social classes have communicated, collaborated, argued, and appropriated one another, as well as separated themselves from others' debilitating conceptions of writing. Even as regional groupings may erase the effects of reading and travel, they urge us to explore and compare writers' working lives.

The work of crossing the lines between race and gender that often implicitly define literary periods has begun. Gloria Hull has discussed the role of women in the Harlem Renaissance.[56] Sidney Bremer highlights the women active in the first Chicago Renaissance.[57] My own work has attempted to restore women and African-American writers to the same period. For their parts, Cappetti, Werner, and Mullen also examine common interests among black and white writers, sociologists, musicians, or activists.

Despite the nonsense of two Chicago Renaissances that bear little scholarly relation to each other, the situation invites a comparison of Chicago to Chicago, in addition to the important discussion taking place within African-American literary studies of the relationship between Chicago and Harlem. Both Mullen[58] and Mason use metaphors of mapping to discuss new approaches to Chicago's literary history and Richard Wright's career respectively.[59] In *Mapping the Invisible Landscape: Folklore, Writing, and the Sense of Place*, Kent C. Ryden points out that maps are "probably one of the most densely packed communications media of any sort."[60] His book examines how narratives, too, structure our understanding of places. Imagining literary history in cartographic terms should lead us to ask about complex networks of literary and other activity. We should wonder about who is inhabiting the same space and whether they are inhabiting it similarly or differently over time. Do these writers know each other? Are they attending the same events and reading the same writers? How does this city or region force them to live separate lives? Do the answers to these questions change from one year to another, and if so, what brings about these shifts? How are interactions between diverse groups of people occupying the same place represented, modeled, normalized, or reimagined in literature? Writing from and about Chicago is well suited to the study of cultural geographers' concerns with the "exclusions in social space which may be unnoticed features of urban life."[61]

Comparing Chicago to Chicago should produce new maps of not only literary production in the city but also of the multiplicity of discourses and traditions that influence individual writers; the connections between writers whose lives are sometimes segregated to different areas, either symbolically or literally; and the circumstances that foster writers and produce renaissance-like conditions for some but not others. My own work has begun to trace some of the links between the first Chicago Renaissance and the Harlem Renaissance and between the two Chicago Renaissances. Werner reminds us of the continued influence of *Poetry* magazine and poetry workshops across the periods that divide Chicago's literary history.[62] Further work remains to be done on the presence of Hull House across both periods, the role of the local and national jazz scene,[63] developments in journalism, and other institutions linking the two movements.

In the American context, then, "renaissance" has little authority left; it is used skeptically, with the understanding that a renaissance is hardly a shadow of the Renaissance and no longer revives the spirit of the American Renaissance, signaling instead a further division in Americans' understanding of themselves and their country. Whether we look to Wright's Bigger Thomas or Brooks's Maud Martha, alienation from the rewards of American capitalism predominates in the third Renaissance discussed here. As a trope, however, "renaissance" remains significant for producing scholarship and rethinking the terrain of American literary history.

Notes

1. I also have discussed literary periodization and the background of the Chicago Renaissance in Lisa Woolley, "From Chicago Renaissance to Chicago Renaissance: The Poetry of Fenton Johnson," *Langston Hughes Review* 14, no. 1–2 (1996), pp. 36–48. I have discussed the Americanness and masculinity claimed by Chicago writers in Lisa Woolley, *American Voices of the Chicago Renaissance* (DeKalb, IL: Northern Illinois University Press, 2000).
2. Robert Bone, "Richard Wright and the Chicago Renaissance," *Callaloo* 9 (1986), p. 448.

3. Bernard Duffey, *The Chicago Renaissance in American Letters* (East Lansing, MI: Michigan State College Press, 1954), p. 6.
4. "Who Reads a Chicago Book?," letter signed J. K., *Dial* 13 (1892), p. 131.
5. Waterloo, Stanley. Letter. "Who Reads a Chicago Book?" *Dial* 13 (1892), p. 207.
6. Nina Baym, "Melodramas of Beset Manhood: How Theories of American Fiction Exclude Women Authors," in *The New Feminist Criticism: Essays on Women, Literature, and Theory*, Ed. Elaine Showalter (New York: Pantheon, 1985), pp. 63–80.
7. "The Literary West," editorial, *Dial* 15 (1893), p. 174.
8. Ibid, p. 175.
9. Ibid, p. 173.
10. 10. F. O. Matthiessen, *American Renaissance: Art and Expression in the Age of Emerson and Whitman* (London: Oxford University Press, 1968), p. xv.
11. William Dean Howells, "Certain of the Chicago School of Fiction," *North American Review* 176 (1903), p. 738.
12. Alain Locke, Ed., *The New Negro* (New York: Albert and Charles Boni, 1925), p. 7.
13. Ibid, p. 8.
14. Ibid, p. 10.
15. Ibid, p. 9.
16. Nathan Irvin Huggins, *Harlem Renaissance* (London: Oxford University Press, 1973), p. 59.
17. Locke, *New Negro,* p. 14.
18. Ibid, p.7.
19. Arna Bontemps, "Famous WPA Authors," *Negro Digest* 8, no. 8 (1950), p. 47.
20. Bone, "Richard Wright and the Chicago Renaissance," p. 448.
21. Ibid, pp. 446–8.
22. Ibid, pp. 450–2.
23. Ibid, 453–7.
24. Ibid, pp. 457–60.
25. Ibid, pp. 460–1.
26. Ibid, p. 466.
27. Ibid, p. 467.
28. Lawrence R. Rodgers, "Richard Wright, Frank Marshall Davis and the Chicago Renaissance," *Langston Hughes Review* 14, no. 1–2 (1996), p. 5.
29. Ibid., p. 7.
30. Ibid., p. 8.
31. Cheryl Lester, "A Response to Lawrence Rodgers," *Langston Hughes Review* 14, no. 1–2 (1996), p. 13.
32. Ibid., p. 14.
33. Deborah Barnes, "'I'd Rather Be a Lamppost in Chicago': Richard Wright and the Chicago Renaissance of African American Literature," *Langston Hughes Review* 14, no. 1–2 (1996), p. 52.

34. Bone writes, " 'Renaissance' is perhaps a pretentious word to describe the output of a literary generation. But if we wish to retain the usage 'Harlem Renaissance,' then we must accept the notion of a 'Chicago Renaissance' as well" (p. 448). Similarly, Duffey writes, "By an inevitable if inexact usage, the continuous wave of literary activity in Chicago, beginning in the last decade of the nineteenth century and continuing through the first two decades of the twentieth, has come to be known as the Chicago renaissance" (p. 6).

35. Bontemps, "Famous WPA Authors," p. 43.

36. Woolley, *American Voices*, pp. 120–46.

37. Carla Cappetti, "Sociology of an Existence" Richard Wright and the Chicago School," *MELUS* 12, no. 2 (1985), p. 26.

38. Carla Cappetti, *Writing Chicago: Modernism, Ethnography, and the Novel* (New York: Columbia University Press, 1993).

39. John Edgar Tidwell, " 'I Was a Weaver of Jagged Words': Social Function in the Poetry of Frank Marshall Davis," *Langston Hughes Review* 14 no. 1–2 (1996), pp. 65–78.

40. Rodgers, "Richard Wright, Frank Marshall Davis, and the Chicago Renaissance," p. 11.

41. Barnes, "I'd Rather Be a Lamppost," p. 52.

42. Theodore O. Mason, Jr., " 'Mapping' Richard Wright: A Response To Deborah Barnes' 'I'd Rather Be a Lamppost in Chicago: Richard Wright and the Chicago Renaissance of African American Literature," *Langston Hughes Review* 14, no. 1–2 (1996): p. 62.

43. Bill V. Mullen, *Popular Fronts: Chicago and African-American Cultural Politics, 1935–46* (Urbana, IL: University of Illinois Press, 1999), p. 23.

44. Joyce Russell-Robinson, "Renaissance Manque: Black WPA Artists in Chicago," *Western Journal of Black Studies* 18, no. 1 (1994), pp. 36–43.

45. Mullen, *Popular Fronts*, p. 5–6.

46. Craig Werner, "Leon Forrest, the AACM and The Legacy of the Chicago Renaissance," *The Black Scholar* 23, no. 3–4 (1993), p. 11.

47. Ibid, pp. 13–14.

48. H. L. Mencken, "Civilized Chicago," *Chicago Sunday Tribune*, sec. 8, October 28, 1917.

49. Woolley, *American Voices*, pp. 12–13.

50. Bone, "Richard Wright and the Chicago Renaissance," p. 449.

51. Carl Sandburg, *The Complete Poems of Carl Sandburg* (New York: Harcourt Brace Jovanovich, 1969), p. 3.

52. Joseph Epstein, "Windy City Letters," *New Criterion* 2, no.5 (1984), p. 43.

53. Maxine Chernoff, Cyrus Colter, Stuart Dybek, Reginald Gibbons, and Fred Shafer, "The Writer in Chicago: A Roundtable," *Triquarterly* 60 (1984), p. 333.

54. Mullen, *Popular Fronts*, p. 21.

55. Ibid, p.24.

56. Gloria Hull, *Color, Sex, and Poetry: Three Women Writers of The Harlem Renaissance* (Bloomington, IN: Indiana University Press, 1987).

57. Sidney H. Bremer, "Willa Cather's Lost Chicago Sisters," in *Women Writers and the City: Essays in Feminist Literary Criticism*, Ed. Susan Merrill Squier (Knoxville, TN: Univerity of Tennessee Press, 1984), pp. 210–29.

58. Mullen, *Popular Fronts*, p. 14.

59. Mason, "Mapping Richard Wright."

60. Kent C. Ryden, *Mapping the Invisible Landscape: Folklore, Writing, and the Sense of Place* (Iowa City: University of Iowa Press, 1993), p. 20.

61. David Sibley, *Geographies of Exclusion*. (London: Routledge, 2002), p.xiv.

62. Werner, "Leon Forrest," p.12.

63. See Sibley for a discussion of the exclusion of W.E.B. Dubois and women associated with Hull House from the canon of Sociology. On the role of jazz criticism, see John Gennari, " 'A Weapon of Integration': Frank Marshall Davis and the Politics of Jazz," *Langston Hughes Review* 14, no. 1–2 (1996), pp. 16–33.

CHAPTER 11

The Present Confusion Concerning the Renaissance: Burckhardtian Legacies in the Cold War United States*

Jane O. Newman

[I]nasmuch as the Renaissance was traditionally regarded as the birth hour of the modern world, its interpretation was inseparably bound up with attitudes toward contemporary civilization and hopes for the future.
Wallace K. Ferguson, *The Renaissance in Historical Thought* (p. 293)

Preliminary Excursus: Imagining the Renaissance in 1952

On February 9, 1952, an article reporting on the talks given on the first day of a three-day conference on the European Renaissance at the Metropolitan Museum of Art appeared on page 13 of *The New York Times*. The *Times* reporter was most interested in those parts of the presentations by, among others, Robert Lopez of Yale that focused on elements of Renaissance history and culture with parallels to the here-and-now. Lopez's sly suggestion at the end of his "Hard Times and Investment in Culture" that the "bankers of New York," if they wanted to "foster" "humanistic culture" in the manner of Renaissance princes, could begin by increasing their financial support of the museum, is thus worth a few lines of print. More seriously, though, Lopez is quoted to the effect that there was a "coincidence of economic depression and artistic splendor" during the Renaissance.[1] The second quote shows that the reporter had obviously gotten the point of the economic historian's remarks; Lopez did in fact give a talk that, when read in full, offers a downbeat allegory for current political and economic events. "[C]loser to us than any other historical period," he writes (21), the Renaissance was a time when "[w]ar and inflation were as familiar . . . as they are, unfortunately, to us" (22). His overall image of the Renaissance as a time that had "little faith and little interest in progress for the whole human race" (30) may well have struck some as somewhat strange, particularly those who might have thought about identifying the Renaissance as a period of renewal and hope.

It is not possible to tell if the *Times* sent the reporter back to the conference the next day. Had he or she attended, however, it would have been obvious that the first speaker, Professor George Sarton of Harvard, also saw it as his task to note similarities between the Renaissance and the present in his "The Quest for Truth: A Brief Account of Scientific Progress during the Renaissance."[2] Sarton's lecture nevertheless represented a significantly cheerier side of the equation than Lopez's, one certainly more easily associated with triumphalist narratives about the Renaissance formulated in a vocabulary of "rebirth." It may have been because he was a historian of science that Sarton was able to pitch the period as an important step in the "revolt against medieval concepts and methods," for example, that, with its "revolutionary . . . growth of knowledge," represented a key and "exhilarating" stage of the scientific "progress of mankind" (35–6).[3] Nevertheless, while Sarton does paint a picture of the Renaissance in terms that are overall much sunnier than Lopez's, his underscoring of the relevance of studying the period for the here-and-now is ultimately also decidedly scarier than his, as when Sarton opines:

> Some of our own contemporaries have not even reached the Renaissance—they are still living in the Middle Ages; others are not even as advanced as that; they are still living in the Stone Age. It is because of such disparities that the progress of technology is so frightening; our ancestors were uneasy when guns were used by children; our own fears are deeper and we shudder to think that atomic bombs might fall into the hands of men who, in every respect (except technology) are still barbarians. (35)

Sarton's ability to see medieval barbarians of all sorts clashing with their "in every respect" (but especially morally) superior antagonists in a Renaissance of the West led by the United States is worthy of note. Even though it had by then already been disputed for quite some time, the notion that the Renaissance had left the Middle Ages in the dust of course relied heavily on the "antithetical conception of the two periods"[4] as it had long been associated with the work of the nineteenth-century Swiss cultural historian, Jacob Burckhardt, who famously wrote in his *The Civilization of the Renaissance in Italy* (1860):

> In the Middle Ages both sides of human consciousness—that which turned outward toward the world and that which turned inward toward man himself—lay dreaming beneath a common veil. The veil was woven of faith, illusion, and childish prepossession . . . Man was conscious of himself only as a member of a race, people, party, family, or corporation only through some general category. In Italy [in the Renaissance] this veil first melted into air; there developed an *objective* consideration and treatment of the state and of all things of this world; at the same time, the *subjective* asserted itself with full power; man became a spiritual individual and recognized himself as such. In the same way the Greek had once distinguished himself from the barbarian.[5]

Sarton may well have relied on Burckhardt for the vocabulary of "barbarism," then, as he sought to make his remarks about the relationship between the Middle Ages and the Renaissance as topical as Lopez's. His version of a Renaissance triumphant is nevertheless much more upbeat, especially in terms of the United States' position vis-à-vis its "medieval" competitors on the vexed geopolitical stage of the time.

What emerges in the dissonant images of the Renaissance offered by these two talks are the parameters of the Cold War contest over modernity's inheritance from this particular past. It is the debate during these years about what Anthony Mohlo has called the dominant "filiational metaphor" said to subtend Burckhardt's thinking in particular, namely, that "our" modernity began in the Renaissance, that is the focus of this essay. Mohlo suggests that in Burckhardt, there is an almost "biological link [that] binds us to the Renaissance, especially to the Renaissance in Italy." "If the Renaissance . . . ushered in the great era of modernity, we, as products of the modern age, are able to recognize and understand our ancestors, the men and women of the Renaissance."[6] As convincing as this argument may be in general, it is important to acknowledge that there have in fact also long been substantial disputes over the exact nature of the "link." Those that engaged scholars during the 1940s through 1960s in particular seem to have dropped off the map almost entirely after approximately 1968, when they were replaced by references to a "Burckhardtian Renaissance" of a rather more homogeneous sort, the dominant legacy of which is said to have been the celebration of the "freedom and dignity" of Man, the inheritance of the Ancients, and an upbeat teleology of a hegemonic western progress, all in one.

In the essay that follows, I argue that it is worth excavating the more heterogeneous versions of Burckhardt's Renaissance that were available during the Cold War in order to provoke a discussion of how—and potentially also why—a more or less one-sided image of both the period and the book said to have created it emerged during these years. This kind of genealogical work is important precisely because of the key role these earlier debates played in shaping U.S. Renaissance Studies during the period that followed directly after them. This period saw the beginning of what some might call the new (and current) era of approaches to a non- or more-than-just "Eurocentric" Burckhardtian Renaissance based on Foucauldian paradigms as well as on attention to race and gender, the histories of imperialism, class struggle, and much more. The vexed nature of the discussions that came to a head in the 1960s about whether what "we" inherited from (Burckhardt's) Renaissance was or was not a good thing may help us understand many of the cultural issues raised by the "other Renaissances" discussed in this volume. Examining these "other Renaissances" in terms of the issues and ideologies associated with the period of European history conventionally associated with the term provides a key to how they fit into a longer narrative about what is and what is not worth "rebirthing" from either Europe's or any other civilization's illustrious past.

Texts as Witnesses: European Scholars and American Books[7]

One way to begin to understand the nature of early-to-mid twentieth-century debates about the Renaissance in the United States is to attend to the material form that these debates took. Perhaps most appealing in its human dimension was the "translation" of the long history of prior European work on the period into the mid-twentieth century United States by a significant number of German-Jewish scholars who fled Nazi Germany in the 1930s. Among them were some of the most prominent members of the guild of scholars that dominated U.S. Renaissance Studies during and after World War II, such as Hans Baron, Ernst Cassirer, Felix Gilbert, Paul Oskar Kristeller, and Erwin Panofsky. Part of a massive intellectual exodus out of Germany that has been exceedingly well documented in recent years, these men had for the most part been well-connected young scholars on the brink of successful careers in European academe in 1933.[8] It is thus not surprising that they sought the roots in a Renaissance past of the horrendous "modernity" that had driven them into an insecure exile, on the one hand, and of some better "modernity," whose values they might hope to save from the catastrophe enveloping Europe, on the other, as they moved in insecure fashion between the Old and the New Worlds' academic, linguistic, and political terrains.

And yet, even though the story of their personal fates has been the aspect of the intellectual transfer that has garnered the most attention to date, these scholars' work and its place in the contest about the legacy of the Renaissance were "carried over" into the United States not just in the refugees' immediate physical presence as human objects of sympathy and largesse (as well as of sheer curiosity—and also a measure of resentment on the part of U.S. academics insofar as the newcomers represented the enormously learned European "competition").[9] The disputes about the legacy of the Renaissance for modernity, deeply embedded in academic traditions reaching back into Burckhardt's nineteenth century,[10] were also quite literally translated into U.S. American textual form during the Cold War and reached the desks of massive numbers of American undergraduates in the form of inexpensive paperback translations published by, among others, trade presses like Doubleday and Harper and Row. The Academy Library series in particular, issued under the Harper Torchbook imprint, included not only the two-volume edition of Middlemore's translation of Burckhardt's *The Civilization of the Renaissance in Italy* (1958) with its Introduction by Trinkaus and Nelson, for example, that many of us who went to college in the 1970s purchased, but also a huge number of texts from the early to the mid-1960s by other well known authors, such as Cassirer, Kristeller, and Panofsky, whose versions of the Renaissance had a clear place in debates about Burckhardt's claims. Also represented, however, in The Academy Library were titles such as *The Sociology of the Renaissance* by one Alfred von Martin (1963) that seem not to have enjoyed such a wide reception or that are at least less familiar today. It was not just trade presses, finally, that were involved in selling the European Renaissance to American undergraduates during these years. August university publishers, including Princeton and Chicago, also got in on the business, producing both handy paperback collections of original documents in translation and English-language versions of European research. The most familiar University of Chicago volume of this sort is probably the 1948 *The Renaissance Philosophy of Man*, edited by Kristeller and his colleague at Columbia, John Herman Randall. Princeton University Press weighed in with a paperback edition of Baron's *The Crisis of the Early Italian*

Renaissance; the original two-volume hardbound edition had appeared some years earlier in 1955. Priced at under $3.00, the new and smaller format, single-volume paperback version of Baron's important work had been stripped of its learned appendices and its notes radically shortened. There is thus every indication that it was designed for a broader market than the original.

For those already familiar with the longer history of the contentious scholarly debates in Europe about Burckhardt's Renaissance, books like these clearly took sides. Both their Introductions and their footnotes teem with indirect and direct references to the work (mostly in German) of methodological and historical supporters and opponents too. For U.S. college audiences of the 1950s and 1960s, however, these learned squabbles might have been less than apparent. Rather, it was the overall image of the period these books presented that either could or could not be made to captivate the students because it either did or did not fit with their and the Cold War professoriate's worldview. Up until the mid-1960s, the degree to which the Renaissance was marketable in both literal and figurative terms may have depended, in other words, on the extent to which it matched up with stories about the period that the United States had begun to tell itself already beginning soon after World War I about the nation's identity as the only legitimate inheritor of western culture left standing;[11] later, the United States was able to extend this narrative to include its role as the defender of the patrimony that Europe had shown itself yet again incapable of protecting during a second destructive war. In the years during and after which Lopez and Sarton gave their talks, finally, books about the Renaissance may well have been assessed as to whether they provided sufficient academic ammunition with which to fight what Saunders calls the "cultural Cold War," defending the legacy of a West now solidly located in America against an ever more menacing Soviet Union and the threat of "barbarian" Communism worldwide.[12] According to this logic, U.S. students of the post-1945 era could presumably move with dispatch into their assigned places in a centuries-long *translatio studii et imperii* that reached back into the Renaissance by piggy backing on the celebration of a glittering tradition of cultural achievement during the period by a learned pantheon of European scholars, whose research was available to them in editions priced to sell.

And yet, as is obvious in Lopez's and Sarton's talks at the Met, there was in fact considerable debate during precisely these years about the exact nature of this tradition, and thus about the benefits of the bequest. My interest here is in examining the respective sides of this debate as they were represented by the images of the Renaissance that the books that were available offered and in calibrating the extent to which the positions their authors took may have helped showcase some versions of the period as the signature ones of the postwar years and caused others to fall out of subsequent discussions almost entirely. Von Martin's slim study, for example, was published in the popular Academy Library series and, like the rest of the Harper Torchbook volumes, cost $1.25. Why is it that his version of Burckhardt, with reservations about the "noble legacy" of the Renaissance that rival those of many of today's most cynical scholars, is practically unknown today? Unlike von Martin's book, Baron's book had an enormous impact at the time, as Witt's and Hankins' remarks attest, and has proven remarkably resilient.[13] It was still in print in 1995. Again, what was this life-long historian of Renaissance Florence saying about the period that made his book so attractive at the time and that has allowed its version, or better, its revision of Burckhardt to survive up to the present day?[14] My hypothesis is that we know less about von Martin's more or less accurate version of Burckhardt's Renaissance as a time of confusion and ultimately, of also corruption and decay, because it did not match up with the ideological needs of the United States during the Cold War. Baron's post-Burckhardtian, if not also anti-Burckhardtian rewriting of the Renaissance as the cradle of modern democracy and civic engagement by an intellectual elite was probably far more attractive at the time precisely because of its amenableness to what Carl Landauer has called the "growing humanistic mythology of the American university" and its charge to take the lead in a United States destined to be the "culture bearer" of the western world.[15]

A Past Not "Dead and Done With": The Renaissance of Alfred von Martin

Alfred von Martin's approach to the Renaissance is driven by his Diltheyian-Weberian charge to understand the "spirit, the essence of [the] period" and its "social conditioning and social function . . . [as] determined by the economic, political and cultural ruling class."[16] This class was the bourgeoisie, not just as a historical *unicum*, however, but as an "ideal type" of "the first modern civilization" (pp. xvii–xviii). His analysis in fact follows Burckhardt's in claiming that there was a great change in the Renaissance and that it represented the beginning of modernity. Von Martin's more specific mission, namely, to "plot certain rhythms which arise from the structural type of bourgeois civilization" from the period of the Renaissance up through "our own time" (p. xviii), nevertheless distinguishes his Renaissance not only from Burckhardt's, which is famously a rich cross-section of the period as a "static" culture, but also from any assessment of the period that would celebrate only its high points, and not discuss its end too. It is thus not just a set of either good or bad cultural artifacts or political ideologies that "modernity" has inherited from the Renaissance, according to von Martin; it is also the determining power of its rhythms on the rise and fall of future "civilizations" too. His original 1932 book makes it clear that this inheritance had already come home to roost, as the Europe of his time was fast approaching, if not already enveloped in a "typical" and inevitable downward slide.

Indeed, a vocabulary harboring extraordinarily timely concerns about the internal decadence of capitalism, the "rationalization" and bureaucratization of both business and the state, as well as the rise and fall of the bourgeois class characterizes the entirety of von Martin's Renaissance book. Machiavelli "diagnosed" how the "democratic regime" of Florence "entered upon its crises" already from a "proto-Fascist point of view" (p. xix), for example, when, in desiring to "adopt [the] way of life" of the "traditional ruling classes" of the feudal aristocracy, the "capitalist entrepreneurs" of the Renaissance from the "very beginning" have "a tendency towards the Right" (pp. 3–4). The elite among the "great merchants" of Florence stood "apart" from the "middle class and working proletariat," moreover, when they made the much vaunted guild system "into the basis for the Florentine constitution," and masked with "the ideological façade" of the "slogan for the masses" ("the rule of the people") that there was in fact only the formal existence of a "broad middle class democracy" (p. 6), and that it was actually the merchant elite that was in charge.[17] Such analyses of the "rise and decline" of a "democratic regime" as run by the "haute bourgeoisie" (pp. xviii–xix) could apply equally well to the city-republic of Renaissance Florence and to the Weimar Republic, of course, and von Martin's choice of words makes it obvious that he intended the structural parallels to be clear. That such prophecies of political doom and gloom for liberal capitalism would certainly have seemed legitimate in Europe in 1932, and perhaps also in London, where the first English translation appeared in 1944, does not cancel out how sinister, indeed, even potentially subversive they would have sounded to U.S. ears in 1963, when the Academy Library edition appeared.

If the vocabulary of von Martin's book on the Renaissance is indebted to the early twentieth-century political, economic, and social crises surrounding him, it is nevertheless clear from the very outset of his book, when he states that "J. Burckhardt's outstanding work is by no means obsolete" (p. xix), that what he sees in modernity is what he saw first in Burckhardt. The most memorable chapter title of *The Civilization of the Renaissance in Italy*, namely, "The State as a Work of Art," and Burckhardt's focus on the rise of Renaissance individualism, echo in von Martin's interest in the "human work of art" that is bourgeois capitalism (p. 8), for example, and in his claims for entrepreneurial individualism as the decisive moment in the Renaissance's disengagement from the Middle Ages. Describing the rejection of "old community ties" as well as "blood, tradition and group feeling" in ways that sound as if he is quoting Burckhardt directly, it became "necessary," following von Martin, "to order the world starting from the individual and to shape it, as it were, like a work of art" (p. 2; see also pp. 9–11). Continuing to shadow Burckhardt in his depiction of the age, von Martin repeatedly notes that "talent and determination (in place of birth and rank)" (p. 9; see also pp. 8, 12, 36) characterized the system of values of the Renaissance, and the "objectivity" styled in Burckhardt's Renaissance. Yet, whatever "freedom of the individual" there was in the Renaissance (p. 20) was the freedom, he argues, only to rationally "work one's [own] will" (20) and to "freely" compete in the marketplace of (one's own) ideas (p. 41). Thus, von Martin's version of the Renaissance updates Burckhardt by highlighting the ruthlessness of the period and the opportunism of its most famous sons.

Von Martin's version of Burckhardt thus produced for U.S. readers in 1963 what must have seemed a decidedly more cynical view of the period than they might have liked. It may have also been rather too materialist in method for Cold War academic tastes. The emergence of the Renaissance out of the Middle Ages is not a moment of spiritual liberation, for example, but a by-product of economic developments; the "capitalist domination by the moneyed great bourgeoisie" only exploits those " 'democratic' tendencies which may have destroyed feudalism," but did so not for the sake of democracy, but "as the best way to ensure its own domination" (p. 2). It is nevertheless when von Martin moves on to account for cultural developments within his overall thesis of the Renaissance that his picture of the period may have seemed the most shocking. The rise of "national languages" (pp. 18–19), for example, and even the grand architectural achievement of Brunelleschi's Duomo in Florence (p. 25) were nothing more than part of the overall "spirit" of a period in which there had been a shift in class hegemony from the aristocracy to what he identifies as the "intellectually supported economic power" of the bourgeois class (p. 2). Von Martin's mission of creating an integrated picture of the relationship between the "outward forms" of "fine art and great intellects" traditionally associated with the Renaissance and the identification of those forms with the "class of 'property and intellect' (*Bildung*)," the haute bourgeoisie (p. xix), thus reduces the great minds of the Renaissance to the status of "individualistic intellectual entrepreneurs" (p. 21) whose interests in the "new sciences" and technologies served primarily rational (and often only military) ends (pp. 22–23). All that later generations celebrated as Humanism's achievements, such as its "rediscovery" of "Antiquity," are characterized in turn as designed merely to give that struggle the dignified aspect of a "halo of age" (p. 28). The scandal of seeing even the art of the Renaissance characterized as no more than "a field in which beautiful illusions have their rights" must have outraged readers who were more accustomed to seeing the Renaissance as a moment of the "apotheosis" of art.[18] Von Martin's linking of cultural achievement to a historical class analysis offered a clear alternative, then, in its less than lofty and optimistic image of the Renaissance, to what has been assumed by such scholars as Leah Marcus, Jonathan Goldberg, and John Martin to have been *the* Renaissance legacy. It has become routine to acknowledge and celebrate that lofty image in the history of ideas and the arts and to associate it with Burckhardt's book—while also excoriating it as a "traditional" Eurocentric one.[19] It was not von Martin's reduction of culture to an appendage of class that most threatened the notion of the Renaissance as the origin of an uplifting "new age" of modernity, however. Rather, it was the ideological punch packed by his method that might have reminded Cold War readers of the real threat that this Renaissance's legacy presented for them. For, as noted above, von Martin was primarily interested in the "complete rhythmic progression of the ideal type of a cultural epoch dominated by the bourgeoisie," a rhythm characterized as one that will always "begin . . . in the spirit of democracy and end[s] in the spirit of the court" (p. 3). He thus traces what becomes the necessary "curve of development" (p. 47) from an inspiring spirit of "enterprise" on both the commercial and intellectual levels in the "heroic" age of capitalism and ideas (p. 48) to the decidedly more "conservative" phase of stasis and "moderation" (pp. 50–1) not as one of progress, but rather, always as one of decline. In the Renaissance, the "fresh and daring energy" of early risk-taking capitalist entrepreneurs eventually flattened out into more conservative business practices and the redirection of profits into luxury goods; the resulting changes belied the notion of an active life of engagement in either the business or the political sphere, since for the sake of economic stability, the "saturated" "haute bourgeoisie" (pp. 61, 62) was always "ready to come to terms with the new absolutist states, indeed even to sacrifice its democratic republican institutions" to "enjoy comforts" of "imposed peace" at their villas (p. 61), where the cultural products of the so-called "Full Renaissance" in the arts were produced and enjoyed. Literary humanists met their politically and socially emasculated artist brothers on the slope of this decline, from the "political ardour" of Salutati (p. 53) to the humanist "littérateur," Petrarch (p. 54), who retreated into a "purely literary and imaginary world . . . without practical application" (pp. 54–5), ending with Pontano, whose "defense of unconditioned obedience towards the established political authority" (p. 59) sealed the fate of the notion of a critical and freedom-loving intellectual class. In its entirety, von Martin's would have seemed a depressing account—and prediction—of the possible fate of the bourgeois capitalist successor class in the Cold War United States. In fact, von Martin's later work traces precisely this curve in the development of the bourgeois class in the United States as well as in a postwar Germany influenced by its values and the need to "consume." As in the Renaissance, so too in the postwar "Free World," the rationalization and functionalization of individuals in society leads to depersonalization ("Entpersönlichung"), and consumer power like that of the Renaissance princes becomes the only way to assert one's self.[20] Fortunately, the way in which the suggestion of such unpleasant afterlives for the Renaissance in the here-and-now was packaged in the Harper Torchbook edition of von Martin's book in fact made it easy for U.S. readers to avoid them. For von Martin's 1963 *Sociology of the Renaissance* was accompanied by an Introduction by one Wallace K. Ferguson, who had himself been another of the Met speakers and author of the well-known account of the historiography of the Renaissance in the West, *The Renaissance in Historical Thought* (1948). In his Introduction, Ferguson does his best to contain both Burckhardt's and von Martin's doubts about the legacy of the period.[21] Indeed, while he quite helpfully uses his pages to locate von Martin's place in the scholarly landscape of the early twentieth century in Germany for its new readership, his discussion focuses primarily on the book's and its author's methodological lineage, beginning with the relationship of von Martin's approach to Dilthey, Weber, and Sombart (pp. vi–viii), and ending, most importantly, I would argue, with his (von Martin's) eclipse by the newer political and economic history of the postwar period (pp. xi–xiii). The fact that, in 1963, Ferguson characterizes von Martin's work as belonging to a "tradition already becoming obsolete" (p. v) and as somewhat "unfashionable" (p. xi), perhaps even "irrelevant" (p. xii) in light of recent work, may not have helped any readers it did find to see the usefulness of von Martin's analysis of the Burckhardtian Renaissance for an understanding not only of the political and social conditions that permitted National Socialism, but potentially also of the way liberal democracy and capitalism can always and quite easily veer away from their allegedly lofty goals. Another book by a scholar whom Ferguson names in his Introduction, namely, Hans Baron (p. xii), would probably have been more useful in preserving an image of a Renaissance whose model the West could follow with good conscience and also a lighter heart.

Appearing in paperback just three years after von Martin's *Sociology of the Renaissance*, the book Ferguson cites, namely Baron's *The Crisis of the Early Italian Renaissance: Civic Humanism and Republican Liberty in an Age of Classicism and Tyranny* (original hardback edition, 1955), found a very different set of patterns in the Renaissance. Somewhat younger than von Martin, but coming of intellectual age in the same milieu, Baron was also conditioned in his understanding of the period by Burckhardt; he understood as well as von Martin that the Swiss historian's description of the epoch as a model for the future was in fact somewhat bleak. But he (Baron) chose the path not of reproducing Burckhardt's analysis of the origins of a morally and culturally brittle modernity in the Renaissance, as von Martin had done, but rather of developing a new and more attractive image of the time as an alternative to it. That there was a sustained controversy up through the end of the twentieth century about the accuracy of Baron's more optimistic version of the Renaissance may well have had the somewhat counter-intuitive result of guaranteeing its longevity. In any case, his celebration of the origins of a liberal-democratic modernity in the work of the Florentine (male) elite was well known in the Cold War years.

Our Ancestors, the Humanists: Hans Baron's Post-Burckhardtianism and the Appeal of Florentine Republican Thinking

Like many of his generation, Baron understood Burckhardt's darker claims about the Renaissance from the very beginning.[22] It was against the pressure of readings of Burckhardt like von Martin's, readings that accepted a vision of the period not only as the bad dream of modernity's beginnings, but also as a critique of Renaissance Humanism in particular, that Baron developed his anti-Burckhardtian or perhaps better "post-Burckhardtian" alternative image.[23] Based on an elaborate calculus whereby he could explain the important "political" role the Humanists played in preserving the grand legacy of the Renaissance for the future of a "free" and democratic West, this project determined Baron's obsessive focus on the figure of Leonardo Bruni of Arezzo (1374–1444) as the personification of the concept of a politically engaged Florentine "civic humanism," on the one hand, and his commitment to a new periodization scheme for the Renaissance, on the other, which demanded that he back the high point of Renaissance cultural achievement up to the late fourteenth century so that it would coincide with the resistance of the Florentine Republic to the Visconti "tyrants" of Milan and thus with the establishment of a stability-ensuring balance of power on the Italian peninsula. Against Burckhardt's by now well-known view of Renaissance "individualism" as produced by political chaos and driven by self interest, Baron thus set a communitarian image of individuals working in concert to preserve liberty in the state; against the view of great art produced in a vacuum of political values, he set the notion of Renaissance cultural workers reaping the benefits of—and contributing to—a new belief in the power of a democratic public sphere. What was not likeable in the postwar United States about this image of the mother culture of one's own time?

Baron's scholarly contributions in defense of his thesis about a Renaissance "we" could be proud to inherit were legion, and he presented them in a number of dense and often polemical articles in learned journals in both German and English over the course of a half a century or more. But Baron's legacy in the United States, as "surely one of the three or four most influential interpreters of the Renaissance in the second half of the twentieth century," as Hankins writes, was based primarily on his synthesis of his earlier work in the complexly choreographed *The Crisis of the Early Italian Renaissance*, originally published in hardback in 1955.[24] The first edition of *Crisis* consisted in two volumes of carefully cross-indexed arguments. Readers were asked to shuttle back and forth between bracing accounts of historical events in Volume One and an elaborate scholarly apparatus in Volume Two, containing learned mini-monographs, which Baron entitles "Annexes," on issues related to the main arguments as well as some two hundred pages of notes. Reference is made throughout *Crisis* to an additional and separate companion volume, *Humanistic and Political Literature*, published by Harvard University Press in the same year; it contains further materials relevant to Baron's case. It is clear that the point of publishing the inexpensive 1966 paperback version of *Crisis* was to provide a more generally accessible version of the "narrative"[25] of his Renaissance, one that "modernity" stood poised to adopt. But Baron's more or less explicit commitment to creating a picture of the Renaissance that is quite different from Burckhardt's—and from von Martin's—was the product of scholarship produced over the course of his long career. Some snapshots of the development of his argument reveal just how much of an alternative *Crisis* really was to earlier versions of the period.

It is important to note that even though Fubini claims that "[t]o those who knew him, Baron seemed essentially apolitical,"[26] Baron's 1942 article, "Articulation and Unity in the Italian Renaissance and the Modern West," published in a collection entitled *The Quest for Political Unity in World History* in 1944, suggests somewhat the opposite.[27] The essay's main task is to challenge the nineteenth-century notion—also articulated by Burckhardt, Baron writes—that "the Renaissance" is to be celebrated only as an era of "national" renewal; such a binding together of "nation and culture" (p. 124) may be the basis of "the penetration of the whole globe [today] by the ideas and energies of European 19th century nationalism" (p. 126), but it obscures the equally as prominent and much more important parallels for the here-and-now between the Renaissance and a more integrated "world-system of states which has emerged in the 20th century" (p. 126). Baron claims that the "mirror" (p. 123) of the Renaissance can help the modern world see the importance of a system of "co-operating nations," each with "abiding self-consciousness and individual independence" (p. 129), to be sure, but all ultimately concerned with "mutual exchange" (p. 135) and resistance to any tyranny that threatens. The parallels between this Renaissance and a league of nations resisting both Fascism and National Socialism are not difficult to discern, and Baron is clearly issuing a political call here. Indeed, if Baron's essay of 1942–1944 is continuously punctuated by such claims as "the Italian Renaissance becomes once more an indispensable testing-ground for fundamental problems of modern history" (p. 127), his 1953 piece in the *American Historical Review*, "A Struggle for Liberty in the Renaissance. Florence, Venice, and Milan in the Early Quattrocento," is even more explicit—even though it still looks backward to the events that drove him from his home.[28] Writing of the great "political conviction and patriotic will" of the Florentines in their struggle against the Visconti in the 1390s and first decade of the Quattrocento, Baron again endorses a reading of the Renaissance as a "harbinger of modern conditions" (p. 268) that enables an understanding of the overwhelming importance of a cooperative "states system." One cannot help, he writes, but be "struck" by the "resemblance [of developments in the Renaissance] to the events of modern history when unifying conquest loomed over Europe. In a like fashion, Napoleon and Hitler poised on the coast of the English Channel. . . . This is the only perspective from which one can adequately reconstruct the crisis of the summer of 1402" when the Visconti leader, Giangaleazzo, died and Milan's tyranny thus failed (pp. 284–5).[29] Baron's "translation" of an analysis of Renaissance politics, and specifically Italian politics, into a more general thesis in 1953 about the virtues of "republican" powers resisting "imperial" tyrannies throughout the ages may have been read as particularly appealing after the war's end; to the liberal intelligentsia of the Cold War United States, that is, Baron's narration of a story of "nations" cooperating in their commitment to "freedom" may have seemed ideal as a way of laying claim to the notion that their country had not only led the choir of nations in the defeat of National Socialism, but also could now engage in a united quest in the West for yet a further rebirth of freedom and democracy, this time as an alternative to a tyrannical Soviet totalitarianism. What better advertisement, indeed, what better conditions for the republication in an inexpensive paperback edition of Baron's book just one year later, where we find the Hitler reference has been kept?[30]

Baron's recognition that Burckhardt had to be rewritten was not merely a postwar phenomenon, however, even though his commitment to the task may have been "sharpened" subsequently by the events of his migratory years.[31] Indeed, already in "A Sociological Interpretation of the Early Renaissance in Florence," an article published in 1939 in *The South Atlantic Quarterly*, but based on campus lectures Baron had given at some nine American universities over the prior year as part of an ongoing search for employment, the central political role that the intelligentsia—and thus humanists—had to play in the preservation of freedom in economically and politically difficult times had become the main point.[32] His argument in this essay that it was the economic savvy of the city's leadership that produced a nonmedieval, indeed antimedieval, ideology in Florence by the fourteenth century (pp. 431–3) was probably a story that American capitalism might have adored: namely, that by hard work, anyone could improve his condition in the world. His original academic audiences might have been more uplifted by Baron's claims about the essential synergism in the Renaissance between both economic and "political factor[s]" *and* "the humanistic mind" (p. 438). The same "free initiatives" that had proven successful in the development of industrial wool and silk production were, in other words, those that the Florentines were defending as they pitched their city-state against the "absolutism" and "despotic rule" of the Viscontis in Milan at the end of the fourteenth century. In Baron's analysis, this energy translated directly into stimulating learned and artistic work on the part of the Humanists, who found models for their city's greatness in texts from the classical past. It was this image of the legacy of the Renaissance that was to be passed on to the student-elite in the work of the man who, according to Fubini, adapted himself to the "climate and values of Anglo-Saxon culture" of his new "republican" home during these years by claiming that he would teach their sons to inherit both the Ancients and their Renaissance custodians in similar ways.[33]

In his 1960 article, "Burckhardt's 'Civilization of the Renaissance' a Century after its Publication," Baron states explicitly that his project is to replace Burckhardt's Renaissance with another version of the period.[34] Above all, the "false image of the unscrupulous, ruthless, and lusty 'superman' of the Renaissance" Humanist must finally be put to rest (p. 207). Baron locates the origin of the amazing resilience of this image in the twentieth century not only in the new edition of *Die Kultur der Renaissance in Italien* edited by his own senior colleague back in Weimar Germany, Walter Goetz, in 1922, however, but also in the countless reprints and translations, particularly into English, of the book since that "re-publication" (p. 207). Ultimately, he claims, the real problem is the historiographic "lacuna" in "Burckhardt's analysis" (p. 215) itself, the marked absence, that is, of sufficient attention to more upbeat interpretations of the period prior to his own, such as the thesis of "the invigorating power of competition within and between free city-states" explicated by Adam Ferguson in 1767, on the one hand, or of the power of "popular sovereignty and direct democracy in small local states" advocated by Rousseau and Simonde de Sismondi, on the other (pp. 215–6). By focusing on the position of the Humanists only at the courts of the despots, according to Baron, Burckhardt had ignored these earlier and thus "already available approaches" to the period in 1860, and thus failed to acknowledge in the history of Renaissance Florence in particular "the molding influence of a society in which citizens were compelled to be rulers as well as ruled" (p. 217). It was thus not more English-language copies of Burckhardt that were needed; indeed, they were precisely the problem. Rather, an entirely new image of the period, based on a different historiographic tradition, had to be substituted for his. By now an American citizen, Baron dismisses, or if that is too strong, then at least puts at arm's length those "European" interpretations of the Renaissance linked with Burckhardt and also with his (Baron's) own German past, especially the legacy of German "neo-humanistic liberalism" (p. 219) that saw Humanism as only a private affair. "[A] good deal of recent study," Baron claims, has signaled the beginning of a new era of scholarship by focusing on the great achievements of the period as the product of the work of men who, "emotionally and intellectually, were deeply involved in the struggles of their age" (p. 219). There is a curious absence of footnotes to substantiate this claim, particularly when Baron refers to "recent stud[ies]" and "present-day scholars" (p. 219) of the post-Burckhardtian persuasion, and perhaps for good reason, as it might have appeared unseemly to footnote primarily his own work.

As noted above, in the 1955 edition of *Crisis*, Baron had unrolled in hugely learned and heavily annotated fashion the new story of the Renaissance that he had been constructing for such a long time, an image of the period that offered an explicit alternative to Burckhardt.[35] A carefully choreographed series of chapters in the first volume narrates in Part One the political struggles of the Milanese Wars and the "effects of this experience on . . . humanistic attitudes" in the "city of the Arno" (p. 37). He then circles back around in Part Two to revisit Humanist versions of antiquity in particular as both the source and expression of their engaged "politico-historical ideas" (pp. 77–8), thus preparing for his close explication of Leonardo Bruni's contribution to the renewal of republican ideology in Part Three. Part Four then takes on the task of deploying this new reading of the political engagement of the Humanists in the service of moving *away* from readings of the "puristic" (p. 249) and "militant Classicism" (p. 254) of Humanism as only a Latinizing "professional" movement uninterested in its "vernacular" civic surroundings and in any case "a veiled or open ally of court and tyranny" (p. 252); the role of Humanists like Bruni is thus redefined as that of the custodians of these and other political lessons crucial to the political health of the republic. Part Five follows the afterlife of early Quattrocento Florentine commitment to "liberty" he has just established into the so-called "late Renaissance" of the mid-fifteenth century, carefully skirting any suggestion that the "youthful proud belief in the democratic liberty of Florentine life" (p. 371) had faded in any way, thus bringing his new version of the period up into the years more commonly associated with grand achievements in culture and art. Underlying all of these claims was a synergistic understanding of politics and ideas not unlike Burckhardt's, to be sure, but antithetical to it, for he advances the belief that key political events (the "crises" of his book's title) like the defeat of Viscontean Milan by "republican" Florence were instrumental in inspiring great things in citizen intellectuals and gifted artists alike. The real legacy of the period and the turn to Antiquity were thus to promote a version of "the civilization of the Renaissance in Italy" as one that could serve as a model of active political and moral health.

Baron's thesis about communitarian humanism clearly rivaled Burckhardt's depiction of the Humanists' self-serving individualism in what we might today call its interdisciplinarity and consistency of message. But, its academic "packaging," with its constant calls to attend to both the additional materials in the eight "Annexes" of Volume Two as well as its two hundred pages of closely printed notes in a variety of languages, was nevertheless considerably more daunting to any other than scholarly readers. The changes he undertook for the 1966 paperback edition of *Crisis* did in fact produce (in the single and somewhat smaller format volume, which has no appendices and only one hundred pages of notes) a genuinely more accessible and thus also more marketable version of his tale.[36] Sensitive that both the original scholarly apparatus and any additional learned detail might "overburden the historical narrative" (p. ix) he so wishes to promote, Baron states in the new Preface that he has made every effort to dis-"encumber" (p. viii) the "historical analysis" in the new edition. He has thus banned all references to the "Annexes" from their intrusive place in the main text to the endnotes and has integrated any "pages" from them that need to be "part of the full historical picture" into the main story (p. ix). Moreover, although he helpfully informs readers (p. viii) that, if need be, they may consult the second volume of the original 1955 text as a kind of parallel reference book (all the note numbers have been left the same as in the original edition, but the notes themselves have for the most part been chopped down to the bare minimum), the materials contained there are now to be considered really as only "preparatory investigations" and can be done without. That Baron in 1966 was quite literally offering a more readable story of the Renaissance that could rival Burckhardt's—or at least one that could stand alongside it as a kind of counterweight on the shelves of college bookstores, if not on students' dormitory bookshelves too—supported the ideological attractiveness of his picture of the period as the intellectual and political progenitor of their land.

A salient detail of the new 1966 edition of *Crisis* makes clear Baron's project to usurp Burckhardt whose bleak message he, like von Martin, understood quite well. In the new Epilogue to the 1966 version, entitled "The Nature and Significance of the Crisis," Baron glosses the central term of his book's title:

> The term "crisis," in recent years, has become a rather hackneyed word in the vocabulary of historical writers. It often means no more than a period of danger or suspense, preserving little of its more precise meaning of a turning-point in the growth of an organism, institution, or people threatened

by some weakness or disease, but finally regaining health and strength by successful resistance or adaptation to vital change. (p. 443)

The choice to unpack the medical meaning of the term "crisis" after arguing for the "immense vitality" of both political and cultural life in Renaissance Florence (p. 443) is a clear nod in the direction, yet also a correction of Burckhardt, who had famously used Dante's reference to Florence's constant revisions of its constitution as the actions of a sick man who continually shifts his position to see if he can find an escape from the pain.[37] Whereas Burckhardt's description of Florence as a suffering patient occurs in the context of narrating the "Schattenseiten" (dark sides) of its culture as an exemplum for the modern world, Baron's rewriting of the image as one that indicates the city's imminent recovery and health turns Burckhardt's tormented Renaissance on its head. Professors might not have needed to assign and students might have not needed to read any more than the Epilogue to get the point, for it reviews and recites in compact form the various stages of the argument Baron had been developing for such a long time: the rise of civic humanism against the "catalyst" background of the victory of Republican Florence over the Milan of the Visconti in 1401–1402, and the importance of developing an integrated state system predicated on the all-important principle of a balance of powers. This Renaissance, like Burckhardt's, did indeed initiate a "new historical epoch" (pp. 446, 453), but, Baron writes, it "transcended in significance the history of Florence and of Renaissance Italy" (p. 459) in ways that surpass Burckhardt's claims. The stirring words with which Baron closes his book call for present-day Humanists to "visualize this contribution to modernity and its historical growth" by revising the "memory of what happened in Florence," the very "developments" that have "been traced" in his book (pp. 461–2), to include the education of "man as a member of [his] society and his state." The "rebirth" of the citizen-scholars of Florence in the expanded student readership of his book would ensure the renaissance of his version of the Renaissance— rather than either von Martin's or even Burckhardt's—in the here-and-now of "the modern world" in the United States.

Coda: Introducing Burckhardt

"To read Burckhardt's pages is to look into a mirror." So ends Nelson's and Trinkaus' Introduction to the two-volume paperback illustrated edition of *The Civilization of the Renaissance in Italy* published by Harper Torchbooks in 1958.[38] It was only one of the three editions of

Civilization published in the 1950s and 1960s in the United States. In the Introduction to the 1954 edition of *Civilization* published by Random House, Hajo Holborn, also a German refugee, writes, for example, that "[t]he experiences of wars and revolutions in our own times make us look at Jacob Burckhardt's work with fresh eyes."[39] But while Holborn's reference to the conflicts of "our own times" is reminiscent of the Met talks, he nevertheless ends his account of the significance of Burckhardt's book with the rapid transformation of the mirror from one that enabled a somewhat pained backward glance (like Lopez's) into a far more hopeful (Sartonian) vision of the period's legacy. While "Burckhardt knew as well as Ranke that man was thrown into the maelstrom of history," Holborn writes, it is "[n]ot the outcome of events . . . [that] decides his worth, but his will to defend his patrimony, the faculty to produce civilization" (p. x). Burckhardt, so Holborn, had an "abiding faith in the creative power of man" and was thus ultimately no "skeptical onlooker," but, rather, a "hopeful visionary" (p. xi) whose picture of the Renaissance would contribute to the future creation of such ideals. Students reading this edition of Burckhardt might have been quite well prepared for Baron's similarly "hopeful" version of the same period.

Nelson's and Trinkaus' Introduction to the 1958 Harper Torchbook edition of *The Civilization of the Renaissance in Italy* nevertheless suggests a much more vexed fork in the road of Burckhardt reception than Holborn's and thus more closely resembles the more problematic version of his Renaissance that I have tried to sketch here. As descriptive as their account initially sounds, it is the pathos that breaks out in the last four pages that draws our attention to the weighty stakes of the debates about the parallels between the Renaissance and modern times that were taking place during these years. They end with a lengthy analysis of the ways in which Burckhardt is to be counted among the "forerunners of contemporary existentialism" (p. 18), and explain:

> [T]he legacy which the Renaissance was to leave the future was not without ambiguity; it was more a summons to responsibility than a release from restraints. In the end, as Burckhardt conceives it, what the Renaissance bequeathed to man was a burden by the bearing of which alone would come whatever creative renewals and rebirths—whatever Renaissances— might henceforth issue from the unregenerate mass of men of the looming Age of Iron and Steel which was his own and ours. (pp. 17–8)

As much as the vocabulary here echoes a kind of lonely Heideggerian "thrownness" into the world (they continue: "[w]estern man has irrevocably been cast out—has cast himself out—of a child-like world of enchantment and undividedness," p. 18); the inevitability of some form of "renewal" and "rebirth" indicates that the version of Renaissance Man offered here is no melancholic intellectual in black, but is, rather, a "modern" Man faced with a choice. While he must bear the "ambiguous" "burden of selfhood," the "grim" mandate "which [was] once laid upon the men of the Renaissance and which are now laid upon us who are their heirs" (pp. 18–19), he can bear it, they write, either as "his sign of Cain" or as "his crown of glory" (p. 19). Despite the fact that Nelson and Trinkaus ultimately suggest that it was Burckhardt's lasting insight to have recognized that the crown and the sign of Cain were one and the same thing, students may well have understood their words as a clear call to choose the crown, to invest in a future of only one of the two versions of modernity offered here, in a Baronian celebration of the glory of democracy as "our" legacy, in other words, rather than in an insistence that it was only ever decline that "we" would inherit that more resembled von Martin's take. That the image of a Renaissance developed by Baron may have seemed more attractive even to those who quite clearly understood, with von Martin, that they were living in a modernity marked by nothing so much as the "sign of Cain" is not surprising. That most of the scholars promoting this version of the Renaissance at the time also recognized the inevitability of the other side of the coin should nevertheless not be overlooked. Modern scholars of the European Renaissance and those who would claim that "other Renaissances" appropriated the European one may want to consider the possibility that there was, is, and always will be an ambiguous politics of choice involved in inheriting this and any period's legacy in only a selective way. Choosing to leave "other" von Martinian Renaissances out of the "other" Baronian Renaissances in the study of how a wide variety of cultures used the concept of the European Renaissance to shape their own modernity may as much obscure as illuminate the internal complexities of rebirth in each case.

Notes

* So describes Wallace K. Ferguson the state of contemporary scholarly debate about the Renaissance in his *The Renaissance in Historical Thought* (Boston, MA and New York: Houghton Mifflin Company, 1948), p. xi. I would like to thank Professors Warren Boutcher, Martin Elsky, Paul Freedman, Lionel Gossman, and Kathryn Reyerson for sharing their work and thoughts with me as I completed this essay. Matt Ancell and Alana Shilling provided invaluable assistance in securing texts.

1. The MMA symposium talks are available as a typescript, entitled *The Renaissance. A Symposium. February 8–10, 1952*, produced by the Museum in

1953. Page references here are to the version of Lopez's talk available in this typescript, pp. 19–33. The talks also appeared as a book. See Wallace K. Ferguson, Ed. *The Renaissance. Six Essays* (New York: Harper Torchbooks, 1962). Hereafter, Lopez's talk is cited parenthetically in the text.

2. Sarton's talk is available in the typescript of the Met talks cited in note 1, pp. 35–49. Hereafter, Sarton's talk is cited parenthetically in the text.

3. Sarton does admit, however, that there were "gloomy parts" of the period, such as the persecution of witches, pp. 44–6. His ability to subordinate precisely these "darker" sides of the Renaissance to a more optimistic narrative is precisely the move deplored by many recent Renaissance scholars, who are interested in gender in ways Sarton was not.

4. See Ferguson, *The Renaissance in Historical Thought*, p. 342.

5. As cited in ibid., pp. 189–90.

6. See Anthony Mohlo, "Burckhardtian Legacies," *Medievalia et Humanistica* 17 (1991), pp. 133–39, here p. 133.

7. For the concept of "texts as witnesses," see French Annalist Lucien Febvre's call for listening to the evidence books and textual materials provide about the "frame of mind" of a period in his *The Problem of Unbelief in the Sixteenth Century. The Religion of Rabelais*, orig. 1942, trans. Beatrice Gottlieb. (Cambridge: Harvard University Press, 1982), pp. 4 and 11–16.

8. See, among others, Kenneth D. Barkin, "German Émigré Historians in America: The Fifties, Sixties, and Seventies," in *An Interrupted Past. German-Speaking Refugee Historians in the United States after 1933*. Eds. Hartmut Lehmann and James J. Sheehan. (Cambridge: Cambridge University Press, 1991), pp. 149–69; Donald Fleming and Bernard Bailyn, Eds., *The Intellectual Migration. Europe and America, 1933–1960* (Cambridge, MA: Harvard University Press, 1969), and Hartmut Lehmann and James J. Sheehan, Eds. *An Interrupted Past. German-Speaking Refugee Historians in the United States after 1933* (Cambridge: Cambridge University Press, 1991).

9. See Carl Landauer, "Erwin Panofsky and the Renascence of the Renaissance," *Renaissance Quarterly* 47: 2 (1994), pp. 255–81, on the largesse of U.S. academe, but also on academic suspicions about the refugees.

10. The history of the German historiographic tradition up through the early twentieth century is of course immensely complex, and involves not only its implication in nationalist state projects that is so often referred to, but also the "export" of its methods to the community of professional historians in the United States even before the war. For an introduction, see Wolfgang J. Mommsen, "German Historiography during the Weimar Republic and the Émigré Historians," in Lehmann and Sheehan, *An Interrupted* Past, pp. 32–66, and Ernst Schulin, "German and American Historiography in the Nineteenth and Twentieth Centuries," in Lehmann and Sheehan, *An Interrupted Past*, pp. 8–31.

11. See Edward Muir, "The Italian Renaissance in America," *American Historical Review* 100: 4 (1995), pp. 1095–118.

12. See Frances Stonor Saunders, *The Cultural Cold War. The CIA and the World of Arts and Letters* (New York: The New Press, 1999).
13. See Ronald Witt, "The Crisis after Forty Years," *The American Historical Review* 101: 1 (1996), pp. 110–18, here p.111, and James Hankins, "Introduction," in *Renaissance Civic Humanism: Reappraisals and Reflections* (New York: Cambridge University Press, 2000), pp. 1–13, here p. 1.
14. William J. Connell and Andrea Zorzi, Eds. *Florentine Tuscany: Structures and Practices of Power* (New York: Cambridge University Press, 2000), Hankins, "Introduction," in *Renaissance Civic Humanism*, pp. 1–13 and Witt,. "The Crisis after Forty Years," pp. 110–18. Of course note the numerous challenges to Baron's work by Seigel, Quint, and others. (See David Quint, "Humanism and Modernity: A Reconsideration of Bruni's *Dialogues*," *Renaissance Quarterly* 38: 3 (1985), pp. 423–45, and Jerrold E. Seigel, " 'Civic Humanism' or Ciceronian Rhetoric? The Culture of Petrarch and Bruni," *Past and Present* 34 (1966), pp. 3–48. These controversies nevertheless appear to have guaranteed the longevity of his work.
15. See Landauer, "Erwin Panofsky and the Renascence of the Renaissance," pp. 271, 276.
16. Here I cite the 1963 version of von Martin's *The Sociology of the Renaisance* (New York: Harper and Row, 1963). Hereafter citations are included parenthetically in the text. Von Martin clearly states that his purpose in assessing the Renaissance is to understand it as an example of a Weberian "ideal type," in this case, of the rise and fall of bourgeois society. "[T]his phenomenon is by no means confined to this specific period alone," he writes in his "Author's Preface." It is thus that he writes "about a past which is [not] dead and done with" (xx) when he writes about the Renaissance. While I am interested less in von Martin's personal history than in the image of the Renaissance available in the U.S. in his book, it is of interest to note that he was a leader in what Kruse calls "Weimar historical sociology" (see Völker Kruse, *Analysen der deutschen historischen Soziologie* (Münster: Lit, 1998), p. 12). It is no wonder that Karl Mannheim arranged for the first translation of his book in 1944. Von Martin was neither a Jew nor was he in the United States during or after the war, however. At the height of his career as a sociologist and cultural historian in the early part of the twentieth century, von Martin had been appointed to a chair in Sociology and as director of the Institute for Sociology at the University of Göttingen in 1931. Two years later, he resigned out of protest at the coming to power of the National Socialists, and went into "inner emigration" in Munich for the duration of the war, writing a subversive analysis of Nietzsche and Burckhardt, for example, as allegories of pro-versus anti-Nazi stances on culture, respectively. *Nietzsche and Burckhardt* made it through two editions before being confiscated by the Gestapo. Von Martin was a spiritual advisor to the students, Hans and Sophie Scholl, who were of course executed for anti-government activities at the University of Munich in 1943, and himself barely escaped arrest. After 1945, he was reappointed as a professor in

Munich and was instrumental in rebuilding Sociology in postwar Germany. He died in 1979. While both *The Sociology of the Renaissance* and most of his postwar work are virtually unknown in the United States, the 1932 book was considered a masterpiece of historical sociology at the time and was translated into four languages. For von Martin's biography, the background of Weimar and postwar sociology in Germany, and for a summary of von Martin's work, see Kruse, *Analysen der deutschen historischen Soziologie*, pp. 9–17, 18–49, and 100–40.

17. Najemy's most recent work appears to bear von Martin out in his analysis of the Florentine guilds. See his "Civic Humanism and Florentine Politics," in *Renaissance Civic Humanism: Reappraisals and Reflections*, Ed. James Hankins (New York: Cambridge University Press, 2000), pp. 75–104.

18. See Landauer, "Erwin Panofsky and the Renascence of the Renaissance," p. 268, on the intersection of Panofsky's and Cassirer's art historical Renaissances with the celebratory "emphasis on the artifact" by the New Critics.

19. See Leah S. Marcus, "Renaissance/Early Modern Studies," in Stephen Greenblatt and Giles Gunn, Eds. *Redrawing the Boundaries: The Transformation of English and American Literary Studies* (New York: Modern Language Association, 1992), pp. 41–63, in which Marcus characterizes a more or less Burckhardtian Renaissance as in one way or another "traditional" fifteen times in her 21-page article; Jonathan Goldberg, "Introduction," *Queering the Renaissance* (Durham, NC: Duke University Press, 1994), pp. 1–14, here p. 1, and John Martin, "Inventing Sincerity, Refashioning Prudence: The Discovery of the Individual in Renaissance Europe," *The American Historical Review* 102: 5 (1997), pp. 1309–42, here p. 1311.

20. See von Martin, "Gesellschaft und Freiheit heute." In *Mensch und Gesellschaft heute* (Frankfurt: Josef Knecht, 1965), pp. 15–40, here p. 22.

21. See Ferguson, "Introduction" in von Martin, *Sociology of the Renaissance*. (New York: Harper and Row, 1963), pp. v–xiv. Hereafter references to the "Introduction" are included parenthetically in the text.

22. There is a small industry of work on Baron's biography and intellectual career, as well as on the intricacies and accuracy of his understanding of early Republicanism. See, among others, Alison Brown, "Hans Baron's Renaissance," *The Historical Journal* 33: 2 (1991), pp. 441–8; Riccardo Fubini, "Renaissance Historian: The Career of Hans Baron," *Journal of Modern History* 64 (1992), pp. 541–74; Hankins"Introduction," in *Renaissance Civic Humanism: Reappraisals and Reflections*, pp. 1–13; John M. Najemy, "Baron's Machiavelli and Renaissance Republicanism," *The American Historical Review* 101: 1 (1996), pp. 119–29; Kay Schiller, *Gelehrte Gegenwelten: Über humanistische Leitbilder im 20. Jahrhundert* (Frankfurt am Main: Fischer, 2000), and Witt "The Crisis after Forty Years," pp.110–18. Born in Berlin in 1900, Baron was a student of the great historians Ernst Troeltsch and Friedrich Meinecke and took his Ph.D. in 1922. His work was also heavily influenced by the great German cultural historian, Walter Goetz. Baron's publication of important articles and

reviews thus reaches back to the immediate post –World War I and Weimar periods; see Tedeschi's and Lewis' bibliography of his writings as well as Epstein on Baron 33–6. A research associate at the Historische Kommission at the Bayerische Akademie der Wissenschaften and *Privatdozent* at the University of Berlin, Baron, who was Jewish, left Germany in 1933 and finally emigrated to the United States (via Italy and England) in 1938. Hard of hearing, he was unable to find a permanent teaching position and survived on short-term grants and temporary jobs until 1949, when, after retraining as a librarian, he finally secured a permanent position as a Research Fellow and Bibliographer at the Newberry Library in Chicago. He died in 1988.

23. The term is Baron's. See his "Burckhardt's 'Civilization of the Renaissance' a Century after its Publication," *Renaissance News* 13: 3 (1960), pp. 207–22, here p. 219.

24. See Hankins, "The 'Baron Thesis' after Forty Years and Some Recent Studies of Leonardo Bruni," *The Journal of the History of Ideas* 56: 2 (1995), pp. 309–38, here pp. 309–10.

25. See Baron's "Preface" to *The Crisis of the Early Italian Renaissance. Civic Humanism and Republican Liberty in an Age of Classicism and Tyranny*: Revised One-volume Edition with an Epilogue (Princeton, NJ: Princeton University Press, 1966), pp. viii–ix.

26. See Fubini, "Renaissance Historian: The Career of Hans Baron," p. 544.

27. See Baron, "Articulation and Unity in the Italian Renaissance and in the Modern West," in *The Quest for Political Unity in World History*. Ed. Stanley Pargellis, (Washington, DC: United States Government Printing Office, 1944), pp. 123–38. (Rpt. As "Politische Einheit und Mannigfaltigkeit in der Italeinischen Renaissance und in der Geschichte der Neuzeit," trans. Marie-Luise Gutbrodt, in *Zu Begriff und Problem der Renaissance*. Ed. August Buck (Darmstadt: Wissenschaftliche Buchgesellschaft, 1969), pp. 180–211.) Hereafter all references to the English-language version of this essay will appear parenthetically in the text.

28. See Baron, "A Struggle for Liberty in the Renaissance. Florence, Venice, and Milan in the Early Quattrocento," *The American Historical Review* 58: 2 (1953), pp. 265–89. Hereafter all references to this essay will appear parenthetically in the text.

29. Fubini, "Renaissance Historian: The Career of Hans Baron," pp. 544–5, has surmised that Baron's political stance in the prewar period resembled that of the so-called *Vernunftrepublikaner* among prominent intellectuals in Germany before the war; they supported the Weimar Republic on the basis of a rational analysis that there were in fact precious few other choices. Hankins, "The 'Baron Thesis' after Forty Years and Some Recent Studies of Leonardo Bruni," pp. 311–12, portrays Baron as a more enthusiastic and committed "supporter of the Weimar Republic, eager to wean Germany away from its chauvinistic and monarchical past."

30. See Baron, *Crisis of the Early Italian Renaissance*, p. 40.

31. See Warren Boutcher, "From Germany to Italy to America: The Migratory Significance of Kristeller's Ficino in the 1930s," in *Weltoffener Humanismus. Philosophie, Philologie, und Geschichte in der deutsch-jüdischen Emigration* (Bielefeld: Transcript Verlag, 2006), pp. 134–5. Boutcher writes compellingly that the "shared pre-war history" of some of these scholars, including Baron and Kristeller, who both spent time in Italy after 1933, may have "sharpened postwar scholarly debates" about the Renaissance.

32. See Baron, "A Sociological Interpretation of the Early Renaissance in Florence," *The South Atlantic Quarterly* 38 (1939), pp. 427–48. (Rpt. in *In Search of Florentine Civic Humanism. Essays on the Transition from Medieval to Modern Thought* 2 vols. [Princeton, NJ: Princeton University Press, 1988], 2: 40–54.) Hereafter all references to the 1939 version of this essay are included parenthetically in the text.

33. See Fubini, "Renaissance Historian: The Career of Hans Baron," p. 568.

34. See Baron, "Burckhardt's 'Civilization of the Renaissance' a Century after its Publication." Hereafter all references to this essay are included parenthetically in the text.

35. See Baron, *The Crisis of the Early Italian Renaissance. Civic Humanism and Republican Liberty in an Age of Classicism and Tyranny* 2 vols. (Princeton, NJ: Princeton University Press, 1955). Hereafter all references to these volumes are included parenthetically in the text.

36. See Baron, *Crisis of the Early Italian Renaissance.* Hereafter all references to this volume are included parenthetically in the text.

37. See Jacob Burckhardt, *Die Kultur der Renaissance in Italien. Ein Versuch*, Orig. 1860. Ed. Walther Rehm, (Hamburg: Nikol Verlagsgesellschaft, 2004), p. 113.

38. See Benjamin Nelson and Charles Trinkaus, "Introduction," in *The Civilization of the Renaissance in Italy* by Jacob Burckhardt, (New York: Harper Torchbooks/The Academy Library, 1958), pp. 3–19, here p. 19. Hereafter all references to this essay are included parenthetically in the text.

39. Hajo Holborn, "Introduction," in *The Civilization of the Renaissance in Italy* by Jacob Burckhardt (New York: The Modern Library, 1954), pp. v–xi, here p. vi. Hereafter all references to this essay are included parenthetically in the text.

Epilogue: When the New is Not New

Sander L. Gilman

The Renaissance is one of the few moments of self-naming in cultural history. "Humanism" (its historical kissing cousin) was a concept coined in 1808 by a German educator, F. J. Niethammer, looking to further connect the amorphous idea of German *Bildung* (education) with the earlier rebirth of classical learning. And certainly no one in the "Dark Ages" ever imagined that they were so. It was only Petrarch in 1330, knowing that he lived in the final of Augustine's six ages, who could designate them as dark: "De sui ipsius et multorum ignorantia."[1] The Renaissance is different: it was a term coined as a brand label for the movement by those who needed to define themselves as belonging to a world quite different to the one in which they had found themselves. It was a moment of self-conscious reshaping; a self-invention of both cultural and individual identity.

The self-invention of any term, however, is no guarantee that it will remain anchored in its original, intended meaning. "Modernity" is a concept that the "moderns" (from the late nineteenth century to the present) coined and use in ways that over the past century has incorporated virtually any ideology. Today retro is modern; the avant-garde was modern; even the aesthetic movement, modern in its own time, can newly be made modern today. Oscar Wilde's comedy *The Importance of Being Ernest* can, according to one contemporary critic, be moved from the preciousness of nineteenth-century, middle-class culture to "a modern world of corporate snobbery."[2] Indeed, it may well be the claims on "authenticity" of those terms such as the "modern" and the "Renaissance" that provide a force for their adaptability. Unlike postfacto epochal labels (such as "Humanism" or the "Dark Ages"), the "Renaissance's" claim that it was coined by thinkers who shaped this new world (such as Petrarch) has made it more powerful. New is not just new but incredibly useful.

But sometimes new really is new. In 1869, Matthew Arnold, in his programmatic essay on "Culture and Anarchy," noted that the two poles of culture he called "Hebraism" (which he did not like) and "Hellenism" (which he did) alternated in

> the effort to see things as they really are, and the effort to win peace by self-conquest, the human spirit proceeds, and each of these two forces has its appointed hours of culmination and seasons of rule. As the great movement of Christianity was a triumph of Hebraism and man's moral impulses, so the great movement which goes by the name of the Renascence.[3]

And here Arnold, before going on to see this moment of the new as the triumph of Hellenism, drops a footnote for the learned reader: "I have ventured to give to the foreign word *Renaissance*, destined to become of more common use amongst us as the movement which it denotes comes, as it will come, increasingly to interest us, an English form." Here is something new: we now know when and in what context the very term Renaissance became "modern," at least in English. "Renaissance" had been used in this form as a label for the architectural style. Indeed, Queen Victoria notes in her quasi-public "diary" for September 14, 1842 visiting a building built in the "Renaissance style."[4] But the notion of the Renaissance as "new" is a Victorian conceit, building on, as Matthew Arnold noted, a French usage. It is foreign and cultured; therefore Hellenic not Hebraic. It is not "merely" a period style in architecture but a way of seeing the world. Ironically, no one in Great Britain before the Victorians in England had adapted the Italian self-label for their or any other age: even Shakespeare does not use the term. It is only through the venue of nineteenth-century French high culture as articulated by Jules Michelet (1798–1874) that the Renaissance becomes modern by becoming French and thus, in Arnold's terms, becoming Hellenic.

Since Matthew Arnold we have entered into a world of Renaissance(s). Some make reference to the distant, unfocused past. We have "Renaissance Faires" throughout the United States and the United Kingdom that evoke Shakespeare's (un-Renaissanced) world. Some evoke the Renaissance as any refiguring of a lost and noble past. We see the reappearance of older styles characterized as a Renaissance as in 1990 when her "self-titled debut album surfaced in 1985, Suzanne Vega sounded fresh and original, heralding a renaissance of the 'sensitive singer-songwriter.' "[5] Lost worlds may not only be five years old; they may be radically repressed and now resurgent. Thus, in an obituary in 1990 it was noted that there was "a renaissance of religion in the Soviet Union under glasnost," heralded by the late Patriarch Pimen, the leader of the 50-million member Russian Orthodox Church.[6] This statement makes sense only if we imagine the Renaissance as a mode of thinking rather than a specific historical moment. Today in Boston and Florida (and I am sure elsewhere) we have corporations that call themselves "Renaissance Properties."[7] I am certain they are not in the business of buying and selling the Sistine Chapel, but they may be in the business of buying and selling various Renaissance Hotels—a brand name for the new and posh.

What has the brand naming of the "Renaissance" done to its aesthetic sensibility? For, whatever we think about the Victorians, they saw the Renaissance, either as art, as architecture, as an epochal term, or as metaphor, in terms of the aesthetic. This quality has clearly been lost in its expansion as metaphor over the past hundred years. Yet contemporary poetry in English has had a "Renaissance" of the Renaissance. It is an epochal term that resonates among poets as few others do (besides the "modern" and its cousin the "postmodern").

Given the power of the idea of a "Harlem Renaissance," as we have seen in this volume, Amiri Baraka, the African-American erstwhile poet laureate of New Jersey (remember that Petrarch was made poet laureate in 1341, not of New Jersey, but Rome), questions its end:

> Did some one say, "The Renaissance
> is over?" Or was that the living
> Dying wind, reality, or the Rags
> of yr future? The living dying wind
> adhesive against wet w/ blood top hats
> souls w/bullet holes. Ex leapers smashed
> against the bankruptcy of bullszit & oppression.[8]

Is the Renaissance something that only the whites can relish, as the American poet laureate (of all the states including New Jersey, but not Rome) Rita Dove implies? In her view it is a quality, not of repressive capitalism, but of the pretensions of white middle-class society with its knowledge of multiple "Renaissances":

> As for the improbable librarian
> with her salt and paprika upsweep,

her British accent and sweater clip
(mom of a kid I knew from school)—
I'd go up to her desk and ask for help
on bareback rodeo or binary codes,
phonics, Gestalt theory,
lead poisoning in the Late Roman Empire,
the play of light in Dutch Renaissance painting;
I would claim to be researching
pre-Columbian pottery or Chinese foot-binding,
but all I wanted to know was:
Tell me what you've read that keeps
that half smile afloat
above the collar of your impeccable blouse.[9]

But is the "real" Renaissance in the racist past and are we post-Renaissance, or do we long for a new Renaissance as the British poet Iain Crichton Smith implies?

We want the Commandments from the gritty deserts
and shadowy ghosts in their post-Renaissance frames,
our underwater programmes. We want your Commandments
suited to a pastoral land in green,
the extinct shepherds with their pilgrim staffs,
their clouds of white sheep and visiting angels
perching on branches with their fathomless eyes.[10]

Or is the Renaissance us (to paraphrase the Renaissance 'possum Pogo: "We have met the Renaissance and it is us"):

Like us, the Renaissance genius puzzled
why rustic deities and lovers
sally into love, arrayed
only in flesh, bruisable flesh,
if the tournament's end is always
willowy mourning:
against the undertow,
your body, siphoned for a while
of sorrow—
will I ever love you more
than in this place
where voices of reproach
can't reach us,
sees it as part of our world.[11]

Or does the Renaissance fill yet another cultural niche in our search for an appropriate discourse to speak of the unspeakable:

> In a battered Volvo, driving through the German Colony
> on the way to Mea Shearim—place of "100 gates"—
> Malka said: *Do you belong to a synagogue?*
>
> "I'm not Jewish, but maybe through my father's father . . ."
> I answered, offering tales of a tattered
> coat of arms, a Renaissance Star of David.
>
> "That won't do any good," she said
> in the kindest way.
> I know. I know a Jew must be born
>
> from the mother, from the bloody
> flesh: the zealots wouldn't
> have bothered to strike me dead—would they?—
> at the hot top of Masada.[12]

Being Jewish is being seen as Jewish, bearing that Renaissance coat of arms with the Star of David, that new logo for Zionism, crafted in the nineteenth-century age of Arnold's Hebrews and Hellenes. This distance will not protect you from foe or friend. The past always comes back to haunt, even the Renaissance past.

In 2005, a local reporter in Bridgeport, Connecticut evoked the Renaissance in the context of a remembered world:

> The annual profusion of cherry blossoms serves as a harbinger of spring, nature's renaissance, life anew.
>
> The flower is special to Anita Schorr, 74, a Westport woman for whom cherry tree blooms signify a second chance at life and a freedom sweeter than the scent of all the delicate pink blossoms on Earth combined.
>
> Schorr is a Holocaust survivor, one of three who last week shared with Central High School students the stories of the horrors and indignities they suffered under Nazi rule.
>
> She spoke to students on Friday, a date which marked the 60th anniversary of her liberation from a Nazi death camp by British soldiers. She was 15. One of her lasting memories from that day were the cherry blossoms just springing to life.
>
> "Until today, cherry blossoms and freedom are synonymous. Whenever I see cherry blossoms I feel free," Schorr said.[13]

If the Holocaust has become a free floating signifier in the twenty-first century, meaning quite whatever one wants it to mean, then the grounding of the term in the real experience and memories of a survivor is an important corrective. "Holocausts" now exist across the world: they exist retrospectively (as in the Armenian Holocaust) or in the contemporary world (the Holocaust in Bosnia).[14] The term is clearly evoked because of its associative power. Indeed, the Holocaust, as recent studies have stressed, has become so ubiquitous as to force the relabeling of the Nazi murder of the Jews as the Shoah.[15] The appropriation of such terms does shape memory. The brand name of the Renaissance adds to this reshaping of memory a sense of the rebirth that is both an inherent part of the history of a concept as well as its extension into the present.

Notes

1. Theodore E., Mommsen, "Petrarch's Conception of the 'Dark Ages'," *Speculum* 17 (1942), pp. 226–42. See also Herbert Weisinger, "The Renaissance Theory of the Reaction against the Middle Ages as a Cause of the Renaissance," *Speculum* 20 (1945), pp. 461–7.
2. "Shots of Modern Wilde," *Canberra Times* (Australia), July 29, 2005, p. 3.
3. Matthew Arnold, *Culture and Anarchy: An Essay in Political and Social Criticism* (Cambridge: Cambridge University Press, 1993), p. 134.
4. Queen Victoria, *Leaves from the Journal of our Life in the Highlands, 1848–61*, Ed. Arthur Helps (London: Smith, Elder & Co., 1868), p. 37.
5. Joe Brown, "Singer-Songwriters Follow Vega's Road," *The Washington Post*, May 4, 1990, p. N28.
6. Michael Collins, "Russian Orthodox Patriarch Dies," *United Press International*, May 3, 1990, Thursday, BC cycle.
7. Jesse M. Harris, "Bank Takes Over S. End Condo," *The Boston Globe*, May 10, 1990, p. C3.
8. Imamu Amiri Baraka, "Y You Ask?" in *Transbluesency: The Selected Poems of Amiri Baraka, 1961–1995* (New York: Marsilio, 1995), p. 238.
9. Rita Dove, *On The Bus With Rosa Parks* (New York: W. W. Norton & Company, 1999), pp. 32–33.
10. Iain Crichton Smith, "Dipping Your Spoon," in *Collected Poems* (London: Carcanet 1995), p. 117.
11. Cyrus Cassells, "The Magician-Made Tree," *Beautiful Signor* (Port Townsend, WA: Copper Canyon Press, 1997)], p. 13.
12. Sandra M. Gilbert, "In a Battered Volvo, Driving through the German Colony," in *Ghost Volcano* (New York: Norton 1995), p. 34.
13. Meg Barone, "Cherry Blooms Hold Special Place for Holocaust Survivor," *Connecticut Post* (Bridgeport, CT), April 19, 2005, p. 1.

14. "Anglicans to commemorate Armenian Holocaust Sunday," *Portland Press Herald* (Maine), April 25, 2005, p. C1; "NGO Pays Tribute to Holocaust Victims, Calls Srebrenica Bosnia's Auschwitz," *Monitoring/BBC International Reports*, January 27, 2005.
15. Peter Novick, *The Holocaust in American Life* (Boston, MA: Houghton Mifflin, 1999).

Bibliography

'Aflaq, Michel. *Fī Sabīl al-Ba'th*. Ed. Michel 'Aflaq. Baghdad: Dār al-Hurrīya lil-Tibā'a, 1959. 37–39.

al-Amīn, 'Abd Allāh Muzaffar. *Jamā'at al-Ahālī: munshu'hā, 'aqīdatuhā, wadawruhā fi'l siyasa al-'Irāqīyya, 1932–1946*. Beirut: al-Mu'assasa al-'Arabīyya li'l dirāsāt wa'l nashr. Amman: Dar al-faris, 2001.

Ahmad, Aijaz. *In Theory: Classes, Nations, Literatures*. London: Verso, 1992.

Akam, Everett H. *Transnational America: Cultural Pluralist Thought in the Twentieth Century*. Lanham, MD: Rowman and Littlefield, 2002.

Alkalay, Yehudah. *Ketavim*. Jerusalem: Mosad ha-Rav Kuk, 1944.

Amin, Samir. *Eurocentrism*. Trans. Russell Moore. New York: Monthly Review Press, 1989.

Anderson, Benedict. *Imagined Communities*. London: Verso, 1983.

Andrews, Walter G. *Poetry's Voice, Society's Song: Ottoman Lyric Poetry*. Seattle, WA: University of Washington Press, 1985.

———. "Literary Art of The Golden Age." In *Süleymân the Second and His Time*. Eds. Halil İnalcık and Cemal Kafadar. Istanbul: The Isis Press, 1993. 353–68.

———. "Contested Mysteries and Mingled Dreams: Speaking for Ottoman Culture Today from Gencebay to Pamuk." In *Cultural Horizons: A Festschrift in Honor of Talat S. Halman*. Ed. Jayne Warner. Syracuse, NY: Syracuse University Press and Istanbul (wga): Yapı Kredi Yayınları, 2001. 518–37.

———. "Stepping Aside: Ottoman Literature in Modern Turkey." *Journal of Turkish Literature* 1 (2004): 9–32.

——— and Mehmet Kalpaklı. *The Age of Beloveds*. Durham, NC: Duke University Press, 2005.

Antonius, George. *The Arab Awakening: The Story of the Arab National Movement*. New York: Capricorn, 1965.

Arnold, Bruce. *Jack Yeats*. New Haven, CT and London: Yale University Press, 1998.

Arnold, Matthew. *Culture and Anarchy: An Essay in Political and Social Criticism*. Cambridge: Cambridge University Press, 1993.

Arooran, N. Nambi. *Tamil Renaissance and Dravidian Nationalism*. Madurai: Koodal Publishers, 1980.

al-Arsūzī, Zakī. *al-Jumhūriyya al-muthlā*. Damascus: Dār al-Yaqza al-ʿArabiyya, 1965.

ʿAzzām, ʿAbd al-Wahhāb. *Rahalāt*. Cairo: Matbaʿat al-Risāla, 1950–1951.

Badr, Abd al-Muhsin Taha. *Tattawur al-riwayah al-arabiyyah al-hadithah fī misr*. Cairo: Dar al-Maʾarif, 1992.

Baram, Amatzia. "Neo-Tribalism in Iraq: Saddām Husayn's Tribal Policies 1991–96." *International Journal of Middle East Studies* 29, 1 (1997): 1–31.

———. "The Ruling Political Elite in Bathi Iraq, 1968–1986: The Changing Features of a Collective Profile." *International Journal of Middle East Studies* 21, 4 (1989): 447–93.

Barash, Nahman. *Ein Mishpat*, Berlin, 1796.

Baraz, Shimon. *Ma'archei Lev*, Königsberg, 1785.

Barkin, Kenneth D. "German Émigré Historians in America: The Fifties, Sixties, and Seventies." In *An Interrupted Past. German-Speaking Refugee Historians in the United States after 1933*. Eds. Hartmut Lehmann and James J. Sheehan. Cambridge: Cambridge University Press, 1991. 149–69.

Barnes, Deborah. " 'I'd Rather Be a Lamppost in Chicago': Richard Wright and the Chicago Renaissance of African American Literature." *Langston Hughes Review* 14, no. 1–2 (1996): 52–61.

Baron, Hans. *Calvins Staatsanschauung und das konfessionelle Zeitalter*. Berlin/Munich: Verlag R. Oldenbourg, 1924.

———. "Einleitung." In Leonardo Bruni Arentino, *Humanistisch-philosophische Schriften*. Ed. Hans Baron. Leipzig: Teubner, 1928. xi–xl.

———. "A Sociological Interpretation of the Early Renaissance in Florence." *The South Atlantic Quarterly* 38 (1939): 427–48. (Rpt. In *In Search of Florentine Civic Humanism. Essays on the Transition from Medieval to Modern Thought*. 2 vols. Princeton, NJ: Princeton University Press, 1988. 2: 40–54).

———. "Articulation and Unity in the Italian Renaissance and in the Modern West." In *The Quest for Political Unity in World History*. Ed. Stanley Pargellis. Washington, DC: United States Government Printing Office, 1944. 123–38. (Rpt. As "Politische Einheit und Mannigfaltigkeit in der Italeinischen Renaissance und in der Geschichte der Neuzeit." Trans. Marie-Luise Gutbrodt. In *Zu Begriff und Problem der Renaissance*. Ed. August Buck. Darmstadt: Wissenschaftliche Buchgesellschaft, 1969. 180–211).

———. "The First History of the Historical Concept of the Renaissance." *The Journal of the History of Ideas* 11, 4 (1950): 493–510.

———. "A Struggle for Liberty in the Renaissance. Florence, Venice, and Milan in the Early Quattrocento." *The American Historical Review* 58, 2 (1953): 265–89.

———. *The Crisis of the Early Italian Renaissance. Civic Humanism and Republican Liberty in an Age of Classicism and Tyranny*. 2 vols. Princeton, NJ: Princeton University Press, 1955.

———. "Burckhardt's 'Civilization of the Renaissance' a Century after its Publication." *Renaissance News* 13, 3 (1960): 207–22.

————. *The Crisis of the Early Italian Renaissance. Civic Humanism and Republican Liberty in an Age of Classicism and Tyranny.* Revised one-volume edition with an Epilogue. Princeton, NJ: Princeton University Press, 1966.

Batatu, Hanna. *The Old Social Classes and the Revolutionary Movements of Iraq.* Princeton, NJ: Princeton University Press, 1978.

Baym, Nina. "Melodramas of Beset Manhood: How Theories of American Fiction Exclude Women Authors." In *The New Feminist Criticism: Essays on Women, Literature, and Theory.* Ed. Elaine Showalter. New York: Pantheon, 1985. 63–80.

Behan, Brendan. *An Irish Sketch Book.* London: Hutchinson, 1962.

————. *The Dubbalin Man.* Dublin: A.A. Farmar, 1997.

Belich, James. *Making Peoples: A History of the New Zealanders: From Polynesian Settlement to the End of the Nineteenth Century.* Auckland: Allen Lane, 1996.

Ben Yehuda, Eliezer. "She'elah Nichbadah." *Hashahar*, 9 (1878): 359–66.

Bengio, Ofra. *Saddam's Word—Political Discourse in Iraq.* New York: Oxford University Press, 1998.

Bergahn, Klaus L. Ed. *The German-Jewish Dialogue Reconsidered.* New York: Peter Lang, 1996.

Berlin, Saul. *Besamim Rosh*, Berlin, 1793.

Bhabha, Homi. *The Location of Culture.* London: Routledge, 1994.

Bhattacharya, Bijoy. *Bengal Renaissance: A Study in the Progress of English Education (1800–1858).* Calcutta: P. Sen & Company, 1963.

Binder, Leonard. *The Ideological Revolutions in the Middle East.* New York: John Wiley, 1964.

Birmingham, George A. *The Lighter Side of Irish Life.* London and Edinburgh: T. N. Foulis, 1912.

————. *Irishmen All.* London and Edinburgh: T. N. Foulis, 1913.

————. [James Hannay] *An Irishman Looks at His World.* London, New York, Toronto: Hodder and Stoughton, 1919.

Blackall, E. A. *The Emergence of German as a Literary Language 1700–1775.* Cambridge: Cambridge University Press, 1959.

Boland, Eavan. *Object Lessons: The Life of the Woman and the Poet in Our Time.* New York and London: W. W. Norton, 1995.

Bombaci, Alessio. *Histoire de la Littérature Turque.* Trans. I. Melikoff. Paris: Librairie C. Klinksieck, 1968.

Bone, Robert. "Richard Wright and the Chicago Renaissance." *Callaloo* 9 (1986): 446–68.

Bontemps, Arna. "Famous WPA Authors." *Negro Digest* 8, 8 (1950): 43–7.

Boucicault, Dion. *Arrah-na-Pogue, or, The Wicklow Wedding. The Dolmen Boucicault.* Ed. David Krause. Leinster: Dolmen, 1965.

————. *Selected Plays by Dion Boucicault.* Gerrards Cross: Colin Smythe, 1987a.

————. *Selected Plays by Dion Boucicault.* Gerrards Cross: Colin Smythe, 1987b.

————. *Selected Plays of Dion Boucicault.* Gerrards Cross: Colin Smythe, 1987c.

Boucicault, Dion. *Selected Plays by Dion Boucicault.* Gerrards Cross: Colin Smythe, 1987d.

———. *Selected Plays of Dion Boucicault.* Gerrards Cross: Colin Smythe, 1987e.

Bourdieu, Pierre. *L'Amore dell'Arte: I Musei d'arte europei e il loro pubblico.* Rimini: Guaraldi, 1972. Orig. *L'amour de l'art: Les musées d'art européens et leur public.* Paris: Editions de Minuit, 1969.

Bourke, Angela. *The Burning of Bridget Cleary.* New York: Penguin Putnam, 1999.

Boutcher, Warren. "From Germany to Italy to America: The Migratory Significance of Kristeller's Ficino in the 1930s." In *Weltoffener Humanismus. Philosophie, Philologie, und Geschichte in der deutsch-jüdischen Emigration.* Bielefeld: Transcript Verlag, 2006: 133–53.

Bratlinger, Patrick. *The Reading Lesson: The Threat of Mass Literacy in Nineteenth Century Britain.* Bloomington, IN: Indiana University Press, 1998.

Breasted, James Henry. *Ancient Times, a History of the Early World: An Introduction to the Study of Ancient History and the Career of Early Man.* Boston, MA: Ginn and Company, 1916.

Bremer, Sidney H. "Willa Cather's Lost Chicago Sisters." In *Women Writers and the City: Essays in Feminist Literary Criticism.* Ed. Susan Merrill Squier. Knoxville, TN: University of Tennessee Press, 1984. 210–29.

Breslau, Mendel. "El Rodfei Zedek Vedorshei Shelom Aheinu Bnei Yisra'el." *Hame'asef* 6 (1790): 301–14.

Brewster, Scott. *Ireland in Proximity: History, Gender, Space.* London: Routledge, 1999.

Brooks, Peter. *The Melodramatic Imagination: Balzac, Henry James, Melodrama and the Mode of Excess.* New Haven, CT and London: Yale University Press, 1995.

Brown, Alison. "Hans Baron's Renaissance." *The Historical Journal* 33, 2 (1991): 441–8.

Brown, Ruth. *Cultural Questions: New Zealand Identity in a Transnational Age.* London: Kakapo Books, 1997.

Burckhardt, Jacob. *Die Kultur der Renaissance in Italien. Ein Versuch.* Orig. 1860. Ed. Walther Rehm. Hamburg: Nikol Verlagsgesellschaft, 2004.

———. *The Civilization of the Renaissance in Italy.* Trans. S. G. C. Middlemore. London: Penguin Books, 1990.

———. *Weltgeschichtliche Betrachtungen.* Ed. Rudolf Stadelmann Basel: Neske, n.d.

Burke, Peter. "Concepts of the 'Golden Age' in the Renaissance." In *Süleyman the Magnificent and his Age.* Eds. Metin Kunt and Christine Woodhead. Harlow, Essex: Longman, 1995. 154–63.

———. *The European Renaissance: Centers and Peripheries.* Oxford: Blackwell Publishers, 1998.

Butterworth, Graham. *Sir Apirana Ngata.* Wellington: A. H. and A. W. Reed, 1968.

Cahill, Thomas. *How the Irish Saved Civilization: The Untold Story of Ireland's Heroic Role from the Fall of Rome to the Rise of Medieval Europe*. New York and London: Nan A. Talese, 1995.

Cappetti, Carla. " 'Sociology of an Existence' Richard Wright and the Chicago School." *MELUS* 12, 2 (1985): 25–43.

———. *Writing Chicago: Modernism, Ethnography, and the Novel*. New York: Columbia University Press, 1993.

Carey, John. *The Intellectuals and the Masses: Pride and Prejudice among the Literary Intelligentsia. 1880–1939*. London: Faber and Faber, 1992.

Caro, David. *Berit Emet*. Dessau, 1820.

Castle, Gregory. *Modernism and the Celtic Revival*. Cambridge: Cambridge University Press, 2001.

Chakrabarty, Dipesh. *Provincializing Europe*. Princeton, NJ: Princeton University Press, 2000.

Chatterjee, Partha. *The Nation and Its Fragments: Colonial and Postcolonial Histories*. Princeton, NJ: Princeton University Press, 1993.

Chattopadhyaya, D. P. "Raja Rammohun Roy: A New Appraisal." In *Nineteenth Century Thought in Bengal*. Eds. Kalyan Sengupta and Tirthanath Bandyopadhyay. Jadavpur: Allied Publishers Limited, 1998. 7–23.

Chen Duxiu. "Wenxue geming lun" (On Literary Revolution). In *Zhongguo xin-wenxue daxi* (Compendium of Modern Chinese Literature). Ed. Zhao Jiabi. Vol.1. Shanghai: Liangyou tushugongsi, 1935. 44–7.

Chen Pingyuan. *Zhongguo xiandai xueshu de jianli* (The Establishment of Modern Chinese Scholarship). Beijing: Beijing University Press, 1998.

Chen Xiaomei. *Occidentalism: A Theory of Counter-Discourse in Post-Mao China*. Oxford: Oxford University Press, 1994.

Chernoff, Maxine, Cyrus Colter, Stuart Dybek, Reginald Gibbons, and Fred Shafer. "The Writer in Chicago: A Roundtable." *Triquarterly* 60 (Spring/Summer 1984): 325–47.

Chow, Tse-Tsung. *The May Fourth Movement*. Cambridge, MA: Harvard University Press, 1964.

Clarke, Austin. *Twice Round the Black Church: Early Memories of Ireland and England*. London: Routledge and Kegan Paul, 1962.

Cleveland, William L. *The Making of an Arab Nationalist: Ottomanism and Arabism in the Life and Thought of Sati' al-Husri*. Princeton, NJ: Princeton University Press, 1971.

Cohen, Margaret. "Travelling Genres." *New Literary History* 34 (2003): 481–99.

Connell, William J. and Andrea Zorzi, Eds. *Florentine Tuscany: Structures and Practices of Power*. New York: Cambridge University Press, 2000.

Connolly, James. "To The Irish People." *Irish Socialist Republic*. 1896. 97–100.

Corkery, Daniel. *The Fortunes of the Irish Language*. Cork: The Mercier Press, 1968.

Cowley, Joy. "Rev. of *the bone people*," *New Zealand Listener*, May 12, 1984. 60.

Daly, Nicholas. *Modernism, Romance and the Fin de Siècle: Popular Fiction and British Culture. 1880–1914*. New York: Cambridge University Press, 1999.

Damrosch, David. *What is World Literature?* Princeton, NJ: Princeton University Press, 2003.

Darling, Linda T. "The Renaissance and the Middle East." In *A Companion to the Worlds of the Renaissance*. Ed. Guido Ruggiero. Oxford: Blackwell, 2002. 55–69.

Darnton, Robert. *The Forbidden Best-Sellers of Pre-revolutionary France*. New York: W. W. Norton, 1995.

Darraj, Faysal. "Al-Riwayah al-arabiyyah: al-wiladah al-mu'awwaqah fi al-tarikh al-muqayyad." *Al-Karmal* 74–75 (Winter/Spring 2003): 99–131.

Dawisha, Adeed. *Arab Nationalism in the Twentieth Century: From Triumph to Despair*. Princeton, NJ: Princeton University Press, 2003.

Datta, Bhabatosh. *Resurgent Bengal: Rammohun, Bankimchandra, Rabindranath*. Calcutta: Minerva, 2000.

Davis, Lennard. *Factual Fictions: The Origins of the English Novel*. Philadelphia, PA: University of Pennsylvania Press, 1997.

Dawley, Alan. *Changing the World: American Progressives in War and Revolution*. Princeton, NJ: Princeton, 2003.

Dawn, Ernest C. "The Formation of Pan-Arab Ideology in the Inter-war Years." *International Journal of Middle Eastern Studies* 20, 1 (1988): 67–91.

Deane, Seamus. "Heroic Styles: The Tradition of an Idea." *Ireland's Field Day*. London: Hutchinson, 1985. 45–60.

———. *Nationalism, Colonialism, and Literature*. Minneapolis, MN: University of Minnesota Press, 1990.

———. *Strange Country: Modernity and Nationhood in Irish Writing since 1790*. New York: Oxford, 1997.

Deleuze, Gilles and Félix Guattari. *A Thousand Plateaus: Capitalism and Schizophrenia*. Trans. Brian Massumi. Minneapolis, MN: University of Minnesota Press, 1987.

Devlin, John F. *The Ba'th Party: A History from Its Origins to 1966*. Stanford, CA: Hoover, 1966.

———. "The Baath Party: Rise and Metamorphosis." *The American Historical Review* 96, 5 (1991): 1396–407.

al-Dīn al-Bītār, Salah. "The Major Deviation of the Ba'th Is Having Renounced Democracy." Interview with Marie-Christine Aulas, Eric Hooglund, Jim Paul. *MERIP Reports* 110 (1982): 21–3.

Dodge, Toby. *Inventing Iraq: The Failure of Nation Building and a History Denied*. New York: Columbia University Press, 2003.

Dolezelova-Velingerova, Milena. "The Origins of Modern Chinese Literature." In *Modern Chinese Literature in the May Fourth Era*. Ed. Merle Goldman. Cambridge: Harvard University Press, 1977. 17–35.

Duffey, Bernard. *The Chicago Renaissance in American Letters*. East Lansing, MI: Michigan State College Press, 1954.

Duggan, C. G. *The Stage Irishman: A History of the Irish Play and Stage Characters from the Earliest Times*. New York and London: Benjamin Blom, 1937.

Dunsany, Lord Edward. *My Ireland.* New York and London: Funk and Wagnalls, 1937.

Eagleton, Terry. *The Truth About the Irish.* Dublin: New Island Books, 1999.

Eber, Irene. "Thoughts on Renaissance in Modern China: Problems of Definition." In *Studia Asiatica: Essays in Asian Studies in Felicitation of the Seventy-fifth Anniversary of Professor Chen Shou-yi.* Ed. Laurence G. Thompson. San Francisco, CA: Chinese Materials Center, 1975. 188–220.

Ehernpreis, Mordechai. "Le'an?" *Hashiloah* 1 (1897): 489–503.

———. "Hashkafah Sifrutit." *Hashiloah* 11(1903): 186–92.

El Beheiry, Kawsar. *L'influence de la littérature francaise sur le roman arabe.* Sherbrooke, QC: Naaman, 1980.

Ellmann, Richard. *James Joyce.* New York: Oxford University Press, 1982.

Eppel, Michael. *The Palestine Conflict in the History of Modern Iraq: The Dynamics of Involvement, 1928–1948.* London: Frank Cass, 1994.

———. "The Elite, the Effendiyya, and the Growth of Nationalism and Pan-Arabism in Hashemite Iraq, 1921–1958." *International Journal of Middle Eastern Studies* 30, 2 (1998): 227–50.

———. "The Fadhil Al-Jamali Government in Iraq, 1953–54." *Journal of Contemporary History* 34, 3 (1999): 417–42.

Epstein, Catherine. *A Past Renewed. A Catalog of German-Speaking Refugee Historians in the United States after 1933.* Cambridge: Cambridge University Press, 1993.

Epstein, Joseph. "Windy City Letters." *New Criterion* 2, 5 (1984): 37–46.

Erasmus, Desiderius. *Opus Epistolarum Des. Erasmi Roterdami.* Eds. P. S. Allen and H. M. Allen. Oxford: Clarendon, 1992.

Erünsal, Ismail E. *The Life and Works of Tâcî-zâde Ca'fer Çelebi with a Critical Edition of his Dîvân.* Istanbul: Edebiyat Fakültesi Basımevi, 1983.

Euchel, Isaac. "Igrot Yitzhak Eichel." *Hame'asef* 2 (1785): 116–21, 137–42.

Fahmy, Khaled. *All the Pasha's Men: Mehmed Ali, His Army and the Making of Modern Egypt.* Cambridge: Cambridge University Press, 1997.

Fallis, Robert. *The Irish Renaissance.* Syracuse, NY: Syracuse University Press, 1977.

Farouk-Sluglett, Marion and Peter Sluglett. *Iraq since 1958: From Revolution to Dictatorship.* 2nd edn. London: I. B. Tauris, 2001.

Febvre, Lucien. *The Problem of Unbelief in the Sixteenth Century. The Religion of Rabelais.* Orig. 1942. Trans. Beatrice Gottlieb. Cambridge: Harvard University Press, 1982.

Fee, Margerie. "Why C.K. Stead Didn't Like *the bone people*: Who Can Write As Other?" *Australian and New Zealand Studies in Canada* 1 (1989): 11–32.

Feiner, Shmuel. "Yitzhak Euchel Ha'yazam' Shel Tenu'at Hahaskalah Begermanyah." *Zion* 52, 4 (1987): 427–69.

———. *Haskalah Beyahasah Lahistoriah—Hakarat He'avar Vetifkudo Bitnu'at Hahaskalah Hayehudit (1781–1881).* A Doctoral Dissertation. Jerusalem, 1990.

Feiner, Shmuel. *Haskalah Vehistoriah*. Jerusalem, 1995. Trans. English *The Jewish Enlightenment*. Philadelphia, PA: University of Pennsylvania Press, 2002.

Ferguson, Charles. "Diglossia." *Word* 15 (1959): 325–40.

Ferguson, Margaret W., Maureen Quilligan, and Nancy Vickers, Eds. *Rewriting the Renaissance. The Discourses of Sexual Difference in Early Modern Europe*. Chicago, IL: University of Chicago Press, 1986.

Ferguson, Wallace K. *The Renaissance in Historical Thought: Five Centuries of Interpretation*. Boston, MA: Houghton Mifflin Company, 1948.

———. "Toward the Modern State." In *The Renaissance. A Symposium* (1953). 1–17. *The Renaissance. A Symposium. February 8–10, 1952*, produced by the Metropolitan Museum of Art in 1953.

———. Ed. *The Renaissance. Six Essays*. New York: Harper Torchbooks, 1962.

———. "Introduction." Alfred von Martin. *Sociology of the Renaissance*. Orig. 1932. New York: Harper Torchbooks, 1963. v–xiv.

Fleischer, Cornell H. *A Mediterranean Apocalypse: Imperialism and Prophecy*, 1453–1550. Berkeley, CA: University of California Press, forthcoming.

Fleming, Donald and Bernard Bailyn. Eds. *The Intellectual Migration. Europe and America, 1933–1960*. Cambridge, MA: Harvard University Press, 1969.

Folgarait, Leonard. *Mural Painting and Social Revolution in Mexico: Art of the New Order*. New York: Cambridge, 1998.

Foucault, Michel. *Discipline and Punish: The Birth of the Prison*. Trans. Alan Sheridan. New York: Random House Vintage Books, 1979.

———. "The Subject and Power." In *Michel Foucault: Beyond Structuralism and Hermeneutics*. Eds. Hubert L. Dreyfus and Paul Rabinow. Chicago, IL: University of Chicago Press, 1982. 208–26.

———. "What Is Enlightenment?" In *The Foucault Reader*, Ed. Paul Rabinow. New York: Pantheon, 1984. 32–51.

Frazier, Adrian. *Behind the Scenes: Yeats, Horniman, and the Struggle for the Abbey Theatre*. Berkeley, CA: University of California Press, 1990.

Friedrichsfeld, David. "Hadlah Mimlitzat Yehudit Hatif'eret." *Hame'asef* 2 (1784–1785).

Fubini, Riccardo. "Renaissance Historian: The Career of Hans Baron." *Journal of Modern History* 64 (1992): 541–74.

Gabbay, Rony. *Communism and Agrarian Reform in Iraq*. London: Croom Helm, 1978.

Gay, Peter. "Burckhardt's *Renaissance*: Between Responsibility and Power." In *The Responsibility of Power. Historical Essays in Honor of Hajo Holborn*. Eds. Leonard Krieger and Fritz Stern. Garden City, NY: Doubleday, 1967. 183–98.

Gennari, John. " 'A Weapon of Integration': Frank Marshall Davis and the Politics of Jazz." *Langston Hughes Review* 14, 1–2 (1996): 16–33.

Gershoni, Israel. "Rethinking the Formation of Arab Nationalism in the Middle East, 1920–1945: Old and New Narratives." In *Rethinking Nationalisms in Middle East*, Eds. Israel Gershoni and James Jankowski. New York: Columbia University Press, 1997. 3–25.

Ghose, Aurobindo. *The Renaissance in India*. Calcutta: Arya, 1920.

Gibb, E. J. W. *A History of Ottoman Poetry*. Vols. 1–6. London: Luzac and Company, 1900–1906.

Gibb, H. A. R. *Studies on the Civilization of Islam*. Eds. Stanford J. Shaw and William R. Polk. Princeton, NJ: Princeton University Press, 1982.

Gilbert, Felix. *A European Past. Memoirs 1905–1945*. New York and London: W. W. Norton, 1988.

———. *History: Politics or Culture? Reflections on Ranke and Burckhardt*. Princeton, NJ: Princeton University Press, 1990.

Goldberg, Jonathan. "Introduction." *Queering the Renaissance*. Durham, NC: Duke University Press, 1994. 1–14.

Gordon, Irene. "Introduction." In *The Civilization of the Renaissance in Italy*. By Jacob Burckhardt. New York: The New American Library and Mentor Books, 1960. v–xxi.

Gossman, Lionel. "Jacob Burckhardt: Cold War Liberal?" *The Journal of Modern History* 74 (2002): 538–72.

———. "Burckhardt in der anglo-amerikanischen Geisteswelt." In *Begegnungen mit Jacob Burckhardt/Encounters with Jacob Burkchardt*. Eds. Andreas Cesana and Lionel Gossman. Basel: Schwabe; Munich: C.H. Beck, 2004. 113–48.

Gottlober, Abraham Baer. "Et La'akor Natu'a." *Haboker Or* 1 (1, 1786), 4–17; (2, 1786), 77–86.

Gramsci, Antonio. *Gli Intellettuali e l'Organizzazione della Cultura*. Turin: Einaudi, 1955.

———. *The Gramsci Reader: Selected Writings*, 1916–1935. New York: New York University Press, 2000.

Gran, Peter. *Islamic Roots of Capitalism: Egypt, 1760–1840*. Cairo: The American University in Cairo Press, 1999.

Greenblatt, Stephen. *Renaissance Self Fashioning. From More to Shakespeare*. Chicago, IL: University of Chicago Press, 1980.

Gregory, Lady Augusta. "Our Irish Theatre." *Modern Irish Drama*. Ed. John P. Harrington. New York and London: W. W. Norton, 1991. 377–86.

Gunn, Edward. *Rewriting Chinese: Style and Innovation in Twentieth-Century Chinese Prose*. Stanford, CA: Stanford University Press, 1991.

Ha'am, Ahad. The Complete Writings of Ahad Ha'am. Tel Aviv: Devir, 1956.

Hacohen, Shalom. *Ktav Yosher*. Vienna, 1820.

Hafez, Sabry. *The Genesis of Arabic Narrative Discourse*. London: Saqi Books, 1993.

Haim, Sylvia. *Arab Nationalism: An Anthology*. Berkeley, CA: University of California Press, 1976.

Hale, Charles. "Frank Tannenbaum and the Mexican Revolution." *The Hispanic American Historical Review* 75,2 (May 1995): 215–46.

Halkin, Shimon. "Tekufat Hatehiyah." *Derachim Vetzidei Derachim Basifrut* 1 (1969): 49–52.

Hankins, James. "The 'Baron Thesis' after Forty Years and Some Recent Studies of Leonardo Bruni." *The Journal of the History of Ideas* 56, 2 (1995): 309–38.

Hankins, James. "Introduction." In *Renaissance Civic Humanism: Reappraisals and Reflections.* Ed. James Hankins. New York: Cambridge University Press, 2000a. 1–13.

———. Ed. *Renaissance Civic Humanism: Reappraisals and Reflections.* New York: Cambridge University Press, 2000b.

Hanna, Nelly. *In Praise of Books: A Cultural History of Cairo's Middle Class, 16th and 18th Century.* Syracuse, NY: Syracuse University Press, 2003.

Hanson, Alan. "The Making of the Maori: Cultural Invention and Its Logic." *American Anthropologist* 91 (1989): 890–902.

Hardtwig, Wolfgang. "Jakob Burckhardt und Max Weber: Zur Genese und Pathologie der modernen Welt." In *Umgang mit Jacob Burckhardt. Zwölf Studien.* Ed. Hans R. Guggisberg. Basel: Schwabe; Munich: Verlag C. H. Beck, 1994. 159–90.

Harris, Aroha. *Hikoi: Forty Years of Maori Protest.* Wellington: Huia, 2004.

Hay, Denys. "Burckhardt's 'Renaissance': 1860–1960." *History Today* 10, 1 (1960): 14–23.

———. Ed. *The Renaissance Debate.* New York: Holt, Rinehart, and Winston, 1965.

Haywood, A. *Modern Arabic Literature 1800–1970.* London: Lund Humphries, 1971.

Heaney, Seamus. *Station Island.* New York: Farrar, Strauss, Giroux, 1985.

Heehs, Peter. *Sri Aurobindo: A Brief Biography.* Delhi: Oxford University Press, 1989.

Heine, Heinrich. *Religion and Philosophy in Germany.* Boston, MA: Beacon, 1959.

Heke, Hone and A. T. Ngata. *Souvenir of Maori Congress, July, 1908: Scenes from the Past with Maori Versions of Popular English Songs.* Wellington: Whitcombe and Tombs, 1908.

Helm, Mackinley. *Mexican Painters: Rivera, Orozco, Siqueiros and Other Artists of the Social Realist School.* New York: Dover, 1989.

Herder, Joh. Gottfried. *Vom Geist der Ebräischen Poesie* 2. Gotha: Cotta, 1890.

Hertzberg, Arthur. *The Zionist Idea.* New York: Doubleday, 1984.

Hess, Moshe. *Roma Virushalayim.* Warsaw, 1899.

H. K. (HayimKeslin) "Toldot Hazman." *Hame'asef* 1 (1784): 111.

Hinnebusch, Raymond A. *Authoritarian Power and State Formation in Ba'thist Syria: Army, Party and Peasant.* Boulder, CO: Westview, 1990.

Hodgson, Marshall G. S. *The Venture of Islam: Conscience and History in a World Civilization.* 3 vols. Vol. 3: *The Gunpowder Empires and Modern Times.* Chicago, IL: University of Chicago Press, 1974.

Hogan, Robert. *Dion Boucicault.* New York: Twayne, 1969.

Holborn, Hajo. "Introduction." In *The Civilization of the Renaissance in Italy.* By Jacob Burckhardt. New York: The Modern Library, 1954. v–xi.

Holbrook, Victoria. *The Unreadable Shores of Love.* Austin, TX: University of Texas Press, 1994.

Hourani, Albert. *Arabic Thought in the Liberal Age, 1798–1939*. New York: Cambridge University Press, 1962.

———. *A History of the Arab Peoples*. London: Faber and Faber, 1991.

Howells, William Dean. "Certain of the Chicago School of Fiction." *North American Review* 176 (1903): 734–46.

Hsia, C. T. *A History of Modern Chinese Fiction, 1917–1957*. New Haven, CT: Yale University Press, 1961.

Huggins, Nathan Irvin. *Harlem Renaissance*. London: Oxford University Press, 1973.

Hughes, Winifred. *The Maniac in the Cellar: Sensation Novels of the 1860s*. Princeton, NJ: Princeton University Press, 1999.

Hull, Gloria. *Color, Sex, and Poetry: Three Women Writers of The Harlem Renaissance*. Bloomington, IN: Indiana University Press, 1987.

al-Husayn, Faysal ibn (King Faysal I). *Faysal ibn al-Husayn fī khuṭubihi wa aqwāli*. Baghdad: Mudīriyat al-di'ayat al-'āmma, 1946.

Hu Shi. *The Chinese Renaissance*. Chicago, IL: The University of Chicago Press, 1933.

———. "Jianshe de wenxue geming lun" (Toward a Constructive Theory of Literary Revolution). In *Zhongguo xinwenxue daxi* (Compendium of Modern Chinese Literature). Ed. Zhao Jiabi. Vol.1. Shanghai: Liangyou tushu gongsi, 1935. 127–40.

———. *Hu Shi liuxue riji* (Hu Shi's Diary While Studying Abroad). Taipei: Commercial Press, 1959.

Hutchinson, George. *The Harlem Renaissance in Black and White*. Cambridge, MA: Harvard University Press, 1995.

Hyde, Douglas. "The Necessity for De-Anglicising Ireland." *The Revival of Irish Literature*. London: T. Fisher Unwin, 1894. 115–61.

Ihimaera, Witi. *Pounamu Pounamu*. Auckland: Heinemann, 1972.

———. *The Matriarch*. Auckland: Picador, 1988.

———. Interview with Mark Williams. *In the Same Room: Interviews with New Zealand Writers*. Eds. Elizabeth Alley and Mark Williams. Auckland: Auckland University Press, 1992.

Imagining Home: Class, Culture, and Nationalism in the African Diaspora. Eds. Sidney Lemelle and Robin Kelley. New York: Verso, 1994.

İnalcık, Halil and Cemal Kafadar, Eds. *Süleymân the Second and His Time*. Istanbul: The Isis Press, 1993.

Isma'īl, Fā'iz. *Bidāyāt al-Hizb al-Ba'th al-'Arabī fī'l 'Irāq: 1944–1950, 1950–1953*. Damascus: Markaz al-Sha'lān/F. Isma'īl, 1997.

Jaber, Kamel Abu. *The Arab Ba'th Party, History, Ideology and Organization*. Syracuse, NY: Syracuse University Press, 1966.

Jamīl, Husayn. *Al-Hayāt al-niyābīyya fī'l 'Irāq, 1925–1946: mawāqif jamā'at al-Ahālī minhā*. Baghdad: Maktabat al-Muthannā, 1983.

Joyce, James. *A Portrait of the Artist as a Young Man*. Ed. R. B. Kershner. Boston, MA and New York: Bedford Books, 1993.

Jung, Thomas. *Geschichte der Modernen Kulturtheorie*. Darmstadt: Wissenschaftliche Buchgesellschaft, 1999.

Kafadar, Cemal. "The Myth of the Golden Age: Ottoman Historical Consciousness in the Post-Süleymânic Era." In *Süleymân the Second and His Time*. Eds. Halil İnalcık and Cemal Kafadar.Istanbul: The Isis Press, 1993. 37–48.

Kalischer, Zvi. *Derishat Zion*. Torun, 1866.

Katz, Barry M. "The Criticism of Arms: The Frankfurt School Goes to War." *Journal of Modern History* 59 (1987): 439–78.

———. "German Historians in the Office of Strategic Services." In *An Interrupted Past. German-Speaking Refugee Historians in the United States after 1933*. Eds. Hartmut Lehman and James J. Sheehan. Cambridge: Cambridge University Press, 1991. 136–9.

Keenan, Danny. "Aversion to Print? Maori Resistance to the Written Word." *A Book in the Hand: Essays on the History of the Book in New Zealand*. Eds. Penny Griffith, Peter Hughes, and Alan Loney. Auckland: Auckland University Press, 2000. 17–28.

Kermode, Frank. "Canon and Period." In *History and Value: The Clarendon Lectures and the Northcliffe Lectures*. Oxford: Clarendon, 1988. 108–27.

Kerrigan, William and Gordon Braden. *The Idea of the Renaissance*. Baltimore, MD and London: The Johns Hopkins University Press, 1989.

Khalidi, Rashid. "Arab Nationalism: Historical Problems in the Literature." *The American Historical Review* 96, 5 (1991): 1363–73.

al-Khalil, Samir (Kanan Makiya). *Republic of Fear*. New York: Pantheon Books, 1990.

Khayrī, Suʿād. *Fahd wa-al-nahj al-Markisi al-Linini fī qadaya al-thawra*. Beirut, Dar al-Farabi, 1974.

Khurshid, Faruq. *Fi al-riwayah al- ʿarabiyyah fī ʿasr al-tajmīʿ*. Cairo: Dar al-qalam, 1960.

Kiberd, Declan. *Inventing Ireland: The Literature of the Modern Nation*. Cambridge, MA: Harvard University Press, 1996.

Kilito, Abdelfattah, *L'Auteur et ses doubles*. Paris: Seuil, 1985.

King, Michael. *Te Puea: A Life*. Auckland: Hodder and Stoughton, 1977.

King, Richard. "The Modern Myth of 'Hinduism.' " In *Orientalism and Religion: Postcolonial Theory, India and " The Mystic East."* London: Routledge, 1999. 96–117.

Klausner, Joseph. *Historiah Shel Hasifrut Ha'ivrit Hahadashah* [History of Modern Hebrew Literature] Vol. 5. Jerusalem: Ahiasaf, 1955.

Knight, Alan. "Racism, Revolution, and *Indigenismo*: Mexico, 1910–1940." In *The Idea of Race in Latin America, 1870–1940*. Ed. Richard Graham. Austin, TX: University of Texas Press, 1990. 71–117.

Kopf, David. *British Orientalism and the Bengal Renaissance: the Dynamics of Indian Modernization 1773–1885*. Berkeley, CA: University of California Press, 1969.

Krause, David. *The Profane Book of Irish Comedy*. Ithaca, NY and London: Cornell University Press, 1982.

———. *The Regeneration of Ireland: Renaissance and Revolution*. Bethesda, Dublin, and Oxford: Academia Press, 2001.

Kristeller, Paul Oskar. "In Memoriam: Wallace K. Ferguson, A Tribute." *Renaissance Quarterly* 37, 4 (1984): 675–6.

Kruse, Völker. *Analysen der deutschen historischen Soziologie*.Münster: Lit, 1998.

Kunt, Metin and Christine Woodhead, Eds. *Süleyman the Magnificent and his Age*. Harlow, Essex: Longman, 1995.

Landauer, Carl. "Erwin Panofsky and the Renascence of the Renaissance." *Renaissance Quarterly* 47, 2 (1994): 255–81.

Lapidus, Ira M. *A History of Islamic Societies*. Cambridge: Cambridge University Press, 1988.

Lawson, Henry. "The Writer's Dream." In *Henry Lawson: Collected Verse, Volume One 1885–1900*. Ed. Colin Roderick. Sydney: Angus and Robertson, 1967. 343–45.

Le Goff, Jacques. *Medieval Civilization*. Trans. Julia Barrow. Oxford: Basil Blackwell, 1988.

Lehmann, Hartmut and James J. Sheehan, Eds. *An Interrupted Past. German-Speaking Refugee Historians in the United States after 1933*. Cambridge: Cambridge University Press, 1991.

Lester, Cheryl. "A Response to Lawrence Rodgers." *Langston Hughes Review* 14, 1–2 (1996): 13–15.

Lewis, Andrew W. and John A. Tedeschi. "A Bibliography of the Writings of Hans Baron." In Anthony Mohlo and John A. Tedeschi, Eds. *Renaissance Studies in Honor of Hans Baron*. Florence: G. C. Sansoni, 1971. lxxiii–lxxxvii.

Lewis, Archibald R., Ed. *Aspects of the Renaissance. A Symposium*. Austin, TX and London: University of Texas Press, 1967.

Lewis, David Levering. *When Harlem Was in Vogue*. New York: Penguin, 1997.

Liang, Qichao. "On the Recent Scholarship." *Xinmin cong-bao* (new citizen journal) (1904): 53–8.

Lionnet, Françoise. " 'Logiques métisses': Cultural Appropriation and Postcolonial Representations." In *Postcolonial Subjects: Francophone Women Writers*. Ed. Mary Jean Agreen. Minneapolis, MN: University of Minnesota Press, 1996. 321–43.

"The Literary West." Editorial. *Dial* 15 (1893): 173–5.

Liu, Lydia. *Translingual Practice: Literature, National Culture, and Translated Modernity in China, 1900–37*. Stanford, CA: Stanford University Press, 1995.

Livingstone, John W. "Western Science and Education Reform in the Thought of Shakyh Rifa'a al-Tahtawi." *International Journal of Middle Eastern Studies* 28, 4 (1996): 543–64.

Locke, Alain. Ed. *The New Negro*. New York: Albert and Charles Boni, 1925.

———. Ed. *The New Negro*. New York: Atheneum, 1992.

Lopez, Robert S. "Hard Times and the Investment in Culture." In *The Renaissance. A Symposium. February 8–10, 1952*, produced by the Metropolitan Museum of Art in 1953. 19–33.

Lukitz, Liora. *Iraq: The Search for National Identity.* London: Frank Cass, 1994.

Lydon, James. *The Making of Ireland: From Ancient Times to the Present.* New York: Routledge, 1998.

Mack, Rosamund E. *Bazaar to Piazza: Islamic Trade and Italian Art, 1300–1600.* Berkeley, CA: University of California Press, 2002.

McKenzie, D. F. *Oral Culture, Literacy and Print in Early New Zealand: The Treaty of Waitangi.* Wellington: Victoria University Press with the Alexander Turnbull Library Endowment Trust, 1985.

McRae, Jane. "Maori Literature: A Survey." In *The Oxford History of New Zealand Literature in English*, 2nd edn. Ed. Terry Sturm. Auckland: Oxford University Press, 1998. 1–30.

Makdisi, Saree. "Postcolonial Literature in a Neocolonial World: Modern Arabic Culture and the End of Modernity." *Boundary* 22, 1 (1995): 85–115.

Makdisi, Ussama. *The Culture of Sectarianism: Community, History, and Violence in Nineteenth-Century Ottoman Lebanon.* Berkeley, CA: University of California Press, 2000.

Mani, Lata. *Contentious Traditions: The Debate on Sati in Colonial India.* Berkeley, CA: University of California Press, 1998.

Marcus, Leah S. "Renaissance/Early Modern Studies." In *Redrawing the Boundaries: The Transformation of English and American Literary Studies.* Eds. Stephen Greenblatt and Giles Gunn. New York: Modern Language Association, 1992. 41–63.

Marlatt, Daphne. *Taken.* Concord, ON: Anansi, 1996.

Marr, Phebe. "The Development of Nationalist Ideology in Iraq, 1921–1941." *The Muslim World* 75, 2 (1985): 85–101.

Martin, John. "Inventing Sincerity, Refashioning Prudence: The Discovery of the Individual in Renaissance Europe." *The American Historical Review* 102, 5 (1997): 1309–42.

Mason, Theodore O., Jr. " 'Mapping' Richard Wright: A Response To Deborah Barnes' 'I'd Rather Be a Lamppost in Chicago: Richard Wright and the Chicago Renaissance of African American Literature." *Langston Hughes Review* 14, 1–2 (1996): 62–4.

Matthiessen, F. O. *American Renaissance: Art and Expression in the Age of Emerson and Whitman.* London: Oxford University Press, 1968.

Mencken, H. L. "Civilized Chicago." *Chicago Sunday Tribune*, October 28, 1917, sec. 8: 5.

Mendelsohn, Moses. Ed. *Sefer Shmot, Netivot Hashalom.* Berlin, 1783.

———. *Jerusalem.* Trans. Allan Arkush. Hanover and London: University Press of New England, 1983.

Migliorini, Bruno. *The Italian Language.* Boston, MA: Faber and Faber, 1984.

Mishkin, Tracy. *The Harlem and Irish Renaissances.* Gainesville, FL: University Press of Florida, 1998.

Mitchell, Timothy. *Colonising Egypt.* Berkeley, CA: University of California Press, 1991.

———. *Rule of Experts, Egypt, Techno-Politics, Modernity.* Berkeley, CA: University of California Press, 1995.

Modern Chinese Literary Thought: Writings on Literature, 1893–1945. Ed. Kirk Denton. Stanford, CA: Stanford University Press, 1996.

Mohlo, Anthony. "Burckhardtian Legacies." *Medievalia et Humanistica* 17 (1991): 133–9.

Mommsen, Theodore E. "Petrarch's Conception of the 'Dark Ages'." *Speculum* 17 (1942): 226–42.

Mommsen, Wolfgang J. "German Historiography during the Weimar Republic and the Émigré Historians." In *An Interrupted Past. German-Speaking Refugee Historians in the United States after 1933.* Eds. Hartmut Lehmann and James J. Sheehan. Cambridge: Cambridge University Press, 1991. 32–66.

Moosa, Matti. *The Origins of Modern Arabic Fiction.* Boulder, CO: Lynne Rienner, 1997.

Morpurgo, Eliyahu. "Divrei Hochmah Umusar." *Hame'asef* 3 (1786): 131.

Mosse, George L. *German Jews Beyond Judaism.* Bloomington, IN: Indiana University Press, 1985.

Mubārak, Zakī. *Laylā al-marīda fī'l 'Irāq: ta'rīikh yufassil waqā 'i Laylā bayna al-Qāhira wa-Baghdād min sanat 1926 ila sanat 1938.* Beirut: al-Maktaba al-'asrīya, 1976.

———. *Malamih al-mujtamā ' al-'Irāqī: ktiāb yusawwiru al-'Irāq fi madhāhibih al-adabiyya wa'l qawmiyya wa'l ijtimā 'iyiya.* Cairo: Matba'at Amīn 'Abd al-Rahmān, 1942.

Muir, Edward. "The Italian Renaissance in America." *American Historical Review* 100, 4 (1995): 1095–118.

Mullen, Bill V. *Popular Fronts: Chicago and African-American Cultural Politics, 1935–46.* Urbana, IL: University of Illinois Press, 1999.

Najemy, John M. "Baron's Machiavelli and Renaissance Republicanism." *The American Historical Review* 101, 1 (1996): 119–29.

———. "Civic Humanism and Florentine Politics." In *Renaissance Civic Humanism: Reappraisals and Reflections.* Ed. James Hankins. New York: Cambridge University Press, 2000. 75–104.

Najm, Muhammad Yusuf. *Al-Qissah, fi al-adab al-arabi al-hadith.* Beirut: Manshurat al-maktabah al-ahliyyah, 1961.

Necipoğlu, Gülru. "Süleymân the Magnificent and the Representation of Power in the Context of Ottoman-Hapsburg-Papal Rivalry." In *Süleymân the Second and His Time.* Eds. Halil İnalcık and Cemal Kafadar. Istanbul: The Isis Press, 1993. 163–94. [Rpt. *The Art Bulletin* 71 (1989): 401–27.]

Nelson, Benjamin and Charles Trinkaus. "Introduction." In *The Civilization of the Renaissance in Italy.* By Jacob Burckhardt. New York: Harper Torchbooks, 1958. 3–19.

Nelson, Norman. "Individualism as a Criterion of the Renaissance." *Journal of English and Germanic Philology* 32 (1933): 316–34.

Neumann, Franz. *Behemoth. The Structure and Practice of National Socialism.* London: Victor Gollancz, 1942.

Norman, Jerry. *Chinese.* Cambridge: Cambridge University Press, 1988.

Novick, Peter. *The Holocaust in American Life.* Boston, MA: Houghton Mifflin, 1999.

Noyes, John. *Colonial Space: Spatiality in the Discourse of German South West Africa 1884–1915.* Chur, Switzerland and Philadelphia, PA: Harwood, 1992.

al-Nusūlī, Anīs. *'Ishtu wa-shāhadtu.* Beirut: Dār al-Kashshāf, 1951.

O'Brien, Edna. *Mother Ireland.* New York: Plume Books, 1976.

O'Casey, Sean. *Autobiographies: Inishfallen, Fare Thee Well.* New York: Carroll and Graf, 1984.

O'Connor, Frank. *A Book of Ireland.* London and Glasgow: William Collins, 1959.

Olivier-Martin, Yves. *Histoire du roman populaire en France 1840–1980.* Paris: Albin-Michel, 1980.

Ortiz, Fernando. *Cuban Counterpoint: Tobacco and Sugar.* Durham, NC and London: Duke University Press, 1995.

O'Toole, Fintan. *The Ex-Isle of Erin: Images of Global Ireland.* Dublin: New Island, 1996.

Pargellis, Stanley. "Introduction." In *The Quest for Political Unity in World History.* Ed. Stanley Pargellis. Washington, DC: United States Government Printing Office, 1944. vii–xi.

Parkinson, Phil and Penny Griffith. *Books in Maori, 1815–1900.* Auckland: Reed, 2004.

Pearson, W. H. "The Maori and Literature 1938–65." In *The Maori People in the 1960s: A Symposium.* Ed. Erik Schwimmer. Auckland: Longman Paul, 1968. 217–56.

Pelli, Moshe. *The Age of Haskalah.* Leiden and Lanham, MD: University Press of America, 1979.

———. *Bema'avkei Temurah.* Tel Aviv: Mif'alim universitaiyim le-hotsaah le-or, 1988.

———. "On the Role of Melitzah [Euphuism] in the Literature of Hebrew Enlightenment." Chap. 4 in *Hebrew in Ashkenaz: A Language in Exile.* Ed. Lewis Glinent. New York and Oxford: Oxford University Press, 1993. 94–110.

———. "Criteria of Modernism in Early Hebrew Haskalah Literature: Towards an Evaluation of the Modern Trends in Hebrew Literature." *Jewish Education and Learning.* Eds. Glenda Abramson and Tudor Parfitt. Switzerland: Harwood Academic Publishers, 1994. 129–42.

———. *Sugot Vesugyot Besifrut Hahaskalah Ha'ivrit.* Tel Aviv: Kibuts ha me' uhad, 1999.

———. "Tehiyat Halashon Hehelah Bahaskalah: 'Hame'asef,' Ketav Ha'et Ha'ivri Harishon, Kemachshir Lehidush Hasafah." *Leshonenu La'am,* Series 50, 2. January–March 1999 (5759): 59–75.

―――. "When Did Haskalah Begin? Establishing the Beginning of Haskalah Literature and the Definition of 'Modernism.' " *Leo Baeck Institute Year Book* 44 (1999): 55–96.

―――. "Hame'asef: Michtav Hadash Asher Aden Beyameinu Lo Hayah." *Hebrew Studies* 41 (2000a): 119–46.

―――. *"Hame'asef* (1783–1811)—Peritzat Derech Baperiodica Ha'ivrit." *Hadoar* 79 no. 19 (August 25, 2000b), 18–21; no. 20 (September 9, 2000b), 18–20; no. 21 (September 29, 2000b): 39–41.

―――. 'Lamenatze'ah Bineginot Maskil'—Melechet Hashir Vetofa'at Hashirah Be'hame'asef.' Ktav Ha'et Harishon Shel Hahaskalah Ha'ivrit. *Dappim Lemehkar Besifrut* 12 (1999/2000c): 65–116.

―――. *Sha'ar Lahaskalah*, Annotated Index (1783–1811). Jerusalem: Hotsa at Sefarim 'a sh. Y.L.Magnes, 2000d.

―――. *Dor Hame'asfim Beshahar Hahaskalah*. Israel: Hotsa' at ha-kibuts ha-me 'uhad, 2001.

―――. " 'These Are the Words of the Great Pundit, Scholar and Poet Herder . . .' Herder and the Hebrew Haskalah." *Hebräische Poesie und jüdischer Volksgeist: Die Wirkungsgeschichte von Johann Gottfried Herder im Judentum Mittel- und Osteuropas.* Hildeshein, Zürich and New York: Olms, 2003. 107–24.

Peres, Henri. "Le Roman, le conte et la nouvelle dans la littérature arabe moderne." *Annales de l'institut d'études orientales* 3 (1937): 266–337.

Pool, D. Ian. *The Maori Population of New Zealand, 1769–1971.* Auckland: Auckland University Press, Oxford University Press, 1977.

Pratt, Mary Louise. *Imperial Eyes: Travel Writing and Transculturation.* London: Routledge, 1992.

Prentice, Chris. "What Was the Maori Renaissance?" In *Writing at the Edge of the Universe: Essays Arising from the 'Creative Writing in New Zealand Conference.* University of Canterbury, 2003. Ed. Mark Williams. Christchurch: Canterbury University Press, 2004, 85–108.

Priestly, Joseph. *Letters to the Jews.* New York: J. Harrison, 1794.

Purkait, B. R. *Indian Renaissance and Education.* Calcutta: Firma KLM, 1992.

Quint, David. "Humanism and Modernity: A Reconsideration of Bruni's *Dialogues.*" *Renaissance Quarterly* 38, 3 (1985): 423–45.

Radford, Jean. *The Progress of Romance: The Politics of Popular Fiction.* London: Routledge Press, 1986.

Ray, Rajat Kanta. *Exploring Emotional History: Gender, Mentality and Literature in the Indian Awakening.* Oxford: Oxford University Press, 2001.

Reeves, William Pember. *The Long White Cloud Ao-tea-roa.* London: Horace Marshall & Son, 1898.

Reflections on the Bengal Renaissance. Eds. David Kopf and Safiuddin Joarder. Dacca: Bangladesh Books Ltd., 1977.

The Renaissance. A Symposium. February 8–10, 1952. New York: The Metropolitan Museum of Art, 1953. Typescript.

Ricoeur, Paul. *Oneself as Another*. Trans. Kathleen Blamey. Chicago, IL: University of Chicago Press, 1992.

al-Rihānī, Amīn. *Qalb al-'Iraq*. Beirut: Matba'at Sādir, 1935.

Rikābi, Fu'ād. *'Ala Tarīq al-Thawra*. Cairo: al-Dār al-Qawmiyya li'l Tibā 'a wa'l nashr, 1963a.

———. *Fī Sabīl al-Thawra*. Cairo: al-Dār al-Qawmīyah lil-tibā 'a wa'l-nashr, 1963b.

Rodgers, Lawrence R. "Richard Wright, Frank Marshall Davis and the Chicago Renaissance." *Langston Hughes Review* 14, 1–2 (1996): 4–12.

Rowe, J. G. and W. H. Stockdale. Eds. *Florilegium Historiale. Essays Presented to Wallace K. Ferguson*. Toronto, ON and Buffalo, NY: University of Toronto Press, 1971.

Ruehl, Martin A. " 'In this Time without Emperor's': The Politics of Ernst Kantorowicz's Kaiser *Friedrich der Zweite* Reconsidered." *Journal of the Warburg and Courtauld Institutes* 63 (2000): 187–242.

Ruggiero, Guido. Ed. *A Companion to the Worlds of the Renaissance*. Oxford: Blackwell, 2002.

Russell-Robinson, Joyce. "Renaissance Manque: Black WPA Artists in Chicago." *Western Journal of Black Studies* 18, 1 (1994): 36–43.

Ruthven, R. K. *Faking Literature*. Cambridge: Cambridge University Press, 2001.

Ryden, Kent C. *Mapping the Invisible Landscape: Folklore, Writing, and the Sense of Place*. Iowa City, IW: University of Iowa Press, 1993.

Sa'id, Nafusa Zakariyyah. *Tarikh al-da'wa ila al-'ammiyyah wa athariha fi misr*. Cairo: Dar qasr al-thaqafah bi al-iskindiriyyah, 1964.

Said, Edward. *Orientalism*. New York: Vintage Books, 1979.

———. *The World, the Text, and the Critic*. Cambridge, MA: Harvard University Press, 1983.

———. *Culture and Imperialism*. New York: Knopf, 1993.

———. "Traveling Theory." In *The Edward Said Reader*. Eds. Moustafa Bayoumi and Andrew Rubin. New York: Vintage, 2000. 195–218.

Sandburg, Carl. *The Complete Poems of Carl Sandburg*. New York: Harcourt, Brace, Jovanovich, 1969.

Saunders, Frances Stonor. *The Cultural Cold War. The CIA and the World of Arts and Letters*. New York: The New Press, 1999.

Schildgen, Brenda. "Dante in India: Sri Aurobindo and *Savitri*." *Dante Studies* 120 (2002): 83–98.

Schiller, Kay. *Gelehrte Gegenwelten: Über humanistische Leitbilder im 20. Jahrhundert*. Frankfurt am Main: Fischer, 2000.

Schulin, Ernst. "German and American Historiography in the Nineteenth and Twentieth Centuries." In *An Interrupted Past. German-Speaking Refugee Historians in the United States after 1933*. Eds. Hartmut Lehmann and James J. Sheehan. Cambridge: Cambridge University Press, 1991. 8–31.

Seigel, Jerrold E. " 'Civic Humanism' or Ciceronian Rhetoric? The Culture of Petrarch and Bruni." *Past and Present* 34 (1966): 3–48.

Selim, Samir. "The Narrative Craft: Realism and Fiction in the Arabic Canon." *Edebiyat* 14, 1–2 (May–Nov 2003): 109–28.

Sengupta, Kalyan and Tirthanath Bandyopadhyay. Eds. *Nineteenth Century Thought in Bengal*. Jadavpur: Allied, 1998.

Shalaq, Ahmad Zakariyyah. *Ahmad Fathi Zaghlul wa qadiyyah al-taghrib*. Cairo: Maktabah madbuli, 1966.

al-Sharif, Hasan. "Nahdah al-adab fi misr." *al-Hilal* 1 (October 1918): 67–71.

Sharma, K. K. "Poetry as 'The Mantra of the Real.'" In *Sri Aurobindo: Critical Considerations*. Ed. O. P. Mathur. Bara Bazar, Bareilly: Prakash Book Depot, 1997. 65–80.

Shavit, Uzi. "Ha'haskalah' Mahi: Leverur Musag Ha'haskalah' Basifrut Ha'ivrit." *Mehkerei Yerushalayim Besifrut Ivrit* 12 (1990).

Shaw, George Bernard. *John Bull's Other Island. The Genius of the Irish Theater*. Eds. Sylvan Barnet, Morton Berman, and William Burto. New York: New American Library, 1960.

Shawkat, Sāmī. *Hadhihi Ahdāfunā*. Baghdad: Majjalat al-Muʿallim al-Jadīd, 1939.

Sibley, David. *Geographies of Exclusion*. London: Routledge, 2002.

Sichel, Edith. *The Renaissance*. New York: Henry Holt, 1914.

Sidney, Sir Philip. *The Poems of Sir Philip Sidney*. Ed. William A. Ringler, Jr. Oxford: The Clarendon Press, 1962.

Simon, Reeva S. "The Hashemite 'Conspiracy': Hashemite Unity Attempts, 1921–1958." *International Journal of Middle East Studies* 5, 3 (1974): 314–27.

———. *Iraq between Two World Wars: The Creation and Implementation of a Nationalist Ideology*. New York: Columbia University Press, 1986.

Smith, G. *Life of Alexander Duff*. New York: A. C. Armstrong and Son, 1879.

Smolenskin, Perez. *Maamarim*, II. Jerusalem: Hotsa at Keren Smolenski, 1925.

Sorrenson, M. P. K. "Sir Apirana Ngata." *The Dictionary of New Zealand Biography, Volume III, 1901–1920*. Auckland: Auckland University Press and Department of Internal Affairs, 1996: 359–63.

Stafford, Jane and Mark Williams. "Victorian Poetry and the Indigenous Poet: Apirana Ngata's 'A Scene from the Past'." *Journal of Commonwealth Literature* 39, 1 (2004): 29–42.

Starn, Randolph. Review of *Aspects of the Renaissance. The American Historical Review* 74, 2 (1968): 542–3.

Stead, C. K. "Keri Hulme's *the bone people* and the Pegasus Award for Maori Literature." *Ariel* 16, 4 (October 1985): 101–8.

Stewart-Robinson, James. "The Ottoman Biographies of Poets." *Journal of Near Eastern Studies* 24, 1–2 (January–April 1965): 57–73.

Stocking, George W. *Race, Culture, and Evolution: Essays in the History of Anthropology*. Chicago, IL: University of Chicago Press, 1982.

Tagore, Rabindranath. *Rabindra Rachanavali*. Vol. 10. Calcutta: Government of West Bengal, 1984.

Tajir, Jak. *Harakah al-tarjamah fi misr khilal al-qarn al-tasiʿ ʿasharah*. Cairo: Dar al-Maʿarif, 1946.

Tauber, Eliezer. *The Emergence of the Arab Movements.* London and Portland, OR: Frank Cass, 1993.

Thiesse, Anne-Marie. *Le roman de quotidien: lecteurs et lectures populaires à la Belle Epoque.* Paris: Chemin Vert, 1984.

Tibi, Bassam. "Islam and Modern European Ideologies." *International Journal of Middle East Studies* 18, 1 (1986): 15–29.

Tidwell, John Edgar. " 'I Was a Weaver of Jagged Words': Social Function in the Poetry of Frank Marshall Davis." *Langston Hughes Review* 14, 1–2 (1996): 65–78.

Tregear, Edward. *The Aryan Maori.* Christchurch: Kiwi Publishers, 1995.

ᶜUmar, Muhammad. *Hadir al-misriyyin wa sirr ta'akhkhurihim.* Cairo: Dar misr al-mahrusah, 2002.

Valensi, Lucette. *The Birth of the Despot: Venice and the Sublime Porte.* Trans. Arthur Denner. Ithaca, NY: Cornell University Press, 1993.

Vasari, Giorgio. *The Lives of the Artists.* Trans. Julia Conaway Bondanella and Peter Bondanella. Oxford: Oxford University Press, 1998.

Velasco, Jesus. "Reading Mexico, Understanding the United States," *Journal of American History* 86, 2 (September 1999): 641–67.

Venuti, Lawrence. *The Scandals of Translation: Towards an Ethic of Difference.* London: Routledge, 1998.

Viswanathan, Gauri. *Masks of Conquest: Literary Study and British Rule in India.* Oxford: Oxford University Press, 1998.

Volosinov, V. N. "Verbal Interaction." In *Semiotics: An Introductory Anthology.* Ed. Robert Innis. Bloomington, IN: Indiana University Press, 1985. 47–66.

Von Martin, Alfred. *Sociology of the Renaissance.* Orig. 1932. With an Introduction by Wallace K. Ferguson. New York: Harper and Row, 1963.

———. "Gesellschaft und Freiheit heute." In *Mensch und Gesellschaft heute.* Frankfurt: Josef Knecht, 1965. 15–40.

———. *Soziologie der Renaissance.* München: C. H. Beck, 1974.

Walker, Ranginui. *He Tipua: The Life and Times of Sir Apirana Ngata.* Auckland: Viking, 2001.

Watenpaugh, Keith D. " 'Creating Phantoms:' Zaki al-Arsuzi, the Alexandretta Crisis, and the Formation of Modern Arab Nationalism in Syria." *International Journal of Middle East Studies* 28, 3 (1996): 363–89.

Waterloo, Stanley. Letter. "Who Reads a Chicago Book?" *Dial* 13 (1892): 206–9.

Watson, G. J. *Irish Identity and the Literary Revival.* London: Croom Helm, 1979.

Webster, Steven. *Patrons of Maori Culture. Power, Theory and Ideology in the Maori Renaissance.* Auckland: Auckland University Press, 1998.

Weisinger, Herbert. "The Renaissance Theory of the Reaction against the Middle Ages as a Cause of the Renaissance." *Speculum* 20 (1945): 461–7.

"Wenxue gailiang chuyi" (Some Modest Suggestions for Literary Reform). In *Zhongguo xinwenxue daxi* (Compendium of Modern Chinese Literature). Ed. Zhao Jiabi. Vol.1. Shanghai: Liangyou tushu gongsi, 1935. 34–43.

Werner, Craig. "Leon Forrest, the AACM and The Legacy of the Chicago Renaissance." *The Black Scholar* 23, 3–4 (1993): 10–23.

Werses, Shmuel. "Yad Yamin Dohah Yad Smol Mekarevet: Al Yahasam Shel Sofrei Hahaskalah Lileshon Yiddish." *Hulyot* 5 (Winter 1999): 9–49.

Wessely, N. H. *Divrei Shalom Ve'emet.* Berlin, 1782.

Wevers, Lydia. *Country of Writing: Travel Writing in New Zealand 1809–1900.* Auckland: Auckland University Press, 2003.

Whitfield, Stephen J. *The Culture of the Cold War.* 2nd edn. Baltimore, MD and London: The Johns Hopkins University Press, 1996.

Wilde, Oscar. "The Decay of Lying." *Dramatic Theory and Criticism: Greeks to Grotowski.* Ed. Bernard F. Dukore. New York and Chicago, IL: Holt, Rinehart and Winston, 1974.

Wilkins, Burleigh Taylor. "Some Notes on Burckhardt." *The Journal of the History of Ideas* 201 (1959): 123–37.

Williams, Herbert W. *A Bibliography of Printed Maori to 1900: And Supplement.* Wellington: Government Printer, 1975.

Winks, Robin. *Cloak and Gown: Scholars in the Secret War, 1939–1961.* New York: William Morrow, 1987.

Witt, Ronald. "The Crisis after Forty Years." *The American Historical Review* 101, 1 (1996): 110–8.

Wölfflin, Heinrich. *Renaissance und Barock: Eine Untersuchung über Wesen und Entstehung des Barockstils in Italien.* Munich: T. Ackermann, 1888.

Woolley, Lisa. "From Chicago Renaissance to Chicago Renaissance: The Poetry of Fenton Johnson." *Langston Hughes Review* 14, 1–2 (1996): 36–48.

———. *American Voices of the Chicago Renaissance.* DeKalb, IL: Northern Illinois University Press, 2000.

Yeats, W. B. "Cuchulain of Muirthemne." In *Explorations.* New York: The MacMillan Company, 1962. 3–13.

———. "Irish Language and Irish Literature." In *The Collected Works: Volume X: Later Articles and Reviews.* Ed. Colton Johnson. New York: Scribner, 2000. 46–50.

Yeh, Michelle. *Modern Chinese Poetry: Theory and Practice since 1917.* New Haven, CT: Yale University Press, 1991.

Young, Robert. *White Mythologies: Writing History and the West.* London: Routledge, 1990.

Yousif, Abdul-Salaam. "The Struggle for Cultural Hegemony during the Iraqi Revolution." In *The Iraqi Revolution of 1958—The Old Social Classes Revisited.* Eds. Robert A. Fernea and William Roger Louis. London: I. B. Tauris, 1991. 172–96.

Yūsuf, Salmān Yūsuf (Fahd). *Kitābāt al-Rafīq Fahd.* Baghdad: al-arīq al-jadīd, 1976.

Al-Zaytuni, Latif. *Harakah al-tarjamah fi 'asr al-nahdah.* Beirut: Dar al-nahar, 1994.

Al-Zayyat, Latifa. *Harakah al-tarjamah al-adabiyyah min al-injiliziyyah ila al-'arabiyyah.* Unpublished Dissertation. Cairo University, 1957.

Zhongguo xinwenxue daxi (Compedium of Modern Chinese Literature). Ed. Zhao Jiabi. 10 vols. Shanghai: Liangyou tushu gongsi, 1935.

Zuʻaytar, Akram. *Min mudhakkirāt Akram Zuʻaytir.* Beirut: al-Muʼassasa al-ʻArabīyya, 1994.

Zubaida, Sami. "The Fragments Imagine the Nation: The Case of Iraq." *International Journal of Middle Eastern Studies* 32, 2 (2002): 205–15.

Index